THE GAELIC MIND AND
THE COLLAPSE
OF THE GAELIC WORLD

THE GAELIC MIND
AND THE
COLLAPSE OF THE
GAELIC WORLD

Michelle O Riordan

Cork University Press
1990

First published in 1990 by
Cork University Press, University College, Cork

Copyright © Cork University Press and
The Irish Committee of Historical Sciences 1990

British Library Cataloguing in Publication Data
O Riordan, Michelle
The Gaelic mind and the collapse of the
Gaelic world.
1. Ireland. Historical sources. Poetry in Irish
I. Title
936.1

ISBN 0-902561-57-X

Printed in the Republic of Ireland by Tower Books,
39 Lavitts Quay, Cork

EDITORIAL NOTE

WITH MICHELLE O'RIORDAN'S, *The Gaelic Mind and the Collapse of the Gaelic World* this present *Studies in Irish History* series, which is being accredited by the Irish Committee of Historical Sciences, enters upon its third volume. The high academic standard of this volume following upon that of its two predecessors, written respectively by Raymond Gillespie and Andrew Gailey, provides evidence that there is indeed a need for a monograph series designed to provide a publishing outlet for scholars who have completed a first major research undertaking in Irish history. The present volume is more venturesome than either of those which preceded it, or than any of the eighteen in the two previous series, because it is the first that has a direct bearing on Gaelic Ireland and the first also that includes a medieval dimension.

The very fact of its publication will undoubtedly inspire other aspirant authors to come forward with manuscripts to join those which are already under active consideration for publication. The editorial committee and the I.C.H.S. will both welcome any such response, but they also point to the need for greater external financial support if the work of publication is to proceed on a regular basis in the years ahead. The three volumes in the series have been made possible by the availability of a voluntary editorial effort, by the willingness of Cork University Press to advance the necessary capital to cover the costs of production, and by small grants from private foundations. The principal grants in aid of publication for the present volume came from the I.C.H.S. itself and from the Senate of the National University of Ireland. While offering grateful acknowledgement for all those essential supports it is the hope of the editorial board that this proof of our ability to sustain a series over three volumes will persuade some generous donors to grant support of the kind that will place the series on a secure financial foundation.

Professor Nicholas Canny,
Series Editor,
University College,
Galway.

CONTENTS

PREFACE

THEIR UNIQUE SOCIAL, political and cultural position lends the work of the bardic poets an authority which is overlooked only at the cost of reducing further the already scant source material for the study of Gaelic Ireland during the expansion of Tudor and Stuart power in the sixteenth and seventeenth centuries. Bardic poetry adds a dimension to our understanding of the contemporary learned and aristocratic mind. This book is concerned with the uses of Gaelic literature as historical source material. It attempts to offer a new approach to possible interpretations of the intriguing corpus of Irish bardic poetry for historians. In it I examine the characteristics of the literary motifs and conceits of Gaelic syllabic poetry from the thirteenth to the seventeenth centuries. I consider the body of poetry as literary artefact and, because of its position as 'official' poetry, as an organ of the political élites. By examining the poetry under both species I arrive at a framework of reference appropriate to the material which makes it useful as a cypher for aspects of the *mentalité* of the Gaelic élites. Within the frame of reference of the poetry as an entire literary structure, the poets' manipulation of the motifs and conceits of the literary genre are made meaningful in a manner useful for the historian. This is especially important for the study of Irish history in the early modern period, when bardic poetry provides the only substantial body of Gaelic source materials outside of the annals. My intention has been to make clear the necessity of considering each historical episode as it is depicted in the literature both as a product of the literary world of bardic poetry and as a possible record of that event in the literary style favoured by the poets. I have endeavoured to develop a methodology which makes use of the poetry in a way which recognizes the importance of different combinations of apologues, motifs and poem-types used by the poet to depict the import of a given occasion without recourse to the schedule of 'conquest' which has

ix

exercised such an influence on our understanding of the poetry to date. Such an approch allows the poetry to speak for itself in a historically meaningful context which is independent of the retrospective timetable of conquest.

ACKNOWLEDGEMENTS

THIS BOOK IS largely based on a doctoral thesis done in University College Cork 1981-1985. During the course of my doctoral work and in the following years of preparing the book for publication, I have incurred many welcome debts. I am particularly grateful for the supervision, advice and support of my studies director, Dr Tom Dunne. I am heavily indebted also to Professor Nicholas Canny, editor of the series of which this book forms part, for his painstaking efforts with my typescripts and for his endless patience with me. I wish to thank the editorial board for accepting my work as a volume of the series and the National University of Ireland for providing me with a grant-in-aid towards the publication costs.

I received stimulation and encouragement from Dr Brendan Bradshaw. I benefitted greatly from a two-year post doctoral Junior Research Fellowship in the Institute of Irish Studies at the Queen's University in Belfast, under the directorship of Professor Ronnie Buchanan, who was also very supportive of my work. For constructive suggestions, advice and encouragement I also wish to thank Dr Cornelius Buttimer, Dr Ciaran Brady, Professor Seán Ó Tuama, Dr Katharine Simms and Liam P. Ó Murchú.

The staffs of the following libraries and institutions were generous with their facilities and co-operative in their dealings with me: Boole Library, University College Cork; the National Library of Ireland; the Public Record Office, Ireland; the Public Record Office, Northern Ireland; the Library of Queen's University; the Institute of Irish Studies and the Royal Irish Academy.

Discussions, arguments and unconscionably long 'coffee-breaks' with the following sustained my interest in the work in hand and forced me to clarify and explain: Colm Breathnach, Dr Louis Power, Finbarr Whooley, Pádraig Ó Flaithbheartaigh, Aidan Doyle, Paula O Riordan and Denis Staunton. Dr Richard Ivens revolutionized my notes and filing systems by instructing me in the use of the word-processor.

I am grateful to the staff of the Cork University Press for their help in the preparation of the book itself and particularly to its Executive Secretary, Donal Counihan.

INTRODUCTION

THE EVOLUTION OF the pre-Christian *file* or seer, into the classical 'bardic' poet of the thirteenth to seventeenth centuries has been outlined by scholars of literature and history.[1] Originally, the *file* enjoyed a semi-sacred rôle in interpreting the world of his fellows.[2] The *file*/poet emerged in the later period as a prop of the secular polity so that by the thirteenth century, his principal perceived function was that of eulogist to the sept chief.[3] The *file*'s evolution from seer to praise poet can be seen as a dilution, so to speak, into a literary form of his more weighty responsibilities of the earlier period.[4] The poet's identity, therefore, came from two sources; the literary and the religious (pre-christian). The literary vehicle, bardic poetry, carried the essence of the poet's former rôle of shaman and seer. The poetry did not necessarily reflect in a factual way, the actual political conditions as experienced at any particular time. Elements of their former sacred rôle remained within the idiom of the poets' literary functions. They operated within two planes of reality — the secular and the sacred.[5]

A certain aura of otherworld powers adhered to the *file* from earliest times. Effective powers of satire, prophecy and anathema were attributed to them long after their occult faculties were redundant. The evolution of the *filí* into a learned literary class was accomplished by the

---

[1] Notably Eleanor Knott, *Irish Classical Poetry* (Mercier Press, Cork, 1960); E. Knott (ed.), *The Bardic Poems of Tadhg Dall Ó hUiginn* (London, 1922); Osborn Bergin (ed.), *Irish Bardic Poetry* (Dublin, 1970) and James Carney, *The Irish Bardic Poet* (Dolmen Press, Dublin, 1967, reprint 1985), Katharine Simms, *From Kings to Warlords: the changing political structure of Gaelic Ireland in the Later Middle Ages,* The Boydell Press, 1987 (Hereafter *From Kings to Warlords*).

[2] J.E. Caerwyn Williams, *The Court Poet in Mediaeval Ireland* (London, 1978), p. 10.

[3] Alwyn and Brinley Rees, *The Celtic Heritage* (Thames and Hudson, London [1961], 1976).

[4] Caerwyn Williams, *The Court Poet in Mediaeval Ireland,* pp 25-6.

[5] Proinsias Mac Cana, 'Notes on the concept of unity', in *Crane Bag,* 2 (1978), p. 63; Caerwyn Williams, *The Court Poet in Mediaeval Ireland,* p. 10, and see also E. Knott, *Irish Classical Poetry,* p. 65.

mid-thirteenth century. They retained their link with the person and position of the king and enjoyed the privileges attending their familiarity with the most powerful individual in the sept.[6] The poets' literary function was underpinned by a coherent and ancient system of values and perceptions. Bardic poetry was therefore imbued with fundamental elements of the Gaelic mentality, particularly those associated with the aristocracy. The poetry is in this way a fascinating and worthwhile source of material in which to explore some of the perceptions of power, authority and the constraints on these, as they are articulated by the poets according to their ancient rationale.[7] The bardic poetry itself as a literary genre had evolved into its classical form by the thirteenth century. Strict rules determined the metrical composition of a number of ornate rhyming and alliterative schemes.[8]

The restrictive nature of the genre highlights the essential reciprocal and mutually beneficial nature of the relationship between lord and poet. This, by extension, reflects the relationship between the two groups; the ruling aristocracy and the literati. The literary event which involved the creation of a poem by an individual poet for an individual chief, and the complementary event of its recitation[9] had its own significance. The two events illustrate the compatibility of the perceptions perpetuated by the lords in their life-style with the life-style and values perpetuated in the works of the bardic poets.

The use of a number of motifs in the poetry of the schools became *de rigueur* within this particular genre.[10] These motifs had their origin in the world of druidic ritual and historical mythology; in the myths, legends and origin tales, rituals, customs and beliefs which formed the bases of the world view and explanations of contemporary events, and those of a problematic hereafter, for the inhabitants of pre-christian Ireland. The Gaelic literati maintained the continuity of this tradition into the Christian period; a veneer of Christianity disguised the more

---

[6] The most recent enlightening article on the poet and the chief is P.A. Breatnach's 'The Chief's Poet', in *R.I.A. Proceedings,* Sect. C, vol. 83, No. 3 (1983), pp 37-79.

[7] Proinsias Mac Cana in B. Ó Cuív (ed.), *A View of the Irish Language* (Dublin, 1969), p. 42.

[8] E. Knott synopsizes the literary style in *Irish Classical Poetry*, p. 51. A full account of 'figurative language' and 'metaphors' is given on pp 58-60 of the same work. See also Liam P. Ó Caithnia, *Apalóga na bhFili 1200-1650* (An Clóchomhar Tta, Dublin 1984).

[9] E. Knott, *Irish Classical Poetry*, p. 53.

[10] E. Knott, *Irish Classical Poetry*, pp 58-60.

blatantly pagan aspects of the tradition.[11] Certain motifs became ritualistically used in the poetry to indicate power, influence, authority and wealth of a certain kind pertaining to the chief. These included the espousal of the king to his territory, the attribution of the fertility of the territory as being among the portents of a rightful monarch, and conversely, attributing its sterility to inappropriate leadership. The bardic themes and motifs also idealized the king's/lord's person and behaviour and articulated the ritual and rhetorical condemnation of all his enemies and rivals, domestic and foreign.

The poets consciously cultivated a sense of the past.[12] They strove to emulate the best features of past masters, and set immense store by oral and written records and the works of former poets, historians, and keepers of genealogy and *seanchas*. Their sense of the past, both mythical and historical, pervades all the works of the poets. This preoccupation, however, is not in any sense retrogressive or morbidly stagnant. It is rather a primitive sense of historical continuity[13] and is perhaps one of the most significant, certainly the most outstanding, of all bardic features. The poets, through the written tradition, and through the oral tradition, inherited a world of precedents, individuals, events, and possibilities, which for them was the stuff of which all existence was made. The articulation of each contemporary situation by the poets was dominated by the literary world which they inherited, and which, with material encouragement from powerful patrons, they sought continually to perpetuate.

Their unique social, political and cultural position lends the work of the bardic poets an authority which is overlooked only at the cost of further reducing the already scant source material of the Gaelic Irish response to the destruction of the Gaelic world during the expansion of Tudor and Stuart power in Ireland in the sixteenth and seventeenth

---

[11] E. Knott, *Irish Classical Poetry*, p. 50.

[12] Caerwyn Williams, *The Court Poet in Mediaeval Ireland,* pp 36-7, and see also David Greene, in B. Ó Cuív (ed.), *Seven Centuries of Irish Learning 1000-1700* (Dublin, 1961), pp 42-3 and also Proinsias Mac Cana in B. Ó Cuív (ed.), *A View of the Irish Language* (Dublin, 1969), p. 42.

[13] Claude Lévi-Strauss, *The Savage Mind* [La Pensée Sauvage], (3rd ed. London, 1974), esp. pp 19-33; Peter Burke, *Popular Culture in early Modern Europe* (London 1978) and Burke, *Tradition and Innovation in Renaissance Italy: a sociological approach* (Fontana, 1974), esp. pp 243-5; and with specifically Celtic reference, see Alwyn and Brinley Rees, *The Celtic Heritage,* pp 105-7.

centuries. Bardic poetry adds a dimension to our understanding of the contemporary learned and aristocratic mind. Through the manipulation of an elaborate structure of motif and symbol, the poets arrived at a language [14] and a mode of expression which articulated for them and their patrons, the nature of their relationships each with the other, and those of each respectively with the world in which they lived. [15] The nature of such material demands that the perceptions of those engaged in its composition must direct our interpretation of it.

In the *file*'s scheme of things, everything is related to previous mythical or historical events. [16] No event is in itself unique; a great event has been preshadowed by a similar one, a great chief or lord is a contemporary version of a historico-mythical figure, or prophecies have heralded his arrival. Historical mythology provides for the 'takings of Ireland' in pre-history. [17] Ireland, under several poetic titles is in a continually beleaguered state, the charter to her sovereignty is always the prize of the most powerful warrior. The most noble and victorious sept or individual will win the right to subdue her, the most valiant and worthy will become her spouse. No chief stands by himself alone, but he is provided with a rearguard of illustrious ancestors and all of his battles or skirmishes have their foreshadowing in antiquity. Each personal attribute is second only to, or surpasses, that of some predecessor. The poets, along with their fellow professionals, the historians and genealogists, recorded each in his own fashion and within his own convention, the mythical and historical experiences of the Gael. The collection of literary and historical and genealogical material thus created, embodying as it did, some expression of the fundamental social and

---

[14] For discussion of some aspects of the evolution of a particular poetic language, see Caerwyn Williams, *The Court Poet in Mediaeval Ireland,* pp 11-4 and E. Knott, *Irish Classical Poetry,* pp 54-60.

[15] Caerwyn Williams addresses the subject of the nature of the poets' spiritual dimension, their shaman characteristics in *The Court Poet in Mediaeval Ireland,* pp 10-17 and *passim*; and see also Clifford Geertz 'Centers, Kings and Charisma: Reflections on the Symbolics of Power', in *Culture and its Creators, Essays in honor of Edward Shils* (University of Chicago Press, 1977), esp. pp 152-61; and J. Goldberg, *James I and the Politics of Literature* (Johns Hopkins University Press, Baltimore and London, 1983).

[16] A. and B. Rees, *The Celtic Heritage,* p. 106, and cf. Caerwyn Williams, *The Court Poet in Mediaeval Ireland,* p. 11.

[17] R.A. Stewart Macalister (ed.), (Dublin, 1939), and see also Mark Scowcroft, 'Miotas an Gabhála i Leabhar Gabhála' in *Léachtaí Cholm Cille* XIII, pp 76-98.

political values of the ruling septs and literati, was never seen as an organically developing pattern by the poets. The 'information' thus amassed by the literati was used rather as a store of precedent to which each new event is contrasted and compared in a purely academic manner. This is the poet's explanation of the past, rationalization of the present and armour for the future. The deeply felt necessity to be able to distinguish the important and lasting, from the transient and superficial, is a need which the poets shared with all mankind in any era.[18] They were the keepers of the written tradition, they drew analogies, inserted apologues and treated of their subject in a manner which placed him in the mainstream of Gaelic tradition. This service was also extended to foreigners with whom the poets must socially or politically and culturally contend. They thus articulated the principles and rationale by which the Gaelic world assimilated extraneous elements into itself.

These basic themes reflect the principal preoccupations of the poets; Banbha will need succour, a spouse will be brought forth, proclaimed worthy of the honour of the task; foreigners will threaten, and in turn be driven away; the sword will confer superior rights on one over others. The reality which the poets endeavour to encompass within this framework, however, is vastly altered over time, and in a manner which threatens the very *raison d'être* of the poetic caste. To coincide with the enormous political and social changes which occurred during the sixteenth and seventeenth centuries, one might expect parallel changes in the poets' works. The poets enjoyed social and political prominence and were personally and professionally abreast of each new situation. Changes in the poetry corresponding directly to political and social changes initiated by the centralized government, do not occur. Throughout the thirteenth and fourteenth centuries and indeed earlier, the genealogists and historians and especially the poets, had categorized all the vicissitudes of Banbha. Their approach to any occurrence, or series of events, must be chosen from a selection of attitudes and 'reactions' stock-piled by them and their predecessors. The framework was not so rigid as to be unable to assimilate new elements, conceptually in accepting the new titles of foreign lords and adjusting to their relations

---

[18] See C. Lévi-Strauss, *The Savage Mind,* esp. pp 217-44 and his notion of 'preconstrained' elements of the units of myth, pp 18-9.

with a foreign monarch, and in a literary sense, by the adaptation of classical and continental material.[19] The fundamental perceptions of the Gaelic world which were given a literary form in the bardic poetry were those also governing the activities of the Gaelic political world under the leadership of the Gaelic political elites. The poets could change their articulation of such principles only when the principles governing the behaviour of the ruling elites became fundamentally altered. The demise of the Gaelic world, indeed its slow foundering in the face of Tudor and Stuart expansion and the unconcerted efforts of the Gaelic leaders to survive only on individual terms indicate that the fundamental concepts of power and the laws governing its maintenance and prerogatives remained fundamentally unaltered in the Gaelic Irish aristocratic mentality, to the end of the seventeenth century.

For this reason, and because the nature of the bardic genre was such that it filtered 'reality' through a structured literary framework and coped with change within the confines of that framework, any alterations to the principles articulated in the poetry had to originate within the depths of the Gaelic mentality and could not be imposed from outside alone. It was only when the Gaelic world eventually proved unable to maintain its integrity and assimilate the changes imposed by the central administration of the crown that the poets' works became obsolete. The Gaelic aristocratic world, as a political entity, crumbled before the poets died away. The collapse of the aristocratic world, however, was a harbinger of the inevitable demise of the poets.

Much of the poets' conventional phraseology disguised a healthy deceit. They were not averse to falsifying and creating genealogies for those in favour. Their exhaustive drawing of analogies must not lead one to believe that the analogy is factually true or figuratively valid. Their appositeness or validity for the twentieth century mind is of no importance. Their importance lies rather in the fact that they formed part of the immense literary structure evolved by the literati over centuries, by which they had created a measure or a rationale of the health of Ireland, culturally, socially, and politically. Their wide fields of reference and manner of expression conveyed a wealth of symbolic meaning, not lost upon their audiences. The bardic structure represents an indigenous ideal of Ireland and what constituted right of belonging

---

[19] See E. Knott, *Irish Classical Poetry*, p. 64.

on a number of levels. The 'fact' of the Elizabethan conquest as it reveals itself in retrospect, warps our view of what must have been the perspective of those involved in the contemporary events. Neglect of two factors especially contribute to the misinterpretation of this material. First, it must be borne in mind that the bardic poetry is the work of professionally trained poets, a literary caste evolved over centuries writing in a genre which is in no way concerned with presenting a chronological account [20] of Gaelic Irish experiences, but which nevertheless of its nature reveals aspects of the nature of Gaelic perceptions. [21] Because of the literary nature of the poets' works, an element of artistic creativity is inevitable in the poetry, preventing any simplistic evaluation of the material. Second, the bardic material is particularly susceptible to the distorting influences of post-colonial historiography. The nationalism of the nineteenth and twentieth centuries in conjunction with the philosophy of many Gaelic revivalists has given rise to an excessively simplified interpretation of bardic motif and mentality, based on the events of two or three centuries posterior to the time of the writing of the poetry in question. [22] In this regard especially, the use of the Irish language as a nationalist vehicle has complicated the interpretation of Gaelic source material which antedates the period of Gaelic revivalism, because it contributes in no small measure to the misinterpretation of material in this language as being imbued with principles and perceptions which formed no part of contemporary political or social thought. Many who succeed in avoiding the trap outlined above, however, produce interpretations of bardic poetry, which, while they may not be dominated by an overriding need to provide anachronistically ancient roots for nineteenth century Irish nationalism, are nonetheless

---

[20] Caerwyn Williams suggests that because of their particular function, and because of their possesion of certain kinds of information to fulfill that function, the poets often were *de facto* historians. See *The Court Poet in Mediaeval Ireland*, pp 40-2.

[21] Cf. Lauro Martines, *History and Society in English Renaissance Verse* (Basil Blackwell, Oxford, 1985), p. 15, and *passim*.

[22] Brendan Bradshaw in *The Irish Constitutional Revolution of the Sixteenth Century* (Cambridge, 1979) makes the following comment:
'The presentation of Irish history from the twelfth century Anglo-Norman invasion to the establishment of the state in 1922 as an epic struggle of resistance against a foreign invader has proved a popular if unwholesome brand of nationalist historiography,' pp 2-3.

dominated by an awareness of 'the Conquest'.[23]

The similarity of the earliest bardic works in the thirteenth century to the latest in the seventeenth century is a testament to the continual and universal significance of the perceptions articulated by the poets for the leaders of Gaelic Irish society. Reliance on precedence[24] is one of the corner-stones of all bardic endeavour, and its continued significance for a powerful class in Gaelic Irish society up to the end of the seventeenth century is central to a true understanding of the whole bardic ethos. Only a firm understanding of the very real part played by the ever-present sense of former ages with which the poets set about the execution of their official duties, can lead one to valid conclusions about their works and their significance as a historical source.

The principal official function of the poet from the twelfth century was to provide support for the reigning or incumbent chief. In exercising this function, the poet expressed the traditional rationale governing Gaelic perceptions of kingship, sources of power and authority, the perception of the threats to which these were subject and the constraints under which they might, legitimately or otherwise, be placed. From this single duty sprang the multiplicity of bardic themes, the presentation of which, in their ultimate literary form, provide the major part of contemporary Gaelic Irish records for the sixteenth and seventeenth centuries.

---

[23] The following recent contributions to the study of bardic poetry as a historical source exhibit in different ways some of the restricting effects of looking to the poetry for statements of passive 'reaction' to the Conquest, rather than as a positive source of independent Gaelic response to, and assimilation of, change over time:
Brendan Bradshaw, 'Native Reaction to the Westward Enterprise: a case-study in Gaelic ideology' in J.H. Andrews, N.P. Canny, and P.E. Hair (eds), *The Westward Enterprise* (Liverpool, 1978) (hereafter 'Native Reaction'). N.P. Canny, 'The formation of the Irish mind: religion, politics and Gaelic Irish Literature 1550-1750', in *Past and Present*, No. 95 (1982), pp 91-116 (hereafter 'Formation'). Tom Dunne, 'The Gaelic Response to the conquest: the evidence of the poetry', in *Studia Hibernica*, No. 20 (1980), 7-30 (hereafter 'Evidence'). Breandán Ó Buachalla, 'Na Stíobhartaigh agus an t-aos léinn; Cing Séamas', in *R.I.A. Proceedings,* Sect. C, vol. 3, No. 4 (1983), pp 81-134 (hereafter 'Cing Séamas').

[24] The repetitious nature of much of the bardic works is explained by Alwyn and Brinley Rees thus:
'Life is meaningful in as much as it is an imitation or a re-enactment of what the gods did in the beginning: reality is acquired through repetition or participation; everything which lacks an exemplary model is 'meaningless'.
A. and B. Rees, *The Celtic Heritage*, p. 106, and see Caerwyn Williams, *The Court Poet of Mediaeval Ireland*, p. 11. See also C. Lévi-Strauss, *The Savage Mind.*

The close social, cultural and political links between the position of the poet and that of the chief created a predictable similarity of fate for both. The fast diminishing power and status of the chief during the seventeenth century was paralleled by the fortunes and status of the poet, though at a slightly slower pace because of their separate functions within the Gaelic world. The functions of poet and chief were complementary. The poet occupied a stronger position culturally than the chief. When a chief became dispossessed of his patrimony by whatever means, his function in the poet-chief relationship, for all practical purposes, ceased. He no longer contributed materially to the welfare of the poet, and his subsequent life-style ceased to provide focus for poetic compositions.[25] The poet, in the event of his chief's eclipse, was deprived of a patron, and of the focus of the official functions of his profession. He likewise fell in status, denied opportunities envisaged in his professional training, and he was materially unprovided for due to the demise of his patron. A deposed chief had to secure a military career abroad or possess negotiable assets in order to be able to survive socially and materially. The poet, however, even without his chief was possessed of a more versatile and flexible profession, the training for which made of him a man of letters; a learned individual whose training and learning were usable under a variety of circumstances.

The long term effects of the end of the Gaelic aristocratic lifestyle meant ultimate death for the professional poet. However, the non-material basis of the profession of the latter meant that the removal of one prop of the support of the poet, notably the chief's patronage, did not immediately reduce the entire literary world of the poet to rubble, or silence their articulation of the traditional perceptions of that world. The distinction between the respective nature and functions of chief and poet within the Gaelic aristocratic world is important for two reasons. In the first place, it highlights the culturally reciprocal element in the poet-chief relationship. Second, and perhaps of more importance for discussion of the seventeenth century, it helps to explain why the two structures, the political structure of the chiefs and the literary structure of the poets, both manifestations of aristocratic Gaeldom, were not coeval. The social and political structure succumbed to the pressure applied, before the literary and theoretical articulation of its position

---

[25] See P.A. Breatnach, 'The Chief's Poet', *passim*.

eventually faded away. It was, however, more a question of when, rather than whether, the collapse of the literary structure would follow the disintegration of the Gaelic aristocratic order.

The compromises the chiefs made with the new order were compatible with the Gaelic aristocratic mentality which was theoretically answerable to a complex body of traditional values, the nature of which one can only attempt to divine from the works of the bardic poets. The belligerent structure of Gaelic Ireland provided the backdrop to the poets' compositions. The proliferation of petty lordships and kingships in later mediaeval Ireland, created a climate in which the poets could exercise their encomiastic and other literary faculties to their fullest extent. Early modern Ireland supported a system of endemic warfare. Cattle-raiding occurred as a common-place of warfare up to and even into the seventeenth century, but 'harrying' and 'plundering' had been the principal form of warfare in Gaelic Ireland up to the end of the fifteenth century. [26] The fragmentary nature of the Gaelic polity and the fissiparous tendencies of the major septs, created a society of continual conflict. [27] The whole structure of the society was based on an understanding of war as an endemic condition; of reciprocal raids and booty-taking, of submissions bought and tributes levied. The system of succession saw to it that the focus of power within the sept changed, with its attendant struggles in at least every generation, usually more frequently. The relations between greater and lesser lords was usually determined by their relative military strengths. [28]

The inhabitants of the country, the aristocracy and the mass of 'followers', grew innured to the constant adjustments which had to be made to accommodate the ever-changing circumstances in a society which experienced constant scenes of power-struggle. No great social or cultural change followed the conquest of territory by one native lord over another. Yet, even where extra-insular influences were concerned, the Gaelic world showed a remarkable ability to adapt the changes imposed by victors and to accommodate novelty. Within the context of the warring Gaelic septs, the process of adaptation usually re-established

---

[26] Katharine Simms, 'Warfare in the Medieval Gaelic Lordships', in *Irish Sword*, vol. XII (1975-6), p. 107.

[27] See Caerwyn Williams, *The Court Poet in Medieval Ireland*, p. 49.

[28] Brendan Bradshaw, *The Irish Constitutional Revolution of the Sixteenth Century* (Cambridge, 1979), p. 16.

the *status quo* following the initial disturbance. This is not to suggest that the Gaelic polity was incapable of development or that ruling septs were not replaced, but that the rationale governing the extent of the changes to be expected under a new regime did not change with every battle. In Gaelic political terms, this meant that a powerful chief met with continual resistance, but that he also collected the submissions of new clients. The most powerful contender for the chieftainship was elected if his support was impressive enough, however tenuous his claims.[29] The successful wielding of power, bought or extorted, ensured the realization of the chief's or the aspirant chief's claims.[30]

The ever-changing fortunes caused by continual warfare taught the Gaelic Irish to be impressed by immediate results and short-term successes, made visible by the substantial spoils that became available for distribution and by the greater support against rivals within the sept. In the context of the piecemeal efforts of the Tudor monarchs to extend crown control over greater areas of Ireland during the sixteenth century, the Gaelic Irish attitude towards the means and goals of warfare became increasingly important.[31] During the Tudor period, the identity, status and position of the Gaelic aristocracy came under pressure from both within and without the Gaelic world. Tudor plantation policy and post-rebellion confiscation accounted for the loss of the traditional sources of wealth and status of many Gaelic leaders.[32] In keeping with the political psyche manifest by the Gaelic Irish in their continual conflict to establish individual supremacy, the Tudor encroachments were for the most part considered as further military incidents in the careers of the individual lords involved. This meant that individual Gaelic chiefs came

---

[29] See, for instance, the conflicting claims within the Uí Néill, in N.P. Canny, 'Hugh O'Neill, Earl of Tyrone, and the changing face of Gaelic Ulster', in *Studia Hibernica, No. 10* (1970), pp 7-35 (hereafter 'The changing face of Gaelic Ulster') — and see also the support gathered by Hugh O'Donnell in his claims to the Uí Dhomhnaill chieftainship in Paul Walsh (ed.), Lughaidh Ó Cléirigh, *A Life of Aodh Ruadh O Domhnaill, transcribed from the Book of Lughaidh Ó Cléirigh,* 2 vols (Dublin, 1948, 1957).

[30] See Brendan Bradshaw's discussion of this in *The Irish Constitutional Revolution of the Sixteenth Century,* p. 16.

[31] See N.P. Canny, *The Elizabethan Conquest of Ireland: a pattern established 1565-76* (Hassocks, Harvester Press, 1976).

[32] The most recent general study of Tudor Ireland is to be found in Steven Ellis, *Tudor Ireland: Crown, Community, and the Conflict of Cultures* (Longmans, London, 1985), in this context see especially pp 212-318.

Introduction

to terms with the Tudor reconquest in a manner which was dictated principally by their own traditional perceptions of war and military or non-
military political initiatives.[33]

The combination of government policy and Gaelic acquiescence in,
and exploitation of it, contributed to the ultimate dissolution of the
Gaelic landholding systems,[34] and with them, their attendant social and
economic institutions. Gaelic sept leaders often welcomed the prospect
of immediate relief from traditional exactions by adopting, in part or in
whole, English landholding practices. Perhaps quite predictably too, the
immediate advantage blinded them to the more complex issues involved
in such alterations. Many Gaelic 'freeholders' who took advantage of the
alternatives provided by the extension of English law and the reduction
of the chief's status, were unable to match their new acquisitions and new
status with the ability or the perceptions to sustain the investments involved.[35] The changes in landownership in County Monaghan, an area
officially excluded from a definite plantation policy, show how the 'conquest' could advance apace, aided in no small measure by the indigenous
population. The Gaelic chiefs were not conscious of the 'conquest' in the
context of such landownership changes. Many Gaelic landowners sold
parts of their freehold to planter elements.[36]

---

[33] See Bernadette Cunningham, 'Native Culture and Political Change in Ireland,
1580-1640', in Ciaran Brady and Raymond Gillespie (eds), *Natives and Newcomers:
essays on the making of Irish Colonial Society 1534-1641* (Dublin, 1986), pp 148-70, and
also Mary O'Dowd, 'Gaelic Economy and Society', in the same volume, pp 120-47.

[34] Patrick J. Duffy's analysis of changes in landholding patterns in sixteenth century
County Monaghan emphasizes the importance, in the late sixteenth century, of the alacrity with which sub-lords exploited the extension of English law to become independent of
their chiefs. See P.J. Duffy, 'The territorial organization of Gaelic landownership and its
transformation in Co. Monaghan, 1595-1640', in *Irish Geography*, vol. 14 (1981),
(hereafter 'Territorial Organization').

[35] P.J. Duffy, 'Territorial Organization', pp 16-7.

[36] Duffy, 'Territorial Organization', pp 16-7, Duffy lists a number of Gaelic landowners who sold land to planters, and he emphasizes the difference in the planters' fortunes and those of their Gaelic entrepreneurs:
'The principal differences therefore between the Gaelic consolidation of estates and the
new colonial estates was the apparent inability of the former to manage their properties
successfully, in contrast to the British investors, who had the capacity and motivation to
make the land work for them.'
See also Allan I. Macinnes, 'Scottish Gaeldom, 1638-1651: The Vernacular Response to
the Covenanting Dynamic' (hereafter 'Scottish Gaeldom') in John Dwyer, Roger A.
Mason, Alexander Murdoch (eds), *New Perspectives on the Politics and Culture of Early
Modern Scotland*, (Edinburgh (nd)), pp 59-95.

Efforts, therefore, by many of the Gaelic Irish to adapt meaningfully to the life-styles of the most advanced of the new English entrepreneurs were undertaken, for the most part, for immediate advantage, without consideration of the complex system of values underlying the attitudes and activities of the newcomers. Their perceptions of authority and even of wealth were not compatible with the values necessary to succeed in long term investment ventures. Their own desire for individual increase in power, obscured their fundamental lack of appreciation for the methods required to secure such power, or wealth. The element of individual aggrandisement characteristic of the power struggles of the traditional Gaelic polity, is manifest once again in the behaviour of such sept leaders. The availability of a further option in the existence of a source of power other than the military strength of one's own sept, or a stronger local ally, namely that of the government, caused many Gaelic chiefs of the sixteenth century to become accomplices in the disintegration of the Gaelic world rather than becoming conscious participants in the 'modernization' of the Gaelic social and political structures.[37]

Along with the demise of the Gaelic Irish elites, the seventeenth century witnessed the tortuous replacement of the Anglo-Irish catholics/Old English, by new English protestants in government administration and as the controllers of wealth, privilege and power. The extension of crown authority over the whole of Ireland during the early seventeenth century reduced the importance of individual Gaelic chiefs to an extent intolerable in its effects, to the majority of them. The Old English who had occupied, uncomfortably, a middle ground between Gaelic Irish and English-born subjects for some decades were now on the brink of social and political dispossession. Much of the political history of the period can be seen in the light of their eclipse as a force in Irish and English politics. They, unlike the Gaelic Irish, had centuries of experience in offices of power in the Dublin administration. Both in education and social orientation they were geared for continued

---

[37] This is a point stressed by T.J. Dunne in his analysis of the impact of the Tudor conquest:
'Political unity and the transformation in attitudes and identity which accompanied it were imposed by English conquest in a manner which involved the destruction of the Gaelic system and political culture rather than its 'modernization' — in Dunne, 'Evidence', pp 11, 12.

participation in government.[38] The Gaelic Irish had rarely taken part in any major way in the Dublin parliament, and usually treated with the king directly, or indirectly through his lieutenants. Shane O'Neill dealt directly with Elizabeth I in the mid-sixteenth century. His kinsman, Hugh O'Neill, earl of Tyrone, likewise preferred to deal directly with the crown than with government officials. He appealed directly to James I over the head of Arthur Chichester in the post-Kinsale settlement in Ulster.[39]

The extent to which a definitive social or cultural distinction can be drawn between the Gaelic Irish and Old English communities in the seventeenth century is quite unclear. Centuries of intermarriage and military alliances had created much common ground between them.[40] The Old English had a tradition of participation in the parliament of the colony. They were proud and jealous of the privileges and duties attached to their rôle in government. The Gaelic Irish traditionally played little part in the Dublin parliament and were not self-consciously jealous of parliamentary rights and procedures as were the Old English. The basic differences in their respective political experiences had far-reaching consequences for the self-perception and especially for the expectations of each group. The difficulties arising from racial and cultural differences in Ireland during the early decades of the seventeenth century, were compounded by the increasingly sectarian nature of the society.[41] The adherence of the majority of the Old English and the Gaelic Irish to Roman catholicism in the seventeenth century further complicates the question of their distinct identities. The reception given to the Counter-Reformation in Ireland by both groups points to another complex network of political and religious overlap of identities and

---

[38] See Brendan Bradshaw's study of the parliament in the mid-sixteenth century in Brian Farrell (ed.), *The Irish Parliamentary Tradition* (Dublin, 1973), Chapter 5, pp 68-87.

[39] See N.P. Canny, 'The Flight of the Earls 1607', in *Irish Historical Studies XVII*, No. 67 (March 1971), p. 383, and see also Aidan Clarke, 'Ireland and the general crisis', in *Past and Present,* No. 48 (1970), pp 79-99, esp. p. 85. However, with regard to the concept of the seventeenth century 'general crisis' see and compare J.H. Elliott, 'Revolution and Continuity in Early Modern Europe', in *Past and Present,* No. 42 (February 1969), pp 35-57, in which Elliott suggests that the sixteenth century too experienced a 'general crisis' period in the 1560s-1570s.

[40] See Aidan Clarke, *The Old English in Ireland, 1625-42* (London, 1966).

[41] Clarke, 'Ireland and the general crisis', *passim.*

ambitions. Whether or not the Counter-Reformation was received differently by the Gaelic Irish and Old English as distinct racial or cultural groups is a problem which will be tentatively explored in the latter part of this study.

The personal commitment of many individuals to the values of Trent is undoubted. Its impact on the religious practice of the majority of the population is less clear.[42] What appears to be more certain, however, is that the individuals involved in the propagation of the Tridentine reforms in Ireland did not subscribe to one goal, one view of Ireland, or share a single political objective. The political implications of the Counter-Reformation were felt throughout Europe — Irish seminarians trained in the continental colleges absorbed both its spiritual and secular implications. On their return to Ireland, some attempted to analyse the Irish situation in terms originally designed to cater for polities which were entirely different to that of Ireland.[43] Many of these continentally trained seminarians and priests became involved in political intrigues involving the catholic continental powers and influential recusant elements at home.[44]

---

[42] The following studies consider the problems faced by the missionaries of the Counter-Reformation including the internal rivalry and problems encountered in the missionary field: Michael Olden, 'Counter-Reformation problems in Munster', in *Irish Ecclesiastical Record*, 104 (1965), p. 42-54; J.J. Silke, 'Hugh O'Neill, the Catholic Question and the Papacy', in *Irish Ecclesiastical Record*, 104 (1965), pp 65-79; P.J. Corish, 'The Reorganization of the Irish Church 1603-1641', in *Proc. of Irish Catholic Historical Committee*, 3 (1957), pp 9-141; John Bossy, 'The Counter-Reformation and the people of Catholic Ireland, 1596-1641', in *Historical Studies*, 8 (1971), pp 155-69, P.J. Corish, *The Catholic Community in the Seventeenth and Eighteenth Centuries* (Helicon, Dublin, 1981), N.P. Canny, *From Reformation to Restoration: Ireland 1534-1660* (Dublin, 1987).

[43] See J.J. Silke, 'Primate Lombard and James I', in *The Irish Theological Quarterly*, 22 (1955), pp 124-50. Preston and O'Neill specified France and Brussels as examples in their demands for freedom of worship in 1646 in the Confederation's propositions. They stated:

'That the exercise of the Roman Catholic religion be in Dublin, Drogheda and all the kingdom of Ireland as free and public as it is now in Paris in France and Brussels in the Low Countries' —

from the *Letter-Book of the Earl of Clanricarde 1645-1647*, (ed.) John Lowe (Dublin, 1983), p. 307.

[44] The Franciscan archbishop of Tuam, Florence Conry, was very active in continental schemes on behalf of the northern chief especially; an elaborate scheme involving the Earls of Tyrone and Tyrconnell was devised in the 1620s. See Tomás Ó Fiaich, 'Republicanism, and separatism in the seventeenth century', in *Léachtaí Cholm Cille* II

Gaelic poetry written during this period has been interpreted as having been imbued to a great extent with the principles of the Counter-
Reformation, and these principles have been said to have exercised a
transforming influence on the traditional bardic world view as articulated in the poetry of this period. Poetry of this period will not be
dealt with in any detail here, but its existence and the problems surrounding its interpretation as possible historical source material will form
part of this study.

While the efforts of the Gaelic chiefs and leaders in the sixteenth and
seventeenth centuries were certainly focussed on survival, their own
world view had a fundamental part to play in determining the lengths to
which they were prepared to go to survive. In order to use effectively, the
bardic poetry of the sixteenth and seventeenth centuries as a possible
source of a Gaelic Irish perspective on contemporary events, one must
consider the whole corpus of bardic poetry as a reference. This poetry
belongs to a distinctively traditional genre, and its entire ethos was one
in which great emphasis was placed on the past as an aid to understanding both the present and the future. [45] The superficial anachronism
of the framework, rigidly adhered to by the poets until their final collapse, has hitherto concealed the major importance of the insights to be
gained into the Gaelic mentality of the sixteenth and seventeenth centuries through examining the carefully constructed framework, preserved and perpetuated by the poets through earlier centuries. The investment of the poets' mode of expression with symbolic and/or allusive
significance over a period of centuries allowed them to adhere to the old
expressions to cope with new situations. Its universal applicability
throughout the cultural unit of Ireland enabled the poets to manipulate

---

(1971) pp 74-87 and F. O'Brien, 'Florence Conry, Archbishop of Tuam 1608', in *Irish
Rosary* (1928). For the careers of the earls involved in Conry's scheme see B. Jennings,
'The career of Hugh, son of Rory O'Donnell, Earl of Tyrconnel in the Low Countries
1607-1642' in *Studies* 30 (1941), pp 219-34. H.F. Kearney considered the Counter-
Reformation hierarchy to be divided into two opposed factions — that of the Spanish
(mainly Old Irish) and the pro-English (mainly Old English). The subsequent politicking
among the Counter-Reformation hierarchy reflected the influence of European politics
on the participants: H.F. Kearney, 'Ecclesiastical politics and the Counter-Reformation
in Ireland 1618-1648' in *Journal of Ecclesiastical History,* vol. XI, No. 2 (October 1960),
pp 202-212. See also John Bossy, 'The character of Elizabethan Catholicism', in *Past and
Present,* No. 21 (April 1962) especially pp 42-3.
[45] Cf. Peter Burke *Popular Culture in Early Modern Europe,* especially pp 178-204.

the structure which they inherited, and which they augmented by their use of it. The ease with which the poets, through several centuries of political turmoil, adapted to ever-changing situations, indicates both their familiarity with their medium and their absolute certainty that those for whom they wrote both understood and appreciated their efforts. Likewise, the stability of the fragile structure carefully maintained by the poets is perhaps a reflection of a similar fragility in the political and social structures of early modern Ireland, which had retained the poets as one of its supports. The poets' survival was of course entirely dependent on the survival of this structure. By the same token, as in many other spheres, that which was created or evolved with a specific and limited purpose, outlived its creators and its function; its original strength becoming finally its greatest weakness. Thus it was with the bardic institution, the poets evolved from an ancient profession of seers and *fili* who performed a specific function within Gaelic Irish society. They supported social structures which maintained a society of which they were an integral part. The paradoxical strength and weakness of the bardic institution is analogous with its political counterpart, the Gaelic Irish segmental and fragmented political structure. This was at once a culturally unified entity and an inherently fractious and fissiparous polity. This fragmented structure initially provided an effective barrier against conquest; the prolonged existence of the same structure finally destroyed any efforts at cohesive united action against sustained attack.[46]

It is as a cypher of the Gaelic Irish aristocratic mentality that the bardic poetry can be examined, but only in its own terms of reference outlined above, in order to provide a referential basis from which to approach the hectic sixteenth and seventeenth centuries. The poetry provides us with a structure of Gaelic responses, albeit in a highly stylized literary form. When the limits of the material are understood and taken into account, this same material can be regarded as an articulation of some of the fundamental perceptions of the Gaelic Irish elites and must be interpreted according to the rationale traditionally articulated in this

---

[46] George Steiner in *After Babel; aspects of language and translation* (London, 1975) outlines a linguistic 'hermeneutic motion' in four parts, pp 296-413. This interpretation in a way, provides a linguistic analogy for the various phases of Tudor involvement in Ireland, and the Gaelic response to it.

medium.[47] This is in contradistinction to the interpretations hitherto offered, which look to the poetry for 'responses' to individual historic and political situations and too often according to the rationale of the initiators of the conquest. The poetry is a positive body of material, articulating positive and long lasting perceptions of the Gaelic mentality.[48] Throughout the late sixteenth century and early seventeenth century, the poetry continued to articulate some of the fundamental perceptions of the world view of the Gaelic Irish, not in spite of encroachments from extra-insular sources, nor indeed because of them, but because the perceptions stylized in form in the poetry were the literary articulation of the *mores* of the Gaelic aristocratic political mentality. The history of Gaelic Ireland during the sixteenth and seventeenth centuries has been almost entirely that of retrospectively anachronistic analysis where the 'conquest' has been seen to dominate the Gaelic mentality even before the English administration felt any security in its position regarding Ireland.

Throughout this study I have resisted the temptation to provide a 'historical context' from the current canon, except in discussions where more than a sketchy background was necessary. Only thus is it possible to consider the poets' compositions independent of the 'milestones' imposed by the historiography of the last two centuries on the historical imagination of the modern reader. This is not to say that the discussion is independent of the considerable body of incisive, thorough and interesting history which has been written in the recent past in this period.[49] It is meant to convey a sense of the Gaelic world, however, from the most immediate of Gaelic source materials without seeking its validation entirely from without itself.

The nature of the Gaelic mentality in the sixteenth and seventeenth centuries, as depicted in the poetry cannot be described and then illustrated. The use of the poetry in this study demands that the poetry be continually called upon in illustration and description rather than in reference alone. The desire to allow the poetry to speak for itself has

---

[47] See Nathan Wachtel, *The Vision of the Vanquished: the Spanish Conquest of Peru through Indian Eyes 1530-1570*, translated by Bert and Sîon Reynolds, (Hassocks Harvester Press, 1977), in which Wachtel attempts to understand the Spanish conquest of Peru through the medium of Peruvian oral literature and cultural rites.

[48] See Martines, *Society and History in English Renaissance Verse,* pp 1-17.

[49] See especially Dunne, 'Evidence', pp 16-17.

posed problems of organization; whether to confine the study to a chronological or to a thematic structure. In the end it was considered that a chronological progression could best provide a framework for a thematic but flexible handling of the material. Therefore, the chapters follow on each other in a chronological sequence, but each one deals with different facets of a number of themes, and forms a complete discussion in itself. The opening chapter thus deals first in a general way with some of the different themes which occur in the earliest and latest bardic poetry. This is done primarily to introduce the tone of the poetry and to indicate the similarity of the earlier material to the later. The second part of the first chapter deals specifically and in some detail with three poems, two from the thirteenth and one from the fourteenth century, which are used to set up a structure of bardic themes and references upon which to build a sense of the bardic mentality for the subsequent centuries.

The second chapter deals with the themes outlined in the first, as they are manipulated by the poets to suit the conditions of the sixteenth century. This chapter deals specifically with the poets' perceptions of unity and the related themes of the rights of battle and the privileges of the victor over the defeated. Poems dedicated to two leaders, an Ormond and a member of the O'Byrne sept, are used to highlight the similarity of treatment accorded to both by the poets — though both leaders operate within their own spheres under the influence of entirely different perceptions of power and warfare and enjoy dissimilar relations with the authorities. The similarity of both poems shows the structure through which the poets view quite different situations. This demonstrates their ability to superimpose their perceptual framework on any situation to suit their own perceptions of events. In this chapter also, some poems of Tadhg Dall Ó hUiginn are studied, which are ostensibly mutually contradictory, but in fact are classic examples of the poets' ability to manipulate their referential framework to accommodate the *fait accompli*, to rationalize the position of the powerful, whoever he/they may be, according to traditional perceptions, enshrined in the poetry. This chapter attempts to see the disparate events, cumulatively recognized as steps forward in the Tudor reconquest, through the poetry, and to accept as consequential only those elements regarded as such by the poets. Chronologically, this is the chapter which deals principally with the mid- to late-sixteenth century.

The third chapter explores the validity of what has been described as the poets' awareness of a sense of impending doom. In the aftermath of the flight of the northern chiefs, the northern poetry was particularly sombre. This has been attributed to the poets' prescient grasp of the imminent collapse not only of the Gaelic polity, but of the Gaelic world. This must be balanced, however, against the euphoric composition of welcome for James I, and both elements must be viewed in the greater context of the bardic referential framework the idiom of which demanded that every loss be lamented as the final and most destructive blow, and every gain regarded as the definitive assurance of future security. This chapter also attempts to deal with the poets' perceptions of the individual Tudor encroachments in Ulster especially, through the poets' treatment of the individuals involved. 'Collaborators' such as Niall Garbh O'Donnell are shown to be just as traditionally motivated as one such as Rury O'Donnell, earl of Tyrconnel, whose name, unlike that of his cousin Niall, conjures no image of a chief for sale. In the Munster sphere, the complexities surrounding land titles, with native interests conflicting with planter interests, provides some interesting background material for the compositions of an O'Daly poet for George Carew, Lord President of Munster (+ 1629), claimant of lands belonging severally to McCarthy, Barry Oge, O'Mahon, O'Driscoll and O'Daly. Once again, this episode is considered as it was encountered through the poets' world view, rather than putting it into the greater 'conquest' picture which has heretofore been the frame of reference for such events with the poetry being used, normally out of its traditional context, to support an anachronistic interpretation of the poets' intentions and perceptions.

In the epilogue which follows the final chapter, an attempt has been made to follow the chosen themes through to the mid- and in some instances, the late seventeenth century, in order to illustrate the longevity of the themes and motifs of the bardic idiom and the problematic question of the appearance of these motifs in poems outside the strictly bardic genere. Since repetition, reiteration and analogy are essential ingredients of the poets' works, any attempt to understand them in their own terms of reference, necessarily involves a familiarization with these essential elements. An attempt has been made to produce an alternative frame of reference from which to work with bardic poetry to that which has hitherto been offered; and thereby return their voice to those who articulated the *mores* of Gaelic society for over four centuries.

I

UNITY, SOVEREIGNTY AND ACCEPTANCE OF THE *FAIT ACCOMPLI*

> *Beag a fhios agad, dar leam*
> *cia misi d'fhearaibh Éireann:*
> *spéis, am dhánuibh dhlighe dhe,*
> *Ó Dálaigh Midhe meise.*
> (Bergin, *Irish Bardic Poetry,* No. 20,
> st. 16, p. 90)

THE IMPLICATIONS OF the survival of the traditional Gaelic perceptions can be understood in a historical sense only by considering the bardic themes which appear to carry the burden of those perceptions. These are the problematic 'unity' of Banbha; the rights to her 'charter' or sovereignty; and the power and prerogatives pertaining to the victor, that is, the poets' acceptance of the *fait accompli,* as they are presented in the poetry at different periods between the thirteenth and seventeenth centuries. While the individual themes mentioned in the introduction will be discussed later in some detail, it is instructive to look in a more general way at the kind of claims the poets made for their profession in relation to the chief. This is especially interesting seen through the perceived role of the poet as the individual whose knowledge of the rationale of the Gaelic world view enables him to articulate the criteria of 'belonging' and legitimacy of position in the Gaelic world.

Sixteenth century material is used in the following discussion in order to introduce a sense of the atmosphere of the bardic world during the early Tudor period; a period when the foundations of the Gaelic world were coming under increasing pressure. This, however, is not evident in the poems presented here, though the prospect of Ireland's imminent

destruction and the demise of the Gaelic world are traditionally cited as motifs of exhortation to the addressee. Through the stanzas presented in the following discussion I hope to create a sense of the independence of the perceptions articulated in the poetry, of what we now, with historical hindsight consider as momentous events in the rapid decline of the Gaelic world. The poets' preoccupations can be seen to have had their roots in a rationale grounded in antiquity and adequate for the expression of the Gaelic mentality without being either anachronistic or self-conscious, if admittedly perhaps precious.

The poets made much of their familiarity with the chief and their claims on his time and attention.[1] In a poem to the O'Hara chief Cormac (+ 1612) Tadhg Dall Ó hUiginn stresses his intimacy with him:

> Do-gheibhinnse, a ghéag Luighne,
> do chogar, do chomhuirle,
> t'uille agus leath do leabtha,
> breath nár thruime toirbhearta,
> (Knott, *Tadhg Dall*, No. 14, st. 17, p. 94)

> [I used to have thy confidence, thy counsel, thou branch of Leyney, thy elbow and half thy couch, an award which no gifts could excel.]

A poem of reproach by the same poet to a different patron, William Burke, contains the following stanza:

> Mé a mhaighistir, mé a dhalta,
> mé a chompán 'sa chomhalta;
> olc fuair i gcéadóir mo chradh,
> éagóir do-chuaidh dom chreachadh.
> (Knott, *Tadhg Dall*, No. 23, st. 10, p. 170)

> [I was his master, his pupil, his companion, his comrade; not well did he forthwith obtain my cattle; unjustly he went to despoil me.]

The diminution of the individual powers of the rulers and septs during the later fifteenth and the sixteenth centuries is not clearly reflected in the work of the contemporary poets. Much of the bardic poetry of the

---

[1] See P.A. Breatnach, 'The Chief's Poet', and see also James Carney, *The Irish Bardic Poet* (Dublin, 1985 reprint).

thirteenth and fourteenth centuries does not appear to be appreciably different in style or content to the bardic poetry of the early seventeenth century for instance. This is important especially where certain themes are involved. The themes, for example, of 'Banbha endangered' and the traditional search for her 'rescuer', an individual who would 'unite' Ireland and defeat her enemies, must be understood for what they are. Examples of similar use of these three connected themes in three poems, one from the late fourteenth century and two others from the later sixteenth century and early seventeenth centuries respectively, illustrate the independence of the use of these themes of the social or political background of the 'conquest'. The themes are used rather by the poets to articulate the traditional perceptions of the poets of the call for a leader, his traditional duties and the dangers from which Ireland must be protected. A poem attributed to Tadhg Camchosach Ó Dálaigh, a poet of the later fourteenth century, calls on Niall Óg O'Neill, a northern chieftain of the Uí Néill, to unite Ireland and to rescue Banbha:

Sí ag Éirionnchaibh dá éis soin;
do bhí ag allmhorchaibh athoidh;
an bhean chomtha lér fhuaigh Art
fuair Orchra agus fuair furtacht.

Cúis athtoirse Insi Fáil:
sochroide Ghall dá gabháil;
tnúth fán mBanbha bhféaraird bhfinn;
faghla in gach énaird d'Éirinn.

Ní raibhe bean ina broid
an chríoch do chabhuir Pádroig
le rígh chláir bhailbhmhilis Bhreagh
airmInis Fáil gur fóireadh.

Teagasg Aodha dá oighre —
ní théid céim don chomhairle;
fuaighfidh le a ghníomh gach gartmhagh;
tuairfidh bríogh na beandachtan.

Niall mhac Aodha, airdrí cáigh —
a-tá i dtairngire Bearcháin,
ní hionráidh nach é bhus fearr
an té do iomráidh Aoibheall,

(Mág Craith, *Dán na mBráthar Mionúr*, Vol. 1, sts. 3, 4, 10, 40, 41, pp 1, 2, 3, 9)

[Having been the property of foreigners for a time, she now belongs to the Irish. The partner with whom Art mated was in trouble and has been rescued. Inis Fáil's being held by a foreign army; lust for the possession of Banbha with the fair rich grass pillaging in every part of Ireland — these have been the cause of Ireland's woe. No woman was ever in a plight like that of Inis Fáil (the land to whose aid St Patrick came) until she was rescued by the king of sweet mute Clan Breagh. (Niall) departs not by (even) a (single) step from the advice of Aodh to his heir. He will unite together every plain and field, by his exploits. He will merit the efficacy of the blessing. It is Niall, son of Aodh, high-king of all, who is (referred to) in Bearchán's prophecy. It cannot be gainsaid that he, whom Aoibheall prophesied, will be victorious.]

Ó Dálaigh describes Ireland as being overrun by foreigners, this fact coupled with the pillaging of internal and external rivals and enemies of Ireland has caused Ireland's downfall. Niall O'Neill, son of Aodh, however, has 'united' Ireland and espoused her. His validation is his actual power and the fact also that he is the 'prophesied' one.

Some two hundred years later (c. 1590s) Mathgamhain Ó hUiginn wrote the following stanzas for the *duanaire* of Feidhlim mac Fiachaidh O'Byrne, chief of the Uí Bhroin of Gabháil Raghnall:[2]

Níor saoileadh go tteacht as-teagh,
fosaidh Gall re gort Gaoidheal
teacht dóibh tar Éireanncha air,
slóigh fá déidheancha ag deabhaidh.

Ní choigleadh a chrú a gcathaibh,
ní fhilleadh ó anfhachain,
ag sníomh lann, ag cor chosguir
gomh Ghall nó gur ghríosasdoir.

2 Seán Mac Airt (ed.), *Leabhar Branach* (Dublin, 1985 reprint).

Treabh na leómhan a leath dí,
aitreabh na nathrach neimhi
san taobh ar-aill don innsi,
nár fhaomh faill 'na feithimh-si.

Na nathracha Goill Ghuirt Breagh,
na leómhain laochruidh Laighean
tug sé a n-aithbheóghadh inn,
is é an flaithleómhan Feilim.

Ní thaobhaid Laighnigh lot Goill,
ní thógbhuid airm dá n-ealchoing;
ortha féin do chló a gconfaidh
ón ló as réidh do Raghnallchaibh.
(Mac Airt, *Leabhar Branach*, No. 50, pp 178-81, lines 4670-3,
4698-701, 4730-3, 4742-5, 4750-3.)

[An encampment of foreigners against the field of the Gael was
not expected, a host who delayed in fighting — until they overwhelmed the Irish, (in spite of Feidhlim).
He was not sparing of his blood in battles, he did not turn from
danger — interweaving spears, creating havoc until he excited the
venom of the foreigners.
The serpents are the foreigners of Gort Breagh, the lions (are) the
warriors of Leinster. He has revived us. Feidhlim is the prince of
the lions.
The Leinstermen yield not to the destruction of the foreigners,
they do not take up arms (in vain?) — from the day that the
O'Byrnes are prepared their rapacity destroys themselves.]

Once again, 'foreigners' have overtaken Ireland and destroyed Banbha.
However, the arrival of Feidhlim has curtailed their activities. He like
Niall has resisted the foreigners. Like the enemies of Niall also
Féidhlim's enemies have undone themselves by their greediness regard-
ing the land of Banbha. Féidhlim O'Byrne's prowess as a warrior has
destroyed their advance. As in the case following O'Neill's victory,
Ireland is saved, she is similarly saved on the occasion of Féidhlim's vic-
tories from a fate similar to that faced by her two centuries earlier in
Niall O'Neill's time.

Fear Flatha Ó Gnímh's poem of the seventeenth century following the
departure of O'Neill, O'Donnell and sundry other northern chiefs, in

September 1607, re-echoes the sentiments of both preceding poems in its perceptions of Ireland's condition in the absence of a leader. Before Niall O'Neill's emergence into power Ireland was overrun by foreigners, likewise before Féidhlim O'Byrne proved his military strength, Ireland was also 'under severe pressure from foreigners'. Now, in Ó Gnímh's case, the absence of the northern chiefs places Ireland in a similar condition of distress:

> Baramhail do-bearar dóibh —
> fuidheall áir d'éis a ndíobhdhóidh,
> 'gá sníomh ó chróluighe a gcneadh,
> nó is líon tóraimhe ar dtilleadh.

> Atá brat ciach ós a gcionn —
> mhúcas glóir Ghaoidheal Éireann,
> mar néall gceath ghrianbháitheas goil
> do leath d'iarghnáicheas orthaibh.

> Treóid Ghall i gcluaintibh a gcean,
> túir aolta i n-áit a bhfoirgneadh —
> margaidh uatha in gach oirear,
> cruacha ar ardaibh aonaigheadh.
> (O'Rahilly, *Measgra Dánta* II, No. 54, ll 5-8, 17-20, 33-6, p. 144-6.)

[They can be compared to the remnants of a slaughter after their destruction, suffering in the gore of their wounds or (they can be compared to) a returning funeral party.
The glory of the Gael is extinguished by a cloud of sorrow which covers them, as a rain-cloud obliterates the sun; so anxiety overwhelms them.
A herd of foreigners in their cattle meadows, lime towers in the place of their buildings — stacks on their assembly mounds, their markets in every quarter.]

The evident survival of the perceptions articulated in both the earliest and latest poems is quite remarkable considering the tremendous changes and development which had taken place in the intervening centuries. These changes had occurred not only in Ireland, but throughout what in the early days of bardic poetry had been known as Christendom, and what in the later period had become divided into the chaotic collection of quarrelling kingdoms and states which constituted Renaissance Europe.

The poet played a substantial political/cultural role, articulating official acceptance of the chief, celebrating his victories and championing his enemies. The poet William Óg mac a'Bhaird extols the dignity and valour of Cú Chonnacht Maguire, a secure lord of Fermanagh from 1566 to 1589.[3] He is a warrior of stature, a generous benefactor of poets and implacable against rivals:

Ní cú míolchon, dá maoidhind,
cú do chuan fhíochmhar Fhéilim,
rogha an chuain an cú luaidhim
luaidhill clú uaidh fá Éirinn.

Lá gliadh a ngar don fherchoin
ní tiad cách d'fhad a orchair;
cú 'na aice ní fhoghthair
cú confaidh craite a chomhthaigh.
(Greene, *Maguire Poems,* No. 18, sts. 7 and 9, p. 161)

[Were I to boast, the hound of the fierce litter of Féilim is not one who hunts small game; the one I mention is the choice of the litter, he has caused a movement of poets throughout Ireland.

His enemies do not go within a spear's cast of the hero on the day of battle; no hound is found to compare with the hound of fury who shakes his rival.]

The Butler earls of Ormond were faithful patrons of the poets and were in the interesting position of being continually dealt with by poets who felt it their duty to celebrate the royalist escapades of many of the Butlers. This the poets accomplished by using the theme of the 'succour of Banbha'. The foreign title 'Earl' proved no insurmountable barrier to the poet:

Do bhoai an t-ainm ar a aire
dá ghnaoi go gairm na sgoile;
don iarmhar, níor fhéag file,
séad fine iarladh oile.
(Carney, *Butler Poems,* No. 18, st. 8, p. 83.)

---

[3] David Greene, *Maguire Poems,* Introduction, p. vii.

[He guarded his name (i.e. that of 'Earl') on account of its fame until given a (new) name by the poetic school; the other the poets regarded not, it being (but) the heirloom of other earls.]

This poem by Uaithne Mac Uilliam Í Chobhthaigh for James Butler, ninth Earl of Ormond makes explicit the poet's role in officially recognizing the lord's title. It also illustrates the poet's ability to absorb or reject titles such as 'earl'. Ormond's military conduct; success against his rivals and enemies (i.e. the O'Neills) and his generosity to poets has been considered by the poet and Ormond qualifies, according to the rationale subscribed to by the poets and articulated in the poetry, as a worthy Gaelic chieftain.

Alternatively, the poet could counsel rejection of such foreign titles and make great play of the superiority of the native titles. This rejection is however, not to be taken at face value. The poet's real complaint in the following poem is his sense of neglect by his patron; he suggests that bad as their relations are now, should Mac William accept the proffered unspecified 'foreign' title, the distance would grow between them. It is poems such as this which cause those unfamiliar with the poets' idiom to perceive 'nationalism' and new nationalistic awareness among the poets:

> San riocht i rabhabhair riamh
> bí id Riocard mhac Mheic Uilliam;
> mairg do ghlac aoinchéim oile,
> a slat mhaoithréidh Mhuchroimhe.
>
> Dá bhfaghtháa ceannus Chláir Floinn,
> níorbh fiú dhuit, a dhreach séaghoinn,
> ainm allmhardha dá rádh ruibh
> fa chlár ndaghBhanbha id dhúthaigh.
>
> Gidh mise féin — níorbh fiú dhuid,
> ar ainm nguasachtach ngaruid,
> a ghríobh thadhaill bhruaigh Bhanbha,
> nach faghaim uain th'agallmha.
>
> Nách mó lámhaim a rádh ruibh,
> gémadh éiric im' aghaidh,
> a ghéag oirnidhe ós fhuil Chuinn,
> go bhfuil oirbhire eadruinn?

(Knott, *Tadhg Dall,* No. 22a, sts. 2, 9, 10, 11, pp 160, 161)

[Be even as thou hast ever been 'Richard son of Mac William', alas, if thou shouldst assume any other rank, thou gentle scion of Mucroimhe.
Didst thou get the headship of Flann's Plain it would not advantage thee, thou gallant form, in thy native place to reign over Banbha by a foreign title.
Even I — it were not worth thy while for the sake of a hazardous and shortlived title, thou warrior who hauntest the border of Banbha, that I should not get an opportunity of speech with thee.
Am I not all the more emboldened to say to thee, though it should mean an *eiric* leviable against me, thou scion ordained above the blood of Conn, that there is a reproach between us.]

In the case of both poems above, the poet translates the contemporary situation into an idiom which allows him to deal with a variety of individuals and situations in a manner conformable to the tradition. This is not merely an exercise in literary manipulation, though such manipulation is a major part of the poets' assimilating machinery; but is also the literary reflection of the rationale and perceptions governing the ability and willingness of the aristocratic polity to accept, absorb and assimilate, if possible, the changes occurring in their world.

'Belonging' in the world of the poets' perceptions was achieved in a number of ways. Along with possessing the military ability to realize one's territorial claims, the successful lord or incumbent might display other hallmarks of validity; the poets praised the lord for his hospitality and his ability to provide adequate patronage (often by indulging in successful reaving), both to protect his own reputation and to attract the most skilled artists to his household. In praising the illustriousness of the patron's household and its visiting company, the poet indicated the wealth of the lord and indirectly the level of reward expected of him.

Tadhg Dall Ó hUiginn describes delightful scenes in his poems praising the household of Conn O' Donnell and his wife Rose in Caisleán Leithbhir, and of Shane O'Neill's dwelling in Lios Gréine. Ó hUiginn praises the company of Caisleán Leithbhir:

Ionmhuin bruidhean 'na mbíd sin;
ionmhuin lucht bhíos san bhruidhin;
slógh an toighe is teach an tslóigh —
mo chean neach foighe a n-onóir.
(Knott, *Tadhg Dall*, No. 5, st. 5, p. 36.)

[Dear is the hostel in which these are wont to be, dear the folk who dwell in the hostel; the people of the house and the house of that people — happy is any who shall get honour such as theirs.]

Again, in 'Lios Gréine', we see the poet exalting the dwelling of Shane O'Neill thereby eulogizing the chief:

Lios Gréine is Eamhain d'Ultaibh,
treabh nách budh tréigthe ar Thailtein
teach nách fuil barr ar bhronntaibh,
bronntair creach Gall san glaintreibh.
(Knott, *Tadhg Dall*, No. 6, st. 1, p. 38.)

[Lios Gréine is the Eamhain of Ulster; a dwelling not to be deserted for Tailte; a house whose gifts are not excelled, booty taken from the foreigner is bestowed in that bright dwelling.]

On another level, 'belonging' and accommodation was achieved by the poets' continual use of analogy and comparison. Inevitably, and almost invariably, comparisons are drawn between the addressee and his ancestors, and/or suitable historical or mythological characters. This of course emphasizes once again the essential continuity of human existence as perceived by the poets in their articulation of Gaelic Irish consciousness, and their perceived necessity to imbue all 'new' events with meaning. Recognizing precedents and foreshadowings and identifying re-enactments is something which Gaelic society shared with most other cultures.[4] Much of this arguably primitive sense of historical continuity lives on in the poets' eternal awareness of the historic and mythological past. Favourable comparison with ancient heroes or

---

4 Alwyn and Brinley Rees stress the importance of precedent and of 'first time of doing' in the early Gaelic world:
'in the *Lebor Gabála* care is taken to commemorate the occasions when things were done or experienced for the first time and to record the names of the persons concerned — the first to land, the first to die, the first to pass judgement, and so on, in this way the prototypes of existence in this world are established one after another',
in *The Celtic Heritage*, p. 106, and see Keating's use of 'first doings' in G. Keating, *Foras Feasa ar Éirinn: the History of Ireland*, ed. David Comyn and P.A. Dineen, 4 vols (London, 1902-14), p. 123. The use of precedent in times of change is discussed at some length in Keith Thomas, *Religion and the decline of magic*, pp 503-5 and see also Claude Lévi-Strauss, *The Savage Mind* (La Pensée Sauvage) (London, 1972).

equation of like attributes places the lauded patron in the mainstream of
the tradition shared by both the poet and the patron, and affords the
lord the respect due his position and prowess. Fearghal Óg mac a'
Bhaird, praising Cú Chonnacht Maguire (lord of Fermanagh,
1566-1589) dares to compare Maguire favourably with the legendary
Art Aoinfhear:

> Cáin Bhanbha do do dáiledh
> tarla so mur do saoiledh;
> nírbh fherr hé iná Art Énfher
> — déinedh sé le Gart Gaoidheal.
> (Greene, *Maguire Poems,* No. 1, st. 11, p. 4.)
> [It happened as was expected, the tribute of Ireland was allotted to
> him; let him move close to Ireland — Art Éinfhear was not better
> than he.]

A poem attributed to Fearghal Óg mac Fearghail addressed to Philip,
son of Aodh Connallach O'Reilly (+1596) illustrates the tendency in a
series of four successive stanzas beginning:

> Nó as tú an tIollánach oirdheirc
> nach umhal d'fhior uabhoirneart . . .
> (Carney, *O'Reilly Poems,* No. 19, st. 35, p. 98)
> [Or you are the noble Ioldánach, who is not humble before men
> . . .]

followed by:

> Nó as tú an déidgheal Ó Dhuibhlinn, . . .
> [or you are the bright-toothed Ó Duibhlinn . . .]

Thus the poet puts Philip O'Reilly on the same level with Lugh
Lámhfhada, fabled hero of the Tuatha Dé Danann, and alludes to the
possibility that he is a reincarnation of Diarmuid Ó Duibhne, Fenian
hero. The same hero (Lugh Lámhfhada) is recalled by Eochaidh (Ó
hEodhusa?) in a poem for Maol Mordha mac Mic Sheáin O'Reilly
(+1617):

> A Mhaol Mhórdha, a mhic ghrádhaigh,
> a aithghin an Ioldánuigh,
> an rí coimhdhe trenár chlá
> ná tí an Coimdhe dá chéddha.
> (Carney, *O'Reilly Poems,* No. 25, st. 39, p. 127.)

[Maol Mhuire — noble son — reincarnation of the Ioldánach . . .
(following lines corrupt)]

A poem by Fearghal Óg mac a'Bhaird celebrates Cormac O'Hara,
lord of Leighne (+ 1612). This entire poem is devoted to the comparison
of Cormac O'Hara with the great names of Gaelic historical mythology
and history:

> Do fághbhudh eighre ó nEadhra
> 'n-a ógmhacaomh oireaghdha
> mar do fágbhadh a fáidh Fionn
> ag clár fhádghlan na hÉirionn.
> (McKenna, *O'Hara Poems*, No. 8, st. 24, p. 118)

[Just as the prophet Fionn was left (heir) to the bright-soiled plain
of Éire, so the famous youth, the heir of Í Eadhra, was left.]

> Do éiridh d'aindeoin gach fhir;
> ar ó nEadhra do imthigh
> dála flatha na Féine,
> brágha chatha Choirrshléibhe.
> (McKenna, *O'Hara Poems,* No. 8, st. 26, p. 118.)

[He grew up in spite of all men; to Ó hEadhra, the vanguard of the
troop of Coirrshliabh, there happened what happened to the
prince of the Fian (i.e. Fionn).]

The victories and glories of Eoghan (Mogh Nuadhat), Murchadh mac
Bhriain Bhóirimhe and Cú Raoi are listed and they are declared
predecessors in temper and spirit of Cormac O'Hara:

> Dá nós súd — ní saobh in reacht —
> fuair tusa inmhe a hoirbheart,
> a bhláth craobh Thighe an Teampla,
> a bhile saor soidheargtha.
> (McKenna, *O'Hara Poems,* No. 8, st. 48, p. 124.)

[Following their example — a wise principle! — thou didst win
wealth by gallantry, O choice hero of the branches of Teach an
Teampla, O noble blushing hero.]

Being of Gaelic Irish lineage was not a necessary condition of belonging in the poets' schema. Foreign origin did not therefore dampen the

zeal of the poet eulogizing his patron, or provide an impediment to the foreigner being accorded the treatment normally the prerogative of the Gaelic chief. Many of those designated 'foreign' had at least one Gaelic Irish ancestor to which the poet skilfully appended often tendentious genealogies. Alternatively, the origins of the patron were explored to provide an equivalent connection for the adressee from his own supposed heritage. Tadhg Dall combines both practices in a poem to William Burke:

Ní aorfuinn, níor aortha dhamh,
gríobh do chloinn Chonaill Ghulban,
ní aorfainn, níor eagal lais,
dreagan do saorchlainn Séarlais.
(Knott, *Tadhg Dall*, No. 23, st. 19, p. 171.)

[I would not, it were not for me to do so — satirize a griffin of Conall Gulban's stock, I would not, he did not fear it, satirize a dragon of the noble race of Charles.]

Thus are Charlemagne, the great Frankish Emperor and Conall Gulban, the fabled mythical Ulster warrior, alluded to in support of William Burke's nobility.

With the same intention, that of accommodating the 'foreign' but suitable lord into the mainstream of the tradition, a sixteenth century poet, compares the castle/dwelling of Theobald Butler with all the great royal seats of Ireland, thereby placing Theobald on a par with those heroes who presided over such dwellings:

Triall gach éinfhir gu cúirt tTeabóid,
ceann na ndámhsgol,
brugh fairsiong fial fleadhach fionmhar,
teisd gan trághadh.
(Carney, *Butler Poems,* No. 6, st. 1, p. 20)

[Every man journeys to Theobald's court, the head of the schools, — a strong, hospitable, generous hostel — abounding in wine, a testimony which does not diminish.]

This dwelling is compared with Conn's Tara, Armagh, Brugh os Bóinne, Nás na Rí and Cashel:

. . . Teamhair Chuinn as choir 'na chonchlann
nó Ard Macha;
. . . nó an Brugh ós Bhóinn, clár na ccuradh,
'na mbíoth Áonghas,
. . . nó Nás na Ríogh a n-iath Laighean
. . . nó ráth Caisil, ríophort Mumhan,
na corn gcráobhach.
(Carney, *Butler Poems,* No. 6, ll. 451-4, 457, 459-60, p. 20.)

Tórna mac Maoilín celebrates the fame of Richard, Viscount Mountgarret (+ 1571) proclaiming him 'onchú Éireann':

Onchú Éireann, éigne Bearbha
nach beag áiriomh,
daor cheannghus a chlú ó chliaruibh
bladh nár báidheadh.
(Carney, *Butler Poems,* No. 1, st. 2, p. 1.)

[Warrior of Erin, salmon of Bearbha, not little his reckoning, his
fame is dearly bought from poets, fame which is not submerged.]

He — Richard — excels over Gaelic families fabled for their valour and
generosity.

Geall coimhleanga do chlú Roisdeard —
ní réim diamhair —
gur sháruigh clú Í Néill náraigh,
béim don Bhrianfhuil.
(Carney, *Butler Poems,* No. 1, st. 4, p. 1.)

[In contest the palm (lit. pledge) goes to the fame of Richard — this
is no secret matter — so that he has outdone the fame of generous
O'Neill, and is a reproach to the O'Briens.]

The poets thus show flexibility in their loyalties as between those of
relatively unquestionable Gaelic Irish descent and those of foreign descent. Similarly, their tradition was manipulated by them to suit the
several styles of encomium and occasional poem which their profession
could demand. Eochaidh Ó hEodhusa feels free to use classical Roman
tales.[5] Tadhg Dall cites Charlemagne among the ancestors

---

[5] See E. Knott, *Irish Classical Poetry*, p. 64.

of William Burke.[6]

The poets were comfortable within the confines of the literary genre. They understood the restrictions and ably manipulated the tradition they inherited and maintained this flexibility by constantly exercising it to its limits. The school poetry was neither the creation of a moribund institution nor a staggering anachronism, but a valid and vital complement to the equally vital world of the Gaelic chief. The poets survived as long as the Gaelic aristocratic world preserved its form, even vestigially, until the final decades of the seventeenth century. It is because of the innate flexibility of the genre and the ability of the poets to operate meaningfully within the bounds of the tradition for both themselves and their patrons which makes their varying uses of the themes and motifs at their disposal a fascinating source for the early modern period.

Three poems of the earlier period of the school's poetry, two from the earlier thirteenth century and one from the mid-fourteenth century, addressed to Cathal Crobhdhearg Ó Conchobhar, Richard fitz William de Burgo and Maurice fitzGerald, second earl of Desmond — respectively exhibit some of the principal and most enduring bardic themes; those themes and motifs which occur and recur with unfailing regularity throughout almost four centuries. The poets' articulation of events of very different periods between the thirteenth and seventeenth centuries in the same idiom suggests that, as has already been indicated, the themes and motifs were not simple literary devices, but represented the literary dilution of fundamental perceptions of the Gaelic aristocratic world.

The earliest of the three poems is one attributed to Muireadhach Albanach Ó Dálaigh — and addressed to a member of the Connacht Uí Chonchubhair, Cathal, brother of Ruaidhrí, the so-called 'last highking of Ireland'. This poem is dated by Bergin between 1213-1224.[7] It represents an early example of bardic eulogy to a well known Gaelic chief. Ó Dálaigh treats of his subject in what one immediately recognizes as the true 'classical' style, and introduces themes which become very familiar indeed to the reader. These include the idealization of warfare, Cathal's strength in battle providing his right to the 'charter' of Ireland, the illustriousness of his ancestry adding weight to

---

6 Knott, *Tadhg Dall*, No. 23, st. 9, p. 171.
7 O. Bergin, *Irish Bardic Poetry*, No. 23, p. 104.

his entitlement and the territory bearing testimony to him in its fruitfulness.

The second poem chosen from the Bergin collection is another poem of Muireadhach Albanach's, this time addressed to Richard fitzWilliam fitzAdelm de Burgo (c. 1213),[8] an Anglo-Norman lord, just about assimilated into the Gaelic world in the early thirteenth century. Ó Dálaigh's treatment of de Burgo in this poem is as a pattern for the relationship between 'foreign' lord and Gaelic poet. This relationship becomes one of unquestioned acceptance of the foreigners' rights through victory, no different in its perceptions of power and valid claims to that put forward by the poets on behalf of Gaelic lords. Ó Dálaigh acknowledges the 'foreigness' of his prospective patron, but simultaneously provides a coveted position for him in the Gaelic world by ascribing to his authority the royal seats of Cruacha and Tara. Again de Burgo's validation is his evident power and his *de facto* position.

The third poem, written about a century later than the two above, serves to illustrate once again the blossoming of entirely comfortable relations between the professional poet and the 'foreign' lord. The addressee is in this instance Maurice fitzMaurice, second earl of Desmond,[9] the poet is Gofraidh Fionn Ó Dálaigh. The poet uses the themes of the lord's espousal of the territory and the resulting fertility of the lordship. In this poem also, Ó Dálaigh makes extensive use of the apologue in order to provide fitzMaurice with his mythical prototype — in this case Maurice is like Lugh Lámhfhada. This foreign lord's expeditions abroad with the King of England merely enhance his stature in the poet's eyes. His power is secure, his connections are impeccable and according to the poet he is a worthy spouse for Banbha.

These three poems provide a touchstone for the themes and motifs which will be followed in this study as they occur in various poems throughout the three centuries following — down to the early seventeenth century. For this reason it is useful to study the poets' use of them in some detail. The rationale governing the poets' perceptions of their lords' activities reflect the underlying rationale of those same activities since the poets articulate the fundamental perceptions of the aristocratic Gaelic world. The survival of both lords and poets into the

---

8 Bergin, *Irish Bardic Poetry*, No. 20, p. 88.
9 Bergin, *Irish Bardic Poetry*, No. 17, p. 73.

mid-seventeenth century says much for the ability of the poets to articulate adequately at least some facets of the fundamental criteria dictating the lords' perceptions of conquest, rebellion, and the uses of war or peace. The poets' idiom remained basically very much the same throughout the period. The Gaelic lords' perceptions of themselves altered relatively little. The attitudes articulated in the three following poems are basically those which endured to the collapse of the Gaelic world in the seventeenth century.

The earliest of the three poems is that of Muireadhach Albanach to Cathal Crobhdhearg O'Connor — king of Connacht. This poem is dated between 1212 and 1224 by Bergin.[10] The poet is seeking the patronage of O'Connor after fleeing from O'Donnell in Tyrconnel. In this poem Ó Dálaigh uses all his powers of flattery to secure Cathal Crobhdhearg's patronage. In his praise of Cathal, Muireadhach Albanach presents us with the Gaelic chief, his idealization of him and of the life-style that produced and supported them both. Cathal Crobhdhearg, the lord, understands the nature of the request and its mode of presentation.[11] Muireadhach Albanach knows too what is expected of him and how to present it; thereby producing not only a poem in reward for patronage but also a record for us of a perception of life and its organization as perceived by and partaken in by both the lord and the poet. For the poet, the exercise is consciously undertaken in his professional capacity as a member of the literati. The lord on the other hand is the living dynamic focus of the efforts of the literati to maintain contact with the gloriously perceived past, the chaotic present and the problematic future.

It is important that Cathal Crobhdhearg O'Connor be entitled to his position as king of Connacht. This entitlement can stem from a number of sources. The use of the idea of the 'charter' as a title testament was very popular with the poets and often used in an oblique way, with extended analogies in keeping with the consciously obscure style often employed by them. Cathal Crobhdhearg was born with his charter in one hand, born with the right of sovereignty over 'Conn's Plain':

As amhlaidh rugadh flaith Fáil
's a sgríbhionn lais 'na leathláimh:

---

[10] See J.E. Caerwyn Williams, *The Court Poet in Medieval Ireland*.
[11] Caerwyn Williams, *The Court Poet in Medieval Ireland*.

branán fearchonta Chláir Chuinn,
láimh ghealchorcra as a ghualoinn.
(Bergin, *Irish Bardic Poetry*, No. 23, st. 9, p. 105.)

[The Prince of Fál was born with his charter in one hand — gallant champion of Conn's Plain — a bright crimson hand from his shoulder.]

He, Cathal, is the Prince of Fál, the 'champion of Conn's Plain'. He deserves his position because of his physical prowess which enables him to maintain his suzerainty. His anger is renowned (st. 8, p. 105). He is well able to protect himself and his patrimony:

Cuiridh sgiath ar sgáth a chnis
risna gáibh nach ttéid thairis:
fuaighfidh risna gáibh géra
an láimh shuaithnidh shoisgéla.

Mór soighiod go seanglúib nglain
do tharruing bas chorr Chathuil;
fagha chas tachair do theilg
bas tana Chathail Croibhdheirg.
(Bergin, *Irish Bardic Poetry,* No. 23, sts. 11-12, p. 105.)

[He sets a shield to protect his skin against the spears that do not go past him; to the sharp spears he will fasten the famous left hand. Many a shaft with bright slender loop has been drawn by Cathal's tapering palm: the graceful palm of Cathal the Redhand has cast a quick battle spear.]

Both on horseback and on foot, his spear-casting is unexcelled.

To add weight to Cathal's undoubted valour, his illustrious ancestors are introduced. His reputed descent from Tuathal Teachtmhar (first century legendary king) and through him Conn Céadchathach and Art Aonfhear are cited, to demonstrate his (Cathal's) worthiness of the praise being showered upon him:

. . . gabhaidh ó Chuinn chleith fá sheól . . .
(Bergin, *Irish Bardic Poetry,* No. 23, st. 13, p. 105.)

[. . . Conn's descendant catches a lance in flight . . .]

. . . nocha sill buachail ar bhoin re linn Uí
Thuathail Teachtmhuir.
(Bergin, *Irish Bardic Poetry*, No. 23, st. 14, p. 106)

[. . . no herdsman watches a cow in the time of the descendant of
Tuathal Teachtmhar.]

The portents of the reign of the true king are manifest in Cathal's territory. The suggested belief that the territory of a rightful ruler is fertile and prosperous is rooted in antiquity and common to the early civilizations of most known cultures. As a literary motif, it was a favourite of the poets. The benefits of Cathal's reign are such that flocks are not in danger from any source:

Maith sén tugadh go Teamhraigh
rí Muaidhe, mac Toirrdhealbhaigh;
nocha sill buachail ar bhoin
re linn Uí Thuathail Teachtmhuir.
(Bergin, *Irish Bardic Poetry,* No. 23, st. 14, p. 106).

[With good omen was the king of Moy, Toirrdhealbhach's son, brought to Tara, no herdsman watches a cow in the time of the descendant of Tuathal Teachtmhar.]

Cathal's reign has been well augured and his espousal to Connacht bears fruit. Having established that much, Ó Dálaigh proceeds to exercise an older poetic privilege; that of a seer calling forth visions; [12] in this instance that of Cathal's projected forays eastwards towards the foreign strongholds. The poet is vouchsafed a vision of the succour of Banbha in the arrival of Cathal Crobhdhearg in Meath driving the foreigners before him:

---

[12] For discussion of the antiquity of the style later known as the *aisling* wherein the poet is vouchsafed a vision of the rescue of Ireland or her rescuer, see an early *aisling* poem in N.J.A. Williams' *The Poems of Giolla Brighde Mac Con Midhe* (Dublin, 1980) and Breandán Ó Buachalla, 'An meisiasacht agus an "aisling" ' in *Folia Gadelica,* ed. P. de Brún (Cork, 1983). For a discussion of the political elements in the poetry see Tadhg Ó Dúshláin, 'Filíocht Pholaitiúil na Gaeilge — a cineál' in *Léachtaí Cholm Cille,* XII (An Sagart, Maynooth, 1982), pp 114-29. European influences in the *aisling* are discussed by Seán Ó Tuama, in 'Téamaí iasachta i bhfilíocht pholaitiúil na Gaeilge (1600-1800) in *Éigse,* II (1965-6), pp 201-13. See also R.A. Breatnach, 'The Lady and the king: a theme of Irish literature', in *Studies,* Vol. 42 (1953), pp 321-36.

Suairc an taidbhsi tárfas damh
aréir do chathuibh Cruachan,
a dhul amach san Midhe,
gach clach 'na tur theinntidhe.

Creithre teineadh tárfas damh
d'fhaicsin ar fhud a margadh:
as í an chrithre, as breath bhunaidh
sirthi creach Uí Chonchubhair.

Do-chiú glastonn mara mir
amuigh ag toidheacht tairrsibh:
as í an ghlastonn mhear mhara
an geal basdonn béltana.
(Bergin, *Irish Bardic Poetry,* No. 23, sts. 15, 16, 17, p. 106.)

[Pleasant was the vision that appeared to me last night of the battalions of Cruacha, how he went forth into Meath and each stone building became a blazing bush.
Sparks of fire I seemed to see throughout its markets; the sparks — 'tis a well-founded judgement — were O'Connor's raiding bands.
I see the green wave of the wild sea coming over them yonder: the wild green wave of the sea is the bright redhanded thin-lipped prince.]

Ó Dálaigh's vision depicts O'Connor accomplishing the banishment of foreigners from Meath (the Pale) with his raiding bands. Cathal is depicted as one who shall banish the 'foreigners' who have seized Tara:

As é an Croibhdhearg chuirfios soir
na Gulla do ghabh Theamhraigh:
an duine ní diombaidh linn
'ga ttiomáin uile a hÉirinn.
(Bergin, *Irish Bardic Poetry*, No. 23, st. 18, p. 106)

[It is the Redhand that will drive eastwards the foreigners who have seized Tara: it were no grief to me that he should banish them all from Ireland.]

Thirteenth century lordly preoccupations predominate, and include raids on the Pale. Setting houses or settlements afire is a mediaeval commonplace: 'Crithre teineadh tarfas damh . . .'. Cathal directs his famous anger at the 'foreigners'. This theme of banishing foreigners, so often encountered, is of major importance. It appears regularly in the poetry from the thirteenth to the seventeenth centuries. It is a bardic theme most open to misinterpretation in the light of later Irish nationalist historiography. The poets' fulminations against foreigners have often been cited as evidence of their consciousness of Ireland as a sovereign political unit; and as an exhortation to the political leaders to identify and vanquish the common foreign enemy. The theme, however, must be considered within the poets' framework where it takes its place alongside other major themes, such as the succour of Banbha, the power of the sword and the rights of suzerainty. And its use is subject to the evident power and aspirations of the individual addressed. Writing for an active Gaelic lord, involved in military expeditions against foreign or domestic rivals and enemies, the poet feels free to draw on the 'banishment of foreigners' theme, and to couple it with the requisite acclamation of the lord's undoubted military ability. Ó Dálaigh has complied with both bardic demands in this poem. Both elements, Ó Dálaigh's praise of Cathal's physical ability and his projected raids on the Pale are in their turn subject to the *de facto* situation. Essentially Cathal O'Connor deserves his lordship because he possesses it; this respect for the *de facto* situation is of major importance to any discussion of the poets' perceptions of the changing political and social world. Cathal maintains his lordship through the strength of his arm, literally implied in the poet's treatment of Cathal's nickname, in this instance supported by the hovering aura of his victorious ancestors.

Such a poem, written as it is with the express purpose of securing patronage will undoubtedly contain a certain amount of flattery. However, that which the poet sees fit to emphasize and praise is significant and remains basically unchanged throughout three succeeding centuries. Of special significance is the treatment of Cathal's 'charter' to Ireland, his military success at maintaining his lordship; his military objectives, notably the driving out of foreigners, and inevitably his generosity to poets. In order to introduce his fairly heavy demands, Ó Dálaigh spends some time describing the wealth of Cathal's person, the expense of his raiment and the luxury of his household; all tending to the enhancement of Cathal's personal and popular stature, and a further validation of his position:

> Ionar corcra mar chaoir nduinn —
> matal sgarlóid, sgiamh ndíoghainn,

is léini chaol mar chailc ngil
fa dhá thaobh uí Airt Aoinfhir.
(Bergin, *Irish Bardic Poetry,* No. 23, st. 22, p. 107.)

[A crimson tunic like a red berry, a scarlet mantle decked with great ornaments, and a fine shirt like white chalk about the sides of the descendant of Art Aoinfhear.]

Thus Ó Dálaigh skilfully combines kingly description with the added effect of typical bardic name-dropping. The nobility of Cathal's person is attested to in the approved traditional description of his kind, the unblemished king:

Súil chochlach uaine aga,
dá bhais mhíne mhérfhada,
is bonn tana saor sleamhain;
mala chaol donn druimleabhair.
(Bergin, *Irish Bardic Poetry*, No. 23, st. 24, p. 107.)

[A blue eye he has with dark lashes, smooth long-fingered hands, a foot slender, noble and smooth, and a brow delicate, brown, long-ridged.]

A man of such wealth, beauty, power and position should prove a generous patron of the arts. Ó Dálaigh opens his poem with praise of Cathal's generosity, comparable to that of Guaire, fabled for his generosity:

Tabhrum an Cháisg ar Chathal,
a hucht Íosa an Ardathar:
a mheic, cuimhnigh ar gcaingne,
dheit . . .
(Bergin, *Irish Bardic Poetry*, No. 23, st. 1, p. 104.)

[Let us spend Easter with Cathal, in the name of Jesus, Son of the High Father! O Son, remember our troubles, to Thee . . .]

Gluaisdior linn d'iarraidh fhaighdhi
go ceann foltchas fionn Aidhne:
dá n-éra ceann Aidhne inn
nocha mbem d'fhaighdhi a nÉirinn.
(Bergin, *Irish Bardic Poetry*, No. 23, st. 4, p. 104.)

[Let us go to seek a boon from the curly-haired ruler of Aidhne: if Aidhne's ruler refuse us, we shall ask no boon in Ireland.]

Such is Cathal's generosity, the best in Ireland, comparable to that of Guaire, that if he refuse, there is no other who would accept the poet. Yet all this praise does not do justice to 'Toirrdhealbhach's heir':

> Minic a luaittear a leabhraibh
> oidhre taoibhgheal Toirrdhealbhaigh
> cúl fiar is fleasga 'na bharr —
> trian a theasda ní thabhram.(Bergin, *Irish Bardic Poetry*, No. 23, st. 25, p. 107.)

[Often in books is told of Toirrdhealbhach's bright-skinned heir: curving locks with ringlets above — one-third of his fame I do not tell.]

This poem praises Cathal — the Gaelic lord, an unvanquishable hero of impeccable ancestry, unblemished appearance and unstinting generosity. These are the qualities demanded of the lord and the poet is satisfied that Cathal possesses them. He has undisputed authority over any area which attracts him; the precise area is invariably and expansively vague, and he is engaged in worthy combat with intrusive foreigners. These shall, as will all his other enemies, be defeated by Cathal. These foreigners have seized Tara, Cathal is within his rights to challenge their possession of it. Ó Dálaigh praises Cathal O'Connor's intention to rid Meath of the foreigners. They have seized it, he must retrieve it. His own patrimony is however held by the power of his 'Red hand'. This in itself is an accepted validation of his claims. It is interesting and vitally important for our comprehension of the poets' and the lords' perceptions of the prerogatives of power, to consider the 'rights of the sword' in another context.

The fundamental bardic perceptions of power and sovereignty contained in the poem above are explored further in another poem by the same poet, this time addressed to a 'foreign' prospective patron. In this poem Ó Dálaigh is again seeking patronage. Anglo-Norman presence in Ireland was hardly a generation old when Ó Dálaigh composed the following poem for the lord of Clanrickard, Richard fitzWilliam fitzAdelm de Burgo. Bergin dates the poem 1212. Ó Dálaigh fleeing from O'Donnell in Tyrconnel must appeal to a foreign lord. It is in the poet's situating this foreigner in an already established tradition which illustrates at once the paradoxical flexibility of this rigid genre, the poets' ability to manipulate the tradition for the purpose of accommodating extraneous elements in their world, and the ability of the literary genre and the perceptions which dictate its tone to articulate the Gaelic world's ability, and interest in, assimilating and accommodating new elements in its own terms of reference.

Ó Dálaigh begins his poem with immediate acknowledgement of the foreign origin of his prospective patron:

> Créd agaibh aoidhigh a gcéin
> a ghiolla gusan ngaillsgéimh,
> a dhream ghaoidhealta ghallda
> naoidheanta sheang shaorchlannda?
> (Bergin, *Irish Bardic Poetry*, No. 20, st. 1, p. 88.)

> [Whence comes it that ye have guests from afar, o youth of foreign beauty, o ye who are become Gaelic yet foreign, young, graceful and highborn?]

The adjustments made by the Anglo-Normans to suit their new neighbours and surroundings, have not escaped the notice of Ó Dálaigh, who addresses de Burgo:

> a dhream ghaoidhealta ghallda . . .
> [become Gaelic, yet foreign . . .]

This compliment is not a wholly disinterested one on Ó Dálaigh's part: in bestowing at least partial Gaelic status on de Burgo, he places the onus of maintaining the traditional obligations of the Gaelic chief, towards the poets at least, on him. If de Burgo is Gaelic yet foreign, the Gaelicized part of him will appreciate the poet's efforts. At the same time, however, fearing perhaps that his patronless state placed him in some unwonted inferior position, Ó Dálaigh endeavours to let de Burgo know that the honour is indeed shared, should de Burgo choose to accept him:

> Meisi a maighistir múinte
> minic mé a measg ghallchúirte
> beag do charaibh chuirim dhíom
> suidhim ar aghaidh airdríogh.

Tárruim dá gach rígh roineart,
aoibhinn damh ar deóruigheacht,
uasal mo riocht sa tír thoir,
ní bhínn gan chniocht am chumaidh.
(Bergin, *Irish Bardic Poetry,* No. 20, sts. 4, 5, p. 89)

[I am their master of teaching; oft have I been amid a foreign court; little ceremony I make; I sit in the presence of a monarch. I attain great power from every prince, pleasant it is to me to be abroad; noble is my state in the eastern land; I had ever a knight attending me.]

Perhaps a deep consciousness of the 'foreigness' of de Burgo, causes Ó Dálaigh to spell out his position in a way that would be unnecessary in the ordinary course of events, as indeed we have seen in the poem above by the same poet for Cathal Crobhdhearg. O'Connor would not be in any doubt about Ó Dálaigh's own status, while the poet seeks to counter-balance his insecure position with de Burgo with typical arrogance:

Beag a fhios agad, dar leam,
cia misi d'fhearaibh Éireann;
spéis am dhánuibh dhlighe dhe,
Ó Dálaigh Midhe meise.
(Bergin, *Irish Bardic Poetry,* No. 20, st. 17, p. 90.)

[Little thou knowest, methinks, who I am of the men of Ireland; thou art bound to give heed to my verses for that I am O'Daly of Meath!][13]

By this spelling out his status and the honour due him, Ó Dálaigh is suggesting that de Burgo should consider himself honoured that Ó Dálaigh should chose to have him rather than any other lord as a patron. Moreover, Ó Dálaigh may be unconsciously suggesting that it is he, the poet, who can most successfully accomplish the integration of a *Gall Gaelach* — a Gaelicized foreigner, into the Gaelic aristocratic world. In so far as the poetry could be, or was actively used as propaganda, the poet could play such a rôle. At any rate, in this poem Ó Dálaigh does

---

[13] See A. and B. Rees, *The Celtic Heritage,* pp 105-6.

achieve the rationalization of a foreigner's claim to Banbha and the status and duties attending it. Denied protection and patronage in Ulster by O'Donnell, Ó Dálaigh justifies himself in turning to de Burgo:

> Rí Easa Ruaidh do-rinne
> bagar orm tré aininne
> do-ghén tréna ngealltaibh dhamh
> mo bhél ré seabhcaibh Saxan.
> (Bergin, *Irish Bardic Poetry,* No. 20, st. 11, p. 90.)

[The king of Assaroe has threatened me in anger. Because of their promises to me I will turn my face to the Saxon champions.]

Here Ó Dálaigh makes little of the difference between Anglo-Norman and Saxon English. 'Saxan' here is used imprecisely to indicate foreign. Indeed, not only does the poet seek protection from de Burgo, repeatedly acknowledging his foreigness, but he is bold enough to complain about O'Donnell's treatment of him:

> Domhnall Doire is Droma Cliabh,
> ná tréig dhó mé, a mheic Uilliam;
> neach dá mbí go cruaidh ad chionn,
> an rí thuaidh nocha tréigeann.
> (Bergin, *Irish Bardic Poetry*, No. 20, st. 9, p. 89)

[Domhnall of Derry and Drumcliff, abandon me not to him, Fitz-William; the northern prince does not abandon one who is bold against thee.]

Wherefore, Ó Dálaigh feels justified in turning to 'foreigners'; protection and patronage is what the poet seeks, he will accept it wherever he finds it. In attributing patriotic motives and leanings to the bardic poets, the essential nature of their function and outlook has been ignored or at least misunderstood by those who seek to identify any anti-foreign sentiment expressed by the poets, with anti-Englishness in particular and more generally with an awareness among the poets of the ultimate political and cultural outcome of the 'foreigners' activities in Ireland. Ó Dálaigh in turning to de Burgo makes his decision quite clear:

> Mé ar h'eineach 's ar eineach nGall,
> 's gach aon iomarchas iarann;
> a nathair sheang ghlan gharccsa,

gabh fád cheann mo chonmharccsa.
(Bergin, *Irish Bardic Poetry,* No. 20, st. 12, p. 90.)

[I put myself under thy safeguard and under the safeguard of the Foreigners, and of everyone who carries steel; o champion, graceful, bright and fierce, take upon thee my quarrel (?)]

However, since Ó Dálaigh has decided that de Burgo is worthy of his addresses, he must fit him into the mould, shape him, as his successors, for centuries to come, were to do with other 'foreign' patrons. Ó Dálaigh must create a niche for de Burgo in order to be able to deal with him in the bardic idiom and to apply to him the standards and rationale governing the acceptance of the 'foreign' or native lords into the Gaelic tradition. Ó Dálaigh does not enter into discussion of the genealogy of de Burgo, a frequent practice with poets dealing with lords of foreign or mixed descent, emphasizing the connections often on tenuous grounds with ancient Gaelic heroes. Instead, Ó Dálaigh proclaims de Burgo's primacy among his own people:

Tusa ceann do chinidh féin,
a mheic Uilliam go n-óirnéimh;
an té as fhearr dá gach aicme,
as hé as ceann don chlannmhaicne.
(Bergin, *Irish Bardic Poetry*, No. 20, st. 16, p. 90.)

[Thou art the head of thine own race, O Fitz-William of the golden sheen; he that is the best in each stock is the head of the family.]

Far from decrying the intrusion of foreigners into the Gaelic world, as the superficial study of Ó Dálaigh's poem to O'Connor might indicate, the poet celebrates the encroachment of a man of de Burgo's calibre upon Gaelic Irish territory. He ascribes the famous royal seats of Cruacha, and Tara to the authority of de Burgo:

As leat Cruacha mhór Mheadhbha,
Teamhair, as tú a tighearna;
ón ló as é do theagh Teamhair,
as mo chean a cóigeadhaigh!
As leatsa Múr Mheic an Duinn,
dan hainm Caislén Uí Chonuing,

as leat anoisi an cladh clach
dar ghabh Mac Coisi an cédrath.
(Bergin, *Irish Bardic Poetry*, No. 20, sts. 19, 20, p. 91.)

[Thine is Meadhbh's mighty Cruacha, thou art lord of Tara; since Tara is thy house, hail to her provincial kings!
Thine is the castle of Mac an Duinn which is named Caislén Uí Chonuing, thine is the stone fence from which Mac Coise won the first success.]

Thus does Ó Dálaigh, the poet, draw de Burgo, the lord, into the mainstream of the tradition of the former; an intentional undertaking on the poet's part, especially when considered in the light of his earlier exhortations to Cathal Crobhdhearg to drive the foreigners from the country and to reclaim Tara. In this exhibition of apparently conflicting loyalties, Ó Dálaigh proves himself a true member of his caste.[14] De Burgo is a secure ruler of Clanwilliam:

A Riocaird óig an fhuinn ghloin,
ó nach mair Uilliam t'athair,
do ghiall Clann Uilliam uile
dod bharr chruinnfhiar chríochbhuidhe.
(Bergin, *Irish Bardic Poetry,* No. 20, st. 18, p. 91.)

[O young Richard of the bright land, since thy father William lives not, all Clanwilliam has obeyed thy round curling saffron-yellow locks.]

Likewise, in the other poem Cathal Crobhdhearg is established in his territory, even to the point of expansion. Such flexibility of loyalties does not indicate anything of an anomalous nature either in the poet's position or in the relative positions of his patrons. The convention of offering the highest possible praise to the addressee of the moment is in the best tradition of the politic poet. It also serves to illustrate forcibly a major bardic concept of power, its sources and its limits: the *fait accompli* always presented a much more attractive case to the poets than the confusion of conflicting rights and tendentious claims. Ó Dálaigh's list of FitzWilliam's 'kingly seats' comprising as they do, two of the more famous mythological royal seats of Ireland, Tara and Cruacha, shows

---

14 The identity of this poet is not certain.

what little difficulty he experienced in granting 'Meadhbh's land' to 'foreigners'.

The most important conclusion to be drawn from this apparently dichotomous situation is that the possession of and successful maintenance of power or authority constituted the single strongest argument of right recognized by the poets, and thus by their supporters. Bearing this fundamental point in mind and tempering it with a number of other considerations, such as the perceived 'nation' of the addressee, whether or not he was, or intended to engage in battle for or against his neighbouring rivals or the crown, and the location of the territory occupied by the lord, we come to a clearer understanding of contemporary Gaelic perceptions of what in retrospect is regarded as the conquest of Ireland.

In preparation for the final repetition of his request, Ó Dálaigh artfully describes the wealth of de Burgo's household and dwelling:

Teagh budh leabhra gile lámh,
teagh budh tana troigh bhonnbhán,
teagh budh connloighe cladhfholt,
's budh lonnraighe lámhanart; —

Teagh budh gile guala is ucht,
is budh bélchorcra banntracht,
teagh budh cromghlanbhuidhe cúil
ós gormabhruighe glasshúil; —

Teagh budh lia uscar órdha,
teagh budh lia fear friothólmha,
teagh budh lia dáileamh deighfhear, —
nár sáidheadh 's nach sáithfidhear!
(Bergin, *Irish Bardic Poetry,* No. 20, sts. 22, 23, 24, p. 91.)

[A house where white hands were longer, a house where white-soled feet were more slender, a house where clustering locks were more brilliant, and where hand-linen was more lustrous.
A house where shoulders and bosoms were whiter, and where ladies were more red-lipped, where locks were more curving, bright and yellow, and blue eyes shaded by darker lashes; —
A house wherein were more golden jewels, a house wherein were more serving men, a house wherein were more spencers of noble birth, — that has not been built and will not be built!]

Thus Ó Dálaigh broadly hints that de Burgo's illustrious house can bear the cost of a poet such as he. The hint is followed by an appeal which might have been made to any native lord, and de Burgo is addressed as 'lord of Bladhma' and 'prince of the Connacht race', no insignificant titles:

> A Rocaird Bheinne Bladhma,
> ná tréig an t-aos ealadhna;
> gibé oirbheirt do-né neach,
> ní hoirdhearc é gan eineach.
> (Bergin, *Irish Bardic Poetry,* No. 20, st. 25, p. 91.)

> [O Richard of Beann Bladhma, forsake not the men of art. Whatever exploit one may do, no one is famous without generosity.]

In the poem by Ó Dálaigh addressed to Cathal Crobhdhearg, he (the poet) calls O'Connor 'mac Thoirrdhealbhaigh'; this Toirrdhealbhach (+1156) was king of Connacht, so too by inference is Cathal Crobhdhearg 'king of Connacht'. Now de Burgo shares that coveted title along with titular possession of Tara and Cruacha. At the same time Ó Dálaigh also appeals to him as 'prince of the Foreigners':

> Ná beir leithbhreith, a fhlaith Gall . . .
> (Bergin, *Irish Bardic Poetry*, No. 20, st. 26, p. 92)

> [Pass no partial sentence, O prince of the Foreigners . . .]

Once a lord had settled (even temporarily) and had fulfilled the social obligations expected of a Gaelic lord, notably support of the literati, his origin caused little bother to the poets. The alleged xenophobic tendencies of the poets is based on a misinterpretation of their use of racial origins and their importance. So completely has Ó Dálaigh written de Burgo into the tradition that the poet concludes his poem with a suggestion that it were not inconceivable that he (Ó Dálaigh) should one day be proud to possess a gift received from de Burgo:

> Fá neimhiongnadh uair eile
> a Riocaird, a ridire,
> each luath ó Gholl 'na nglaicne
> nó cuach corr go gcubhairchre.
> (Bergin, *Irish Bardic Poetry*, No. 20, st. 29, p. 92.)

[It was nothing strange one day, O knightly Richard, that I should hold as my own a swift steed bestowed by a foreigner, or a smooth and lidded goblet.]

Ó Dálaigh is capable of addressing a Gaelic chief and an Anglo-Norman lord and giving each one the treatment traditionally accorded the Gaelic chief. In his accommodation of both patrons he exercises the poets' prerogative of manipulating the tradition to articulate a number of different perceptions fundamental to the aristocratic Gaelic mentality. The poets' accommodation of foreign encroachment into Gaelic territory is of particular importance since it is this faculty especially which became increasingly important in the sixteenth and seventeenth centuries. The criteria governing the acceptance of foreign victories, native defeats and other such changes are articulated in Ó Dálaigh's poems for O'Connor and de Brugo respectively, and are the fundamental criteria maintained by the poets throughout the following three and a half centuries.

Another Ó Dálaigh poet, writing, it has been suggested by Bergin about 1357, also found himself engaged in composing encomiastic verse for 'foreigners'. This time the object of the Ó Dálaigh praise is Maurice fitzMaurice, second earl of Desmond who was to die in 1358. His father, Maurice, had been a justiciar. Gerald the Poet, (Gearóid Iarla) was his half-brother. Gofraidh Fionn Ó Dálaigh to whom this work is attributed died about 1387. He also enjoyed the patronage of the O'Brien's of Thomond, and the McCarthy's of Desmond. The occasion of this poem appears to be the absence of fitzMaurice while he travelled to England paying his respects to his liege, the King of England.

In this poem (Begin, *Irish Bardic Poetry*, No. 17), a broader spectrum of bardic themes is explored. These include the ruler's espousal of Ireland, her dejection in his absence, and the equation of fitzMaurice with noteworthy Gaelic heroes in extended apologues and analogies. This poem has been the subject of an interesting misinterpretation in which the opening line of the first stanza has been construed, in a political sense, as a bitter rebuke to the king of England.[15] The misinterpretation is interesting because it illustrates the danger of superficial

---

[15] The stanza in question is isolated out of context by Pádraig Ó Fiannachta in *Léas ar ár Litríocht* (An Sagart, Maynooth, 1974), p. 120, and misinterpreted thus:
'I bhfad siar sa triú haois déag sular luigh an t-éigean chomh géar sin ar chine Gael d'fhógair an file cneasta Gofraidh Fionn Ó Dálaigh cé air a bhí an milleán le cur.'

analysis of the bardic 'anti-foreigner' theme and anachronistic appraisal of its implications. The poem begins on an apparently sharp note of displeasure with the monarch of England:

> Mór ar bfearg riot a rí Saxan,
> a sé a dhamhna,
> do-raduis, gér mhór a meanma,
> brón for Bhanbha.
> (Bergin, No. 17, st. 1, p. 73.)

[Great is our anger against thee, O king of England; the ground therof is that, though her spirit was high, thou hast brought sorrow upon Banbha.]

Before one goes on to place this stanza in its correct context, it is instructive to consider the longevity of this particular bardic sentiment into a later period. Such an opening is easily transposable to the seventeenth century. Compare, for instance, the sentiments expressed by Fear Flatha Ó Gnímh [16] in the early seventeenth century:

> Mo thruaighe mar táid Gaoidheal!
> annamh intinn fhorbhaoilidh
> ar an uair-se ag duine dhíobh,
> a n-uaisle uile ar imshníomh.

> Atá brat ciach ós a gcionn
> mhúchas glóir Ghaoidheal Éireann,
> mar néall gceath ghrianbháitheas goil,
> do leath d'iarghnáicheas orthaibh.
> (O'Rahilly, *Measgra Dánta* II, No. 54, sts. 1 and 5, pp 144 and 145.)

[Woe, the condition of the Gael, seldom now is any one of them in good spirits, their entire nobility are anxious.
The glory of the Gael is extinguished by a cloud of sorrow which covers them, as a rain-cloud obliterates the sun; so does anxiety overwhelm them.]

---

16 See Bernadette Cunningham and Raymond Gillespie, 'The East Ulster Bardic Family of Ó Gnimh' in *Éigse,* 20 (1984).

Ó Dálaigh in 1357 tells us:

Ma a leannán d'fosdadh na hégmuis,
d'uaim lé mór-rath,
inis Éirionn an gheal ghríanach,
as bean bhrónach.

Brón ar éicsibh innsi Fódla
's ar a bfionnmhnáibh,
ó do fáguibh dún geal Gabhráin
fear úr Iomhdháin.

(Bergin, *Irish Bardic Poetry,* No. 17, sts. 2 and 5, pp 73, 74.)

[Because her lover is kept away from her, who had knit great fortune to her, the isle of Erin, the bright sunny one, is a sorrowful woman.

The poets of the island of Fódla are sorrowful, and their fair ladies, since the young hero of Iomghán left Gabhrán's bright fortress.]

Again in the seventeenth century Eoghan Rua mac a' Bhaird indicated the desolation of Banbha after the departure of O'Neill and O'Donnell:

Mór tuirse Ulltach fá n-airc
d'éis Í Dhomhnuill do dhíobairt
sní lugha fá Aodh Eanuigh
cumha ar an taobh thuaidheamhain.

Gan gáire fa ghníomhraibh leinbh
cosg ar cheól glas ar Ghaoidheilg
meic ríogh mar nár dhual don dream
gan luadh ar fhíon nó aithfreann.

(Paul Walsh, (ed.), *Beatha Aodha Ruaidh Uí Dhomhnaill* part 2, st. 4, 5, pp 138-9.)

[Great the sorrow of Ulster in her difficulty since Ó Domhnaill has been banished, and not less in grief is the North because of Aodh of Eanach.

No laughter at children's play: an end to music: Gaelic is silenced: sons of kings unhonoured: no mention of winefeast or Mass.]

In all three poems, Ireland is in distress, her poets are sorrowful, a cloud of sorrow covers her. The similarity of the sentiments expressed in the extracts from these three poems give rise to the questions which are central to our understanding of the nature of the perceptions of the Gaelic aristocracy articulated in the poetry. In each case Ireland/Banbha is deeply distressed. In the fourteenth century Ó Dálaigh's poem (*IBP*, No. 17), addressed to fitzMaurice, the reason for such desolation and anger against the Saxon are part of an intricate form of compliment both to the addressee and his liege — the king of England. Ó Dálaigh admits that the anger he expresses in the opening stanza:

> Mór ar bfearg riot a rí Saxan . . .

is both absurd and excessive since the journey upon which his patron has embarked, illustrates the exalted position of fitzMaurice. FitzMaurice is apparently on a customary visit of a client to his liege, an occasion of which the poet is proud:

> Iongnadh dhúinn reacht ré rígh Saxan
> na slógh meanmnach,
> tré bheith aigi go mear muirnioch
> don gheal ghreadhnach.
> (Bergin, *Irish Bardic Poetry,* No. 17, st. 8, p. 74.)

> [Strange that I should rage against the king of England, of the gallant hosts, because he keeps with him the bright joyous one in mirth and revelry.]

In explanation of his pride in his patron, Ó Dálaigh elucidates the relationship between fitzMaurice and the king of England:

> Dalta rígh Saxan Sior Muiris,
> maith a chaomhna,
> trén ina mhúr mac an íarla,
> slat úr aobhdha.
> (Bergin, *Irish Bardic Poetry*, No. 17, st. 9, p. 74.)

> [Sir Maurice is the fosterling of the king of England, good is his protection; secure in his palace is the earl's son, the fresh lovely scion.]

and he outlines the reason for fitzMaurice's absence:

> Lé a oide, lé hairdrígh Saxan,
> siobhal díoghainn,

téid isan bFraingc n-ealaigh n-áloinn
bfleadhaigh bfíonduinn.
(Bergin, *Irish Bardic Poetry*, No. 17, st. 12, p. 75.)

[With his fosterer, the King of England — a mighty expedition —
he goes to France, the beautiful land of swans, of feasts, and of
dark wine.]

Far from harbouring any resentment against the king of England, Ó
Dálaigh is proud that his patron should be the 'fosterling' of such a
prestigious individual. Indeed, the poet works the feudal relation between fitzMaurice and his liege into a Gaelic relation between powerful
fosterer and fosterling, and fitzMaurice's knights' service to the king
becomes a traditional Gaelic foray in a foreign country. The suggestion
that Ó Dálaigh was directing either politically or culturally motivated
hostility towards the king of England in a conscious effort to signify his
disapproval of the monarch, is clearly not borne out by the evidence of
this poem. To heighten the stature of fitzMaurice, Ó Dálaigh uses the
conceit of the desolation of Banbha for the purposes of emphasizing
how much his departure is felt in his own territory and throughout
Ireland as a major loss. Banbha is desolated because her lover, spouse,
ruler, is gone away. Fear Flatha Ó Gnímh in the seventeenth century
makes use of the same theme also bemoaning the departure of the northern chieftains,[17] and their replacement by numbers of unsympathetic
foreigners. Finally, the poet Eoghan Rua mac a' Bhaird in 1607,
describes an Ireland bereft of all joy and cultural integrity upon the
abandonment of the country by O'Donnell and O'Neill.[18] The cause of
Banbha's distress is attributed to the same source in each instance; the
departure of the legitimate ruler/spouse. This is not to say, however,
that the consequences of each departure were the same or even perceived
to be similar by the poets. This cannot be divined from the poets' use of
the theme of Banbha's distress. The poets maintain the bardic themes,
motifs and conceits as a referential source and a mode of articulation.
The combination of different motifs, their literary context and the position and aspirations of the individual are addressed to modify the

---

[17] O'Rahilly, *Measgra Dánta* II, p. 206.
[18] Lughaidh Ó Cléirigh, *A Life of Aodh Ruadh Ó Domhnaill*, trans. and ed. by Paul
Walsh, 2 parts (Dublin, 1948, 1957), p. 138.

impact and the implications of the use of such themes. This has been amply illustrated in the poets' use of the celebration of military force and the proper status of foreigners. In one selection of themes a Gaelic chief can be praised for his indefatigable military forays against foreigners, while the same poet can use the selfsame motif of military strength and the rights accruing thereto to celebrate the entrenchment in power of a foreigner. Such flexibility within a rigid literary and traditional structure is manifest in the case of all major bardic themes. It is of special importance that the poets' attitude towards the departure of the legitimate ruler and the conquest of Ireland by foreign elements are not necessarily linked in the poets' use of the 'desolation of Banbha' theme. For this reason it is necessary to be aware of the breadth of choice open to the poets in the use of similar themes for situations which are quite dissimilar in import. Likewise such themes and conceits cannot be interpreted literally. The celebration of the status of the individual addressed is thus manipulable to suit his *de facto* power or aspirations.

The question of fitzMaurice's status is introduced by Ó Dálaigh with the theme of Banbha's espousal to her lord. Her lover/spouse is in this case a scion of a major Anglo-Norman house of Munster. Like Muireadhach Ó Dálaigh a century earlier, Gofraidh Fionn Ó Dálaigh treats fitzMaurice exactly as if he were a Gaelic chief. Once again the poet filters the perception of the position of the Anglo-Norman lord through the prism of the traditional Gaelic rationale. This is expressed in fitzMaurice's auspicious reign over his territory:

> Ma a leannán d'fosdadh na hégmuis,
> d'uaim lé mór-rath. . . .
> (Bergin, *Irish Bardic Poetry,* No. 17, st. 2, p. 73.)
> [Because her lover is kept away from her, who had knit great fortune to her. . . .]

His sovereignty over Ireland (meaning his own territory), and his right to rule, an abiding concern of the poet, is assured by a number of factors. Of primary importance is the nobility of fitzMaurice's blood. Gaelic genealogy is not provided for him — so his position as liegeman of the English king is advanced as proof of his nobility. The natural attributes of fitzMaurice prove his worthiness, physically and mentally:

> Fúair búaidh gcéille is gcrotha is gcónaigh
> ceann an fionnshlóigh

gá ttám acht do-fuair gach iolbhúaidh
go mbúaidh mbionnghlóir.

Treisi fá rath, rath go gconách,
croidhe adhnáir,
cíall dá choimhéd,
ciabh na bfoighég arna bfagháil.
(Bergin, *Irish Bardic Poetry,* No. 17, sts. 15 and 17, p, 75.)

[The leader of the fair host has excelled in understanding and comeliness and success — in short he has won all the varied excellences, with the excellence of sweetness of voice.
Strength in luck, luck with success, a modest heart, understanding to keep him, curling tresses he has gotten.]

Even the celestial bodies declare the propriety of fitzMaurice's position:

Na hairdrionnaigh agá faisnéis
dá fult ngéigfíar
d'fior a anbhraith
cion ar an ardflaith as égciall.
(Bergin, *Irish Bardic Poetry,* No.17, st. 19, p. 76.)

[The planets declare it to his curling hair: whoever betrays him, crime against the prince is senseless.]

Again, because of his foreign origin, fitzMaurice is without ancient Gaelic ancestry. However, Ó Dálaigh produces a likely comparison for the exaltation of fitzMaurice in a manner typical of the poets. He presents a lengthy analogy between fitzMaurice and Lugh Lámhfhada — a hero of the Tuatha de Danann, the Ioldánach; skilled in every art and craft:

Lugh Lámhfada leithéid Muiris,
mhóras dámha,
comhmór bfeasa an conchlann cródha,
comhthrom gcána.
(Bergin, *Irish Bardic Poetry,* No. 17, st. 20, p. 76.)

[The like of Maurice, who exalts bards, was Lugh Longhand: equally great in knowledge was the valiant compeer, equal in sway.]

FitzMaurice is another Lugh, neither his attributes nor position is new, novelty is not sought or appreciated by the poets.[19] The poet needs to link fitzMaurice to a traditional character adequately to accommodate him in the tradition. Lugh Lámhfhada, the multi-skilled leader of the Tuatha de Danann was a very useful character for the poets. Since he was accomplished in every skill, any talent possessed by any chief could be compared to those of Lugh Lámhfhada. In a poem by an unknown poet (dated by James Carney to around 1583)[20] to Philip O'Reilly, Lord of Breifne, the same analogy is produced:

> Fear fhóireas gach éindeacuir,
> mac leanus lorg a athar,
> do-ní a mbeirn do Bhréifneachaibh
> feidhm Logha na Lámh bhFada.
> (Carney, *O'Reilly Poems,* No. 8, st. 35, p. 47.)

> [A man who relieves every hardship — a son who follows the steps of his father — in time of danger for the men of Breifne — he performs the part of Lugh Lámhfhada.][21]

In his use of Lugh Lámhfhada as a foreshadowing of fitzMaurice, Ó Dálaigh leads us to another very popular bardic theme, perhaps one of the most popular of all, surviving into the latest bardic period, that is, the delivery of Banbha. Lugh Lámhfhada, henceforth to be understood as a proto-fitzMaurice, delivered Banbha in antiquity:

> A n-áois Muiris mic an íarla
> do fóir Banbha,
> dá ttug leagadh d'fine Fomhra
> bile Bladhma.
> (Bergin, *Irish Bardic Poetry*, No. 17, st. 21, p. 76.)

> [At the age of Maurice, the earl's son, he delivered Banbha, when he, the mighty tree of Bladhma, defeated the race of the Fomorians.]

---

[19] See Caerwyn Williams, *The Court Poet in Medieval Ireland,* pp 10-11.

[20] J. Carney, *Poems on the O'Reillys,* p. 199.

[21] A further example of the use of the same mythological figure occurs in a poem by Domhnall Ó hUiginn in a *duanaire* for Fiach MacHugh O'Byrne (+ 1597) in S. Mac Airt, *Leabhar Branach* No. 32, stanzas 13 and 21, pp 132.

Lugh travelled the world in search of Tara, to which his many talents failed to gain him admittance until he demonstrated his superiority in skills. Maurice fitzMaurice is explicitly compared with this Lugh. Maurice is Lugh, returned to rescue Banbha once again:

> Aithghin Logha nó Lugh a-rís,
> go ráith Luimnigh,
> a thréidhi acht gan teacht go Teamhraigh,
> ceart ro chuimhnigh.
> (Bergin, *Irish Bardic Poetry*, No. 17, st. 48, p. 79.)

> [The equal of Lugh, or Lugh himself again, to Limerick's fort; save that he came not to Tara, truly he has recalled his qualities.]

Like Lugh, it falls to Maurice's lot to 'rescue Banbha'. From what, or from whom, we are not told. The poet leaves the source of Banbha's peril quite vague. This theme is again used at the poet's discretion to cover a number of eventualities from the death of a chief to the overrunning of territories by foreigners. In this case the rescue of Banbha is introduced as a fitting task for one as worthy to do so as is fitzMaurice, it enhances the compliment built into the poem:

> Mac Eibilín, airgnioch Gaoidhiol,
> gearr go ttora,
> dár gcabhair tar mearthuinn mhara,
> leathchuing Logha.
> Ag deaghoil Éirionn re hurchra
> do folt cloidhfionn
> ar Lugh 's ar Thúath Dé Danann
> é 's a foirionn.
> (Bergin, *Irish Bardic Poetry*, No. 17, sts. 51, 52, p. 80.)

> [Avelina's son, slayer of the Gael, soon will he come to our aid across the wild surge of the sea, he the counterpart of Lugh. When his hair in fair ridges severs Erin from decay, he and his men stand for Lugh and the Tuatha Dé Danann.]

'Severing Erin from decay' seems to be the task before fitzMaurice. This idea of 'succouring Banbha', rescuing Ireland, perhaps takes its roots from the earliest tales of the *gabhála*; the 'takings' of Ireland in which the sovereignty was successively claimed by several different spouses —

enumerated in the *Lebor Gabála*,[22] a standard text of the schools of poetry. This motif became so widely used as to be considered a suitable task for the most unlikely people, including fitzMaurice who was an Anglo-Norman encroacher on McCarthy and O'Brien territory in the south. Clearly the use of the motif is not restricted to Gaelic Irish chiefs, but is applicable to anyone whom the poet considers strong in his own territory and whose status demands that he receive all the accolades traditionally ascribed to the successful chief.

The 'taking of Ireland' and her rescue are branch themes of the ancient ritual and concept of the king's marriage to his territory. These are linked with the concept of the able suitor being the most worthy; the most successful military hero deserves the spoils of his victories. This, in turn, logically extends to the fundamental principle of might is right. The alacrity with which the poets acquiesce in the *de facto* power of the addressee and in the *fait accompli* whether the victor be native or foreign can only be expected in a polity and culture in which military escapades played a prominent role and where the concept of a continual struggle for mastery in Ireland was enshrined in the oral and written tradition.

The idea of 'rescue' is that of the rightful suitor saving the prospective bride from the attentions of the boorish usurper, the latter rôle being played by local enemies and imaginary or real rivals, and the 'foreigner' or the 'English' as occasion demands. Fearghal Óg mac a' Bhaird's sixteenth century encomium for Cúchonnacht Maguire, Lord of Fermanagh (1556-1589) makes great use of this theme — stressing the dual nature of the king's rôle; ruler and spouse of the territory.[23] It is his enforcement of his rule throughout his territory which validates Maguire's position, though he has traditional title to it. Banbha is willing to be subdued by the strongest arm. The winner is right because of his victory. The attraction of power well wielded, regardless of its origins; the *fait accompli* impresses the poet. That which the lord holds is his simply because he holds it; his success in retaining it adds to his stature. It is thus with the earl of Desmond, usurping much McCarthy territory in the south, to him are due all the hereditary prerogatives of his position, regardless of his origin:

---

22 MacAlister, *Lebor Gabála*.
23 David Greene, *Maguire Poems*, No. 4, st. 3, p. 34.

Íarla óg Deasmhumhan dlighidh
díon na ttrumshlógh
tugsat do ghéig Ruidhe roghrádh
uile d'urmhór.
(Bergin, *Irish Bardic Poetry*, No. 17, st. 60. p. 81.)

[The young earl of Desmond is entitled to the defence of the
mighty hosts; well-nigh all of them love the branch of Ruidhe.]

Gofraidh Fionn Ó Dálaigh thus presents us with a foreign lord, aban-
doning his territory temporarily to accompany his liege and guardian,
the king of England, on a trip to France. He is hailed by his Irish poet as
spouse of Erin which is rendered desolate by his absence. His journey to
London is likened to the mythical journey made by Lugh Lámhfhada to
gain entrance to Tara. This Maurice will deliver Banbha from 'decay'
and bear out his similarity to his father in his generosity to poets. Such a
picture becomes very familiar over time as chief after chief, lord after
lord, is hailed as the final hope of Banbha; the only hero to effect her
rescue. Likewise, mythical characters, with or without apposite
qualities are chosen as prototypes of the individual being addressed.

The three poems examined above are examples of the work of two of
the most famous of the earlier poets, Gofraidh Fionn Ó Dálaigh and
Muireadhach Albanach Ó Dálaigh. The former practised mainly in
southern Ireland in the fourteenth century, the latter in the north and
west in the thirteenth century. Two of the poems are addressed to lords,
acknowledged by the poets to be of foreign origin,[24] the third to a
renowned member of an ancient Gaelic Irish household.[25] As encomia
and poems of bardic entreaty for patronage they each contain some of
the most basic of all bardic themes and motifs which are modified by,
and manipulated by and repeated by the poets for over three and a half
centuries. The chapters following will deal with the major themes
outlined above and their expansion and modification to suit different
events and situations.

---

[24] William fitzAdelm de Burgo, Bergin, *Irish Bardic Poetry,* No. 20, Maurice fitz-
Maurice, Bergin, *Irish Bardic Poetry*, No. 17.
[25] Cathal Crobhdhearg O'Connor, Bergin, *Irish Bardic Poetry,* No. 23.

II

BARDIC INTERPRETATIONS OF THE TUDOR RECONQUEST

Nó an fíor Niall ag cagar chniocht,
nó ag bagar ghliadh um gach gort,
nó an bhfuil gá dhreich réidh n-a reacht
gan teacht fa bhreith Néill a-nocht?
(McKenna, *Magauran Poems*, No. 14, st. 16, p. 107)

THE POETRY OF the sixteenth century can be studied for its handling of the three major themes introduced in the earlier chapter; the problematic unity of country, the sovereignty of Banbha and to whom it rightfully belonged; and most important of all, the respect shown by the poets for the *fait accompli* and the various themes emerging therefrom. These same themes reassert themselves in the poets' explanations of events for themselves and their audiences in the sixteenth century. Modifications and alterations have naturally occurred over two hundred years in their treatment. What has altered very little however are the underlying perceptions and the world view articulated in the poetry.

The developments taking place in the contemporary English polity were revolutionary in their own right and part of domestic English cultural, social and political processes. Such developments were not concurrent in the Gaelic world; and it could be suggested that similar or comparable development was thwarted by the escalating intensity of Tudor activity in Ireland.[1] The lengths to which the Gaelic Irish were able to go in accommodating new political values and new mental attitudes to power and authority say much for the flexibility of their

---

[1] See N.P. Canny, *The Elizabethan Conquest of Ireland,* passim.

civilization. These accommodations and compromises are articulated in the poetry following, which will illustrate the poets' manipulation of the traditional themes in a new century. The poet's tone is modified to suit the allegiances and aspirations of his lord; he (the lord) must unite Banbha by the sword; or he must wrest power and authority from the usurper (foreigner or domestic rival) and thus save Banbha's glory. In any event, the power he wields must be celebrated and he must be exhorted to strive after the power to which he aspires. Any compromises he has made or defeats he has suffered are deftly worked into a pattern of compliment or exhortation to vengeance. The poems of Gofraidh Fionn Ó Dálaigh and Muireadhach Albanach Ó Dálaigh for Cathal O'Connor, Mac William and Maurice fitzMaurice in the thirteenth and fourteenth centuries, studied in the earlier chapter, can be regarded as patterns for the use of motifs and themes which will reappear in different historical contexts in the sixteenth century. While the historical context undoubtedly changed between the thirteenth and sixteenth centuries, the use of the motifs and themes are used in the same way by the later poets, for the same reasons and to articulate the identical world view.

The poets' themes of the 'unity' of Banbha was popular from the earliest bardic period. In retrospective appraisal of the sixteenth and seventeenth centuries it seemed to acquire a new significance during the period of the Tudor reconquest.[2] The theme of the inherent 'unity' of Ireland however, was not only a bardic commonplace prior to the sixteenth century, but had its roots in Indo-European antiquity. For the poets it was a theme and a concept which was not linked to the 'politics' of any period and could not reflect a 'political' ideal which was aspired to in any objective sense. The theme of the inherent unity of Banbha, a situation never paralleled in reality was a motif inherited by the sixteenth century poets. Proinsias Mac Cana points out that the spiritual concept of the unity of Ireland did not have a coincidental political existence in the secular realm.[3] This interpretation of the poets' sense of

---

[2] B. Bradshaw, 'Native Reaction', p. 76.

[3] Mac Cana deals at some length with this theme in his article 'Notes on the Early Irish Concept of Unity', (hereafter 'Concept of Unity') in *Crane Bag*, Vol. 2 (1978), p. 63:

'According to the view of the world by which they were conditioned, the spiritual concept of a national unity did not require a mirror image in the realm of secular politics; in other words religious concept and political structure did not necessarily coincide.'

contemporary or historical reality appears particularly appropriate in the continual use of the theme of 'unity' by the poets. Such a concept seems to have had its origins in the Indo-European past.[4] The theoretical and literary theme of unity was deeply ingrained in the poets' consciousness. It was not a development ushered into existence by the prospect of Tudor conquest, not a modernization of the Gaelic mind in a post-conquest context, but a shade of an Indo-European cultural past.[5] The concepts of the essential unity (political) of the island and 'the cult of the centre' had both a religious and political dimension. Their respective strengths in myth and ritual was not however reflected in 'reality'.[6]

The chasm between promulgated ideals and ultimate concepts of the identity of Ireland as put forward by the poets throughout the centuries is no less evident in the later period when the literature itself became highly conventionalized and structured. It provided a uniquely consistent framework of reference for both the aristocracy and the literati, in many respects reassuming the rôle enjoyed by their cultural predecessors without the overt spiritual dimension. To suggest that the concept of 'unity' in particular, acquired a newly relevant urgency in the sixteenth century, however, is to mix in a misleading way, the two planes of reality in which the poets worked.[7] This would seem to indicate that the poets were beginning to relate the ancient motifs of their literary conventions directly to actual political situations, in a manner which had never been their wont, and which ill-suited the tradition of their profession. Not only does this assume an unnatural use of the

---

[4] This is discussed in some detail by Alwyn and Brinley Rees in the *Celtic Heritage.* The discussion is based on the principle of the division of Ireland into four constituent provinces and a central province making five in all. See especially pp 145-9, and see also 'A new version of the Battle of Mag Rath', ed. and trans. by C. Marstrander, *Ériu* V, 1911, p. 226-47.

[5] Marstrander, 'A new version of the Battle of Mag Rath', p. 233.

[6] Alwyn and Brinley Rees, *Celtic Heritage,* pp 147 and 148.

[7] Following on from the theme of ambiguity which existed between the sacred and the profane nature of the poets' profession, Mac Cana points out that in early Irish religion:
'. . . even the concept of national unity and the cult of the centre are common to both religion and politics, as indeed we might expect in a society dominated by the notion of sacred kingship: the important difference is that in the realm of politics the impressive centralist theory so richly supported by myth and ritual was almost impossible to translate into practical reality.' — in 'Concept of Unity' p. 65. And see Benveniste, E., *Indo-European Language and Society*, Coral Gables, Florida 1973.

historico-literary motifs of the poets, but it implies an interest in political objectives on the part of the poets which was not shared by their patrons at any time during the sixteenth century. Mac Cana quotes a poem from the late fourteenth century by Tadhg Óg Ó hUiginn addressed to Niall Óg Ó Néill: [8]

Ón aird thuaidh thig an chobhair,
tig gach aird d'uaim a hEamhain,
as a n-ucht do uair chabhoir,
gabhoir ón lucht thuaidh Teamhair

Réidh faoi gach fiadh dá bhfuaighionn
Niall Ó Néill na naoi ngéibhionn,
téid ar ndéanaimh chóig [gcórrann]
d'fhéaghain tórann fhóid Éirionn.
(McKenna, *Aithdioghluim Dána* 1, No. 15,
sts. 1 and 36, p. 55 and 59.)

[From the north comes succour; from Eamhain all quarters are joined in union; let the men of the north take Tara, they who came to her aid in the past.
Niall Ó Néill of the nine fetters brings peace to the lands he unites; having established the five equal divisions, he goes forth to inspect the borders of Ireland's territory.][9]

The theme of the five provinces is very distinctly treated here. The Uí Néill of the fourteenth century were as far from assuming control over the five provinces as the Maguire chieftain addressed in the following stanzas in the late sixteenth century. The poem book, *duanaire* of the Maguires[10] contains several poems to Cú Chonnacht Maguire, Lord of Fermanagh (1566-1589). In most of the poems Cú Chonnacht's sway over all Ireland is celebrated. He levies rents on the five provinces:

---

[8] Mac Cana suggests that the iteration of the essential unity of Banbha '. . . acquired a new and more urgent relevance during this (post-Norman) period, and especially from the mid-sixteenth century onwards.' — 'Concept of Unity', p. 68.

[9] Mac Cana did not quote the stanza in Irish which I have used here from McKenna's *Aithdioghluim Dána*. I use the translation used by Mac Cana, however, in 'Concept of Unity', p. 68.

[10] D. Greene, (ed.), *Duanaire Mhéig Uidhir* (Dublin, 1972).

Sibh co nóin i nbeirn bhaoighail
ag seilg ar na cóig cánaibh;
ní dheachaidh riamh clú a ccéimibh
nár éiligh tú a ngrian ghábhaidh.
(Greene, *Maguire Poems*, No. 4, st. 27, p. 40)

[You stay until evening in the gap of danger seeking the tributes of
the five provinces; never was another's fame enhanced that you
did not challenge it on the field of battle.]

The same Maguire is exhorted to strive for the 'unity' of the five provinces:

Síol cCuinn uaidh fa anfholaidh
go huaim an Fhuinn Fhuinedhaigh;
nír bhen re mnaoi Muiredhaigh
a fer fa dhlaoi duilleabhair.
(Greene, *Maguire Poems*, No. 7, st. 33, p. 66)

[Till Ireland has been united under his sway, the Ulstermen are
under a heavy tribute from him; Ireland's husband has openly
united with his wife.]

The poet links thematically two kinds of 'unity' dealt with in the poetry;
the unity of Banbha as a territory consisting of five provinces, and the
unity of the chief's territory with the chief, a concept of rightful
kingship popular in the earliest theories of kingship throughout
Europe.[11] Casually, as part of a description of Maguire's prowess as a
provider of booty for the poets, a poet simply identified as 'Mac a'
Bhaird' tells us:

Díon Gaoidheal do ghabh do láimh
triall ós aird ar ua Seáain;
cur a shealbha ar Fhiadh Uisnigh
a dtriall menma an Mhanchaighsin.
(Greene, *Maguire Poems,* No. 14, st. 21, p. 134.)

[He has undertaken the defence of the Irish, the descendant of
Seáan is to march openly; in the movement of the mind of that
Maguire, there is the bringing of Ireland under his sway.]

---

[11] See Caerwyn Williams, *The Court Poet in Medieval Ireland,* pp 48 and 49.

The literary conceit involving the presentation of the chieftain as one who will hold sway over the five provinces recalls the ancient semi-sacred, ritualistic belief of the *filí* in the essential mystic unity of the island, a unity never experienced in any political sense. Exhortations to 'unity' by the poets in the sixteenth century poems are in the same spirit as those of two centuries before. The 'unity' involved appreciation of an aspect of the cultural integrity of Ireland which did not necessitate a political expression at this time. In any event, its political expression involved an appreciation of values which had no lasting existence in the contemporary Gaelic mentality.

The Gaelic lords of the sixteenth century were unaware of any major 'threat' to their civilization. The piecemeal advances of the English penetration into the administration and to the remoter parts of the country was regarded as neither serious nor final. The English court likewise felt no security in their conquest effort. The 'conquest' was not at any time before the early eighteenth century regarded by the settlers themselves as a completed task.[12] The theme of the essential unity of the territories of Banbha is closely related to that of resistance to encroachments from extra-insular forces. Fulminations against foreigners abound in the early annals. References to foreigners recognizable as Norsemen, and later Normans are very common. The English interest in Ireland following on the collapse of the Anglo-Norman colony presented the chroniclers with a further group of foreigners. At no stage in the Viking period, the Norman period of the twelfth century or the earlier phase of Tudor conquest, did military resistance give rise to any concerted efforts on the part of the Gaelic Irish to translate their sensitivity to the innate unity of Ireland into a political consciousness of the use of the united Gaelic Irish effort against foreign encroachments. In fact the two concepts; the unity of the territories of Ireland in the abstract almost mythical sense, and the principle of resistance to outside interference were not related in a way which could be construed as having a realistic political dimension.

The theme of 'unity' and of 'uniting' Banbha in the face of foreign encroachments did not have a political existence, nor did its corollary; that foreigners should be excluded from Ireland, either because of their foreigness, or because of any threat they might pose for the Gaelic Irish

---

[12] Cf. Sir William Petty, *The Political Anatomy of Ireland,* ed. by John O'Donovan [reprint Shannon] (Irish University Press, 1970), pp 25-35.

polity. In the poetry this is evidenced in the various ways in which the poets accommodated the foreigness of their patrons in a tradition which catered almost exclusively for Gaelic perceptions of power and the rights pertaining to it. One of the principal guiding factors in the poet's acceptance or rejection of a chief was his *de facto* position. If the addressee had secured a position, then the rights accruing thereto were automatically his. A foreign lord who had succeeded in carving a social and political niche for himself in the Gaelic world, was eulogized as a Gaelic chief. The constant readjustments demanded by a polity in which war was endemic fostered a respect for the *fait accompli* in the values of the Gaelic Irish; a fundamental consideration in our evaluation of the perceptions articulated in the poetry.

In order to understand the apparent flexibility of the loyalties of the poets in the sixteenth century, it is necessary to understand the part played by victory and defeat in the Gaelic Irish mind. Poets saw no contradiction in eulogizing an Anglo-Norman lord who engaged in campaigns for the crown against a Gaelic lord.[13] Just as Gofraidh Fionn Ó Dálaigh was proud to declare that his patron was a liegeman of the king of England in the mid-fourteenth century, so is the poet Flann mac Eoghain Mac Craith(?) proud to describe the favour in which his patron, Thomas, 10th Earl of Ormond is held by the king of England in the mid-sixteenth century:

> Cion mhic airdríogh a Ching Hannrí
> fuair an seang-mhín séimh-ghlacach,
> 's do bhí an tréinfhear ag Cing Éadbhard
> 'na fhior aobhdha éinleabtha.
> (Carney, *Butler Poems*, No. 16, st. 2 lines 1749-1752, p. 74.)

> [The smooth-fisted, slender, fine one received the share/portion of the son of a high-king from King Henry, the champion was the cheerful companion of King Edward's bed.][14]

The poet Diarmaid Dall mac an Fhir Léighin in a poem dated about the final decade of the sixteenth century describes his very favourable relations with the chiefs of a number of septs of both Gaelic-Irish and Anglo-Norman or other foreign descent. The poem itself is one expressing dissatisfaction with Cormac O'Hara, lord of Leighne:

---

[13] E. Knott, *Irish Classical Poetry,* pp 67 and 68.
[14] And cf. Bergin, *Irish Bardic Poetry,* No. 23, st. 19, p. 106, and No. 20, st. 29, p. 92.

Fine Chonoill is cland Néill,
tairrngeartoigh Éiriond iaidséin,
fir chumoind fa cruaidh gcogoidh
urroim uaim ní fhuarodair.
Ní um gabh eagla rompa riamh,
síol gConchobhoir, cland Uilliam,
ná síol lond toirbheartoch Táil,
drong fa hoirbheartach n-iomráidh.
Síol na gColla gidh iad and,
cland Charrthoigh chríche Frémhann,
nó Gearaltoigh grádh gach fhir,
deaghaltroimh na ndámh nduillidh.
(McKenna, *O'Hara Poems,* No. 17, sts. 10, 11, 12, p. 200.)

[The races of Conall and Niall were the prophesied ones of Éire, and yet those hard-fighting friends of mine had not (always) got respectful homage from me.
I had felt no fear before the Í Chonchobhair or Clann Uilliam or the vigorous generous race of Tál (Í Bhriain), folk of well-established fame.
Or even the race of the Collas (Mac Mathghamhna, Mág Uidhir, etc.), or the race of Carthach of the land of Fréamhainn, or the Gearaltaigh, beloved of all men, good fosterers of the exigent(?) poets.]

The poet makes no distinction whatsoever here between Mac William and Geraldines on the one hand, and O'Donnell, O'Neill and O'Brien on the other. The poets simply respected power; power which was visible or implied and which was competently wielded. The whole society revolved on this acceptance of the reality of the *fait accompli.* For this reason the inter-dependence of the three themes one upon another is a characteristic of most of the poems addressed in this study. It also prevents a neat and exclusive categorization of the themes of 'sovereignty' and 'unity' from the fundamental acceptance of the *fait accompli.*

The perceptions of power underlying this attitude can be divined in the works of the literati since the beginning of the written tradition. The earliest wonder-tales and sagas were adapted after the fifth century to suit the values of a newly christianized society, by christian clerics who compiled the earliest collections of tales and kept monastic records. The *Lebor Gabála* itself and the race-origin tales were worked over to create a pseudo-historical synchronization of pre-historic tales with the Book of Genesis. The annalistic entries in different areas, and under the patronage of different septs reflect the political ambitions of the patron. Genealogists in their computations and compilations were adept propagandists for their employers, creating precedents and illustrious family connections for the chiefs of newly emerging septs. In the later period of the seventeenth century, the celebrated 'Four Masters'.[15] evaluated the activities of prominent Gaelic Irish, Old English, and even newly arrived English, to reflect the loyalties of their patron, Fearghal Ó Gadhra, a successful M.P.; so much so indeed that their obituary for John of Desmond, brother of the earl of Desmond, who was killed in 1582, was qualified thus:

> Were it not that he was opposed to the crown of England, the loss of this good man would have been lamentable on account of his liberality in bestowing jewels and riches and his valour in the field of conflict.[16]

O'Donovan, editor of the so-called 'Annals of the Four Masters', found it necessary to add an explanatory footnote to this entry:

> . . . but these annals were compiled for Farrell O'Gara who was loyal to his Protestant sovereign Charles I, and it is quite evident that the Four Masters adopted their language to his, not their own notions on this subject.[17]

The fate of the Earl of Desmond himself, who was betrayed by a follower while in hiding, is judged similarly by the same annalists:

> Were it not that he was given to plunder and insurrection, as he [really] was, this fate of the Earl of Desmond would have been one of the mournful stories of Ireland . . . It was no wonder that the vengeance of God should exterminate the Geraldines for their

[15] *Annála Ríoghachta Éireann: Annals of the Kingdom of Ireland by the Four Masters from the earliest period to the year 1616*, ed. and trans. by John O'Donovan, (Dublin, 1851, reprint, New York, 1966) (hereafter *AFM*).

[16] *AFM, sub anno* 1582, p. 1779.

[17] *AFM, sub anno* 1582, footnote 4, p. 1776.

opposition to the Sovereign, whose predecessors had granted to their ancestors as patrimonial lands, that tract of country extending from Dún Chaoin in Kerry, to the Meeting-of-the-Three-Waters and from the Great Island of Ard Neimidh in Hy-Liathain to Limerick.[18]

The Four Masters needed no prompting to know how to approach any question of conflicting loyalties which presented itself in the course of their work. The victory of the victor must be rationalized and the defeat of the vanquished must be attributed to some weakness, physical or moral, or to an act of divine intervention or alternatively ignored. The ever-changing fortunes caused by the continual warfare which characterized the Gaelic polity taught the Gaelic Irish to be impressed by immediate results. This helps to explain the poets' celebration of short-term successes, made visible by substantial spoils which became available for distribution by the successful lord to win him greater support against his rivals within the sept.

On the individual level, the same trend can be recognized in the celebration by the poets of individual forays of the chiefs and the latters' acceptance of crown titles. The oscillating and all-embracing but short-lived loyalties of the Gaelic lords are all matched by those of the poets whose professional services were offered to anyone who provided the material incentive. No xenophobic qualms prevented them from, on the one hand, hailing a Gaelic chief as the 'succour of Banbha', and on the other, celebrating some Anglophile Old English lord's impressive forays against Gaelic chiefs. 'Conquest' in the national sense, in the sixteenth century meant nothing to the Gaelic chiefs. The poets supported the traditional life-style of the chiefs and also supported any innovations which the chiefs saw fit to introduce; provided the undertaking had a good chance of success. The immediate discomfort or humiliation of dispossession by fellow Gaelic chiefs or by 'foreigners' obscured all wider considerations. The authority to make contracts of peace or declarations of war — prerogatives the execution of which were jealously guarded by the chiefs and were the true enemies of unity of effort — persisted throughout the sixteenth century and were unchecked by any new perceptions of statehood or nationality. The poets praised the

---

[18] *AFM, sub anno* 1583, pp 1796-8.

chiefs for embarking on military forays because the use of battle was enshrined in the life-style of the Gaelic Irish and their own social and
political existence depended upon it.

The English advances provided further opportunities for warfare.
Their system of consolidation of victory was, however, entirely foreign
to Gaelic concepts of the use of warfare. The determining factor in the
longevity of loyalty was success, and the consequences of warfare and
the ensuing compromises were part of the mental schema of the Gaelic
Irish. Their perceptions of local wars were carried into those wars with
outsiders as can be seen from the poets' treatment of any of the English-
Irish battles; but so do their perceptions of the prerogatives of the more
powerful. If might is all important, then the victors, no matter how un-
palatable, deserve their spoils. Such is the scheme presented to us by the
bardic poets in their encomia for various chiefs, Irish, Old English and
English. The literary structure within which they operated had its own
rationale. This is what must be interpreted, not the literal expression of
their genre, but the perceptions from which they emanated.

The battle roll (*caithréim*) of Hugh mac Shane O'Byrne is typical of
its kind. It celebrates the depredations perpetrated by O'Byrne between
1550 and 1579. The O'Byrnes of Gabhal Raghnaill became increasingly
distinguished from their senior branch whose territory was *Críoch
Branach*.[19] Hugh mac Shane took advantage of the downfall of the
Kildares and the power vacuum this created to enlarge his relatively
small territory. This *caithréim* of O'Byrne is found in the *Leabhar
Branach*,[20] an impressive collection of bardic poetry comprising the
duanairí of four generations of the O'Byrne chiefs of *Gabhal Raghnaill*.
It presents us with interesting material concerning the poets' work for
one of the more active Leinster septs.[21] The collection has also been used

---

[19] See L. Price, 'The Byrne's country in the County Wicklow in the sixteenth century',
in *Journal of the Royal Society of the Antiquities of Ireland,* vol. lxiiii (1933), pp 225-41
and also, L. Price, 'Notes on Feagh McHugh O'Byrne', *R.S.A.I. Jn.* vol. lxvi (1936), pp
42-66.

[20] S. Mac Airt, *Leabhar Branach.*

[21] The editor of the collection, Seán Mac Airt, describes it thus:
'The Leabhar Branach, apart from its linguistic value, is important in that it affords us
some insight from an Irish standpoint into the life and fortunes of a sept bordering the
Pale, during an interesting if unhappy era of our history. In contrast with Anglo-Irish
political documents of the period, it reflects the outlook, policy and culture of the *more
patriotic Gaelic nobility.*' — S. Mac Airt, *Leabhar Branach,* p. vii (italics mine).

to illustrate the theory that a 'new self-conscious nationalism' was articulated in sixteenth-century bardic poetry in response to Tudor advances.[22] By examining the content of some of these poems and comparing them to those written for lords whose behavior hardly let them open to the charge of patriotism or Gaelic nationalism, for example Thomas Butler, 10th Earl of Ormond, it can be shown that a literal interpretation of such material, especially when the interpretation or analysis is dictated by knowledge of historical denouements relevant for a later period, can be quite erroneous. Indeed, it can be shown that what is interpreted as nationalistically belligerent anti-English tone and sentiment in the *Leabhar Branach,* appear as standard traditional forms of encomium in the published collection of Butler poems.[23] The issue is not simply a matter of comparing lines of highly cryptic and conventionalized poetry, but rather of identifying identical perceptions underlying the works for both O'Byrne and Butler, and appreciating their identical cultural and socio-political background.

The *caithréim* of Hugh mac Shane[24] celebrates Hugh's activities against Gaelic Irish and English alike. The poem is stylistically presented as a

> . . . rough clockwise *deiseal* circuit through the counties of Wexford, Carlow, Leix, Offaly, Kildare, Dublin and Wicklow.[25]

Only in Co. Wicklow do the O'Byrnes have any hereditary rights since the twelfth century, and it was only in the early sixteenth century that the *Gabhal Raghnaill* branch of the O'Byrnes came to prominence.[26] What is being celebrated therefore in this poem of Fear gan Ainm Mac Eochadha are the reavings and forays traditionally undertaken by Gaelic chiefs, endeavouring to occupy the energies of their followers,

---

[22] It is this collection which Brendan Bradshaw uses in his 'case-study' of Gaelic nationalist ideological content in sixteenth-century bardic poetry: 'For instance, if it can be shown in this particular case, as I think it can, that a new self-conscious nationalism is articulated in the poetry, then this will be sufficient to explode the hypothesis that the Gaelic polity in the sixteenth century could not, or at least, did not generate a nationalist ideology.' — in 'Native Reaction', p. 65.

[23] James Carney, *Poems on the Butlers,* (Dublin, 1945).

[24] S. Mac Airt, *Leabhar Branach,* No. 18, p. 61.

[25] S. Mac Airt, *Leabhar Branach,* p. 356.

[26] S. Mac Airt, *Leabhar Branach,* p. ix.

and to provide revenue for them and their own fairly extensive households.

Bordering the Pale, as their territory did, and their consequently being familiar with the first waves of any and all intrusions through the east coast, the O'Byrne could be expected to raid the *Gall* and engage in hostile activities against them without being considered particularly patriotic or singularly politically motivated. The poem begins on a note of sorrow for the loss of Aodh. The poem thus combines elegy with battle-roll:

> Ceana Aodha an fhabhra mhoill,
> barr bróin ar n-éirghe oroinn
> ar mbéin fá chuimhne na gcean;
> ní duilghe céim dá chaoineadh.
> (Mac Airt, *Leabhar Branach,* No. 18, st. 1, p. 61.)

[Love of Aodh of the slow eye (lit. eyelash) has caused this excess of sorrow in us; no occasion is more sorrowful than our duty to remember him, the beloved.]

The poet's 'remembering' Aodh involves his exhaustively recounting the many conflicts in which Aodh was involved as befitted his position. The poet's treatment of these numerous and varied conflicts is instructive. Gaelic neighbours, though they were not very plentiful, since O'Byrne's immediate neighbours were Ormonds, Kildares and the Pale, were attacked with vigour equivalent to that with which he reputedly attacked the *Gall*. The poet records his depredations against both with equal pride:

> Tuar teasda táinig do ghoin
> Niocoláis Fhinn do Hóraidh;
> ní sealg nárbh adhbhar antnúidh
> sealg fhaghladh Í Fhogharthúin.
> (Mac Airt, *Leabhar Branach,* No. 18, st. 7, p. 62.)

[The wounding (killing?) of Nioclas Finn do Hóradh was an omen of fame, the plundering of Í Fhogarthúin was indeed an occasion of dread.]

Pride is taken in the death of Maithias Breac mac Seoin:

Deimhin marbhtha Maithias Bhric
meic Seóin dob eachtra oirdhric;
a-tá uain in gach éineing,
lá do bhuail fá Bheigéirinn.
(Mac Airt, *Leabhar Branach,* No. 18, st. 8, p. 62.)

[The reality of the death of Maithias Breac was a noble deed of Seán's son, one day when he attacked Beigéire, every land has its turn.]

Tadhg was certainly a Gaelic Irish name, and three individuals of that name were slain by Hugh mac Shane:

A ló marbhtha na ttrí tTadhg
Domhnach Mór fá réim roard;
scél do leathadh as dual damh,
do creachadh uadh 's do hadhnadh.
(Mac Airt, *Leabhar Branach,* No. 18, st. 24, p. 64.)

[On the day upon which the three Tadhgs were killed; at Domhnach Mór, it was a ferocious course — it was burned and destroyed by him. It is my duty to spread tidings.

The death and destruction of fellow Gaels is lauded and recorded with as much pride as that in the visiting of destruction on a Butler town:

Tug Aodh (dob am dá féghain)
gleó a nGráinsigh an Bhuiltéraigh;
ón Ráith Mhóir do chruinnigh cion,
tuillimh ris an gcóir cuirthior.
(Mac Airt, *Leabhar Branach,* No. 18, st. 19, p. 63.)

[Aodh brought destruction into Gráinseach of the Butlers, — it was time to look to it — he collected tribute from Rathmore, a fit reward for the justice that is delivered.]

In their turn Mac Eochadha, the poet, mentions the capture of two English officials along with the destruction of the dwelling of one Murcadha. There is no special significance attached by the poet to Hugh's treatment of the two officials. It is as important or as memorable an incident as those mentioned in the other commemorative stanzas, including those recording the raiding of Gaelic Irish territories or the death of Gaelic neighbours:

Master Dáibhídh a láimh leis,
Masteir Hairbhidh ón aoinghreis,
faghail Mhorchadh dá thaobh tig,
ar Aodh do chonfadh cuirid.
(Mac Airt, *Leabhar Branach*, No. 18, st. 29, p. 65.)

[Aodh repulsed Master Dáibhidh and Master Hairbhidh in a single expedition; the attacking of Morchadh comes on account of him.]

These two gentlemen (Hairbhidh and Dáibhidh) are identified by Seán Mac Airt as Henry Davell and George Harvey 'for whose capture and detention Aodh Mac Seáin and Fiachaidh mac Aodha were pardoned in 1563'.[27] Aodh was pardoned several times for outrages committed against his neighbours. These pardons themselves show the lack of interest Hugh mac Shane felt in following up these many victories, or in consolidating his position beyond his own immediate sphere of interest. The undiscriminating way in which the various forays of Hugh are listed, present a graphic picture of the habitual skirmishing of the Gaelic lords.[28] The burnings and preyings undertaken by Hugh are proudly listed in over eighty stanzas:

Cuimhin linn an lá do chreach
Baile Í Chíog, céim áirmheach;
Cill Áine Duibhe fá dheóidh,
na h-Áile as tuile troimleíon.

Trí huaire do hairgeadh lais
Ráith Bhile tar druim dóchais;
ní toisc ar m'aire nach uil
a thoisc go Baile Bhaltuir.
(Mac Airt, *Leabhar Branach,* No. 18,
sts. 10 and 20, pp 62 and 63.)

[We remember the day he destroyed Baile Í Choig — a deed of note

---

27 Price, 'The Byrne's country in the County Wicklow in the sixteenth century', pp 42-66.

28 See P. Mac Cana, 'Concept of Unity': 'So far as the poets were concerned, raiding and skirmishing among native chieftains was little more than a well tried social lubricant that conferred certain benefits and carried few dangers for the system', p. 68.

— and following that Cill Áine Duibhe, Aile [is] overwhelmed with grief.
In a burst of confidence he plundered Rath Bile three times. The expedition he makes to Baile Bhaltuir is not an expedition I had not considered.]

Many raids are undertaken in the spirit of a cattle prey or *creach*:

> Fá Ráith Iomgháin (?) ar ndul dáibh
> ar mbreith bhuadh Bhaile Cormáin; foghlaidh bó Bhaile Philib,
> mó ar m'aire ná a n-éilighid.
> (Mac Airt, *Leabhar Branach*, No. 18, st. 18, p. 63.)

[After they went throughout Ráth Iomgháin and had taken Baile Cormáin, he plundered the cows of Baile Philip, I have more in mind than what they demand(?).]

and again:

> Ré cois bhó an Bholgáin Riabhuigh
> Aodh 'na fhíorchoin airdfhiadhuigh;
> tug an chreich ón Bhuaile Bhán
> ar mbreith buaidhe ar an mBolgán.

> Baile Éamainn Tiobar tug
> ar díoth cruidh (níor chuairt charad);
> Cúirt an Easpuig gan dol de,
> measgaid a gcrodh tre chéile.
> (Mac Airt, *Leabhar Branach*, No. 18, sts. 43,
> and 65, pp 67, 70.)

[Along with the cattle of Bolgán Riabhach, Aodh, fierce warrior in hot pursuit, took a prey from Buaile Bhán after defeating Bolgán.
He bereft Baile Eamoinn Tiobar of cattle — not a friendly visit — Cúirt an Easpuig could not avoid him, they mix their cattle together.]

Hugh mac Shane O'Byrne certainly revelled in the exercise of this 'social lubricant'. The senior branch of the sept in *Críoch Branach* meanwhile existed in relative quiet in their crown-organized territory complete with sheriff.

The same enthusiasm which the poet exhibited in the description of victories however negligible, was transferred into overpowering grief in the composition of elegies. Just as Hugh mac Shane's victories as a reaver cause his name to be remembered among the '*Danar*' — so his death would cause unprecedented desolation. The death of a chief brings forth declarations of irreparable loss and major calamity from the poets. The exaggerated idiom of grief is consistent with the poet's emphasis on the importance of the immediate situation. This interest in the immediacy of everything must also be seen against the background of the poet's sense of history; the historico-literary framework to which every occasion is ultimately answerable. Therefore in an elegy to Hugh mac Shane by Fear gan Ainm Mac Eochadha it is not surprising to read that the fame of the Leinstermen is at risk because of Hugh's death:

> Cia choimhédfas clú Laighion?
> mór bhfile le bhféchfuidhior;
> bíodh a-nú [a] fhala ar an ég
> muna bhfagha an clú a choimhéd.
> (Mac Airt, *Leabhar Branach*, No. 17, st. 1, p. 56.)

[Who shall maintain Leinster's glory, (it is) a great number of poets from whom it will be expected. Let his displeasure be upon death today if that fame fail to be upheld.]

An end has been put to the glory of the Gael because of Hugh's death:

> Glóir Gaoidhiol ar gcúl do chur,
> do dhruim tnúith tig a turnamh;
> a bhuain dín ní cás coimsi,
> dá bhrígh do fhás m'atuirsi.
> (Mac Airt, *Leabhar Branach*, No. 17, st. 10, p. 57)

[It (his death) caused the deterioration of the glory of the Gael, defeat follows upon expectations, his being taken from us is not a moderate sorrow, my affliction increased because of it.]

The fate of the O'Byrnes following Hugh's death is almost comparable to that of Christ on Good Friday:

> Barr cumhadh do thoirsi thruim
> d'éis imtheachta d'ua Rémainn;

a ttás oirne san Aoine,
doilghe cás na cédAoine.
(Mac Airt, *Leabhar Branach,* No. 17,
st. 14, p. 58.)

[An excess of sorrow from heavy affliction after the departure of Raymond's grandson; only the plight of the first Friday is more harsh than that which affects us on this Friday.]

Neither is the life of the poet assured when his lord is dead. The theme of the poet preferring to die as his patron dies is quite popular:

Ní buan ollamh d'éis a ríogh,
baoghal damh dul a ndimbríogh;
sé ar gach taobh ag teacht ruinne,
neart ag gach aon oroinne.
(Mac Airt, *Leabhar Branach,* No. 17, st. 23, p. 59.)

[A poet lives not after his king, I am in danger of dejection of spirits — a bout with us on every side — the forces of everyone upon us.]

In Knott's collection of Tadhg Dall's poetry an elegy on Cathal O'Connor makes use of the same intense grief motif:

Ó nach féadaim teach thoraibh,
a Chathail Í Chonchobhair,
bheith 'ged luadh is doiligh dhamh;
truagh gan m'oidhidh it fharradh.
(Knott, *Tadhg Dall,* No. 14, st. 31, p. 96.)

[Since I cannot relate of these sufficingly, Cathal O'Connor, it is grievous to me to speak of thee, alas that I did not perish by thy side.]

In the same century the poet Lochluinn Mac Taidhg Óig Í Dhálaigh lamented the death of Philip O'Reilly, lord of Breifne in 1596. Because of the special relationship between the lord and his territory, the weather and fertility of the land all suffered on the demise of the chieftain. Philip O'Reilly having enjoyed the headship of his sept for a mere six weeks, died at the hands of some of O'Neill's followers.[29] The elegy begins:

---

[29] See Carney, *Poems on the O'Reillys,* No. 11, p. 202, notes.

> Frémh gach uilc oidheadh flatha,
> de tig tús gach neamhratha;
> cleachtuidh sein síolaghadh uilc
> 's neimh gach fhíorfhaladh d'adhuint.
> (Carney, *O'Reilly Poems,* No. 11, st. 1, p. 54.)

[The untimely death of a prince is the source of all evil, from it springs every misfortune. The elders sow evil and kindle rancour and every treachery.]

The expression of grief thus, cannot be separated in its function of facilitating the transfer of allegiance from one individual to another; an integral part of the acceptance of the *fait accompli.* This is a useful illustration of the interdependence of the bardic themes one upon another. In expressing such grief the poet respectfully and appropriately disposes of a chief/lord. The grief expressed in elegy is transformed into euphoric welcome for the successor. The capacity of the poetic structure to cope with the many political, social and material and indeed emotional changes which confronted them is manifest in the flexibility of such works and the highly developed philosophy which underlie them.

If one is to regard Hugh mac Shane O'Bryne as a member of the 'more patriotic Gaelic nobility', and see reflected in his *duanaire* the stirrings of an Irish nationalist consciousness, and if this in turn can be said to indicate a burgeoning nationalist awareness among the poets as a body, then the poems addressed to an Old English lord of different loyalties and different religion should reflect some of this new political awareness in the poet's treatment of his household and activities. Carney's collection of poems on the Butlers includes some poems for the earl of Ormond. The position of the House of Ormond is described by Carney thus:

> The House of Ormond, the chief representative of this family was consistently loyal to the English interest, and unlike any other Anglo-Irish families, was not Gaelicized to any great extent in either habits or speech.[30]

However, until the time of James 1st, duke of Ormond, this family and especially its junior branches were generous patrons of the poets and

---

[30] Carney, *Poems on the Butlers,* p. 9.

were the subjects of elegy, panegyric and encomium as their Gaelic and Gaelicized fellows.

Thomas, 10th Earl of Ormond (1534-1614), was a man of immense political stature in Ireland and a court favourite of Elizabeth. His active life in military affairs was spent campaigning in the interests of the crown, protecting his own territory from the encroachments of Tudor bureaucracy and pursuing the traditional Ormond-Desmond rivalry. He was the recipient of royal honours and of confiscated lands following the disturbances in Munster connected with the Desmond rebellions. Ormond sought jurisdiction not only over his own palatinate territory but over the whole of Leinster as well.[31] He was clearly a man about whom a 'patriotic' Gaelic poet should have very little to praise. He was such however, as a Gaelic poet of the sixteenth century would find very impressive and worthy of a battle roll fit for any illustrious son of Mil. The battle roll of Ormond was written *circa* 1614[32] by Flann Mac Eoghain meic Craith. The poem opens with a stanza expressing the poet's familiarity with the battle-standard of Ormond — evidently because of the frequency of its display — following which the poet mentions the areas all over Ireland and indeed in England in which this standard has been a portent of havoc and destruction:

Eólach mé ar mheirge an iarla,
an bhratach bhláith bhoirdniamhdha,
an eang mhór chréachtach chorcra,
an sróll éachtach onchonta.

An eang-soin gan iomlot ngliadh,
minic do chuir chuaird imchian
fá chíghibh Banbha na mbeann
a ttíribh amhra Éireann.
(Carney, *Butler Poems*, No. 15, sts 1 and
4, p. 67.)

[I know the Earl's standard, the noble brilliant flag, the great wound-dealing, purple pennant, the satin powerful standard.
The standard undamaged by conflict, has often journeyed afar, about the breasts of Banbha of the peaks, in the countries of noble Ireland.]

---

[31] N.P. Canny, *Elizabethan Conquest of Ireland*, p. 22.
[32] Carney, *Poems on the Butlers*, p. 129.

Thus does the poet launch immediately into the celebration of one of the most important activities of the lord; his battles. The first victory recorded by the poet in his favour is that of Ormond's part in the suppression of the Wyatt rebellion in 1554, a matter of English domestic politics:

> Gabháil Bhoëit — beag dá shéan —
> táinig le Tomás Builtéar;
> anbhuain re gonaibh nír ghabh
> a ccoraidh chrannruaidh churadh.
> (Carney, *Butler Poems,* No. 15, st. 6, p. 67.)

[He effected the capture of Wyatt — a fraction of his fortune — he never felt anxiety in the face of wounding, in the strenuous contention of warriors.]

This victory is recorded by the poet in the same spirit in which Hugh O'Byrne's poet, Fear gan Ainm mac Eochadha, records that O'Byrne captured Master Davell and Master Harvey. It is an individual victory gained by the patron and lauded as such by the poet.

Ormond attacked Shane O'Neill in the North in 1557,[33] a battle which was to all appearances indistinguishable from a traditional cattle-prey:

> Ar Seaán neartmhar Ó Néill
> tug maidhm gér dheacar dhoi-séin;
> as ní théarnó uaidh, gidh eadh,
> éanbhó do bhuaibh a bhailteadh.
> (Carney, *Butler Poems,* No. 15, st. 8, p. 68.)

[He defeated the strong Seaán Ó Néill though it was difficult for him, nevertheless, not one cow of the cattle of the towns escaped from him.]

The Lord Deputy Sussex was involved in many forays northward between 1556 and 1563 accompanied by Ormond who always distinguished himself in service.[34] These stanzas were written in a post-Kinsale context (c. 1614) in the aftermath of Hugh O'Neill's efforts to maintain a loose federation of septs, and after the first Stuart plantations had been

---

[33] Carney, *Poems on the Butlers,* p. 131.
[34] Carney, *Poems on the Butlers,* pp 130 and 131.

undertaken. The poet evidently feels no qualms at recording the defeat of a kinsman of Hugh O'Neill at the hands of the Lord Deputy's principal supporter in Ireland. A raid on O'Byrne's territory is acclaimed in the same tone:

> Lá a Ránallchaibh ag roinnt chreach,
> athlá a ndúthaigh Dhéiseach-
> táinig adhbhar iarghná de-
> is grianlá a nglanMhagh Ghaillmhe.
> (Carney, *Butler Poems,* No. 15, st. 34, p. 71.)

> [A day (spent) in O'Byrne's territory dividing spoils, another day in Déise, cause for sorrow came of it, and a bright day in the clear plain of Galway.]

This stanza is the direct counterpart of that of Fear gan Ainm mac Eochadha in Hugh mac Shane's *caithréim.* In both poems the addressee is hailed as a reaver of some note:

> Tug Aodh (dob am dá féghain)
> gleó a nGráinsigh an Bhuiltéraigh;
> ón Ráith Mhóir do chruinnigh cion,
> tuillimh ris an gcóir cuirthior.
> (Mac Airt, *Leabhar Branach,* No. 18, st. 19, p. 63.)

> [Aodh brought destruction into Gráinseach of the Butlers (it was time to look to it) — he collected tribute from Rathmore, a fit reward for the justice that was delivered.]

Expeditions north against the Scots, in which Ormond probably took part as a member of the Lord Deputy's forces, are listed:

> A cCeann Tíre láimh do láimh
> tug airgthe as fhochuin iomráidh,
> 's a Manuinn na míneas nglan,
> daghfhuinn nár dhíleas dó-san.
> (Carney, *Butler Poems,* No. 15, st. 29, p. 71.)[35]

> [It is related that he harried Ceann Tíre, and Manainn of the smooth fresh falls — a great land which was not loyal to him — in hand combat.]

---

[35] See also Carney, *Poems on the Butlers,* p. 134.

The Mac Donnells attacked on this occasion by Ormond, are of the same family welcomed to Banbha's side in a poem for Somhairle Mac Donnell by Tadhg Dall *circa* 1567:

Rogha leannáin Leasa Cuinn,
Somhairle mhac Meic Domhnuill,
brath céile do Mhoigh Mhonaidh
's re bhfoil Éire ag anamhain.
(Knott, *Tadhg Dall*, No. 24, st. 13, p. 175.)

[The choice of Conn's dwelling, Sorley, son of Mac Donnell, the expected mate of Monadh's Plain, he for whom Ireland is waiting.]

Mac Craith proudly recalls how Ormond subdued this same family *Síol Domhnaill*:

Do chuir — fa cóir a chuimhne —
rian madhma ar Mhac Samhuirle,
's ar Shíol nDomhnaill leath ar leath,
breath an fhorluinn dob áirmheach.
(Carney, *Butler Poems,* No. 15, st. 16, p. 69.)

[He put the mark of defeat — it is right to remember it — on Mac Somhairle — and on all sides of Síol nDomhnaill, the judgement of oppression were splendid.]

The poet deals with Ormond's depredations in every province of Ireland. Their success is their own justification.

Lord Deputy Sidney complained that Ormond's territory was the 'sinke and receptacle of innumerable cattle and goods stolen'.[36] Munster, a traditional Butler target because of the Desmond earls, was twice ravaged in the later sixteenth century. Ormond assisted Lord Justice Pelham in the destruction of Munster that ensued. The Four Masters record:

A great muster was made of the men of Meath, Fingal and Leinster, and all those who were subject to the laws [of England] from the Boyne to the Meeting of the Three Waters, by the Lord

---

[36] Cited in Canny, *Elizabethan Conquest of Ireland,* p. 145.

Justice and the Earl of Ormond, about the festival of St Bridget, for the purpose of marching into the territory of the Geraldines.[37]

Of this expedition the poet writes:

Eas Geitin do lingeadh lais,
feidhm nár mhór le mac Séamais;
nír tharbha faire ar an bhfonn
baile a ttarla 'na thiomcholl.
Carruig an Phuill na bport nglan,
Cloch an Ghleanna do ghabh-san;
bruidhne daingne ar ar chóir cion,
a ndaingne dhóibh nír dhídion.
(Carney, *Butler Poems,* No. 15, sts. 14 and
15, pp 68, 69.)

[He took Eas Geitin — a town in which he found himself — by assault, a deed of no great moment for James' son, it were no benefit to guard the territory.
He took Carruig an Phoill of the clear harbours and Cloch an Ghleanna, strong dwellings deserving of respect — their fortresses were no protection for them.]

There is no hint or suggestion here that the poet acknowledges any greater significance in these victories other than that they contribute to the stature of his patron. No greater consideration is given them other than that Ormond was successful in defeating his enemies, whoever they may be. The effect of his success on the ultimate political situation is entirely ignored. His incidental reavings are those of any Gaelic chief:

Aonbhó dá mbuaibh ceann a cceann,
Bréifne, Béarra agus Boireann,
nír fhéad siad d'anacal air
gé radhocar iad d'argain.
(Carney, *Butler Poems,* No. 15, st. 23, p. 70.)

[Breifne, Bearra and Boireann, one by one could not protect one single cow of their herds from him, though it was difficult to plunder them.]

---

[37] *AFM, sub anno* 1580, pp 1728-9.

This stanza reads exactly like that of Mac Eochadha's for Hugh mac Shane:

Fá Ráith Iomgháin (?) ar ndul dáibh
ar mbreith bhuadh Bhaile Cormáin;
foghlaidh bó Bhaile Philib,
mó ar m'aire ná a n-éilighid.
(Mac Airt, *Leabhar Branach,* No. 18, st. 18, p. 63.)

[After they went throughout Rath Iomgháin and had taken Baile Cormáin, he plunders the cows of Baile Philip, I have more in mind than what they demand(?)]

Ormond ravaged the O'Brien stronghold at Bunratty in 1558 ousting the popular Domhnall O'Brien in favour of the royal nominee Conor — his [O'Brien's] nephew.[38] This event was noted by the Four Masters, who added a sentence to the effect that the Irish were greatly alarmed at such a development:

In consequence of this deed, i.e. the expulsion of Donnell O'Brien, the Irish of noble Banbha were seized with horror, dread and fear and apprehension of danger . . .[39]

Mac Craith who described the event some fifty years afterwards, presumably aware of the instability which such events caused within the septs, recounts the humiliation of O'Brien with no hint of such horror or trepidation:

An Clár is Bun Raite a-rís
do ghabh bhós — beag dá sheirbhís;
do chreach an t-iath go humhal
fá seach ar thriath Tuadhmhumhan.
(Carney, *Butler Poems,* No. 15, st. 11, p. 68.)

[He took Clár and Bun Raite again, a little of his service, on another turn he harried the lord of Thomond into submission.]

Clearly, the wider implications of this substitution of the Queen's man for the elected *tánaiste* strikes no latent 'patriotic' chord in the poet.

---

[38] Carney, *Poems on the Butlers,* p. 131.
[39] *AFM, sub anno* 1559, pp 1562-3.

Hugh mac Shane's victories over his own Gaelic neighbours recorded by Ó Eochadha are on a par with those over English neighbours and indeed some future supporters of Hugh and his son Fiachadh:

> Rolónt Iúsdás lingthior leis,
> as mó ná Máistir Síleis;
> siad a-raon 'n rian madhma
> re triall d'Aodh dá athardha.
> (Mac Airt, *Leabhar Branach*, No. 18, st. 22,
> p. 64.)

[Roland Eustace along with Master Sileis are overwhelmed by him. Both are spectacles of defeat as Aodh journeys to his patrimony.]

This Roland Eustace, second Viscount Baltinglass died in 1579. He was the father of James Eustace, leader of the Baltinglass rebellion in which Fiachadh mac Hugh took part in 1580.[40] The almost identical tone of both poems, addressed to two people of such different backgrounds, whose behaviour, however, strikes the poets in the same way, illustrate clearly those things which impress them. The two following stanzas could equally be attributed to either poet in praise of either patron:

> Sé creacha déag, dál a chean,
> a n-aonló leis do léigeadh
> ó chrích Luimnigh na learg sean,
> ceard budh duilbhir do dhéineamh.
> (Carney, *Butler Poems*, No. 15, st. 25, p. 70.)

[He delivered sixteen plunderings in one day — division of the chief, from Limerick of the ancient swardes, an achievement of a melancholy nature.]

and

> Ocht mbaile dhég mhaoidhfe mé,
> do loisc am Chaisléan Cairbre;
> said dá thaobh ar díoth daoine,
> fríoth le hAodh a n-iolmhaoine.
> (Mac Airt, *Leabhar Branach*, No. 18, st. 37, p. 66.)

---

[40] Mac Airt, *Leabhar Branach*, p. 359, notes.

[I will boast of eighteen towns burnt around Caisleán Cairbre,
their great wealth was found (taken) by Aodh.]

The poet's glorying in the successful warlord is manifest in the concluding stanzas of both poems. For Ormond, Mac Craith concludes
with stanzas of lamentation on the loss of the earl. He is hailed as the
plunderer of Banbha, the poet reminds us that he has dealt with only a
fraction of his plunderings:

> Iomdha críoch do creachadh lais
> nach maoidhim ar mac Séamais,
> gur chuir triath na ngéirreann nglan
> iath Éireann ar a fhocal.
> (Carney, *Butler Poems,* No. 15, st. 44, p. 73.)

[Many lands of which I boast not were destroyed by James's son.
He brought Ireland under his authority (lit. he put Ireland at his
word) lord of the bright constellation (division).]

His loss as a plunderer of Banbha is the cause of grief to the poet:

> Saoth leam — do chailg mo chroidhe —
> bheith dá a ccill 'na chomhnoidhe,
> creachthóir beann mbruachdhubh mBanbha
> as gleann n-uathmhur n-allmhurdha.
> (Carney, *Butler Poems*, No. 15, st. 43, p. 73.)

[I am distressed and my heart is stung by the death of the destroyer
of the dark bordered peaks of Banbha and of the fearful foreign
valleys.]

The praise for plundering Banbha is part of the celebration of the
ethos of the warlord/reaver. The *duanaire* compiled for Cú Chonnacht
Maguire, lord of Fermanagh (1566-1589), contains several stanzas from
works acclaiming Maguire's ferocity in battle:

> Gan chosg uile d'imeirghe
> d'fhuil Uidhir is fhorfhuidhle;
> ben Éimhir ge hinshuirghe
> déinimh cen a comhuirle.
> (Greene, *Maguire Poems,* No. 11, st. 3, p. 100.)

[That none should be restrained from campaigning are the words of Maguire; though Ireland is ready to be wooed, his advice is that raids should be made.]

and further (presumably relating to a fellow chief):

Beg dá iath nár fholmhuighiss
triath dá chead gur chuibhrighiss,
tug sein gan écht indleighis
neimh do chrécht do chuimhnighiss.
(Greene, *Maguire Poems*, No. 11, st. 15, p. 104.)

[So much of his land did you lay waste that you fettered a chieftain by his own will; the memory of the pain of your wounds causes them to be incurable without some deed of vengeance.]

He indulges in the duties appropriate to his status and:

Na cóig críocha comhchosnaigh
fíorfaidh móid an mhanchaighsin
léim ar áth 'gun onchoinsin
as cach ag bein bharrthuislidh.
(Greene, *Maguire Poems,* No. 21, st. 16, p. 196.)

[He is contending for the five territories, it will bring true the vow of that Maguire; that hero's vigour in the ford overthrows everybody.]

It is no surprise that the poet Mac Craith should proudly declare that no quarter of Ireland remains unmarked by the hooves of Ormond's horse:

Ní fhuil éineang d'Inis Fáil
gan lorg each Iarla Gabhráin,
as rian a chéimeann 's a chath
ar fhiadh Éireann dob eólach.
(Carney, *Butler Poems,* No. 15, st. 46, p. 73.)

[No area of Inis Fáil is unmarked by the hooves of the earl of Gabhrán's horse. His knowledge of Ireland is marked by his triumphs and his battles.]

Mac Eochadha's *caithréim* for Hugh mac Shane concludes with a further emphasis on his victories:

Maidhm do-chuaidh ar deightheisd dó
maidhm oirdheirc Átha Seanbhó;
fada do-chóidh ainm ón fhior
dár chóir an mhaidhm do mhaoidhiomh.
(Mac Airt, *Leabhar Branach,* No. 18, st. 87, p. 73.)

[A victory which enhanced his reputation, the noble victory of Áth
Seanbhó; the man's fame spread a-far, so that it were right to
boast of the victory.]

Any suggestion that the works of these two poets contained the ger-
minating seeds of nationalism or a concept of faith and fatherland, in
the late sixteenth century, must be rendered meaningless when one considers the two poems above. Their stark celebration of the use of force,
of the excitement of battle, the glory of frenetic plundering regardless of
the wider implications of what are traditionally laudable occupations,
support a different argument. The poets, and with them the Gaelic
lords, had perceptions of power, its maintenance and its prerogatives
which were at a considerable remove from those entertained at the
Tudor court.[41] The Gaelic Irish had little use for the concept of the consolidation of victory or of influence. The 'social lubricant' nature of the
warfare in the Gaelic mentality reduced the significance of any one battle in general, but conversely, made it quite important at a particular and
local level. Therefore, while the activities of the O'Byrnes on the borders
of their own territory were not of great moment to anyone not directly
involved, they represented the *raison d'être* of the sept pursuing its
traditional life-style. Submissions and compensatory payments concluded the hostilities until a new challenge emerged in the defeated sept.

The poets, as an integral part of the Gaelic polity, indeed as a
characteristic of that polity, could hardly be attributed a vanguard rôle
in analysing and commenting upon the developments within that polity
— as from a vantage point outside the influence of those same events
and of that society. Mac Cana suggests that the poets were 'better
placed' than their patrons to see 'signs' of the extinction of the native
order and that they 'read them clearly'.[42] The poets were professionally

---

[41] See Lauro Martines, *History and Society in English Renaissance Verse,* passim and
also Martines, *Power and Imagination: City States in Renaissance Italy* (London, 1980),
especially Chapter XV, 'The High Renaissance, a fractured consciousness'.
[42] Mac Cana, 'Concept of Unity', p. 69.

equipped to articulate the experiences of their patrons, but could hardly be said to enjoy a political perspicacity which would imbue their works with ideological nuances foreign to the nature of their profession and the tradition which bound their imaginations. However, in support of his statement, Mac Cana chooses Tadhg Dall Ó hUiginn's poem to Brian O'Rourke. Ó hUiginn's poems to O'Rourke, Maguire and Turlough Luineach O'Neill illustrate Ó hUiginn's appreciation of the war aims of the individuals addressed and his adaptation of the goals they might strive for to the power they actually enjoyed. This is in effect his acceptance of the *fait accompli* and it is in the context of this understanding that Ó hUiginn introduces the other traditional themes such as the unity and sovereignty of Banbha. It is interesting to note that none of the individuals mentioned shared identical political goals or made politic efforts to pursue solid victory at the cost of individual victories. Ó hUiginn's traditional treatment of them is not dependent on their expressing political aspirations consistent with Mac Cana's suggestion that the poets were aware of the inherent dangers of the fissiparous nature of the Gaelic polity. Their ambivalent attitude towards the centralizing efforts of the crown administration is reflected in Ó hUiginn's acceptance of whatever decision the chiefs arrive at. There is no way in which Ó hUiginn can be portrayed as being a political innovator in theory or in practice. Neither can it be shown that his professional compositions were made subservient in theme or sentiment to political aspirations which formed no part of his patron's perceptions of their political situation.

Since the themes introduced in the poetry depend on each other for their coherence in the bardic framework, it is impossible to deal with them separately. Therefore, Ó hUiginn's emphasis on the necessity to unite Banbha, or rid Banbha of the 'foreigner', for instance, dictate his use of or neglect of a theme such as the right of the strongest sword to rule Ireland. His use of the right of the sword theme indicates very forcefully the implications of the poet's interest in maintaining the *status quo*; the *fait accompli* situation. Tadhg Dall's rationalization of *de facto* power is neither a new element in bardic poetry nor a condition of compromise forced upon him by the contemporary political situation. His professional predecessors can be shown to have used the identical referential framework into which to place the events of their period.

While the poets were therefore well placed to read political signs of victory or defeat, they were neither the articulators of nor agents of innovation in perceptions of power, where those innovations were not part of the rationale of their lords. Indeed, their reliance on the bardic referential framework and the genre itself made it easier for them to reiterate the traditional perceptions rather than otherwise. Mac Cana indicates that Tadhg Dall's poem to Brian na Murrtha O'Rourke illustrates the poet's awareness of what Mac Cana perceives as the long-term threat of Tudor encroachment. Ó hUiginn's compositions for others indicate that such an interpretation of an individual poem ignores the vast web of theme and motif which could be woven into a number of different shapes by a poet well learned in the tradition. This, Ó hUiginn and other poets continually do. In so far as they illustrate the independence of the bardic poetry written in the late sixteenth century of the necessity continually to provide a 'response' to the Tudor conquest, the motifs and themes of some of the poetry of that period will be examined in this section.

The Brian O'Rourke addressed in Ó hUiginn's poem was nicknamed 'na Murtha':

> . . . [he] attained the headship of his kindred in 1566, and in 1567 was knighted by Sidney, who records that he was the proudest man he ever dealt with in Ireland. In the autumn of 1580 he was 'easumhal do Gallaibh' [FM] (disrespectful to the foreigners) and was attacked by Malbie. In 1585 he again made peace with the English government, and attended Perrott's parliament.[43]

O'Rourke's career was therefore not one of relentless anti-English activity. He presided over a beleaguered territory in the present Cavan/Monaghan area, a local lord continually struggling for survival. The poem quoted by Mac Cana begins with the well known stanza:

> D'fior chogaidh comhailtear síothcháin,
> seanfocal nách sároighthear;
> ní faghann síoth acht fear faghla
> feadh Banbha na mbánfoithreadh.
> (Knott, *Tadhg Dall*, No. 16, st. 1, p. 108.)

[Towards the warlike man peace is observed, that is a proverb

---

[43] E. Knott, *The Bardic Poems of Tadhg Dall Ó hUiginn,* vol. 2, p. 251.

which cannot be outdone; throughout the fair forests of Banbha none save the fighting man finds peace.]

Tadh Dall thus ostensibly exhorts O'Rourke to engage in warfare to preserve peace. The enemy against whom he should direct his warlike energies is made explicit in the second stanza:

> D'ógbhaigh Bhreagh gi bé lén feirde
> fir Saxan do síodhghadh,
> ní beag so dá dhíon, mar dearar,
> bíodh sealadh dá síorfoghal.
> (Knott, *Tadhg Dall*, No. 16, st. 2, p. 108.)

[If anyone amongst the warriors of Bregia deem it well to pacify the Saxons, this will suffice for his protection, so it is said, let him spend a while in continually spoiling them.]

Continual forays against the Saxons is the only guarantee of protection against them and peace with them. The advice given to O'Rourke effectively accommodates two contingencies; the prospect of war and the option for peace. This attitude of the poets towards the proper uses of war is in essence the characteristic of Gaelic warfare which Mac Cana aptly describes as a 'social lubricant'.[44] The earl of Ormond and his Gaelic neighbour (O'Byrne) had been commended for similar behaviour, though they entertained quite different goals.

Cú Chonnacht Maguire, lord of Fermanagh is addressed in the same vein by the poet Irial Ó hUiginn.[45] The poet declares that continual reaving and warring is the best protection for the patrimony:

> Tuar ríghe rath oirbherta,
> rath do dhísligh deghbherta;
> fer do-gheibh geall oirbherta
> mur sein is fherr n-eighreachta.
> (Greene, *Maguire Poems*, No. 11,
> st. 1, p. 100.)

[Success in prowess cultivates kingship, it is a success which fair

---

44 Cf. Katharine Simms, 'Warfare in the Medieval Gaelic Lordships'.
45 See D. Greene, *Maguire Poems,* p. xiii.

deeds have made their own; he who is most successful in defence has thus the best chance of inheritance.]

Warfare, judiciously conducted, is beneficial for the kingship. The successful military undertaking improves the reputation of the lord in his territory. Therefore the poet continues,[46] let none put a stop to the reavings and other military activities of the chief. In a further poem to Maguire, Ó hUiginn compliments him on his numerous hosts, raiding and plundering the neighbouring territories:

> Do tháin laoch, a mhic Mhég Uidhir,
> ós iath Temhra togbhaid brat;
> ní ró le coin acht a chédchion,
> mó iná soin a léighthior lat.
> (Greene, *Maguire Poems,* No. 12, st. 11, p. 112.)

[Your host of warriors, Maguire, spreads a cloak over Ireland; a dog is allowed only its first bite — you are permitted more than that.]

The celebration of the prowess in war of the chief and his retinue is not particularly related to efforts at defending autonomous Gaelic territories against sixteenth century English encroachment. Cú Chonnacht Maguire, no less than Brian na Murtha O'Rourke, displayed the characteristic expediency of the Gaelic chiefs. Like O'Rourke he too presided over his territory in uncomfortable conditions:

> balanced precariously between O'Neill and the English.[47]

He preferred to enlist the aid of the English against the depredations of Turlough Luineach than to 'unite the five provinces' under his tribute, as he is exhorted to do by Ferghal Óg Mac a' Bhaird:

> Sibh co nóin a mbeirn bhaoghail
> ag seilg na cóig cánaibh . . .
> (Greene, *Maguire Poems,* No. 4, st. 27, p. 41.)

[You stay until evening in the gap of danger seeking the tribute of the five provinces]

---

46 Greene, *Maguire Poems,* No. 11, st. 3, p. 100.
47 Greene, *Maguire Poems,* p. ix.

By November 2, 1567, Cú Chonnacht is complaining to Dublin that Toirdhealbhach Luineach 'is waxen so proude, that he will abyde no manner of order that Sir Henry have taken between him and me' and warning that 'yf you do not helpe nowe in haste to withstande oneyll [h]is malyce your honours may be sorye hereafter . . .'

Furthermore, Maguire cautioned his English allies against letting O'Neill know of his communications with them saying:

> I sow professe befor God if O Nell did now that I should complain to your worship [or] to any Englyshe man within this realme that he would syek me destrucyon to the outermost of his power. (September 25, 1573) [48]

O'Rourke, Maguire and indeed Turlough Luineach all exhibited the ambivalent attitude shared by all the Gaelic lords towards the authority of the crown; submitting to it when immediate protection against a hereditary rival was needed, rejecting the attendant restrictions on individual martial enterprise. This was a period during which O'Rourke along with O'Connor Sligo and several others including Thomas Butler, submitted to Lord Deputy Sidney in return for security of their patents. [49]

The exhortation to princes and chieftains, by the poets, to warlike and valorous deeds is not remarkable. The familiarity of the Gaelic Irish with almost continual warfare as part of the social structure, bred in them an attitude of relative complacency to the fluctuations of fortunes connected with such a life-style. This mentality is reflected in the literature and because of the special position of the poets, is perpetuated through it. The attitudes, manifest in the poetry, to the vicissitudes of war — the acquiescence in the results of decisive ventures, in victory or defeat — were the counterparts of the political perceptions of the Gaelic aristocracy. They were mirrored in the activities of the chiefs whose speed in signing treaties was rivalled only by their corresponding facility in breaking them. The frequency with which the Gaelic chiefs were the recipients of royal pardons, [50] each recorded in the State Papers, is

---

[48] Greene, *Maguire Poems,* pp vii, viii.

[49] See Canny, *Elizabethan Conquest of Ireland,* p. 112.

[50] See T.F. O'Rahilly (ed.), 'Irish Poets, Historians and Judges in English Documents. 1538-1615' in *Proceedings of the Royal Irish Academy,* vol. XXXVI, sect. C. (1921-4), pp 86-120.

ample testimony of this. Acceptance of the *fait accompli* is perhaps the most enduring trait to emerge from the accumulative influences of the warlike society which was the world of both the poet and the chieftain, each entirely dependent on the demands made of and rewards offered by the society. In the following selection of poems dealing with the concepts of the unity of Ireland, the rights to her sovereignty and the protection of both, the dependence of each of the themes on the poets' tacit or explicit acceptance of the *fait accompli* is well illustrated. The antiquity of the themes thus addressed highlights the vanity of seeking to tie the poetry too closely to the passing contemporary events.

Tadhg Dall Ó hUiginn, one of the foremost poets of the late sixteenth century, wrote for several different families of Gaelic Irish and mixed Gaelic/Old English alike. Eleanor Knott's edition of his poetry provides a very convenient register of his sometime patrons. Among the more important were Turlough O'Neill, O'Donnells, O'Haras, Burkes and Mac Williams. Tadhg Dall himself is reputed to have had his tongue cut out by irate members of the O'Hara sept, who felt insulted by some satirical work of his. A poem written by Tadhg Dall for Brian O'Rourke is cited by Proinsias Mac Cana as evidence of the poet's ability to forsee the results of Tudor expeditions in Ireland and the ultimate destruction of the Gaelic way of life. The poem opens with a directive to action:

> D'fior chogaidh comhailtear síothcháin
> seanfocal nách sároighthear; . . .
> (Knott, *Tadhg Dall*, No. 16, st. 1, p. 108.)

> [Towards the warlike man peace is observed, that is a proverb which cannot be outdone . . .]

The general popularity among the poets of such an observation has already been indicated. This poem, however, continues in a more urgent tone; the poet graphically describes the miserable state of the nobility of Ireland, and bemoans the fate of her warriors who are thrust, by grasping foreigners, to the verges of the island:

> Beag nách deachsad go díoth n-éinfir
> uaisle fola fionnGhaoidhil,
> fiú a feabhas a dhóigh na dronga
> tóir arra nach ionmhaoidhimh,
> Siad dá gcur i gciomhsaibh Banbha,

buidhne Ghall 'na glémheadhón;
airc leithimil díobh ar ndéinimh,
síol Éibhir is Éireamhón.
(Knott, *Tadhg Dall*, No. 16, sts. 5 and 6,
p. 109.)

[The nobility of the blood of fair Gaoidheal is vanished almost to a man; such hopeful quarry are they that pursuit of them is nothing to boast of.

They are being thrust on to the outskirts of Banbha, whilst regiments of foreigners are in the centre; of the seed of Eber and Eremon a one-sided(?) hath been made.]

Thus according to Ó hUiginn, the 'centre'[51] is overtaken by foreigners. This theme of the 'centre' is related closely to the consciousnesss of the unity of the five provinces; or four provinces and the centre, making up the fifth. Ó hUiginn likewise develops the theme from the warriors banishment from the centre, to the extension of O'Rourke's power over the five nations and with the purpose of uniting them.

Urusa dhó déanamh cogaidh
tre chombáigh cóig saorphobal,
leis ón tuinn chalaidh go' chéile
raghaidh Éire ar aonchogadh.
(Knott, *Tadhg Dall,* No. 16, st. 14, p. 110.)

[Easy it is for him to give battle, from sympathy of the five noble nations, from one coast to the other Ireland will join him in a united war.][52]

The antiquity of the motif of the inherent unity of the 'five provinces' has already been discussed; Mac Cana's interpretation of Tadhg Dall's exhortation to O'Rourke not only interprets the use of the themes and motifs of unity and war in a way that ignores traditional usage, but the

---

[51] See Alwyn and Brinley Rees, *Celtic Heritage,* Chapter VII, pt. 2, pp 146-73.

[52] Of this poem, presumably on the evidence of such stanzas, Mac Cana says: 'Tadhg Dall himself realized the inappropriateness of the traditional dissipation of energy and in this poem is urging Brian Ó Ruairc to engage the English in all-out war he counsels in a different mode of action.' — in 'Concept of Unity', p. 69, but cf. McKenna, *Magauran Poems,* No. 13, sts. 1, 2, 3, p. 191 and No. 23, sts. 3, 4, 7, 13, 14.

further development of this particular interpretation tends to warp the entire structure of what is essentially a traditional praise poem for a warrior chief. The elaboration of the theme of Banbha's choosing a worthy spouse, causes Ó hUiginn to stress the necessity of Banbha's choice resting on Brian O'Rourke. Ireland is weakened because of disunity. This disunity stems from the fact that the superior qualities of O'Rourke as a warrior are going unheeded by the Irish in general:

> Díoth a dteaguisg tug ar daoine
> fán droing fíochmhair foirneartmhair,
> truagh nách faghaid lucht a laoidhidh
> a hucht aoinfir oirbheartaigh.
> (Knott, *Tadhg Dall*, No. 16, st. 9, p. 109.)

> [Lack of counsel it is that has rendered the people subservient to the wrathful, tyrannical band; alas that they do not find those who would exhort them through any single man of valour.]

The final couplet in this stanza is the introduction to the principal object of the whole poem; the celebration of Brian O'Rourke as a great warrior, a worthy spouse of Banbha. The whole exercise, the denigration of the weakness of the 'men of Ireland' and this exhortation to unity, far from representing a breakthrough in political perceptions on the part of the poet, as suggested by Mac Cana's interpretation, is rather part of an elaborate compliment to O'Rourke. Brian O'Rourke is, of course, the inspiring individual awaited by the enervated, frivolous, native warriors. The required 'aoinfhear oirbheartach' is O'Rourke, waiting and working to succour Banbha:

> Tuigeadh Brian mhac Briain mheic Eóghain
> gan éinneach d'féin ghlan-Bhanbha
> do theacht slán gan mheing gan mheabhail
> ón dreim d'fearaibh allmhardha.
> (Knott, *Tadhg Dall*, No. 16, st. 43, p. 114.)

> [Let Brian, son of Brian, son of Owen, understand that none of bright Banbha's warriors come from the foreigners safe from treachery or betrayal.]

and

> Ós é ár gcuidne do chloinn Mhíleadh
> mac Briain bhronnus airgheadha,

an ghéag do sluagh lúthghrod Luimnigh,
múnfad d'fuighlibh ailgheanna.
(Knott, *Tadhg Dall*, No. 16, st. 11, p. 109.)

[Since our darling amongst the race of Mil is the son of Brian, lavisher of herds, with gentle utterances, I shall counsel the scion of Limerick's vigorous humble host.]

The foreigner's hatred of O'Rourke is itself indicative of his success at harrassing them; it is his claim to the espousal of Banbha, that is, his intrepidity in pursuit of battles with the foreigner proves his valour and worthiness:

Méad a fuatha ag ógbhaidh danar
dhó féin bhíos do bharamhail;
cách dhó dá fógra re fada —
Fódla aga ar aradhain.
(Knott, *Tadhg Dall*, No. 16, st. 47, p. 115.)

[The hatred of the foreigners for him is his testimony[?] all have been proclaiming for long that she is his — he holds Fódla by the bridle.]

The poet, Tadhg Camcosach Ó Dálaigh, addressed a poem to Niall O'Neill, urging him to unite Ireland against the foreigner in a vein remarkably similar to that which Ó hUiginn addressed to O'Rourke. Again, Ireland is in bondage under the tyranny of foreign hosts. Ó Dálaigh urges O'Neill to unite Ireland under his sway in order to repulse the foreigner:

Cúis athtoirsi Insi Fáil;
sochraide Ghall dá gabháil,
tnúth fan mBanbha bhféaraid bhfinn,
faghla in gach énaird d'Éirinn.
Beirt othruis Insi Banbha,
is é a t-earradh allmhardha
fér agus luibhe a gort nglan,
duille agus folt a fiodhbhadh.
(Mág Craith, *Dán na mBráthar Mionúr*, No. 1,
sts. 4 and 8, p. 2.)

[Inis Fáil's being held by a foreign army; lust for the possession of Banbha with the fair rich grass; pillaging in every part of Ireland

— these have been the cause of Ireland's woe.
That Banbha's grass, the herbs of her fair fields and the leaves and foliage of her woods are the apparel of foreigners — that is Ireland's weeds of woe.]

Ó Dálaigh attributes Ireland's woes to the fact that foreigners inhabit her territories, taking possession of Inis Fáil and plundering the surrounding territories. The poet then relates Niall's father's advice to his family before his death:

Dob hí a chomhairle dá chloinn
ria ndol d'Aodh Mhór, mhac Domhnaill,
bíodh um chongnamh re chéile
dáibh ger orlamh aimhréidhe.
(Mág Craith, *Dán na mBráthar Mionúr,* No. 1, st. 37, p. 8.)

[The advice of great Aodh, son of Domhnall, before death, to his family, was this: to set their minds on co-operating with one another even though they were disposed to quarrel.]

Ó Dálaigh is quite specific about the advantage given to enemies when the lordship is split. This might seem to indicate his appreciation of presenting Banbha's enemies with a united effort:

"Ní do ísleochadh ibh féin
— mian bhur n-easgarad eiséin —
ná déanaidh" ar Aodh Eamhna,
"féaghaidh fur gaol geineamhna".
(Mág Craith, *Dán na mBráthar Mionúr,* No. 1,
st. 38, p. 9.)

[Said Aodh of Eamhain: 'Do not do anything that might weaken yourselves — that is what your enemies desire — be mindful of your blood relationship.]

Niall's father, Aodh, advised him to overcome the tendency to quarrelsomeness and internecine strife which characterized internal relations in the septs. This motif as manipulated by the poet in this instance provides at least one good reason why this Niall should be obeyed as uncontested leader of his sept. Niall follows his father's advice implicitly, forcibly 'uniting' territories which he wishes to subdue. The conceit of unity against foreign aggression is that of Tadhg Dall to O'Rourke, proclaiming the individual to whom the poem is addressed as the chief worthy to assume the responsibility of subduing the 'five provinces':

> Teaagasg Aodha dá oidhre —
> ní théid céim don chomhairle;
> fuaighfidh le a ghníomh gach gartmhagh;
> tuairfidh bríogh na beandachtain.
> (Mág Craith, *Dán na mBráthar Mionúr*, No. 1,
> st. 40, p. 9.)

[(Niall) departs not (even) a (single) step from the advice of Aodh to his heir. He will unite together every plain and field, by his exploits, he will merit the efficacy of the blessing.]

This Niall died in 1397, the poem was written by Tadhg Camcosach *circa* 1365-66.[53] The text of it resembles that of Tadhg Dall in sentiment and in its thematic use of the sorrows of Banbha, her ill-use by foreign hordes, the necessity to unite the warriors for her protection and the choosing of one in particular to fulfil this obligation. The exhortations to unite Banbha in the face of foreign encroachment occur in the fourteenth century poem with a regularity explained not by the political events of the period, but by the exigencies of the bardic tradition. Their basis is not in a tradition of cultural oppression or territorial dispossession which relate in a special way to the mid- and late-sixteenth century. They are the literary distillation of the tradition of the mythical past of Ireland and of the legendary 'takings' of Ireland; essentially part of the origin-tale of the Gaelic world. Their political content relates to intersept politics and its principles are applied to foreign elements in exactly the same spirit. Gofraidh Fionn Ó Dálaigh's early thirteenth-century composition for Maurice fitzMaurice comfortably accommodates this foreign magnate within the tradition, as does Muireadhach Albanach in his poem for Richard fitzAdelm de Burgo in the early thirteenth century.

The poems of the sixteenth century are to be interpreted entirely within this tradition and they conform effortlessly to its strictures. Tadhg Dall's composition for Mac William in the late sixteenth century

---

[53] Mág Craith, *Dán na mBráthar Mionúr*, vol. 2, p. 95.

conforms signally to the bardic tradition of accommodating the victor. Set against a background of consciousness of the nature and strength of this tradition, and of its functions, it becomes increasingly evident that there is no room for anachronistic appraisal of the work of even the most ostensibly belligerent poets. Bradshaw's suggestion that such poems were vehicles for the transformation of

> the flattering poetic conceits . . . into emotive ideological symbols

and that

> traditional themes are made to reflect a new ethos, the political nationality of Gaelic Ireland[54]

symbolizing the 'revolutionization' of the 'medieval tradition' falls into the latter category. Within the logic of Bradshaw's interpretation the above statement should be applicable also to Tadhg Camcosach's poem to Niall O'Neill in the fourteenth century, leaving us with the ludicrous prospect of a patriotically/nationalistically motivated *file* in that most Gaelic of territories; Ulster in the fourteenth century.

The poetic themes which had always transcended political 'fact', while reflecting a concept of Gaelic political perspectives, never descended from that lofty somewhat abstracted position; not because the poets were somehow 'outside' of the society in which they flourished but because the nature of their profession and its essential tradition represented a political and social conceptual world. Tadhg Dall's poem for O'Rourke concludes on a crescendo of aggressive exhortation:

> Lasfaid cách do chombáigh rision
> idir rígh is ríoghdhamhna,
> mar loisgthear teach re teagh oile,
> ar feadh moighe míonBhanbha.
> (Knott, *Tadhg Dall*, No. 16, st. 15, p. 110.)

> [Throughout fertile Banbha's plain, the rest, both kings and princes will kindle in sympathy with him, even as one house takes fire from another.]

and:

> Muidhfidh ainnséin ar fóir Saxan
> ré síol Ghaoidhil ghéirreannaigh,

---

[54] See Bradshaw, 'Native Reaction', pp 75 and 76.

nách bia do síor ón ágh d'fógra
ós chlár Fódla acht Éireannaigh.
(Knott, *Tadhg Dall*, No. 16, st. 68, p. 118.)

[Then will the Saxon tribe be vanquished by the seed of keen-weaponed Gaedheal, so that from the proclamation of war there will never be any save Irishmen over the land of Fódla.]

A stanza from the early thirteenth-century poem of Muireadhach Albanach for Cathal Crobhdhearg O'Connor exhorting him to drive the foreigners 'eastward'[55] could without any distortion of sense be appended to this sixteenth-century poem of Ó hUiginn. Ó Dálaigh wrote a poem for the 'foreigner' de Burgo, consigning two important regnal centres, Cruachan and Tara, to his authority.[56] Tadhg Dall in the sixteenth-century poem for a later de Burgo, in the same manner celebrates the ascension of a 'foreign' lord over the traditional regnal centres of Ireland. Ó hUiginn's poem to Mac William Burke [c. 1570],[57] who became Mac William in 1571, seneschal of Connacht in 1575 and died in 1580, places Ó hUiginn's poem for O'Rourke, for instance, in its proper perspective. The tone which superficially appears to contradict everything he wrote for O'Rourke in the poem above, contributes greatly to our understanding of what must have been the underlying rationale of the Gaelic aristocracy towards the events of their 'history' and the perceptions which underlay their approach to those of the contemporary world. The central function of the poem is similar to that of his composition for O'Rourke; a celebration of the incumbent Mac William. Its central theme is a discussion of the criteria governing the claims to the sovereignty of Ireland and to whom it rightfully belongs. These criteria listed by Ó hUiginn as being appropriate to Mac William indicate the breadth of accommodation in the tradition. Tadhg Dall's poem, addressed to a descendant of an Anglo-Norman family who had favourably impressed the government, to the extent that he was awarded the seneschalship of Connacht, is a magnificent celebration of the right of arms, the privileges of the victor and his right to the spoils of his victory.

---

[55] Bergin, *Irish Bardic Poetry*, No. 23, st. 18, p. 104.
[56] Bergin, *Irish Bardic Poetry*, No. 20, st. 19, p. 91.
[57] E. Knott, *Tadhg Dall*, Vol. 2, p. 254.

The influence of the *Lebor Gabála* — the several 'takings' of Ireland is clear in Ó hUiginn's treatment of Mac William's right to suzerainty over Connacht. The argument of might being right is very much to the fore in this elaborately structured encomium for Mac William. It celebrates the acceptance of the *fait accompli* and deals with the themes of unity and sovereignty within the context of Ó hUiginn's rationalization of Mac William's — a foreigner's rights. Far from recommending that:

> . . . nách bia do síor ón ágh d'fógra
> ós chlár Fódla acht Éireannaigh.
> (Knott, *Tadhg Dall,* No. 16, st. 68, p. 118.)

[. . . so that from the proclamation of war there will never be any save Irishmen over the land of Fódla.]

as Ó hUiginn suggested to O'Rourke, he (the poet) now repeatedly insists that birth, heredity or race do not matter where the sovereignty of Ireland is concerned, the strongest is necessarily the most worthy. The poem opens with a declaration concerning the nature of the suzerainty of Ireland:

> Fearann cloidhimh críoch Bhanbha,
> bíoth slán cháich fá chomhardha
> go bhfuil d'oighreacht ar Fiadh bhFáil
> acht foirneart gliadh dá gabháil.
> Ní fuil cóir uirre ag aoinfear-
> críoch suaitheanta seanGhaoidheal,
> bheith fa neart an té is treise —
> is é ceart na críchese.
> (Knott, *Tadhg Dall*, No. 17, sts. 1 and 2, p. 120.)

[The land of Banbha is but swordland; let all be defied to show that there is any inheritance to the Land of Fál save that of conquest by force of battle.

No one has any lawful claim to the shining land of the ancient Gaels. The law of this territory is that it shall be subjugate to him who is strongest.]

While establishing the theme of the poem in these two vigorous stanzas, Ó hUiginn introduces us to a very convincing display of the respect due

to the victor; the perceptions of victory and defeat underlying the acceptance of the *fait accompli*, a fundamental guiding principle of the activities of the Gaelic chiefs and likewise of the writings of the poets.
Tadhg Dall throws open the question of claims to the sovereignty of
Ireland, thereby immediately creating a situation in which any victor
may be acclaimed with enthusiasm regardless of race. This preference
for accommodation rather than confrontation and of acceptance of the
powerful victor in order to preserve status and life-style characterizes
the Gaelic polity during the sixteenth and seventeenth centuries. This
leads to apparently entirely contradictory statements in the poetry;
poets on the one hand ostensibly championing united anti-English efforts, on the other, counselling compliance.

   The two attitudes which emanate from the same basic principle of the
strongest foremost, are independent of the advent of Tudor conquest.
Tadhg Dall's denunciation of disunity and his urging belligerence upon
O'Rourke, is in the same spirit and the same tradition as Tadhg Camcosach Ó Dálaigh's exhortations to Niall Óg O'Neill some two centuries
earlier. The problematic 'awareness' of the eventual fate of the Gaelic
system does not dictate either response. For the same reasons, Tadhg
Dall's composition for Mac William is not the work of a craven
hypocrite but represents the other side of the coin of Gaelic attitudes
towards the functions of war and the rights of the victor. Denying the
superior claims of antiquity of Gaelic lineage, in order to validate Mac
William's *de facto* position Tadhg Dall specifies that not even the fabled
family of Míleadh can claim priority in the quest for the sovereignty of
Banbha:

   Ní fuil do cheart ar chrích bhFáil
   ag Macaibh Míleadh Easbáin,
   's ní bhí ag gach gabháil dar gheabh,
   acht sí d'fagháil ar éigean.
   (Knott, *Tadhg Dall,* No. 17, st. 4, p. 120.)

   [Neither the sons of Mil of Spain nor any who have conquered her
   have any claims to the land of Fáil save that of taking her by force.]

In order to give prominence to the Norman ancestry of Mac William, Ó
hUiginn gives specific mention to them. By force were the Tuatha De
Danann and of late, the sons of Mil, displaced by conquest; Ó hUiginn

thus recognizes the Norman occupation of the twelfth and thirteenth centuries:

> Má tá gur ghabhsad Ghaoidhil
> ag gcrích bhfairsing bhforbhfaoilidh,
> do hathghabhadh í orthaibh,
> sí ar n-athraghadh d'eachtronnchaibh.
> Teaguid tar tuinn teóra cath,
> óig na Fraingce, fian Ghréagach,
> lucht amhsaine an tíre thoir —
> gasraidhe sídhe a Saxaibh.
> (Knott, *Tadhg Dall*, No. 17, sts. 9 and 10, p. 121.)

[Although the Gaels conquered the spacious, kindly land, it was reconquered in despite of them, and has passed into the power of foreigners.
There came across the sea in three battalions the warriors of France, the soldiery of Greece and mercenaries of the eastern land, the wondrous youth of England.]

Interestingly, in the ensuing division of Ireland, redivision was customary following on each 'taking',[58] not only the Normans are granted their due from the spoils of victory but so are the English:

> Cuid an mheicsin Mhogha Néid
> gabhaid na fir a finnGhréig,
> 'sna Goill ó gharbhShaxain ghil
> an chloinn armarsaidh Éibhir.
> (Knott, *Tadhg Dall*, No. 17, st. 12, p. 122.)

[The men from fair Greece and the foreigners from bright, fierce England wrest from the war-seasoned race of Iber the share of Mugh Néid's son.]

The Burke's own territory is identified and placed in its position in tradition:

---

[58] Cf. *Lebor Gabála* and see also Geoffrey Keating's compositions in which he addresses the same theme — E. Mac Giolla Eáin (ed.), *Dánta, Amhráin is Caointe Sheathrúin Ceitinn* (Dublin, 1900), especially No. 14, p. 63, sts. 6, 8, 9, 10.

Ó Luimneach go Leith Cathail —
cuid ronna Chuinn Chéadchathaigh
gabhaid garsaidh síl Séarlais
don tír arsaidh oiléanghlais.
(Knott, *Tadhg Dall*, No. 17, st. 13, p. 122.)

[The warriors of the seed of Charles conquer from Limerick to
Lecale, Conn, the Hundredfighter's share of the ancient green-
sided land.]

The Burke ancestor is of course a descendant of 'Charles', by whom is
meant Charlemagne; and that their subsequent success is entirely explicable in the light of their kinship with such an illustrious ancestor.
Before he launches into the main body of the poem, consisting of a
genealogical perusal of the Burkes from their earliest ancestor —
Charlemagne,[59] Ó hUiginn delivers a challenge which must be borne in
mind at all times when dealing with the work of Tadhg Dall and indeed,
the poets as a body:

Gi bé adéaradh gur deóraidh
Búrcaigh na mbeart n-inleóghain —
faghar d'fuil Ghaoidhil nó Ghoill
nách fuil 'na aoighidh agoinn.
Gi bé adeir nách dleaghar dháibh
a gcuid féin d'Éirinn d'fagháil —
cia san ghurt bhraonnuaidhe bhinn
nách lucht aonuaire d'Éirinn?
(Knott, *Tadhg Dall*, No. 17, sts. 17 and
18, p. 122.)

[Should any say that the Burkes of lion-like prowess are strangers
— let one of the blood of Gael or Gall be found who is not a so-
journer amongst us.
Should any say they deserve not to receive their share of Ireland,
who in sweet, dew-glistening field are more than visitors to the
land?][60]

---

[59] E. Knott, *Tadhg Dall*, No. 17, sts. 13-19, pp 122-3.

[60] An anticipation of Petty's remark almost a century later; see Petty's *Political
Anatomy of Ireland* ed. by John O'Donovan, p. 24.

A tradition of 'conquest', or rather, 'takings' is part of the structure from which the poet approaches the question of the sovereignty of the country. The ever-present awareness of bygone centuries; traditional, historical and mythical, lends the bardic poetry a depth of historical perspective not always appreciated by those insufficiently familiar with their framework of reference. Ó hUiginn's almost overwhelming sense of the inevitability of historical continuity, such as he sees it, and the complacency with which he views the turbulent history of his people lends this poem a mysterious power. He broadly surveys several centuries of Gaelic history in a succession of cryptic stanzas, each one giving utterance to deeply ingrained facets of the perceptions of the Gaelic aristocracy of themselves, their territorial neighbours, and their position within the overall scheme of their collective existence. Ó hUiginn's casual summary of the events of several centuries, his relating of that to the contemporary situation of the Mac William, and his apparently frivolous use of such material to form an elaborate compliment for Mac William leads one back to the realization that the poets evinced a willingness to acquiesce in all and any successful venture — provided they were numbered among the beneficiaries of the new regime. The reality of Mac William's contemporary position of authority and the prospect of its continuance, causes Ó hUiginn to highlight Mac William's rights to his position. The temporarily beleaguered position of O'Rourke in the same period calls on the use of a different 'formula' from the poets' wide-ranging referential framework. The various attitudes articulated by Ó hUiginn have their origin in the selection of perceptions preserved in, and articulated by, the bardic ethos. They are drawn upon as demanded by the necessities of the Gaelic world and are independent of any prospect of conquest that might have been evident in the sixteenth century.

It would be extremely simplistic, however, to conclude that the following sentiments, expressed by Ó hUiginn in his poem to Mac William preclude or cancel the validity of the expression of anti-English sentiment in the other Ó hUiginn poem addressed to O'Rourke:

Gé adeirdís sliocht Ghaoidhil Ghlais
coimhighthe le cloinn Séarlais —
clocha toinighthe bheann mBreagh
coimhighthe an dream adeireadh.
(Knott, *Tadhg Dall*, No. 17, st. 19, p. 123.)

[Though the descendants of Gall Glas used to speak of the race of Charles, set stones of Banbha's hills — as foreigners — foreigners were they who spoke thus.]

The tone which the poet adopts is dictated by the current position enjoyed by the person to whom the poem is addressed. This is of course firmly rooted in the function of the poet; praise of his chieftain. Thus Richard fitzAdelm de Burgo, a well-established Anglo-Norman and thirteenth-century lord is praised by Muireadhach Albanach for his success in wresting Cruachan and Tara, for himself, from Gaelic rivals. His contemporary Cathal Crobhdhearg O'Connor is exhorted by the same poet to banish the foreigner from the island. In Tadhg Dall's case, his poem to Mac William, seneschal of Connacht, reflects in a traditional way, the latter's established, stable position. Another Burke, Éamonn, (not conclusively identified by Knott) who is in a position of contention, apparently for the Mac Williamship (c. 1580s) elicits a slightly modified response from Ó hUiginn. The poet, on this occasion, draws on the tradition of Banbha awaiting succour:

Créad anois fuirgheas Éamonn?
eadamar ní fuiléangam,
mar gach brághaid ar breith nGall,
bheith mar támaid re tamall.
(Knott, *Tadhg Dall*, No. 18, st. 1, p. 132.)

[What now delays Edmund? Surely we shall not endure to be as we have been for some time, like any captive at the mercy of the foreigners.]

Though this addressee is also a Burke, he is exhorted to rout the foreigners and not to be intimidated by them:

Ní feadar créad do chongaibh
mac ríogh an fóid Umhallaigh
mar ghiall i ngeimhleachaibh Ghall,
riamh fa feilbhreathaibh eachtrann.
(Knott, *Tadhg Dall*, No. 18, st. 3, p. 132.)

[I know not what has hitherto kept the prince of the soil of Umhall like a hostage in English fetters, under the treacherous enactments of the foreigners.]

These inflammatory stanzas begin a very exhortative poem:

Do bhí cách 'ga chor i suim;
fad an fuirighsin Éamuinn
suil do hadhnadh uaill an fir,
suil fuair adhbhar far éirigh.
(Knott, *Tadhg Dall*, No. 18, st. 2, p. 132.)

[Everyone has noticed the length of this delay of Edmund's, ere the man's pride was enkindled, ere he found a reason for a rebellion.]

This Edmund's position, scrambling as he was possibly for the Mac Williamship, was not one of stability. He could not be hailed as a settled chief or as a conquering warrior. The poet must therefore present the presumptive chief with hypothetical opportunities to display his military prowess and to prove his worthiness to the chieftainship by the sword. This poem is an interesting synthesis of the two elements; ridding Ireland of the foreigner to be achieved by successful military campaigns. The addressee's unsettled state and his indicated preference for rebellion against the crown allow the poet to combine the 'succour of Banbha' theme with that of the right accruing to the successful warrior to produce a poem of very belligerent sentiment.

Encouraging his patron to battle is the prerogative, indeed often the duty of the poet. That Tadhg Dall encourages Edmund Burke to deeds of rapine and plunder against the English is not at variance with his praise for the Mac William in the earlier poem, and his declaration in that same poem that since Seán mac Oilibhéir was in command, no warfare had taken place between the English and the Gael:

Gan adhbhar le a mbiodhgfadh bean,
gan leattrom Ghoill ag Gaoidheal;
gan éadáil Ghaoidhil ag Gall,
gan éagáir aoinfir d'fulang.
(Knott, *Tadhg Dall*, No. 17, st. 67, p. 131.)

[Nothing which might make a woman tremble, no Gael committing injustice against any Englishman, nor any Englishman despoiling a Gael, no wrong of any man permitted.]

The tradition from which Ó hUiginn writes, encompasses all the ritual and vicissitudes of war. This included the eventuality of defeat. When defeat occurs the tradition is enabled by its inherent paradoxical flexibility to adjust to it and accommodate the new situation. Therefore, Ó hUiginn can with perfect consistency according to his perceptions, at once issue exhortations to battle to one chief,[61] and to another declare that the spoils of victory are the legitimate due of the victor. The poets championed their choice of contender but always welcomed the victor. The chiefs always contested any challenges to their position but always acquiesced in any settlement which offered them something in personal advancement, no matter how transitory. Traditionally, chiefs worsted in battle were generally awarded a compensatory stipend in return for their submission.[62] The relative ease with which this system coped with the complex changes continually occurring in the country, both through internecine warfare and intermittent waves of invasion, was made possible because of the fundamental cultural homogeneity of the inhabitants of the country.

Acculturation existed to a convenient extent between provincial magnates and their Gaelic neighbours, and an uneasy balance was struck in the Pale. This held true for the greater part of the sixteenth and early seventeenth centuries. Until the final decades of the sixteenth century poets continued to praise patrons as warlords. The political goals of such patrons varied from those of the rebel O'Rourke to the expedient O'Hara and the court favourite, Ormond. Success in their martial enterprises and also success in their dealings with the crown, providing they achieve or maintain social and political prominence, is the key to the poet's interest in the addressee. A cursory glance at some material produced for these patrons reveals the endurance of the poet's perceptions of power and authority and the realization of these perceptions in the activities of the chiefs.

The ultimate source of the power of any lord was, as has already been suggested, his success in wielding the sword. This criterion refers alike to Gaelic lord and foreigner. Poems to Gaelic chiefs whose major concerns are the maintenance of their own boundaries, and the accumulation of wealth through raids to support their households and armed retainers,

---

[61] See E. Knott, *Irish Classical Poetry*, p. 65.

[62] S. Mac Airt, *Annals of Inisfallen, sub anno* 1011, pp 180-1: 'Sluagad mór le Brian co cenél Conaill eter muir agus tír co táinic Hua Mail Doraid, rí cenéuil Chonaill, lais co Cend Corad, agus co ruc ennarrad mór ó Brian agus co tuc a ógréir do Brian.'

are many. They deal with the source of the power of the chief in question and the rationale governing the validity of his claims. The complicated confusion of loyalties and expedient political swapping of loyalties are regarded as part of the struggle for survival. The terms of treaties and submissions were binding only in so far as their desired effect or objective was manifest.

Fearghal Óg mac a' Bhaird articulates the reliance on this source of power and security in a poem to Cú Chonnacht Maguire. Maguire is a worthy chief because he has subdued Ulster; he has taken tribute from her and has proved himself valiant enough to be counted as a worthy suitor of Ireland. Ireland is personified as the spouse of Maguire. He deserves her because he claimed her forcibly:

> Dá reic a ndiaigh a diomdha
> biaidh ac an Leic a labhra,
> ní léir dí acht fer a foghla,
> ben Chonnla ar a thí tarla.
> (Greene, *Maguire Poems*, No. 4, st. 2, p. 34.)

> [The Leac will speak, proclaiming him after her sorrow; she sees none but the man who plundered her, the wife of Connla is pursuing him.]

Ireland herself is willing to be dominated by the most successful warrior, Maguire having enforced his will can now claim her:

> Reic a ghníomh as dál doilidh;
> do sgríobh ar chách an ccomhaidh;
> móide a mhian do Mhág Uidhir
> Fád Fuinidh riamh ag roghain.
> (Greene, *Maguire Poems,* No. 4, st. 3, p. 34.)

> [It is a hard task to tell of his deeds; he has enforced a tribute on everyone. The desire of Ireland for Maguire is the greater because the best man has always held her.]

Eoghain Mág Craith in his praise of the 10th Earl of Ormond, similarly rejoiced in the fact that all Ireland bore the marks of Ormond's raiding; his enforcement of his authority over Banbha and validating his power according to the Gaelic perceptions of the chiefs rights.[63] Ormond and

---

[63] Carney, *Poems on the Butlers,* No. 15, st. 46, p. 73.

Maguire are welcomed as 'plunderers' of Banbha. The claims over Ireland are attained through skill in battle. Tadhg Dall in his poem for Mac William, reiterates the superiority of this claim over all others.[64]

The chiefs are lauded because of their repute in battle. Their success in power is traced to their proficiency with the sword, their theoretical right to the reality of their victory. Victory is a swift and transitory experience — to be exulted in while it lasts. Likewise, while the chief is victorious, he defies the government of the English crown; when defeated, or under threat from other chiefs, he appeals to this same government for protection and pardon — against chiefs who are also following their traditional conflicts against him. Maguire and O'Donnell humbly submit to the government:

> O Donnell . . . and Maguire, Lord of Fermanagh, who wrote humbly unto me, live wealthfully and deny not to pay rent and service to her Majestie so as they may be discharged from the exactions.[65]

Tadhg Dall Ó hUiginn spent some time as poet to Cormac O'Hara, lord of Leighne (1584-1612). Cormac experienced many setbacks in his efforts to succeed to leadership of his sept, battling with both native and foreign hosts, now both resigned to his supremacy:

> Do aomhsad Gaoidhil is Goill
> — bheith agaibh is as thoghoim —
> rí fíréanda do rádh ribh,
> a ríréadla ó chlár Chaisil.
> (McKenna, *O'Hara Poems,* No. 3, st. 14, p. 54.)

> [For this have I chosen to be with thee, thou royal star of Cashel's plain, both Gaels and English have agreed to give thee the title of righteous king.]

Both English and Gaelic Irish alike resisted the instalment of O'Hara; Fearghal Óg mac a' Bhaird points this out in a lengthy poem congratulating Cormac on his survival in spite of Gael and *Gall*:

> Ó aois leinb gus an lá a-niodh
> do éiridh d'aimhdheoin Gaoidhiol,

---

[64] E. Knott, *Tadhg Dall*, No. 17, st. 2, p. 120.
[65] D. Greene, *Maguire Poems,* p. vii.

damh na ríghealbha ó ráth Cuirc,
fáth mímheanma do mhaluirt.
(McKenna, *O'Hara Poems,* No. 8, st. 9, p. 114.)

[From his childhood's days till to-day this ox of the royal herd
from Corc's Fort has grown up in spite of the Gaoidhil — a story
to dispel despondency.]

The Gael thus hindered Cormac's advances. The *Gall* did likewise but
now accept his victory:

Táinig dhíot díon do shleachta;
fuair tusa a hucht t'oirbhearta
mar nar fhaláir, a bharr Breadh,
anáir Ghall agos Gaoidheal.
(McKenna, *O'Hara Poems,* No. 8, st. 52, p. 126.)

[Thou hast succeeded in defending thy race; by thy gallantry thou
hast got honour from both Goill and Gaoidhil; it had so to be, O
Lord of Breacha.]

Cormac's position was more settled in 1578:

By 1578 he must have attained to a position of security and
strength as we find a grant being made to him in that year among
the Fiants of Elizabeth (3390) 'Grant to Cormocke O'Harrea of
Collanye (Cúil Áine) Co. Sligo'; of the office seneschal of the
country of Maherye Leynye alias O'Harrea Bue's country. To
hold for life with all lawful customs hitherto received by the
seneschal or captain of the country i Aug. XX.[66]

No sense of latent patriotism or any consciousness of a possible invidious element in this royal appointment prevented O'Hara from accepting the foreign office of seneschalship. It did not interrupt the
copious stream of bardic encomium to him. Cormac deserves his land
because of his vigour in wresting it from his enemies and maintaining it
when he did so. This praise of Cormac is based on an analogy with Fionn
mac Cumhaill:

---

[66] McKenna, *O'Hara Poems,* p. xxiv.

Gá dám ris acht ráinig Fionn
cuid a shean d'inis Éiriond;
críoch a oirbhearta as sé sin
an té as oirrdhearca ag eolchaibh.
(McKenna, *O'Hara Poems,* No. 8, st. 23, p. 118.)

[In short Fionn won his patrimony throughout the Isle of Éire; that was the result of the battling of this man most honoured by poets.]

The tortuous battling of Cormac in retaining his land is graphically presented:

Goin san ghoin is creach san chreich
gur chuir an iomáin d'éinleith
— nír bhean a ghníomh re gníomh tais! —
do-níodh ag díon a dhúthchais.
(McKenna, *O'Hara Poems,* No. 8, st. 29, p. 120.)

[In defence of the land he inflicted wound for wound, raid for raid, till he reached his goal; his deeds had nothing weak about them.]

The poet glories in recounting the difficulties experienced by O'Hara before he could declare his land subject to him:

Triath Luighne na dtoirbheart dtrom,
mór fhuair Ó hEadhra dh'fhorlonn
fa chlár mín na magh sreaphghlas
gur ghabh tír is tighearnas.
(McKenna, *O'Hara Poems,* No. 8, st. 36, p. 122.)

[Ó hEadhra, Lord of Luighne, bestower of weighty gifts — great was the hardship he bore for the smooth land with its verdant stream-fed plains until in the end he won his land and his chieftain-ship.]

The successful chief must have swift visible victories accompanied by outward signs of triumph and success. The literary motifs that accompany this confidence in the competence of the successful warlord are expressed with almost excessive indulgence by Giolla Riabhach Ó Cléirigh in a poem for Cú Chonnacht Maguire:

Barr fedh as tuar tromáirmhe
ó chnuas do chleacht mailldéinmhe;
benaidh fa Fhiadh fhinnÉirne
grian a fedhaibh fainnéirghe.
(Greene, *Maguire Poems,* No. 7, st. 26, p. 64.)

[The tops of the trees are an omen of heavy counting; they have become languid through weight of fruit; throughout the fair land of the Erne, the sun causes the trees to rise only slightly.]

Cormac O'Hara enjoyed the seneschalship of Connacht, having struggled vigorously against natives and foreigners alike to secure his position. He, however, did not relax his warring activities after 1578. The events of his reign illustrate the importance of expedience, rather than patriotism which directed the chiefs' choice of war or peace. After signing the papers of the Composition of Connacht in 1585,[67] O'Hara apparently remained 'loyal' the following year. He was involved with Governor Bingham in the subjection of the Scots mercenaries who marched on Sligo in that year at the behest of O'Donnell who traditionally claimed suzerainty over Connacht. It is perhaps in oblique reference to O'Hara's favour with the English and Irish alike after much striving that Fearghal Óg mac a' Bhaird says:

Táinig dhíot díon do shleachta;
fuair tusa a hucht t'oirbhearta
mar nar fhaláir, a bharr Breadh,
anáir Ghall agos Gaoidheal.
(McKenna, *O'Hara Poems,* No. 8, st. 52,
p. 126.)

[Thou has succeeded in defending thy race; by thy gallantry thou hast got honour from both Goill and Gaoidhil; it had so to be, O Lord of Breagha.]

During the defection into rebellion in 1589-90, O'Hara was attacked presumably because of previous participation in the crown campaigns against the Burkes. McKenna assures us that this 'loyalty' was of short duration:

---

[67] See Canny, *Elizabethan Conquest of Ireland,* pp 47-8 and see also Steven G. Ellis, *Tudor Ireland, Crown, Community and the Conflict of Cultures 1470-1603,* pp 288-91.

When the fall of Sligo town held by George Bingham for the Governor of Connaught, had loosened the bonds of English power, Cormac O'Hara with several other chieftains went into revolt.[68]

He later submitted again in 1602 after the influence of O'Neill (a traditional enemy) and O'Donnell (another traditional rival) subsided following the escape of O'Donnell to Spain, and the defeat by the English and Munster forces of the combined Ulster hosts and their allies at Kinsale. Far from being released from a stranglehold of English power, it is more likely that O'Hara preferred to ride the crest of every change in balance of power. The conclusion of any offensive left the Gaelic lord scrambling to emerge on the victorious side, regardless of long term effects.

The willingness of the poets to acquiesce in the *fait accompli* and their praise of the strongest, is illustrative of their belief in the value of the obvious. The complexities of the Pyhrric victory are not part of the poet's philosophy. Maguire's resentment subsides when he is mollified by the crown's writs of possession, protecting him momentarily against O'Neill. Poets and chiefs alike respect the *de facto* power, and are ever aware of power changes and alert to realign themselves. To inherit a patrimony from a renowned ancestor and to extend its boundaries by raiding was the most honourable occupation of a lord. The risks attending this system; continual harassment and short-lived triumph, were tacitly recognized by the society, and the mental equipment of the Gaelic lords and their social and academic counterparts catered for the hazards and fortunes of the life-style. The wisdom of any action is judged by its immediate effects and consequences. The heroic motto of Cú Chulainn:

Acht ropa airdeirc-se, maith lem ceni beinn acht oen-laa far domun.[69]

in a sense pervades the entire philosophy of the aristocracy, expressed in the works of the poets; fame for generosity and valour, immortality in the works of the poets, is the ideal fate of a chief.

---

[68] McKenna, *O'Hara Poems*, p. xxv.

[69] J. Strachan (ed.), *Stories from the Táin,* Dublin 1944, [reprint 1976], p. 12. It is in this respect perhaps more than in that suggested by Bradshaw in 'Native Reaction' (pp 79 and 80), that Pearse was influenced by what he saw as the Gaelic tradition.

In reality, expedience in political undertakings and survival are the overriding principles, lending a contradictory character to the unpredictable behaviour of the chiefs, for example in their several dealings with the crown. This is attested to by the records of pardons continually sought by, and granted to the wayward lords whose native cultural bias was entirely in favour of the advantage of the present. Therefore, it is the immediate deed which ultimately surpasses all other considerations when the poet attempts to exercise his duties. Elegies, eulogies, battle rolls and occasional poems all betray an underlying awareness of that which is accomplished, be it victory or defeat. This is why Tadhg Dall Ó hUiginn could counsel war to O'Rourke for the purpose of securing his territory against the foreigner and counsel war also to Mac William that he might secure that territory over which he presided as a foreigner, and achieved by the sword.

This apparently extremely pragmatic, if not indeed cynical, approach is, however, made explicit through the medium of a literary tradition which exercises a strong influence on the expression of those deeply rooted Gaelic perceptions. It must be borne in mind that the literary tradition is of indigenous origin — doubtless influenced greatly by contemporary events of varying kinds, but essentially representing independent Gaelic responses to one period of intense political and social change. The gradually increasing presence in the country of a culturally distinct and aggressively expansionist element against whom the Gaelic Irish failed to present a viable military resistance gradually rendered the cultural and social equipment of accommodation and defence of the aristocracy as evinced in the bardic poetry, meaningless in so far as practical measures were concerned. By the close of the seventeenth century, both the Gaelic aristocracy and the poets were no longer socially or politically powerful.

III

THE BARDIC THEMES
IN A POST-KINSALE
CONTEXT

Assuredly these Irish lords appear to us like glow worms,
which afar off seem to be all fire; but, being taken up
in a man's hands, are but silly worms.

Sir John Davis

THE PREVAILING atmosphere for the Gaelic Irish aristocracy in the late sixteenth century was one of accelerating decline — politically and materially. The poets were affected socially and materially by the diminishing power and status of the chiefs. The background to their compositions in the first half of the seventeenth century is in most cases one of instability and unpredictability. This condition of political uncertainty was one to which the chiefs and poets were innured politically and culturally. This can be illustrated by the poetry occasioned by the flight of the northern chiefs abroad.[1]

The attitude of poets like Eochaidh Ó hEodhusa and Feargal Óg mac a' Bhaird, for instance, to the flight of the Earls, taken in isolation would appear to usher in a new era of bardic awareness of 'impending doom'; the 'new attitudes' and the 'new awareness' mentioned by Tom Dunne,[2] leading to the 'sudden transformation'[3] of Canny's thesis. Rather than seeking novelty in the approach of the poets to contemporary political events — one is forced to recognize their traditional approach; their continual obsession with patronage, their preoccupation

---

[1] See N.P. Canny, 'Flight of the Earls'.
[2] See T.J. Dunne, 'Evidence', *passim*.
[3] N.P. Canny, 'Formation'.

with maintaining their status. It is in their exposition of the fundamental precepts of unity, sovereignty and their tradition of acceptance of the *fait accompli* that the poets of the early seventeenth century manifest their adherence to the traditional values and perceptions enshrined in the literary medium and which remained valid for them and the majority of the Gaelic aristocracy until their decline at the end of the century.

The works of the professional Gaelic poets of the seventeenth century reveal very little that is new in terms of altered perceptions in areas already discussed with regard to sixteenth-century bardic poetry. The poets attribute the rights of the sovereignty of Ireland to various individuals, they alternatively bewail the lack of unity among the warriors of Ireland and champion individuals to the detriment of that same unity. Invariably, the poets rationalize the success of the victorious and powerful and also conversely rationalize the defeat of the weak and vanquished. In the case of some compositions, the literary structures are more relaxed; the accentual metre becomes more popular, so do the more complex metres of *crosántacht* and *droighneach*.[4] Just as the poets of the earlier century performed their cultural functions of articulation of the fundamental precepts of the aristocracy, so did those of the later sixteenth century; champions of the powerful Gaelic Irish, Old English and indeed New English. In their works they reiterated the traditional preoccupations of sovereignty and unity of Banbha, and rationalized the circumstances in which Banbha and her nobles were placed. What one finds in the poetry of the late decades of the sixteenth century, and the first decades of the seventeenth, is the poets' accommodation to an increasingly changing world. The poets compassed the changes in their compositions in a manner which is fascinatingly illustrative of their confidence in their ability to cope with the alternatives with which the political developments presented them.

It is in the context of the Kinsale defeat and of an Ulster bereft of the two earls and some lesser chiefs that the poetry of Ó hEodhusa and Mac a' Bhaird especially have been interpreted. A brief survey of some northern poetry written on and around the turn of the century, illustrates something of the complexity which characterizes the bardic poetry of every period, but perhaps especially of this crucial period in the history of the Gaelic world. The poets' necessity to secure patronage provides

---

4 B. Ó Cuív, *New History of Ireland,* Vol. III, p. 528.

some of the more interesting compositions of the early 1610s. While Fearghal Óg Mac a' Bhaird about 1616, appealed for aid to Flaithrí Ó Maolchonaire, archbishop of Tuam (1609-1629),[5] Tadhg Óg Ó Dálaigh, about the same time, welcomed Sir George Carew, president of Munster (+ 1629) into his rightful ownership of an estate in south Cork.[6] Apocalyptic declarations about the death of Ireland abounded in Ulster poetry in the first decade of the seventeenth century. An anonymous poet bewailed the disappearance of the Gael in 'C'áit ar ghabhadar Gaoidheal'[7] — supposedly written at the beginning of the reign of James VI and I, and impressively laments Ireland's death following the departure of the Ulster chiefs. During the same decade another Ulster poet Eochaidh Ó hEodhusa provided a glowing welcome to James I, the principal analogy contained in the poem being based on Ovid's 'Metamorphosis'.[8] These poems in their turn were the direct successors to their fourteenth-century counterparts for instance, those in a collection such as that of *The Book of Magauran*.[9] Ó hEodhusa's contemporary and fellow Ulster poet Feargal Óg Mac a' Bhaird also found it fitting that he too should compose an encomium for James Stuart — 'Trí coróna i gcairt rí Shéamais'.[10]

Since 'Kinsale' has been raised into the position of a watershed in Irish history in the historiography of the recent past, poems such as those being considered here, have, in the context of 'Kinsale', been regarded as being illustrative of the poets' awareness of the 'watershed' nature of the inconclusive events of 1601. However, as with the poetry of the sixteenth century, these poems, placed in the poets' literary and historical context and thus viewed from the perspective of the Gaelic Irish élites, show themselves to be eloquent of traditional Gaelic attitudes towards defeat and victory, which are independent of any awareness of 'Kinsale' as an historical milestone in the Gaelic world. The poetry of the early seventeenth century illustrates the survival of the

---

[5] Mág Craith, *Dán na mBráthar Mionúr*, Nos 23, 24, 25, pp 117-26.

[6] Anne O'Sullivan, 'Tadhg O'Daly and Sir George Carew' in *Éigse*, 14 (1971), pp 27-38.

[7] William Gillies, 'A Poem on the Downfall of the Gaoidhil', in *Éigse*, 13 (1970), pp 203-10.

[8] Pádraig A. Breatnach, 'Metamorphosis, 1603', in *Éigse*, 17 (1977-8), pp 169-80.

[9] Lambert McKenna (ed.), *The Book of Magauran* (Dublin, 1947).

[10] McKenna, *Aithdioghluim Dána*, vol. I, No. 44, p. 177. See also J. Goldberg, *James I and the Politics of Literature*, pp 1-25.

Gaelic aristocratic rationale. The apparently increasing incongruity of their perceptions against a background of increasingly inassimilable 'reality' must not blind one to the strength of the perceptions which endured among the Gaelic aristocratic elements, political and literary.

The poets celebrated a civilization and a culture which proved unable to compete on the same terms as its increasingly robust rival; it failed to preserve its integrity in the face of major political reverses. Both poet and chief struggled for survival in an ever more uncongenial atmosphere.[11] Their efforts, however, were contained within a cultural perimeter; the Gaelic Irish could not adopt measures which did not fit into their ingrained perceptions of the order of authority and power. Their adherence to indigenous traditional values, ideals and perceptions militated against their survial efforts. This adherence to their traditional world view came, not exclusively, and in some cases, not at all from a desire to resist English influence, or conscious efforts to preserve a failing culture. Set in the centuries-old context of Gaelic consciousness in the bardic poetry, dating from at least mid-thirteenth century to the seventeenth century, the perceptions articulated by the latest and final phase of bardic endeavour are spared the contorting strait-jacket of retrospective expectations. Rather than prefacing the poetry of the early 1600s with suggestions of a new awareness, impending doom and millenarian melodrama, one might more profitably look backwards, as the poets themselves were inclined to do, and recognize the intriguing continuity of perception surviving into the new century.

It is interesting therefore to consider some poems which have hitherto been generally looked upon as works reflecting a new sense of imminent doom and impending catastrophe. Tom Dunne, for instance, sees this 'new awareness' in the works of Eoghan Rua mac a' Bhaird, '. . . four of whose *more perceptive* poems have been put at the beginning of Bergin's anthology'.[12] These include a poem to Hugh O'Donnell (nephew of Rory, earl of Tyrconnel), two poems to Rory O'Donnell and a poem to Red Hugh O'Donnell. Mac a' Bhaird's poem to Rory O'Donnell 'On a Peace Conference' has been interpreted as a rebuke or a

---

[11] 'A new awareness was most apparent in those poets whose patrons had been involved in the Nine Years' War, like O'Donnell's poet Eoghan Rua Mac a' Bhaird . . .' in Dunne 'Evidence', p. 16.

[12] Italics are mine, Dunne, 'Evidence', p. 16.

warning to Rory; [13] when it is more profitably to be read as an example of the bardic practice of turning defeat to victory and rationalizing the *fait accompli*. The second poem mentioned above is by the same poet to the same man; to Rory on his illness while in Rome, it is prefaced by Bergin thus:

> The poet seems to have had some difference with his patron, but his private resentment and his personal grief are now swallowed up by a sense of national ruin. [14]

The remaining poem of Eoghan Rua mac a' Bhaird of this foursome is to Red Hugh O'Donnell on his departure to Spain, wishing him every good, and inevitably, comparing his journey to journeys made by figures in historical mythology. From the same Bergin collection, a poem by Fear Flatha Ó Gnímh is regarded by Dunne as displaying characteristics of the 'new awareness' — 'a deeply pessimistic response' — and 'a spirit of fatalism' recording the 'catastrophe'. [15]

First, it must be understood that the poets were always, as a class, and as a professional group, particularly 'politically aware'. Their special function within the Gaelic system had a major political, mainly pro-pagandist, dimension. Their facility for riding the crests of the waves of change, as they successfully did throughout the centuries, necessitated an acute political awareness. Ó Gnímh's own sense of politics is evident in this poem, his patrons are fled, their replacements have not yet come forward, his lamentations on their departure are a professional duty and a cultural necessity, perhaps also an expression of personal grief. Such a poem is a particularly good and appropriate example of the influence of the superimposition of a historical framework, which comes from a source quite foreign to the poet's own framework, can have on one's understanding of the work in question. Bergin's interpretation is clear in this introduction:

> If the date [1609] is correct, it belongs to the period immediately following the flight of the earls, when Fear Flatha Ó Gnímh might

[13] Bergin, *Irish Bardic Poetry,* Introduction to No. 2.

[14] Bergin, *Irish Bardic Poetry,* p. 35.

[15] Dunne, 'Evidence', pp 16 and 17.

well believe that Ireland was dead, and that it only remained to pray for her soul.[16]

The flight of the earls undoubtedly had an enormous impact on events in Ulster, on the social structures, political balance of power and on the social and personal lives of the dependents.[17] One must, however, look at Ó Gnímh's poem in assumed ignorance of the ultimate consequences of such a flight. The most important element in the flight for the poet is the unexplained departure of his patrons. The loss of their company and perhaps more importantly, their patronage, has bewildered the poet. Another poem ascribed to Fear Flatha Ó Gnímh beginning 'Mo thruaighe mar táid Gaoidhil'[18] deals with the same theme; Ireland is dead, her lands are held by foreigners, her fields are empty, her poets silent.

Poems such as those by Ó Gnímh and Mac a' Bhaird have been regarded as examples of the awakening of bardic consciousness to an understanding of the finality of events such as the Kinsale defeat, and the flight of the earls, enjoyed by historians at a distance of some centuries. The poets participated in, witnessed and recorded events such as the disappearance of their patrons, their patron's travels, illnesses and deaths in a time-honoured manner, fashioned by influences far stronger, far more complex than the immediacy of the political situation. They did not live out their daily professional lives with bated literary breath, awaiting the final gasp of their civilization. By examining these poems in their own literary, social and cultural context, one can appreciate the warping effect that the anachronistic superimposition of unrelated frameworks of reference can have on the historical value of the poems. Two of the above-mentioned poems, both by Fear Flatha Ó Gnímh, convey a sense of overwhelming loss. The death of Ireland is imminent because of the loss of her chiefs. Principal among these are of course Ó Gnímh's own patrons. The emphasis in the two poems is a litttle different. The poem entitled by Bergin 'The Death of Ireland', presents a roll-call of afflicted Gaelic septs. Ó Gnímh feels degraded by the disappearance of the nobility.[19] The flight of her

---

[16] Bergin, *Irish Bardic Poetry,* p. 115.
[17] See N.P. Canny, 'Flight of the Earls' and see also M. Kerney Walsh, *Destruction by Peace': Hugh O'Neill after Kinsale,* (Armagh 1986).
[18] T.F. O'Rahilly, *Measgra Dánta* II, p. 206. O'Rahilly dates this poem 1609.
[19] See P.A. Breatnach, 'The Chief's Poet', pp 54 and 78.

aristocracy is the same thing as the death of Ireland:

Deacair nach bás don Bhanbha
d'éis an tréid chalma churadh
do thriall ar toisg don Easbáin
mo thruaighe beangáin Uladh.
(Bergin, *Irish Bardic Poetry,* No. 26, st. 3, p. 115.)

[It were hard for Banbha not to die after the gallant company of champions who went journeying to Spain [Italy] — alas for the princes of Ulster.]

The author of an anonymous poem dealing with the same event comes to a similar conclusion on realizing that the Ulster aristocracy have disappeared:

Ar dtriall Aodha Í Néill anois
ar n-imtheacht mic mic Maghnois
na Gaoidhil aniú sa neart
go fiú an aoinfhir ar n-imtheacht.
(Walsh, *Beatha Aodha Ruaidh Uí Dhomhnaill,*
vol. 2, p. 118, st. 6.)

[Since Aodh Ó Néill has gone now, and also Maghnus' grandson, the Gaels and their power to-day have vanished to the last man.]

The equation of the chief's life with the life of his lordship and the sovereignty of his territory is as old, and older than the bardic genre. The basic intention is complimentary; the loss felt in the patron's absence is proportionate to his power and stature before he departed; the greater the loss, the greater his stature. Such is the stature of O'Neill or Maguire that the loss of either one is equivalent to an insurmountable defeat. This is the burden of the stanza quoted above. In the same poem the poet emphasizes the illustriousness and stature of those who sailed from Ireland:

Do chuaidh oireachus bhfear bhFáil
anonn uainne don Easbáin
tar sál re lucht na luinge
tár as a ucht oruinne.
(Walsh, *Beatha Aodha Ruaidh Uí Dhomhnaill,*
vol. 2, p. 120, st. 7.)

[The supremacy of the men of Fál has gone from us to Spain, across the sea with the ship's company; we are in disgrace because of it.]

The supremacy of the Gael has left. Ireland is without leaders, the poet feels disgraced that his country is without leading nobility. With them the leaders have taken the life of Banbha; they are coeval:

Ní mhaireann déis an eathair
n-ar imthigh síol saoir-Eachach
uch a Dhé as damhna cumhadh
dé don Bhanbha ar beathughadh.
(Walsh, *Beatha Aodha Ruaidh Uí Dhomhnaill,*
vol. 2, p. 120, st. 8.)

[After the vessel went away with the descendants of noble Eacha, there remains not a spark of Banba alive; alas! O God, it is a cause of grief.]

A similar feeling of shame, on the departure of his patron and protector is indicated by Fear Flatha Ó Gnímh:

Ní mhaireann aicme Chonaill,
dream budh rothoil i n-iomrádh,
no síol Eoghain na mbéimeann —
d'fhearaibh Éireann is iomnár.
(Bergin, *Irish Bardic Poetry*, No. 26, st. 8,
p. 116.)

[The race of Conall is no more, a company that was most eager for fame, nor the seed of Eoghan of the strokes — to the men of Ireland it is a disgrace.]

The sense of shame is further emphasized in a later stanza:

D'éag a huaisle 's a hoireacht
gan toidheacht aice ón oilbhéim,
dá lamhadh sinn a mhaoidheamh,
d'fhine Gaoidheal is oilchéim.
(Bergin, *Irish Bardic Poetry*, No. 26, st. 16, p. 117.)

[That owing to the death of her nobility and her courts, she cannot recover from the stigma, if we dared proclaim it, it is an infamy to the race of the Gael.][20]

Part of the status of the poet accrued from the status of his patron. A poet sought the most illustrious patrons, a poet without a patron felt degraded and unprotected. Tadhg Dall Ó hUiginn, appealing to Cormac O'Hara for the latter's patronage in the 1580s, expresses his unease and vulnerability in the want of a strong patron:

A-tú a mbeol ghuaisi do ghnáth
re ndeachaidh oroinn d'iomráth
gan neach do-ní dísle dhamh
muna thí dhíbhse a dheunamh.
(McKenna, *O'Hara Poems,* No. 3, st. 6, p. 50.)

[I am continually in the jaws of danger, because of all the gossip that has been made about me, having no one to protect me, unless thou canst undertake it.]

Conchubhar Crón Ó Dálaigh, a Munster poet, was bereft of three patrons in succession during the Munster disturbances of the 1580s.[21] He, the poet, appeals to Maguire to accept him as his poet. Ó Dálaigh suggests that it will reflect on the honour of the chief if he fails to receive him as his poet:

Gabh m'égnach, a Chú Chonnacht,
a chnes síthe séghonnacht;
ar n-éra dhaoibh ní dleghair
a rélla an taoibh tuaidhemhain.
(Greene, *Maguire Poems,* No. 19, st. 1, p. 170.)

[Receive my complaint, Cú Chonnacht, fair noble bright skin; you should not refuse me, o star of the northern province.]

If the chief refuses his patronage, it displays his lack of appreciation for a poet, once worthy to serve some powerful Munster leaders. His failure

---

[20] Cf. Breatnach, 'Marbhnadh Aodha Ruaidh Uí Dhomhnaill' in *Éigse,* 15 (1973), pp 31-50. In st. 25, p. 38, Ó Gnímh suggests that the elements are ashamed too, following Red Hugh's departure through his death. And see also McKenna, *Magauran Poems,* No. 22, st. 3, p. 181.

[21] Green, *Maguire Poems,* p. 218.

will disgrace him for a man either parsimonious or ignorant of the poet's value. Such men bring ignominy on those over whom they preside. An extension of this pretence is that of the poet's shame at the chief's departure — especially since the poet yet lives. The chief has neglected him on his death, or in the 1607 context, his departure; the poet is ashamed and patronless. Ó Dálaigh challenges Maguire's own security in his search for patronage. The challenge lies in the implication of disgrace on Maguire's side should he refuse. Ó Dálaigh, however, is making a preemptive strike in order to avoid the continued embarrassment of having no patron:

> Aithnim díbh, más doiligh libh,
> mé dot togha, a thuir Uisnigh,
> ná bí ad lán bheoil na Banbha
> a fhádh eoil gach ealadhna.
> (Greene, *Maguire Poems*, No. 19, st. 14, p. 174.)

> [I command you, if you think it hard that I should choose you, o chief of Ulster, that you should not be spoken of all over Ireland, o instructor in every art.]

Considering, therefore, how affected the poets professed to be by the death of patrons, and how eagerly and proudly[22] they sought new patrons, poems like those of Ó Gnímh or Mac a' Bhaird should not be a cause of surprise in their intensity of feeling at the loss of very substantial patronage. It is against a background of the poets' relations with their patrons that such poems must be considered; whether the relation was actual or theoretical, the expression of it in the bardic poetry cannot be interpreted as figurative in one period and literal in another. Ó Gnímh therefore declares that Ireland has died in the wake of the earls' departure:

> Beannacht ar anmain Éireann,
> inis na gcéimeann gcorrach;
> atá Treabh Briain nam bogglór
> dom dhóigh ar dhobhrón torrach.
> (Bergin, *Irish Bardic Poetry*, No. 26, st. 1,
> p. 115.)

---

[22] Cf. Bergin, *Irish Bardic Poetry,* No. 20, st. 17, p. 90.

[A blessing on the soul of Ireland, island of the faltering steps:
methinks Brian's home of the soft voices is pregnant with sorrow.]

The poet Maol Seachluinn Ó hEodhusa, lamenting the death of Thomas
Magauran in 1343 expressed his loss thus:

Ní beag easbhaidh Inse Fáil,
ní headh nach easbhaidh anbháil;
tug an Coimdhe do chach cor
[a fháth] nír dhoilghe dhosun.
(McKenna, *Magauran Poems,* No. 31, st. 1, p. 271.)

[Not slight is this loss to Inis Fáil — nay, it is a heavy loss; the lord
has cast down all folk; the cause of it (i.e. of general gloom, viz.
Tomas' death) was less hard on him than on men.]

Inis Fáil, Ireland as a whole, is cast under gloom and oppression by the
death of an individual chief. God has seen fit to depress the people of
Inis Fáil by depriving them of Thomas Magauran. Banbha grows weak
at the loss of Thomas:

Iomdha tír atá go sé
i leon uile dhá éise;
do thraoth méad borrfaidh Bhanbha
ar n-éag d'oinchoin Eachlabhra.
(McKenna, *Magauran Poems,* No. 31, st. 20, p. 275.)

[Many is the land in misery today owing to his death; Banbha's
swelling spirit has grown faint after the death of Eachlabhra's
wolf.]

Not only Magauran's own territory but Banbha and Inis Fáil are the expressions used by the poet to indicate the extent to which the loss is felt.
The individual loss of a chief could be considered the greatest such loss
ever at any time. Tadhg Mór Ó hUiginn lamented the death of Brian
Magauran in 1298. This Brian's death was the most disastrous loss for
Ireland.[23] A hierarchy of loss prevailed; the loss of the poet's most
favoured or most powerful patron is regarded as being more grievous
than that of a less favoured or less important chief. Tadhg Mór Ó

---

[23] McKenna, *Magauran Poems,* No. 4, st. 27, p. 37.

hUiginn in the same poem lamenting Brian Magauran places the loss of Brian above that of other kings or nobles whose actual deaths were as cruel or more cruel.[24] Ó hUiginn consciously exalts his own patron above the other admittedly noble and heroic chiefs. Just as Ó hUiginn reckons Brian a greater loss than all the nobles together — though they too are deserving of some note — so too is it with Ó Gnímh in the first decade of the seventeenth century, lamenting the loss of the race of Conall and Eoghan — O'Donnells and O'Neills respectively. He also notes on the same occasion, the loss of O'Rourke and Maguire, with some qualification however in regard to the latter; the loss of Maguire and O'Rourke is but a passing thing compared with the massive loss of the O'Neills and the O'Donnells:

> Ó Ruairc and Mág Uidhir,
> laoich nár fhuirigh ó ghábhadh;
> is cealgach croidhe an chriothshluag,
> mo bhraon diombuan a mbádhadh.
> (Bergin, *Irish Bardic Poetry,* No. 26, st. 12, p. 116.)

[Ó Ruairc and Mág Uidhir, warriors who never shirked danger — treacherous is the heart of the trembling host — the overwhelming of them is to me but a passing drop (?)]

A primary consideration therefore in Ó Gnímh's composition here, is to identify the individuals whose loss is greatest, that is to say posthumously compliment his own great patrons even if it is at the expense of some lesser individuals — who however also receive due mention. Ó Gnímh calculates the relative losses of one chief over another, not according to their respective performances in the 'Nine Years' War' or according to their consistency in anti-English activity, or according to any recognizable proto-nationalistic rationale. Rather, he highlights the loss of the powerful by comparing it to that of the less so, in a manner following the example of Ó hUiginn of the thirteenth century, and not in a self-consciously, innovative awareness of the collective loss at that time of such men for the ultimate fate of the Gaelic system.

Ó Gnímh in another poem of the same period (1609) lamenting the change in his circumstances occasioned by the departure of his patrons,

---

[24] McKenna, *Magauran Poems,* No. 4, st. 28, p. 37.

declares that Banbha has been brought to a state in which only God can help her:

> Muna gcuirid dóigh i nDia
> síol Éibhir Sguit ón Sgithia;
> a gclár foirne — gá dám dhó?
> ní clár d'oighre ná d'iarmhó.
> (O'Rahilly, *Measgra Dánta,* No. 54, lines 93-96,
> p. 147.)

[If the seed of the Scythian Eibhear Scot, put not their faith in God, their chess board will not be that of their heirs or sons.]

This is ostensibly appropriately apocalyptic in Ó Gnímh's particular situation and appears to reflect his own awareness of the hopelessness of Banbha's circumstances so much so that recourse has to be made to the deity rather than to the host of Gaelic chiefs traditionally awaiting Banbha's cry for help. The loss of his chief causes the poet Tadhg Óg Ó hUiginn to fear for the future of Banbha in the same way. Again, only God can aid her in the strait to which the death of Ó hUiginn's patron has brought her:

> Fuilngidh bhur léan, a Leath Coinn!
> bhur gcosnamh cia dar tualaing?
> ní fhuighthe acht ó Dhia a dheimhin;
> cia ó bhfuighthe fóirdhin?
> (McKenna, *Aithdioghluim Dána,* No. 39, st. 1, p. 158).

[Bear your misfortune, O Leath Cuinn; who can protect you? Who can help you? Only God can tell you surely.]

This opening stanza by Ó hUiginn if written in the early seventeenth century, would perhaps in the context of the bereavement of Leath Coinn (the Northern Half) after the earls' departure, be regarded as evidence of a new awareness of the dissolution of the Gaelic world on the part of the poets. However, the stanza in question was written at the beginning of the fifteenth century. It is the opening quatrain of an elegy on the death of the chief of an Anglo-Norman, albeit Gaelicized sept; Ulick Burke, 'Uilleag an Fhíona', chief of Clann Rickard from 1387 to 1424. He was the son of Richard Óg by Mór (+ 1383) daughter of Murchadh Ó

Madagáin.[25] Eoghan Rua Mac a' Bhaird, like Ó Gnímh, distracted by the sudden, ostensibly unexplained departure of the chiefs of Ulster, sees an end to the traditional pastimes and interests because of the departure of his own patron O'Donnell, and along with him Hugh O'Neill:

> Mór tuirse Ulltach fá n-airc
> d'éis Í Dhomhnuill do dhíobairt
> sní lugha fá Aodh Eanuigh
> cumha ar an taobh thuaidheamhain.
> (Walsh, *Beatha Aodha Ruaidh Uí Dhomhnaill,*
> vol. 2, p. 138, st. 4)[26]

[Great the sorrow of Ulster in her difficulty since Ó Domhnaill has been banished, and not less is grief in the North because of Aodh of Eanach.]

In spite of the fact that O'Donnell left for the continent of his own volition, both himself and Hugh O'Neill having secured favourable terms at Mellifont,[27], Mac a' Bhaird sees it as a banishment. Because of this banishment, depriving the poet of his patron, depriving the territory of her mate — the life-style is upset:

> Gan imbeirt gan ól fleidhe
> gan aithghearradh aimsire
> gan mhalairt gan graifne ghreagh
> gan tabhairt aighthe ar éigean.
> Gan rádha rithlearg molta
> gan sgaoileadh sgeóil chodalta
> gan úidh ar fhaicsin leabhair
> gan chlaistin ghlúin ghenealaigh.
> (Walsh, *Beatha Aodha Ruaidh Uí Dhomhnaill,*
> pp 138 and 140, st. 6 and 7.)

[No game, nor drinking festival, nor amusement: no fair, nor racing contest, nor facing of high enterprise.
No reciting of panegyrics: no telling of sleep-inducing story: no wish to examine a volume, nor hear a roll of genealogy.]

---

25 McKenna, *Aithdioghluim Dána,* p. 158.
26 Cf. Greene, *Maguire Poems,* No. 19, st. 1, p. 170.
27 N.P. Canny, 'Treaty of Mellifont'.

Similar changes were feared by Tadhg Óg Ó hUiginn on the death of
Ulick Burke in 1424:

> An mbia mar do bhí roimhe
> ól aguibh nó aonoighe?
> gá fisidh aga bhfuighthe
> an fissin dá bhfiarfuighthe?
> (McKenna, *Aithdioghluim Dána*, No. 39, st. 2, p. 158.)

> [Will you ever again have the old feasts and assemblies? What seer
> could answer if you asked that?]

Their wonted interest in gaming is no more among the Gael because of
their grief:

> Gan fhear ar tí a theilgthe i dtoigh
> — ní hathtoirse gan fhochain —
> do-bheir bhur léan, a Leath Cuinn,
> dá mbeath an t-éan san ursuinn.
> (McKenna, *Aithdioghluim dána*, No. 39, st. 4, p. 158.)

> [There is no man in any house who could shoot a bird were it in the
> doorway; such is the result of your grief, O Leath Cuinn, a grief
> with good cause.]

All this misfortune, grief, debility and change has one source; the loss
through death, banishment or departure of the chief. In Ó hUiginn's
case the blow is insufferable:

> Fuarabhair — fada ó chobhair —
> bás an ríogh ga rabhobhair;
> a aos cumtha, ní fhoil ann
> ó shoin acht urchra d'fhulang.
> (McKenna, *Aithdioghluim Dána*, No. 39, st. 3, p. 158.)

> [You have lost your king — a blow not to be healed; my friends,
> naught remains now but to bear ruin.][28]

Ruin follows the death of a patron, the departure of a chief from his territory. The fertility of the area, the prosperity of the poets, the soul of

---

[28] Cf. O'Rahilly, *Measgra Dánta* II, No. 54, and McKenna, *Magauran Poems*, No. 12.

the country, attach themselves to the person of the chief. They go with him into the grave. This is in essence the logic which underlies even the most complicated bardic panegyric. Defeat, bringing loss of face or territory often leaves Banbha in a disgraced position.

Three poems by different poets, composed at different times and for different occasions, illustrate the flexibility and at the same time the limitations of the poet's referential reserves. They illustrate also the persistence of traditional perspectives, in a literary sense in the poetry, and actually in the adamantly individualistic policies pursued by the chieftains; advocated and castigated alike by the poets alternately and with equal conviction. The mid-fourteenth century poet, Maol Pádraig Mac Naimhín, in a poem on the release of Thomas Magauran by his enemies, presents us with two pictures. First, he depicts the distress of Leath Cuinn — expanded to Fódla — on the capture or death of Magauran. His departure, albeit temporary in this instance, wreaks enormous change throughout Fódla. The news of his release and imminent return alters the tragic situation once again; poets return, cattle prosper, fields become fruitful. The territory and the important subjects respond to the presence or absence of the chief and this motif is used continually by the poets to indicate harmony or disharmony. This poem provides an interesting comparison for a poem by Tadhg Óg Ó hUiginn a century later (*c.* 1441-3). This poem is a propaganda piece for Maolruanadh O'Carroll, chief of Éile. McKenna synopsizes the contents thus:

> The poet urges Maolruanaidh to seize Cashel, unite all the men of Mumha and his kinsmen the Luighne, and then drive the Goill out of the land, Conn Céadchathach's race (i.e. chiefly the Í Néill) will be sure to help him in his enterprise; they cannot but be mindful of the help which Cian and the other sons of Oilill Ólum gave to Art Aoinfhear at the battle of Magh Mucromha.[29]

This poem in turn provides an interesting bardic background for an elegy written by Fearghal Óg Mac a' Bhaird on the death, in Spain, of his patron Red Hugh O'Donnell in 1602.[30] That Red Hugh died abroad places him in a category shared with other major Gaelic heroes; such heroes as Niall of the Nine Hostages, Dáithí mac Fiachrach and Brian

---

29 McKenna, *Aithdioghluim Dána,* p. 100.
30 Breatnach, 'Marbhnadh Aodha Ruaidh Uí Dhomhnaill', in *Éigse,* 15 (1973).

Boru's son. Ireland is left unprotected and spiritless. Red Hugh has taken her spirit with him into the grave. His death, like that of Hercules who took his weapons with him, leaves Ireland without his arms. He did not receive the reward of his efforts — like Caesar who died before he could enjoy his just victories, dying like Red Hugh to protect his empire; 'Tara's honour has perished' with Red Hugh's death. This poem also includes a stanza of lamentation for another patron, one Mag Aonghusa to whom the poet dedicates one quatrain — possibly a duty incumbent upon him as part of his contract with Mag Aonghusa. His death also has severely reduced the honour of the Ulstermen.

During the course of the three hundred odd years covered by the span of the three poems, the relations between lord and poet are seen to have changed not at all. The articulation of sorrow, joy, grief, pride and anxiety, and the sources of all these are remarkably similar. One must remember throughout that the poets illustrate and articulate abstract planes of perspective and consciousness of reality. In many ways, sentiments or concerns mentioned in the poems can hardly be regarded as expressions of the poets' or their patrons' actual beliefs, for instance regarding the prosperity supposedly evident in the territory on the accession of a rightful ruler. As the articulation of a fundamental principle of the correct order of the world, however, such reasoning persisted in the literature to the close of the seventeenth century. Understanding its expedient manipulation is part of the challenge offered in the problem of interpreting bardic poetry in general. Canny suggests that in the pre-seventeenth century period such cause and effect determinism based on the worthiness of the ruler was a firmly held belief; but that this 'belief' was abandoned in the seventeenth century. The poems under discussion, however, illustrate the nature of this bardic 'motif' rather than 'belief'.[31] The complexity of the motifs which in many cases appear to have had their origins in pre-history, enabled the poets to manipulate the tradition successfully for several centuries.

The poet, Maol Pádraig Mac Naimhín, celebrated Thomas Magauran's release from the captivity of some rival Gaelic enemies (*c.* 1338).[32] The poem, however, opens on a note of despair in which the poet indicates the depression suffered by Ireland in Thomas' absence:

---

[31] N.P. Canny, 'Formation', pp 93-4.
[32] McKenna, *Magauran Poems,* p. 422 and poem no. 22, p. 181.

Ní bheag an léansa ar Leath Cuinn,
a dhíoth d'áiriumh ní fhéadfuinn;
léan ag fóbra chuir d'íbh Céin
do chuir an Fhódla i n-aimhréidh.
(McKenna, *Magauran Poems,* No. 22, st. 1, p. 181.)

[Heavy is the affliction on Leath Cuinn, I can not tell how great a loss it is; affliction overthrowing Cian's race has disturbed Fódla.]

Ireland is ruined because of the capture of Brian's son Thomas:

Gabháil mheic Bhriain gá mbí sinn
cúis an leoinse as léan d'Éirinn;
gor gabhadh gríobh fhuinn Uladh,
gan shíol Cuinn do chumhsgughadh.
(McKenna, *Magauran Poems,* No. 22, st. 5, p. 181.)

[The capture of Brian's son with whom I live is cause of this ruin; ruin to Éire till the Griffin of Uladh was captured, Conn's seed has never been scattered.]

Almost three hundred years later, the poet Fearghal Óg Mac a' Bhaird in an elegy for Red Hugh O'Donnell (+ 1602) makes a similar observation on the consequences of O'Donnell's death:

Teasda Éire san Easbáinn,
do deaghladh a díleasdáil;
an sén fuair tre theasdáil thoir
uainn san Easbáinn do fhágaibh.
(Breatnach, 'Marbhnadh Aodha Ruaidh Uí Dhomhnaill', st. 1, p. 34 (hereafter 'Marbhnadh AOD')

[Ireland has perished in Spain; her faithful tryst has been broken; the prosperity she found, he through dying in the East has left it in Spain; out of reach.]

With Red Hugh's death has ended the honour of Ireland; as with Magauran, his capture/death has ruined Ireland:

Bás a n-aoinfheacht re hAodh Ruadh
fuair cadhus na gcóig ríoshluagh;
mar sin terna Banbha Bhreagh:

dá térma tarla toirneamh.
(Breatnach, 'Marbhnadh AOD', st. 4, p. 35.)

[The honour of the five provinces (lit. kingly hosts) has died along with Red Hugh; thus it is that Ireland has departed: her term has been cut short.]

Mac Naimhín, Magauran's poet in 1338, described just how Ireland suffered the loss of the chief; the Gael are left unprotected; the whole territory has become waste, unproductive:

Léan do loigh ar lacht a chruidh
léan nach leig cnuas tre chraobhuibh,
léan dá dtarrla cor do chách,
nach tarbha crodh ná conách.
(McKenna, *Magauran Poems,* No. 22, st. 2, p. 181.)

[Affliction striking the milk of her kine, and leaving no fruit on her branches, and casting every man down and taking all value from kine and treasure.]

As a result, shame overcomes the heroes of Fál, the poets are ruined:

Léan ar bronnudh bhó agus each,
léan dar heasgradh an t-eineach,
léan ba scéal ar fianaibh Fáil,
léan ar chliaraibh do chongbháil.
(McKenna, *Magauran Poems,* No. 22, st. 3, p. 181.)

[Ruin on the bestowing of kine and horses, ruin to all generosity, ruin to shame the Fianna of Fál, ruin on the poets' maintenance.]

The integrity of the territory is threatened, the border is unprotected:

Léan do fhás i gcoimhsaibh críoch,
léan do leig fhás don eissíoth,
léan mór ar teacht an toraidh
le gcleacht gach slógh síorfhoghail.
(McKenna, *Magauran Poems,* No. 22, st. 4, p. 181.)

[Ruin coming on the borders of the land, and letting dissension grow apace, ruin on the coming of fruit, ruin letting all foes' hosts continue raiding.]

Fearghal Óg Mac a' Bhaird expressed the same anxieties after the death of Red Hugh O'Donnell:

> Ní hionand is Éire iar nAodh;
> danair indte in gach éntaobh
> iar mbás gach duine dhíobh soin;
> re bhíodh ruire acht don ríoghraidh.
> (Breatnach, 'Marbhnadh AOD', st. 12, p. 36.)

[After Hugh, Ireland is no longer the same: there are foreigners in her on every side following the death of all those; it used to be that a chieftain came only from the royal line.][33]

The territory likewise laments Red Hugh in its infertility:

> Laithe gruamadh, guirt tana
> dá chaoi bhíd mar bhrughadha;
> bíd mar ollamhna chraoi Chuinn
> lomabhla ag caoi Í Chonaill.
> (Breatnach, 'Marbhnadh AOD', st. 19, p. 38.)

[A gloomy day, sparse fields — they mourn him as farmers. Bare apple trees are mourning the descendant of Conall like the learned men of the race of Conn.]

Were Red Hugh alive, so too would the land thrive:

> Tiocfaimis tar tairthibh feadh
> Aodh Maonmhuighe dá maireadh:
> ní in thráth teasda in toradh;
> gach blath feasda ag feodhughadh.
> (Breatnach, 'Marbhnadh AOD', st. 20, p. 38.)

[If Hugh of Maomhagh were living we would speak of the fruits of the forests; the crop was not wanting in his time; henceforth every flower (will be) withering.]

Mac Naimhín declares that Thomas Magauran's capture is the true disaster of Ireland, the Gael are left unprotected, the nobles have been dispersed, God will have to avenge the wrong:

---

[33] Breatnach, 'Marbhna Aodha Ruaidh Uí Dhomhnaill', *Éigse,* vol. 15 (1973), sts. 8, 9, 10, 11, p. 36.

Gidh mór n-oilbhéim uair Éire
re ngabháil chinn Choirrshléibhe,
ioth Banbha ní béad [ro] bháidh
acht géag Gabhra do ghabháil.
(McKenna, *Magauran Poems,* No. 22, st. 6, p. 183.)

[Many the disaster Éire knew before Coirrshliabh's chief was captured, yet no real disaster came to ruin Banbha's corn till the capture of the Branch of Gabhair.]

Magauran is powerful enough, however, to have important pledges on
hand, these and God's vengeance will secure his release:

A bhfuil ar cleith n-Úire d'airc
suaithnidh linn Dia gá dhíoghailt;
iomdha geall re géag n-Eanaigh
nach téid tar ceann cóigeadhaigh.
(McKenna, *Magauran Poems,* No. 22, st. 10, p. 183.)

[The strait-jacket in which Ur's pillar lies — we know well that
God will avenge it; there is many a pledge available for Eanach's
branch which is not available for (any other) provincial ruler.]

The poet of the early fourteenth century, Mac Naimhín, and the poet of
the early seventeenth century, Fearghal Óg Mac a' Bhaird, both consider the loss of their patrons in the same way. Both patrons are departed
for different reasons. The effects of their respective departures are
nevertheless the same. The grief, despondency and anxiety for the
future displayed by Ó Gnímh and Eoghan Rua Mac a' Bhaird and
Fearghal Óg Mac a' Bhaird and the anonymous authors of such works
as 'Mochean don loing sin tar lear'[34] and 'C'áit ar ghabhadar Gaoidhil'
is one expression of the poets' attitude to changing conditions, which involved the loss of patronage, death of a chief and fear for their future.

It is in relation to poems such as these that the temptation arises to
suggest that 'reality' has finally overtaken the poet and his interminable
prophecy of the death of Banbha, the loss of her nobles and her poets.
That is to say that what was once admittedly part of a complex combination of literary conceit, historico-mythological tradition and

---

[34] Walsh, Paul (ed), Lughaidh Ó Cléirigh, *A Life of Aodh Ruadh Ó Domhnaill,
transcribed from the Book of Lughaidh Ó Cléirigh* (hereafter *BAR*), p. 118.

aristocratic theory, had suddenly become reality; Banbha is in real
danger, the nobles are being scattered, poetry is no longer valued, the
foreigners have conquered all. Not only has this literary scenario
become harsh reality, but the poets, almost simultaneously consciously
forsake an entire world view, mental schema, and transfer their complex
literary structure and attendant references, expressions and precedents
to the service of their new reality. A selection of poems from outside the
Ulster sphere, also written in the early seventeenth century, emphasize
the inadvisability of seeking new perceptions in the poetry, the evidence
for which is based on historical events extraneous to the perceptions and
awareness articulated in, and present in the tradition.

One of the fundamental values underlying the Gaelic Irish mentality
in its approach to power was the strength of the individual wielding the
power, and the possible benefits accruing therefrom for the dependent.
The 'dependent' position, could in the political sphere, be held by the
chief. The willingness of the Gaelic chiefs to accept favourable terms
from a strong adversary is part of the fabric of Gaelic history. Gaelic
chiefs rarely allowed difference of race to interfere with their individual
efforts to stay on the winning side or to blunt the consequences of having
chosen the losing side. Encomiastic verse written for Gaelic and Anglo-
Norman lords alike, form a major part of the corpus of bardic
literature.

The Gaelicized life-style of many Anglo-Norman lords has often been
mentioned in explanation of the poets' willingness to accommodate the
latter in the bardic schema. This explanation is simplistic and hardly accounts for the existence of an impressive encomium by a poet of
disputed identity[35] for Queen Elizabeth I: to the same poet is attributed
also a panegyric for Thomas 10th Earl of Ormond, second cousin of the
Queen. Both these poems were written at the close of the sixteenth century. Standish Hayes O'Grady suggested that the poem for Elizabeth
was written in high irony — deliberately attributing good qualities to the
Queen, which were manifestly absent in her.[36] A poem written by
Dáibhí Ó Bruadair praising James II was based on this poem, and

---

[35] See Carney, *Butler Poems,* p. 136, and cf. J.C. McErlean (ed), *Duanaire Dháibhidh Uí Bhruadair: The Poems of David Ó Bruadair* 3 parts (London, 1910-17) pt. 3, pp 64-5.
[36] *Dáibhí Ó Bruadair*, p. 65.

likewise said by O'Grady to have been written in mock emulation.[37] McErlean in his introductory note to the poem to Elizabeth denies such a possibility, on the grounds that no poet

> attached to the Ormonde family would have ventured to satirize the Queen, for Thomas Dubh was a favourite and a second cousin of Queen Elizabeth's.[38]

Linking the sentiments expressed both in the Elizabethan panegyric and the other poem (supposedly) by the same author, for the earl of Ormond, McErlean observes that:

> A poet who could praise in exaggerated terms the plundering expeditions of Thomas Dubh against the Irish of N.E. Ulster and S.W. Munster was hardly likely to be restrained by national sympathies or prejudices from writing a panegyric on his patron's cousin and suzerain.[39]

'National sympathies or prejudices' were hardly the determining or motivating factors behind the work of the poets for those whom they deemed worthy of their attention. As I have pointed out in relation to the sixteenth century, *de facto* power, confidently wielded was one of the principal factors taken into account by the poets. Whether or not a single individual was responsible for the two poems referred to above is immaterial for the comprehension of the greater implications of the fact that bardic poets addressed poems to such patrons as a matter of course.

Thomas Butler was a considerable power in his own right. His military campaigns are described in detail by Flann mac Eoghan Mág Craith (*c.* 1614) in a battle roll of his exploits. This Flann Mág Craith is unlikely according to Carney to have been the author of either of the two poems mentioned above.[40] In the course of the battle roll, Mág Craith proudly lists Ormond's depredations on Gaelic Irish and foreign lords

---

[37] 'Doubtless Ó Bruadair thoroughly understood the drift of our article, but it was common practice of the bards to carry on such mock controversies with all gravity' — McErlean, *Dáibhí Ó Bruadair*, pt. 3, pp 64 and 65.

[38] *Dáibhí Ó Bruadair,* p. 65.

[39] *Dáibhí Ó Bruadair,* p. 65.

[40] Carney, *Butler Poems*, pp 136-7.

alike;[41]   Captain Wyatt, or equally, Shane O'Neill[42] are deserving of
Ormond's rough dealing. The author of another poem for Ormond,
beginning 'Taghaim Tomás rogha is ríoghradh' saw the earl in the same
light as Mág Craith did; a very successful warlord, who was at once an
eminent member of a renowned house, a favourite of the English court,
a much decorated courtier, and perhaps most important of all, a successful campaigner whose success earned him the right to his position.
As a successful lord, Ormond is represented as having accomplished the
usual tasks of the Gaelic lord; he has taken hostages from all Ireland:

> . . . iarla fuilteach Chille Cuinne
> rug géill na n-uile Éireannach.
> (Carney, *Butler Poems*, No. 16, st. 2, lines 1746 and 1747, p. 74.)

> [the valourous (lit. bloody) Earl of Kilkenny has taken the
> hostages of all the Irish.]

Tadhg Óg Ó hUiginn wrote a poem for Niall Óg O'Neill, chief of Tír
Eoghain from 1395 to 1403[43] celebrating his warlike pursuits. This Niall
had ruled in a joint kingship with his father, until in 1403 his own
nephews replaced him. Two stanzas of this poem illustrate the poet's interest in power effectively wielded, battle is the deciding factor, cess levying and hostage-taking are the symbols of success:

> Sreath do chomha ar cró nEachaidh;
> dá thogha is mó ná mithidh
> ríghe lat i dtaoibh tachair
> far chathuigh mac Maoil Mithigh.
> (MacKenna, *Aithdioghluim Dána,* No. 15,
> st. 11(a), p. 56.)

> [The series (i.e. toll) of thy tributes is laid on Eochaidh's steading;
> 'tis time that the realm for which Maol Mithidh's son strove, be
> thine by ordeal of battle.]

He urged him on further:

---

41 Carney, *Butler Poems*, No. 15, sts. 5, 6, 7, p. 67.
42 Carney, *Butler Poems*, No. 15, sts. 8, 9, 10, p. 68.
43 McKenna, *Aithdioghluim Dána*, p. 54.

Bráighde ag mac Ultaigh uainne,
budh leat a hUltaibh Éire;
tugais druim re trian tíre,
síne is fiadh Cuinn re chéile.
(McKenna, *Aithdioghluim Dána*, No. 15, st. 14, p. 56.)

[We all give hostages to the son of Ulaidh's prince; Éire shall be given thee by them; thou hast refused to be satisfied with a third of the land; thou (i.e. thy ambition) and Conn's land are the same in extent.]

Both the poems to Thomas Butler and that to Elizabeth I are lavish in their praises of the addressees. They are hailed as Gaelic chiefs are, their beauty is traditionally described, their victories glorified, in short, their power is acknowledged and celebrated in a predictable bardic fashion. Ormond's victories against English and Irish are described alike, against Wyatt:

Tall ar Wyat tug an céadchath
an triath baoghlach béimeannach . . .
(Carney, *Butler Poems*, No. 16, st. 6, lines
1777 and 1778, p. 75.)

[He dealt first battle to Wyatt yonder — the dangerous violent lord.][44]

Against O'Neill on whom Ormond inflicted a signal defeat in Glenconkeine;[45]

Fá dhó ['na] dhoibhir Gleann Con Cadhain
ón triath shaidhbhir shaor-bheartach, . . .
(Carney, *Butler Poems,* No. 16, st. 6, lines 1781
and 1782, p. 75.)

[This affluent, determined lord burnt Glenconkeine.]

Ormond's acquisition of the Cistercian monastery of Abington, County Limerick [46] is proudly listed in his battle roll:

---

[44] See Carney, *Butler Poems*, pp 129, 130, l. 1573n., for details of this engagement.
[45] Carney, *Butler Poems*, p. 133, l. 1625n.
[46] Carney, *Butler Poems*, p. 138, l. 1787-9n.

Leis do buaidhreadh Mainistir Uaithne
dá ttug ruaig do réim Ghearuilt; . . .
(Carney, *Butler Poems,* No. 16, st. 7, lines 1787
and 1788, p. 76.)

[He it was who harried the monastery of Uaithne, which banished
the Geraldines triumph.]

Ormond's triumphs over the south Munster chiefs are not at all seen in
the light of a national tragedy. In the eighth stanza of this panegyric the
defeat of the Gaelic chiefs who combined with fitzMaurice in the Ormond wars is further proof of Ormond's valour:

Ní nár bhfeárr-de le Clainn Chárthaigh, do
bhí sé lá a nUíbh Laoghuire.
Leis do lasadh d'éis a leagtha
Dún Lóich lasrach laocharsaidh;
d'éis a tháirdil go hUíbh Ráthach
ní raibh áird ar aoghuire,
Teagh hÍ Ghláimhín leis do háitigheadh,
ní nach áirmhíonn aonduine.
(Carney, *Butler Poems*, No. 16, st. 8, p. 76.)

[He (Ormond) spent a day in Uíbh Laoghuire, not that Clann Car-
thaigh were the better for it [i.e. Clann Cárthaigh suffered because
of his spending a day in their territory.][47] Having knocked Dunloe
Castle (the flaming, noble, warriorlike place) he burnt it.[48]
Following his expedition to Uíbh Ráthach, there was no sign (lit.
no mention) of a herdsman. He occupied Teagh Uí Ghláimhín,[49]
an event mentioned by no one.]

The poem in which the above stanza occurs is dated *c*. 1588.[50] This is of
course before the defeat at Kinsale and the subsequent departure of the
northern lords for the Continent. One might therefore suggest that the
poet celebrated Ormond's depredations in ignorance of the ultimate
consequences of such gradual erosion of Gaelic Irish autonomous

---

47 Carney, *Butler Poems*, p. 139, l. 1793-1803n.
48 Carney, *Butler Poems*, p. 132, l. 1602n.
49 Carney, *Butler Poems*, p. 136, l. 1696n.
50 Carney, *Butler Poems*, p. 137.

lordships. The above stanza is followed by one yet more exultant over the demise of more Gaelic strongholds, Bantry monastery, the territory of the Mic Amhlaoibh[51] of Duhallow, Mag Finghín and the O'Briens of Thomond are numbered among Thomas' victories in the following stanza:

Do bhí a champaí a Mainistir Bheanntroighe
's a cClainn Amhlaoibh éintseachtmhuin.
Leis do mínigheadh Mág Fínghin,
an triath fíorchaoin féilfhairseang.
Tug an Bhrianfhuil ar díth iarla,
tréinfhear diadha daonnachtach,
's do chuir don Fhraingc soir é re haimsir,
cá mó geall ar Ghaodhaluibh?
(Carney, *Butler Poems,* No. 16, st. 9, p. 76.)

[In one week, his camps were in Bantry and in Clann Amhlaoibh Mág Fhínghin, the gentle, bountiful lord was subdued by him. He bereft the O'Briens of an earl,[52] the pious, humane, strong one, and he sent him east to France for a while, what greater pledge for the Gael (can there be)?]

This section possibly refers to events which occurred in the 1570s:

In March 1570 Ormond was sent by Sidney with some force to 'parley with, protect or prosecute' (*CPSI* 1509-73) Conchobhar Ó Briain, Earl of Thomond. He gave up Cluain Rámhfhada, an Clár Mór and Bun Raite to Ormond, and shortly afterwards fled to France. He returned in the winter of the same year and received pardon.[53]

The poet lists these victories without judgemental comment, beyond reiterating Ormond's valour and success. The battle roll[54] composed for Ormond on his death in 1614 by Flann Mág Craith provides an interesting compliment to this early panegyric. The poem by Mág Craith is

---

51 Carney, *Butler Poems*, p. 160.
52 Carney, *Butler Poems*, p. 131, l. 1593-1600n.
53 Carney, *Butler Poems*, p. 131, l. 1593-1600n.
54 Carney, *Butler Poems*, No. 15.

dated by Carney to 1614 or after.[55] The poem by Mág Craith celebrates Ormond's triumphs, of which there were many, in forty-six stirring stanzas. For the most part his escapades were part of a more general undertaking by the queen's lieutenants, in which Ormond played a decisive role. The poet treats them as the forays of a powerful chief, protecting his lordship, extending its boundaries. The major Gaelic and Gaelicized strongholds of South Munster and Thomond and the impenetrable northern territories of Uí Néill, all experienced the consequences of Ormond's prowess and valour, until all Ireland was subject to his word:

> Iomdha críoch do creachadh lais
> nach maoidhim ar mac Séamais,
> gur chuir triath na ngéirreann nglan
> iath Éireann ar a fhocal.
> (Carney, *Butler Poems,* No. 15, st. 44, p. 73.)

[I do not begrudge James's son the many territories he has raided, until the lord of the clear sharp constellations put the land of Ireland at his word.]

His victory roll is similar to that of the earlier panegyric written about 1588.[56] His first significant victory is seen again as his campaign against Sir Thomas Wyatt in the 1540s,[57] a campaign undertaken as Lieutenant of the Horse under Henry VIII. The poet who wrote 'Taghaim Tomás . . .' (*c.* 1588) mentions the favoured position he enjoyed under Henry VIII:

> . . . Cion mhic airdríogh ó Ching Hannrí
> fuair an seang-mhín séimh-ghlacach,
> 's do bhí an tréinfhear ag Cing Éadbhard
> 'na fhior aobhdha éinleabtha.
> (Carney, *Butler Poems,* No. 16, st. 74, lines
> 1749 to 1752, p. 74.)

[The slender, graceful, smooth-palmed one received a prince's portion from Henry VIII, and the warrior was the comely

---

[55] Carney, *Butler Poems*, p. 129.
[56] Carney, *Butler Poems*, No. 16.
[57] Carney, *Butler Poems*, pp 129, 130, l.1573n.

confidant (lit. bedfellow) of King Edward.][58]

The victorious campaign for the king in Scotland is mentioned in the same spirit as are his other victories in Ireland. Ormond, as part of the Lord Lieutenant Sussex's party in the 1550s, conducted a series of inconclusive campaigns against Shane O'Neill which included a considerable cattle prey.[59] The poet describes a similar incident thus:

Ar Seaán neartmhar Ó Néill
tug maidhm gér dheacar dhoi-séin;
as ní théarnó uaidh, gidh eadh,
éanbhó do bhuaibh a bhailteadh.
(Carney, *Butler Poems,* No. 15, st. 8, p. 68.)

[Though it was difficult, he defeated strong Shane O'Neill, indeed, he did not recover from him a single cow of the cattle of his homestead.]

A further victory against O'Neill is proudly recorded along with another victory in the territory of the Uí Bhroin in Leinster and in Mayo:

Gleann Con Cadhuin do chreach sin
is Gleann Mo-Lura a Laighnibh;
lá oile do hionnradh lais
na moighe um fhionnmhagh Iorrais.
(Carney, *Butler Poems,* No. 15, st. 19, p. 69.)

[He raided Gleann Con Cadhuin and Gleann Mo-Lura in Leinster, another day he attacked the fields about the fair plain of Iorrus.]

The raiding of Ulster, Leinster and Connacht are worthy expeditions for Ormond. The poet mentions Ormond's escapades in Munster, the

---

[58] P.A. Breatnach discusses the possible origins and implications of this conceit of the poet's 'feminine rôle' in complement to the 'masculinity' of the chief in 'The Chief's Poet', pp 38-45; and see James Carney, 'The Féuch Féin Controversy' pp 243-266 in Carney, *Studies in Irish Literature and History,* Dublin 1955.

[59] An account of a journey made by the earl of Sussex in 1563 described how the expedition '. . . came into a great plain by the Lough Naha. Mr Marshal with a few light horsemen discovered about 80 of Shane's kine which we took' (*CSPC, 1515-74,* p. 351) as cited in Carney, *Butler Poems,* p. 131, l. 1581-60. Cf. Carney, *Butler Poems,* st. 6, ll. 1781-4, p. 75.

defeat of Donal O'Brien, his banishment from the lordship of Thomond to France, and his nephew Conor being installed in his place as earl of Thomond.[60] There is no mention of the lord deputy, his soldiers or any crown initiative in this event, by the poet. Ormond is represented as making a raid, successfully on O'Brien's territory — taking the strongholds, subduing the chief:

> Bun Raite, gér thuar troda,
> an Clár is Cluain Rámhoda,
> siad re lúdh glanáigh do ghabh,
> gabháil na ndún géarbh iongnadh.
> (Carney, *Butler Poems,* No. 15, st. 10, p. 68.)

[Although it was a portent of fighting, he took Bun Raite, An Clár and Cluain Rámhoda in a swift successful movement, even though the takeover of the fortress was a surprise.][61]

The poet feels no compulsion to specify the role Ormond played, or indeed to see the replacement of Donal O'Brien 'chief of all his name', by his nephew Conor O'Brien as earl of Thomond as being in any way significant enough to warrant comment or mention. The same incident could be said to be referred to in the earlier poem 'Taghaim Tomás' in which the same attitude is taken towards Ormond's rôle and the significance of the event:

> Tug an Bhrianfhuil ar díth iarla,
> . . .'s do chuir don Fhraingc soir é re haimsir, . . .
> (Carney, *Butler Poems,* No. 16, st. 9, lines 1805
> and 1807, p. 76.)

[He left the O'Briens without an earl . . . and banished him east to France for a while.]

It is interesting to note that the earl was not banished, but rather Donal, chief of the O'Brien's was removed to make way for Conor who was the first earl so called. The poet used the term 'iarla' indiscriminately to denote illustrious status rather than a true title. The entire incident was not part of the process of the conquest of Ireland under the Tudors, but

---

60 See AFM, sub anno 1581, and see also Carney, *Butler Poems,* p. 131 l. 1593-1600n.
61 *CSPC.* 1515-74, p. 276, as cited in Carney, *Butler Poems,* p. 131, l. 1589-92n.

rather one of a number of victories attributed to Ormond by his Gaelic poet, on a par with several other skirmishes equally recorded. Likewise, the defeat of the Uí Bhriain, which was a government initiative, is listed simply as an Ormond event rather than as an official undertaking in which he played a prescribed rôle. Mág Craith, the poet, sees no reason here to bewail the destruction of the O'Brienship. The surrender of the O'Brien towns is recorded with pride as a tribute to Ormond:

> An Clár is Bun Raite a-ris
> do ghabh bhós — beag dá sheirbhís;
> do chreach an t-iath go humhal
> fá seach ar thriath Tuadhmhumhan.
> (Carney, *Butler Poems,* No. 15, st. 11, p. 68.)

[Yet again he took An Clár and Bun Raite — little to him the labour, he harried the territory in its turn into submission on the lord of Thomond.]

The earlier poem, 'Taghaim Tómás', written in accentual metre for Ormond deals with his victories over the Uí Shúilleabháin, the Uí Bhriain and the Uí Néill. His great status in England, as a court favourite, and a recipient of major titles and decorations is recorded in some detail:

> Fuair ón bprionnsa — mór a tharbha —
> spríos na Banbha braonghlaise;
> Libir lánmhur Tiobrad Árann
> fuair triath cráibhteach caomhChalluinn.
> Fuair tar oilbhéim bheith 'na Threisinér
> ós Iath inisréidh Fhéidhlime.
> Fuair sé d'airdchéim Ridireacht Gáirtéir,
> ainm nár ghnáth é ar Éirionnach.
> (Carney, *Butler Poems,* No. 16, st. 3, p. 74.)

[He received from the prince — great his benefit — the wine prisage(?) [62] of Banbha of the clear streams; he pious lord of gentle Callan received the liberty of plentiful Tipperary. Despite obstacle, he became Treasurer of Ireland (lit. of the land of Feidhlim's smooth island). In distinction of his nobility he received a knighthood of the garter, a title unusual among the Irish.]

---

[62] Carney, *Butler Poems,* p. 171.

It has been pointed out already that this poem was written about 1588 before the defeat of the Northern chief at Kinsale, before the same lords departed for the Continent in 1607. These events, however, and their supposed consequences have not influenced Mág Craith in his treatment of Ormond's victories over the Gaelic chiefs. His elegy for Ormond, written in or later than 1614, displays no sensitivity to, or even awareness of, the wider implications of Ormond's identity as an arm of the ever strengthening central administration. He deals with all of Ormond's campaigns in the context of the earl's identity as a raiding lord. There is no 'spirit of fatalism' pervading Mág Craith's poem for Ormond, no 'new awareness' following the 'massive psychological blows of the defeat at Kinsale'.[63]

The sorrow expressed by Mág Craith for the loss of Ormond is the sorrow of the poet after his lord's death/departure: the raider of Banbha has gone from his poet into the church/burial place:

Saoth leam — do chailg mo chroidhe —
bheith dó a ccill 'na chomhnoidhe,
creachthóir beann mbruachdhubh mBanbha
as gleann n-uathmhur n-allmhurdha.
(Carney, *Butler Poems*, No. 15, st. 43, p. 73.)

[It is distressful for me, my heart is pierced that he is living in the churchyard (lit. church, i.e. burial place); that he is dead, the raider of Banbha of the peaks of dark streams, and the fearful foreign valleys.]

Maol Seachluinn Ó hEoghusa wrote an elegy for Thomas Magauran (+ 1343) and stated:

Mág Shamhradháin an bheoil bhinn
ní beag an easbhaidh d'Éirinn;
mé [go] croidhe [gum] chneasghuin
[is é] like ar n-aoineasbhaidh.
(McKenna, *Magauran Poems,* No. 31, st. 4, p. 271.)

[Sweet worded Mág Shamhradháin is a great loss to Éire; it means my utter ruin piercing me to the heart.]

---

63 Dunne, 'Evidence', p. 16.

Mág Craith declares proudly, having proved it in several successive stanzas that there is no part of Ireland which Ormond has not visited i.e. subdued:

Ní fhuil éineang d'Inis Fáil
gan lord each Iarla Gabhráin,
as rian a chéimeann 's a chath
ar fhiadh Éireann dob eólach.
(Carney, *Butler Poems,* No. 15, st. 46, p. 73.)

[No area of Inis Fáil is unmarked by the hooves of the earl of Gabhrán's horse. His knowledge of Ireland is marked by his triumphs and his battles.]

It is interesting to consider the same motifs used by the poet Niall Ó hUiginn in reference to Thomas Magauran's (+1343) prodigious warlike feats throughout Ireland:

I ngach crích dar thaisdil Tomás
talamh naomh do-ní don chriaidh,
acht sleachta bróg gríbhe Gabhra
gan fhód fíre i mBanbha Bhriain.
(McKenna, *Magauran Poems,* No. 10, st. 26, p. 76.)

[The soil of every land where Tomás marched has become a holy land; no sod in all Brian's Banbha seems a rightful one if not marked by the shoe of the Griffin of Gabhair.]

The tone of the Ormond panegyric of the 1580s 'Taghaim Tómás' and that of the elegy by Mág Craith (*c.* 1614) show no development of any kind in the poets' perceptions of Ormond's power and position. In the poets' own context, therefore, from their particular perspective an event such as the Kinsale defeat, a retrospective watershed, has no existence as such in the composition of Mág Craith in 1614 for Ormond at any rate. Both poems are in a battle roll and encomiastic tradition of bardic composition.[64] That of Mág Craith combines these characteristics with the principal elements of the traditional elegy presented in traditional fashion. The poets' reality once again asserts itself above the restrictions placed upon it by later retrospective interpretation.

---

[64] Cf. Mac Airt, *Leabhar Branach,* No. 18, p. 61.

One can enter more fully into the mentality of those Gaelic Irish who sought to continue their lives within a recognizable or at least manageable framework, by refuting the postulation of a new bardic awareness; the development of new perceptions among the Gaelic aristocracy — articulated by the bardic poet — following the Kinsale defeat and the departure of the northern chiefs. This struggle for survival need not necessarily be looked upon as heroic, courageous, patriotic or foolhardy, but rather simply as the effort of a weakened, continually declining aristocratic class, whose survival techniques had stood them in good stead throughout the centuries to keep abreast of the changes occurring in their lifetime. These 'techniques' were applied in confidence, not in their success, but in their appropriateness for the occasion. It was, for instance, with confidence in his professional ability, the worthiness of the object of his work and some hopes of benefit or remuneration that the poet (now anonymous) undertook a panegyric for Elizabeth I.[65] The author is quite conceivably identical with that of the poem for Elizabeth I's kinsman Ormond — 'Taghaim Tomás'. Both poems were composed in the 1580s, both are in accentual metre.

This poem for Elizabeth I celebrates her personal beauty, and her power as a ruler. It opens with a pious dedication to 'an Airdmhic' [Christ] and a declaration of the poet's intention to write a poem for the princess of England [an phrionsa Shacsan]:

> I n-ainm an áirdmhic doghnídh grása
> is éinmhic álainn óghMhuire
> doghéan aiste do phrionnsa Shacsan
> cúmtha cneasta cóirighthe . . .
> (McErlean, *Dáibhí Ó Bruadair,* Pt. 3, No. 12,
> st. 1, p. 64.)

> [In the name of the High Son, maker of Grace, the beautiful only son of the Virgin Mary, I shall make a well-formed, suitable, correct poem for the prince of England . . .]

The poet provides a succint genealogy indicating the nobility of Elizabeth's antecedents:

> Dá theagh Sacsan no slógh seasmhach
> do ba cneasta comharsanacht

---

65 Mac Erlean, *Dáibhí Ó Bruadair,* pt. 3, No. 12.

an seachtmhadh Hannraí cathach
campaidheach
do na planndaoibh pórghlana
tug chum éintighe cuid dá séimhidheacht
an dá thigh réidhlígheach róschrothach
is í dar liomsa an cúigeadh prionnsa
ós a gcionnsa comhnaidhtheach.
(McErlean, *Dáithí Ó Bruadair*, Pt. 3, No. 12,
st.2, p. 66.)

[Two Houses of England of the steadfast hosts lived in mild
neighbourliness, warlike Henry VII of the camps, scion of the noble seeded plant, united them in one house, the two brilliant-hued,
rose-appearanced ('rose-emblemed' McErlean, p. 67) houses, she
is, I think, the fifth prince abiding over them.]

The praise of her physical beauty and attributes is that of any fair
patroness; hair, lips, teeth and eyes all conform to the poet's ideal; she is
fond of embroidery and significantly, generous to poets and learned
men:

. . . atá sí gréasach, scéimheamhail,
scéimheach
béarlamhail béasach beoilchliste
cuid do thréidhthibh na mná séimhe
a grádh d'fhéile is d'eolachaibh . . .
(McErlean, *Dáithí Ó Bruadair*, Pt. 3, No. 12,
st. 3, p. 66.)

[. . . she is skilled in embroidery, beautiful, graceful, voluble,
well-mannered, clever one of the traits of this graceful woman is
her love of poets and the learned . . .][66]

The poet's description of Elizabeth's physical appearance is that of any
noble Gaelic woman:

Atá ar an mbainríoghain . . .
— muarfholt muirearach, dualach,
druimneach

---

[66] Cf. McKenna, *Magauran Poems*, No. 17, sts. 28 and 32, pp 137, 139.

cuachach, cruipineach comhdhlaghthach
suanrosc soilbhir ós gruadh dheirgghil
mar ghual gcrithearach gcróluisneach . . .
(McErlean, *Dáibhí Ó Bruadair,* Pt. 3, No. 12,
st. 4, p. 66.)

[This Queen has . . . great heavy masses of braided ridged hair,
[which is] curled, wavy and interloped, a cheerful languid eye, a
bright red cheek, like a blood-red sparkling coal.]

Brian Magauran's daughter Gormlaidh (*c.* 1300) shared these physical
characteristics with Elizabeth I, as both are typically described;
Gormlaidh is depicted by Maol Pádraig Mac Naimhín thus:

I bhfult Ghormlaidhe as ghorm súl
dan mongbhuidhe gach corn caomh
casaidh fannmhuine fionn fiar
ós chionn chiabh gclannbhuidhe gclaon.
(McKenna, *Magauran Poems,* No. 9, st. 21, p. 65.)

[In blue-eyes Gormlaidh's hair which makes every fair ringlet
bushy and yellow, a great waving bush bends down over the soft
yellow curling tresses.]

Elizabeth I's military exploits are recounted in the same fashion and
with the same zeal as that displayed by Ormond's eulogists and that of
Hugh mac Shane O'Byrne. The poet naturally chooses some legendary
and mythical proto-types for Elizabeth; Caesar, King Arthur and Hector are the ancestors of Elizabeth in prudence, valour and power:

Ó d'éag Caesar sluaghach séiseach
buadhach béasach beoneartmhar,
nó cing Ártúr iongantach árdchlúdhach
cumasach cáirdeamhail comhgairseach
níl 'na bheathaidh is ní dheachaidh
tar éis hEachtoir óigchleasaigh
rí mar Eilís ghrádhmhair gheilchlídhigh
bhláthmhair bheigchíghigh bheoltsoithimh.
(McErlean, *Dáithí Ó Bruadair,* Pt. 3, No. 12,
st. 6, p. 68.)

[Since Caesar of the hosts and companies, victorious, exemplary, vigorous, or wonderful, famous, King Arthur — the powerful, friendly neighbourly one — died, there lives not, nor has there departed after Hector, the wiley youth, a sovereign like the loving bright-bosomed, beautiful, small-breasted, smooth-lipped Elizabeth.]

The poet in time-honoured fashion thus provides analogous figures from historical mythology for Elizabeth I's attributes. She is a Caesar, an Arthur, a Hector in power, victory and hosts.

The poet goes on to list her individual exploits throughout Europe and the Americas. Ireland is protected too by her powerful hosts:

> . . . féach Éire aice i gcléith Sacsan
> re taobh Breatan bórdghlaine
> is cuid dá cródhacht is lé Plóndras
> an tír nóghlan nóschruthach.
> (McErlean, *Dáibhí Ó Bruadair,* Pt. 3, No. 12,
> st. 7, p. 68.)

[Behold she has Ireland under the English hosts, (McErlean: 'she holds Erin in Ireland's protection) on the borders of bright-surfaced Britain, and part of her valour, she owns Flanders, the fresh bright, nobly-fashioned country.][67]

Elizabeth also holds the tribute of France, the wealth of Scotland, the treasures of Philip of Spain; but all this wealth flows to and from her with the regularity of the waves because of her generosity:

> Cíos na Fraince ionnmhus Alban
> 'na múr dealbhach dóibhriste
> stór cing Philib 's a chuid cupard
> 'na cúirt chrutha chomharba
> cíos na cruinne sa bheith aice,
> níl air filleadh feoirlinne
> acht uaithe is chuice do nós tuinne
> do gach fine i bhfóirithin.
> (McErlean, *Dáithí Ó Bruadair,* Pt. 3, No. 12,
> st. 8, p. 70.)

---

[67] Mac Erlean, in *Dáibhí Ó Bruadair,* pt. 3, p. 69, notes that in 1588 Elizabeth I was chosen by the clergy of Friesland as their sovereign.

[In her well-formed, impregnable fortress is the tribute of France and the wealth of Scotland, in her shapely inherited court are King Philip's treasures and his cupboards, though she has the tribute of the world [68] not a farthing is returned, rather, after the fashion of the waves it comes to her and leaves her, giving help to each sept.]

As with other great chiefs and lords, God himself and the elements assist Elizabeth I to her victories which include the defeat of Spain [69] and the sack of Lisbon:

> Atá dia ag congnamh le triath Lonndan
> na n-iath bhfonnmhar bhfódtar thach
> atáid na gaethe, atáid na spéire
> atá gach réalta rósholas . . .
> (McErlean, *Dáibhí Ó Bruadair*, Pt. 3, No. 12,
> st. 13, p. 72.)

[God is helping the lords of London of the cheerful, fertile lands, the winds (or 'rays of sunlight') the skies, and every brightly shinging star [is helping her] . . .]

The poet celebrates Elizabeth's battalions and their European escapades:

> D'fhág a gárda fá chás Spáinigh
> 's a mná cráidhte comhthuirseach
> thugadar goradh géar uatha don
> Phoirtingéil
> le sluagh borblaoch beochroidheach
> dia 's a tionól gliadhmhar groidbheo
> 's iad tug Liosbóin leonuighthe
> aicme laoch ainmhear thairgthréan
> thairpeach
> each (radh) dhaorarmthach orduightheach.
> (McErlean, *Dáibhí Ó Bruadair*, Pt. 3, No. 12,
> st. 14, p. 74.)

---

[68] Or 'Corunna', see Mac Erlean, *Dáibhí Ó Bruadair*, pt. 3, p. 71, note 2.

[69] In the context of the later sixteenth century, the poet's pride in Elizabeth's defeat of Spain is to be noted, considering FitzMaurice's recourse to Spain a decade earlier and the northern overtures to Spain a decade later.

[Her guards left the Spaniards in distress, and her women (of Spain) afflicted and grieving, a host of arrogant, bright-hearted warriors dealt Portugal a severe burning; God and her battling, rapid hosts took injured Lisbon; a battalion of pompous, strength-producing [McErlean 'resourceful'] overbearing warriors, expensively armed, mounted and orderly.]

This poem to Elizabeth cannot be regarded merely as an uncharacteristic aberrative work by a self-seeking poet, whose dependence upon Elizabeth's kinsman, Ormond, demanded that he curry favour with his patron's monarch.[70] Neither can it be read as an unusually oblique example of poetic irony. This panegyric by an unknown poet is rather a perfectly acceptable example of bardic panegyric written in honour of the English monarch — acknowledging the power of that monarch, and utterly indifferent, within the confines of the literary medium, to the complex questions of Anglo-Irish relations.[71]

The poets flourished in and celebrated an aristocratic life-style and condition of existence. They also worked on the basis of individual experience where the erosion of their status was concerned. The affliction of the northern poets in the immediate aftermath of their patron's departure is confined to them, and to poems written for the patrons involved. For instance, Fearghal Óg Mac a' Bhaird's lament for Red Hugh O'Donnell: 'Teasda Éire san Easbáinn . . .', is quite compatible with his later eulogy for James I: 'Trí coróna i gcairt Shéamais . . .' from the poet's perception of his position and that of his patron. O'Donnell was his departed patron, dead in a foreign country — Ireland because of his death, is ruined and leaderless. Just as the elements proclaimed Elizabeth I's glory, so they commiserate with Ireland in her great loss:

Arthrach gan sdiúir Banbha Breagh
do bháidh a bhás glóir Ghaoidheal;
tug tar tealaigh Dha-Thí thuinn

---

[70] Mac Erlean, *Dáibhí Ó Bruadair,* pt. 3, introduction to poem no. 12, pp 64-5.

[71] The poet's knowledge of contemporary European events is noteworthy in the light of Canny's comment regarding the ignorance of European current affairs and politics prevalent among the poets in the pre-seventeenth century period. Canny, 'Formation', p. 93, and cf. Ó Cuív, *New History of Ireland,* vol. III, chapter 20.

deaghail dí ris Ó nDomhnaill.
(Breatnach, 'Marbhnadh Aodha Ruaidh Uí
Dhomhnaill', st. 14, p. 37.)

[Ireland is a ship without a rudder. His death has drowned the glory of the Gaels. Her parting with O'Donnell has brought a wave over Ireland.]

furthermore:

Tuar uathbháis treathan na dtonn:
tuar uilc ruithneadh na réltonn:
tuar díbheirge niamh na néll:
sgiamh fhírfheirge ar an aiér.
(Breatnach, 'Marbhnadh Aodha Ruaidh Uí Dhomhnaill', st. 24, p. 39.)

[The fury of the waves is a portent of horror; the shining of the stars is an omen of evil: the colour of the clouds is a presage of vengeance; sky has a look of true anger.]

The atmosphere of menace can hardly have been more vividly depicted in this stanza by Fearghal Óg Mac a' Bhaird. The traditional use by the bards of the elemental sympathy is compounded with the popular widespread belief in apocalypic omens and natural premonitions in the early seventeenth century.[72] The anguish and torment so graphically and so traditionally described thus give way to great jubilation on the accession, in 1603, of James I to the throne. Fearghal Óg Mac a' Bhaird was joined in his celebration of James in 'Trí coróna . . .' by another northern poet, Eochaidh Ó hEodhusa in 'Mór theasda dh'obair Óivid . . .'[73]

There is, of course, nothing remarkable about the fact that either or both poets should see fit to hail the new monarch of England as the new hope of Ireland, the saviour of Banbha. That James Stuart could rightfully claim descent from a historico-mythical family, the three Collas, endeared him all the more to genealogically sensitive poets. The phenomenon of the poets writing in favour of the crown, the monarch

---

[72] Keith Thomas' *Religion and the Decline of Magic,* is an authoritative work on the prevalence of millenarianism and superstition of various kinds in England during the sixteenth and seventeenth centuries.
[73] Breatnach, 'Metamorphosis 1603', in *Éigse,* 17 (1977-8).

or the administration does not arise from the peculiar circumstances of the early seventeenth century. Indeed, a selection of poems from the fourteenth century to the seventeenth century, inclusive, could be made to indicate the willingness of the poets to support the claims of the monarch of England in proportion to the success of the claims and, or, the known allegience of the patron. Quite often the situation is hardly as complex as that. Gofraidh Fionn Ó Dálaigh's eulogy for Maurice fitz-Maurice, second Earl of Desmond (+ 1358)[74] involves an interesting compliment to fitzMaurice based upon the fact that Maurice is a liegeman of the King of England, and is at the time of writing the poem, visiting him. The poet is not concerned that Sir Maurice should have such connections with an extra-insular monarch. The English king is a powerful, prestigious, individual, his relationship with the poet's patron reflects honour on both patron and poet.

In a poem to Éamonn na Féasóige Burke, Mac William Íochtair (+ 1458), the poet Tadhg Óg Ó hUiginn bewails the lawlessness of Gael and *Gall* in Ireland and their failure to recognize the king's writ:

> Do briseadh riaghail ríogh Sacsann,
> seadh cairte ní chomhaill Gall;
> gan neach ann do réir a riaghla
> gach Gall féin is iarla ann.
> (McKenna, *Aithdioghluim Dána,* No. 38, st. 1, p. 152.)

> [The law of the Saxon's Kings has often been broken; the Goill set no store by legal document; none of them obeying the king's law, each of them is an Earl for himself.]

Ó hUiginn deplores the laxity of the new Earls, unlike their ancestors, they have ignored the law, that of the English king:

> Lorg na n-Iarladh ní headh leantar
> gan luadh cirt ag an chath Ghall;
> a grás nochan fhuighe oidhreacht
> duine go fás oirbheart ann.
> (McKenna, *Aithdioghluim Dána,* No. 38, st. 3, p. 152.)

> [The way of the old Earls is not followed, the Gall making no account of justice; a man's inheritance will get no recognition except when he has strength to fight.]

---

[74] Bergin, *Irish Bardic Poetry,* No. 17.

As though in explanation, Ó hUiginn's next stanza informs us that for some time now Gaelic law is being replaced by that of the king; a law, by inference, superior:

> Do haithigheadh d'éis a chéile
> fa chrích Fódla fada an ré
> dligheadh an ríogh ar reacht nGaoidheal,
> reacht nach gníomh le haoinfhear é.
> (McKenna, *Aithdioghluim Dána,* No. 38, st. 4, p. 152.)

[For long past throughout Éire the King's law has been gradually coming into use instead of the law of the Gaoidhil, which is not held binding by folk now.]

Here we must remember to whom Ó hUiginn is addressing the poem; Éamonn na Féasóige, Mac William Íochtair is of course an Anglo-Norman lord, member of the great de Burgo family. Consequently, Ó hUiginn can be expected to support the extension of English law, in as much as it increases Mac William's power:

> Iomadh ó Luimneach na learg n-uaine
> go hArd Macha — mór an gníomh,
> go dtí cobhair ann ó Iarla-
> Gall i n-aghaidh riaghla an ríogh.
> (McKenna, *Aithdioghluim Dána,* No. 38, st. 6, p. 153.)

[From green-sloped Luimneach up to Ard Macha many a Gall, alas! is set against the King's law; let an Earl now come to set this right.]

Éamonn is to reclaim Eamhain Macha from the Uí Néill — the ancient charter of the de Burgo granted Ulster to that family. Éamonn must demand his birthright. Far from indicating his dismay or horror at the impositions of foreigners upon legendary Macha, the poet declares that Eamhain Macha is ruined following the departure of the Goill:

> Ná héagcaoin [a] Eamhain Macha
> — mithidh dhúinn gan déanamh thort —
> a bhfoighe do bhroid a mbliadhna
> 's a ghoire dhoid Iarla ort.
> (McKenna, *Aithdioghluim Dána,* No. 38, st. 7, p. 153.)

[We can no longer do without thee, O Eamhain of Macha; weep not for the trouble thou mayest now endure, an Earl is now coming so soon to thee.]

An Anglo-Norman lord must rescue (Eamhain Macha) Ulster from the Uí Néill. The poet is quite willing to countenance the replacement of the Gaelic Uí Néill by the Anglo-Norman Mac William. No consideration of the appropriateness of Uí Néill over Mac William as titular or actual ruler of Ulster enters into his treatment of the subject. Anyone who can sustain his claim to 'Eamhain Macha' is its true ruler. This is the fundamental principle which supports the poet in the following verse:

Ní bhia [áit i raibh] ráith Eamhna
ar iasocht ag aicme Néill;
is í as aitreabh do na nIarlaibh
faicthear í ga fiadhnaibh féin.
(McKenna, *Aithdioghluim Dána,* No. 38, st. 8, p. 153.)

[The site of the fort of Eamhain shall be only for a short time held by Niall's race on loan; it is the dwelling of the Earls; let it be seen testifying to this.]

Ó hUiginn accuses the Uí Néill of usurping the birthright of the Mac William to the ancient Ulster seat. The departure of the foreign earls has reduced Eamhain Macha and the Uí Néill as a result of Mac William's absence in Ulster, have usurped Clann William's birthright:

Eamhain Macha na múr bhfairsing
a bhfuair d'anshódh ar éis Ghall
ag urra muna bhé a mbliadhna
cuma lé gan Iarla ann.
(McKenna, *Aithdioghluim Dána,* No. 38, st. 9, p. 153.)

[As for the woes afflicting big-walled Eamhain Macha after the departure of the Goill, unless some one stop them this year, she (being destroyed) will not care about the existence of an Earl.]

The disposition of the charter of at least half of Ireland (northern half) is in this instance in the hands of the King of England. Ó hUiginn is willing to abide by the King's charter to Mac William even in the case of Eamhain Macha. His allegiance in this regard is directed by the ideal allegiance of his patron to the English king:

Ná sirthear libh acht leath Banbha,
ná beiridh acht an bhreath rug;
do bhreith an ríogh is í t'oidhreacht;
do sgríobh an rí an toirbheart thug.
(McKenna, *Aithdioghluim Dána,* No. 38, st. 15, p. 154.)

[Demand then only half of Banbha, abide by the King's decision;
that decision states it to be thy inheritance; he put in writing what
he gave thee.]

Ó hUiginn emphasizes the martial origin of Mac William's claims on
Ulster. These, he emphatically supports as legitimate grounds for claims
by Mac William to Uí Néill territory. Once again the rightful authority
of the Saxon king over the disposition of territories in Ireland is not only
undisputed but insisted upon. Deference to the King's wishes, laws and
charters are the advice of Ó hUiginn to Éamonn Burke. In support of
Burke's claims in Ulster and Connacht he sketches the sept's successful
career from 'Uilliam Conquer', the first Earl who conquered Banbha
with the King's permission:

Muinntear an ríogh fa rian cogaidh
do chosmanmh Fhódla an fheoir thigh
do bhí d'aontoil aga fhastadh;
do aontoigh rí Sacsan sin.
(McKenna, *Aithdioghluim Dána*, No. 38, st. 19, p. 154.)

He was eagerly mustering in battle-array the King's folk to conquer soft-grassed Fódla; the Saxon's king had agreed to this.]

to Éamonn, whose numerous victories over the Gael, were they recounted, would cause resentment:

Do shluaighidh mheince, a Mhic Uilliam,
a n-áireamh ar t-earla nocht
ní bheinn gan fholaidh dá n-áirmhinn;
omhain leinn a n-áirmhim ort.
(McKenna, *Aithdioghluim Dána,* No. 38, st. 40, p. 156.)

[To tell of all thy many raids, O Mac Uilliam of the flowing locks,
would rouse resentment; even what I have said makes me fear.]

The main body of the poem consists of lists of victories of William the
Conquerer and Éamonn's over the powerful Gaelic septs. This poem is

the poet's articulation of one of the major principles in aristocratic Gaelic Ireland, as expressed by the poets from the thirteenth century to the end of the seventeenth. Tadhg Óg Ó hUiginn supports Mac William's claims against the Uí Néill in Ulster, because William the Conquerer — ancestor to Éamonn, won them by the sword, under the patronage of the English king. [75] As an Anglo-Norman lord, his ultimate allegiance is to the English monarch: Ó hUiginn therefore demands that all Ireland be subject to Éamonn, and thus to the laws of the king:

A-taoi, a Éamoinn mhac mheic Éamainn,
d'fhuil Iarladh as uaisle crú;
críoch Banbha go ndeach fad dhaoirse
leath a tarbha dhaoibhse is dú.
(McKenna, *Aithdioghluim Dána,* No. 38, st. 46, p. 157.)

[O Éamonn, son of Éamonn's son, thou art of the most noble blood of the Earls; thou shouldst enjoy a half of Banbha while waiting for the whole of it to be beneath thy sway.]

The sixteenth century Ó hUiginn poet, Tadhg Dall, eulogized a later Burke chief. The fundamental theme of his eulogy is celebration of rule by right of conquest. [76] Just as Tadhg Óg Ó hUiginn validated Éamonn na Féasóige's claims in the 1450s, so does Tadhg Dall in the sixteenth century validate the contemporary Mac William's position. Both poets wrote in full consciousness of the *de facto* power of the chief, exult in his glory and accommodate him within the framework of bardic historico-traditional rationale.

In the poem for Elizabeth I, the poet suggests that '(atá) Dia ag congnamh le triath Lonndan . . .' [77] [God is helping the lord of London . . .] so too does Tadhg Óg Ó hUiginn declare that God helped William the Conquerer in his initial struggle for mastery in Banbha:

Do-rinnis creich re cois abhann,
a Éamoinn, 'n-a haithle sin
go Dún nDoidhre is í do fhásaigh;
do bhí an Coimdhe an lásain libh.
(McKenna, *Aithdioghluim Dána,* No. 38, st. 30, p. 155.)

---

[75] McKenna, *Aithdioghluim Dána,* No. 38, sts. 17-19, p. 154.
[76] E. Knott, *Tadhg Dall,* No. 17, p. 120.
[77] Mac Erlean, *Dáibhí Ó Bruadair,* pt. 3, No. 12, st. 13, p. 72.

[When thou didst plunder along the river (i.e. Síonann) as far as Dún Doidhre, that raid left it destroyed; the Lord helped thee that day.]

Neither poet considered the foreign 'lord' for whom they wrote to be unworthy in any way of God's help in their efforts to subdue Ireland. The acquisition of power and its maintenance by the sword is a value deeply entrenched in the bardic ethos. Those wielding power already acquired were lauded in their strength — as Mac William by Tadhg Óg, Ormond, by Flann Mág Craith and Elizabeth by the unknown poet. Individuals seeking to extend their power were also equally emphatically exhorted to do so. The two Ó hUiginn poets, Tadhg Óg of the fiteenth century and Tadhg Dall of the sixteenth century, were also the authors of some of the most memorable poems of exhortation to their respective Gaelic patrons.

Tadhg Óg Ó hUiginn's poem for Maolruanadh Ó Cearbhaill, lord of Éile (*c.* 1441-1443),[78] exhorts the chief to seize his territory. Ó hUiginn makes extensive use of the 'unity of Banbha' motif in his exhortation. He is the same poet who urged Mac William to seize 'half of Banbha' of his right according to the King's charter. To Ó Cearbhaill, lord of Éile, however, he emphasizes the ignominy of Banbha's disunity and cites the '*Goill*' as the ever-ready enemy:

Déanaidh comhaonta, a chlann Éibhir,
budh iomdha i n-aghaidh bhur gclann,
náir gan bhur gcungnamh re chéile,
urlamh mbáigh an ghléire Gall.
(McKenna, *Aithdioghluin Dána,* No. 26, st. 1, p. 100.)

[Be ye united, O children of Éibhear; many are your foes; shame on you not to help each other; the bravest of the Goill are ever ready to attack you.]

Ó hUiginn goes on to describe the usurpation of the south by the *Goill*:

Fear a cosanta i gcloinn Eoghain
ná agaibh féin — féachaidh sin —
ó nach faicim, a chlann Cháirthinn,

---

[78] McKenna, *Aithdioghluim Dána,* introduction to No. 26, p. 100.

aicill Gall do ráidhfinn ribh.
(McKenna, *Aithdioghluim Dána,* No. 26, st. 3,
p. 101.)

[As I see not in Eoghan Mór's race any man able to save Éire or
among you either, O race of Cáirtheann — you see it yourselves —
I can only tell you to look out for the Goill.]

The same poet had exhorted Mac William Íochtair to reclaim Uí Néill
territory for themselves — foreigners who had been granted Ulster in an
English king's charter. Now, however, he presents a dismal picture of
the chiefs of Leath Mogha in bondage — waiting for Ó Cearbhaill's
emergence:

A-tá ag Gallaibh an glas céadna
ar chloinn Táil — cá truaighe ceas!
ní fhuil acht deoraidh i ndaoirse
d'fhuil Eoghain don taoibhse theas.
(McKenna, *Aithdioghluim Dána,* No. 26, st. 5, p. 101.)

[The Goill, alas! have fixed their chains on the race of Tál; also the
race of Eoghan in the South are exiles in bonds.]

Tadhg Dall Ó hUiginn's poem for Brian O'Rourke, lord of Breifne
(*c.* 1566-1591),[79] a century and a half later impresses upon the chief the
necessity for warfare with the Goill, that, indeed, the only way to remain
peaceful with them is to make war with them. This poem, far from con-
tradicting his poem for Mac William in the same period, merely further
illustrates the attitude towards power and its acquisition in the rationale
of the bardic poets and of facets of the world view of the Gaelic
aristocracy: power is to be sought by war and maintained by war if
necessary. Victory is an automatic vindication of the victor's position.
Ó hUiginn can therefore with perfect consistency declare to Ó
Cearbhaill:

D'ógbhaidh Bhreagh gi bé lén feirde
fir Saxan do síodhoghadh,
ní beag so dá dhíon, mar dearar,

---

[79] Knott, *Tadhg Dall,* vol. II, p. 251, note 16.

bíodh sealadh dá síorfoghal.
(Knott, *Tadhg Dall*, No. 16, st. 2, p. 108.)

[If anyone amongst the warriors of Bregia deem it well to pacify
the Saxons, let this will suffice for his protection, so it is said; let
him spend a while continually spoiling them.]

It is fascinating to note that both poets remark upon the principle of the
right of the sword, each time for different reasons, with different intent;
but its frequency certainly indicates the pervasion of this principle in the
functioning of the Gaelic aristocratic polity and of its characteristic
endemic warfare. Tadhg Óg, addressing Éamonn Burke, castigates this
tendency to seize power arbitrarily and remarks that this situation
prevails because of widespread flouting of the King's law:

Orraim ag an fhior bhus treise
tiomchall Éireann — anba an tnúdh —
is eadh budh áil le gach n-aicme;
do-cháidh seadh na cairte ar gcúl.
(McKenna, *Aithdioghluim Dána,* No. 38, st. 2,
p. 152.)

[About Éire the principle of them all is respect for the strong man;
fearful their greed; all respect for law is gone.]

In Tadhg Dall's case, when supporting a later Mac William, it behoves
him to support this very system, to validate Mac William's claims:

Ní fuil cóir uirre ag aoinfear
críoch suaitheanta seanGhaoidheal,
bheith fa neart an té is treise —
is é ceart na críchese.
(Knott, *Tadhg Dall,* No. 17, st. 2, p. 120.)

[No one man has any lawful claim to the shining land of the ancient Gaels. The law of this territory is that it shall be subjugate to
him who is strongest.]

However, exhorting Brian O'Rourke to rid the country of foreigners, he
manipulates this principle by suggesting that only in war can the Gael
secure peace from the Gall, throughout Ireland only the warlike man

secures peace; Brian must do battle with the English.[80] Yet another Ó hUiginn poet, Irial, in a eulogy for Cú Chonnacht Maguire, lord of Fermanagh, (1566-1589), lauds Maguire for his appreciation of the 'raiding' principle. Maguire understands the necessity and desirability of war in the context of the Gaelic polity:

Tithe Cláir Chuinn do chomhdha
do bhí i ndán do dhruim fhaghla,
sé re ccath do légh liobhra
iomdha sgeul ac brath Bhanbha.
(Greene, *Maguire Poems,* No. 10, st. 12, p. 92.)

[Ireland was fated to be ruled as a result of raiding; before battle he read books — many stories in which this was revealed concerning Ireland.]

The complexities of the allegiances articulated by the bardic poets are not therefore identifiable as being racial or sectarian in origin. The eulogy for Elizabeth I illustrates both elements since she was both English and head of the established church. It was sufficient that Elizabeth was enthroned and successful in her martial undertakings. Against such a background, therefore, one does not need to 'justify' Eochaidh Ó hEodhusa's or Fearghal Óg Mac a' Bhaird's eulogies for James I. Many catholics welcomed the prospect of a monarch disposed, as it was thought, to religious toleration,[81] especially those for whom religious differences created increasing cases of conflict of loyalty between crown and pope. It is not necessary, however, to be aware of this essentially catholic expectation in order to account for the existence of

---

[80] Knott, *Tadhg Dall,* No. 16, st. 1, p. 108.

[81] See Carol Z. Weiner, 'The Beleaguered Isle: a study in Elizabethan and Jacobin Anti-Catholicism', in *Past and Present,* No. 52 (May 1971). See also John Bossy, 'The Character of Elizabethan Catholicism' in *Past and Present,* No. 21 (April 1962), p. 43 in which he makes the following remark concerning the values which directed the loyalties of the catholic gentry:

'Whatever disturbed this hierarchy, they resented. Heresy disturbed it by upsetting the spiritual order which sanctioned it; fidelity and heresy were incompatible because heresy was infidelity to God. Protestantism particularly disturbed it because it was a religion of "basket-makers and beer-brewers". But the Pope had no more right to interfere with it than anyone else, and they took no notice when he relieved them of their duty of fidelity to the Queen.'

those accountable to a different schema. The world view accommodated within the literary framework of the bardic poets had its own rationale for the praise of an English monarch or any other individual. For James I was an illustrious and powerful king. His position as liege of their patrons exalted both them and the poet. Their evaluation of his worthiness of bardic eulogy was made not according to what modern historians see as the contemporary 'political reality' of the Kinsale defeat, the imminent plantation of Ulster, but according to the traditional bardic perception of the status of a powerful monarch. The poet's depiction of the status and power of individual chiefs has been shown to be drawn from a perspective which ignored our sense of 'political reality'. So also does their eulogizing of James I assume a traditional tone, suited to the poet's own perception of the accession to the throne of a king to whom they felt they could lay legitimate claim. James I's Gaelic Irish connections were hotly disputed by two poets as part of the famed mid-seventeenth century contention; 'Iomarbháigh na bhFileadh'.[82] This element in the dispute centered not around James I's descent from the Dál Riada kings, but rather whether Leath Mogha or Leath Chuinn had greater claim to be regarded as his ancestors' birthplace. The Northerner, Aodh Ó Domhnaill, claimed James I for Leath Chuinn, and listed the septs with whom he could claim kinship:

De shíol Iughoine as bhuan bladh
ríoghradh uaisle na hAlban
le Séamus aniú ma le
Sacsa, Alba agus Éire.
Dá shíol fós i nÉirinn uill
Osraidhe, Laighin, Leath Chuinn
Dál bhFiatach, Dál Riada a-le
Baisgne Músgraidhe Déise.
(McKenna, *Iomarbháigh na bhFileadh* I, No. 15,
sts. 26 and 27, p. 138.)

[Of Iughoine's ever-glorious stock are the princes of the nobility of Alba. To James belong to-day England, Alba, Éire.
Of his seed in great Éire are the Osraidhe, the Laighin, all Leath Chuinn, Dál bhFiatach, Dál Riada too, Baisgne, Músgraidhe, Déises.]

---

[82] Cited in Breandán Ó Buachalla, 'Cing Séamas', p. 126.

These claims were countered by those of the Southern poet Tadhg Mac Dáire, supporting the claims of the Munstermen who saw Máine Leamhna Mac Coirc — King of Munster — as James I's ancestor:

An rí deire — Dia dá dhíon —
fada go léighfinn duit díom,
d'fhuil Mhaine Leamhna Mhic Chuirc
Leamhnach Alban go hordhuirc.
(McKenna, *Iomarbháigh na bhFileadh* II, No. 18,
st. 55, p. 184.)

[The king you mention — God preserve him! — far be it from me to yield him up to you! He is of the race of Maine Leamhna, Corc's son, Alba's famous Leamhnach.][83]

For both poets, Fearghal Óg Mac a Bhaird and Eochaidh Ó hEodhusa, one of James I's most significant characteristics was his acknowledged authority over three kingdoms: England, Scotland and Ireland. Neither poet finds it necessary to emphasize James I's undoubted Gaelic connections. This element is taken for granted in their treatment of him.

Eochaidh Ó hEodhusa's poem 'Metamorphosis' (*c.* 1603) is a straightforward eulogy in which the poet ascribes the revitalization of the kingdom to the accession of the new and rightful monarch. The poet makes use of Ovid's 'Metamorphosis' to develop his theme of the transformation of Banbha under the auspicious influence of James's reign. He suggests that Ovid's work would now have to be revised since a new stage had been achieved owing to the miraculous changes wrought by James I's ascent to the throne of three kingdoms:

Mór theasda dh'obair Óivid
leis ar tús do tionóilid
(sgéala suthain láimh ar láimh)
fréamha cruthaidh is claochláidh.
(Breatnach, 'Metamorphosis', st. 1, p. 171.)

---

[83] Breandán Ó Buachalla summarized the barrage of genealogical ramifications claimed for James I on his ascent to the throne:
'Acht ní amháin go raibh gaol ag Séamas le ríthe Uladh agus le ríthe na Mumhan araon, bhíothas ábalta a thaispeáint chomh haithitheach céanna go raibh gaol díreach freisin aige le Cathal Crobhdhearg agus ríthe Connacht, agus le Diarmaid Mac Murchadha agus ríthe Laighean — ginealach gan smál gan aon agó.' In 'Cing Séamas', p. 126.

[Much is wanting from Ovid's work; he first gathered together the roots of creation and metamorphosis a lasting seal balanced equally.]

Ó hEodhusa makes extensive use of contrasting evil and good, attributing everything bright and good to James's presence, everything dark and evil to his absence. This is the traditional bardic practice of associating prosperity and fertility with a good or popular ruler, and conversely association deprivation and loss with his absence. Everything is utterly changed by the arrival of James, dark changes to light, the timid are protected, war is banished:

Tillidh deallradh gach doircheacht,
díbridh eagna anfhoirfeacht;
an ghlóir a n-oighreacht re headh,
foirneart gach bróin do báitheadh.
(Breatnach, 'Metamorphosis', st. 4, p. 172.)

[Brightness repulses all darkness, wisdom banishes imperfection; for a time glory is their heritage; the violence of all sorrow has been vanquished.]

James is credited with the 'unification' of the energies of the rival powers, this is left sufficiently obscure to facilitate its application in general:

Do éirigh d'aithrighthibh ann
éincheann ar iomad colann,
cosg gach uilc d'aobhdhacht ré a n-ucht
cuirp a n-aonchorp ré hannsacht.
(Breatnach, 'Metamorphosis', st. 10, p. 173.)

[Amongst the changes now a single head has risen up on many bodies; a joy to restrain all harm is in store for them — (many) bodies united in one body by affection.]

The cause of this new 'unity' and joy is directly attributable to James:

An ghrian loinneardha do las;
sgaoileadh gach ceó Cing Séamas;
tug 'na glóir comhorchra cháigh:
móir na comhortha claochláidh.
(Breatnach, 'Metamorphosis', st. 13, p. 174.)

[The brilliant sun lit up; king James is the dispersal of all mist; the joint mourning of all he changed to glory; great the signs of change.]

His good will and the benefits of his reign will be felt in more than one kingdom:

Ionann san uile dhomhan
as oircheas a fhiadhoghadh
luibh fhóirthe chiach gach cridhe,
ní fhóirfe ar iath dh'áiridhe.
(Breatnach, 'Metamorphosis', st. 19, p. 175.)

[Equally it befits all the world to welcome him; the herb that relieves the grief of every heart will not succour any one land in particular.]

It is especially interesting to see how Ó hEodhusa's perception of English monarchic succession mirrors that of the perceptions of the transfer of power traditionally articulated by the bardic poets. Elizabeth I dies before James's accession, her death is unwelcome in itself, it is the fortuitous occasion, however, of the raising of James to the throne. [84] This is the poet's typical treatment of the transfer of power involved in death or defeat or victory; the intensity of the disruption or desolation they feel is measured to emphasize the elation they experience at the advent of a new lord, or king, in this instance. Ó hEodhusa notes that the death of Elizabeth was fortuitous only in that it provided the occasion by which James VI of Scotland became monarch of England. Though Eochaidh Ó hEodhusa must have been very much aware of recent military reverses suffered by his own Ulster chiefs at the hands of Elizabeth's generals, the death of Red Hugh in Spain and the unsettled condition of Ulster in general, no mention is made of Elizabeth's part in this. The poet's composition is not concerned with reflecting the local contemporary political events, but with appropriating for the Gaelic world the new order being ushered in by the new monarch. He achieves this by providing a traditional interpretation of the major events such as the accession of a new king to the throne, the implications of which he rationalizes by dealing with them in a manner which accommodates

---

[84] Cf. J. Goldberg, *James I and the Politics of Literature,* especially pp 24-6.

them in the Gaelic world view. Therefore Elizabeth is described as 'an céad shoillse' (the first brightness); her death 'bearradh flaithis bhfear Lunndan' (the curtailment of the sovereignty of the men of London):

> Óig Lonndan lór do ghrádsa
> fuairsiod fios na cclaochládh sa;
> deallradh éagcoimse as an tig
> an chéadshoillse an tann tairnig.
> (Breatnach, 'Metamorphosis', st. 11, p. 173.)

[The warriors of London — sufficient favour — got knowledge of these transformations; when the first brightness died then comes brilliance beyond measure.]

No sooner indeed had the English grieved over the death of Elizabeth, when without delay an even greater monarch emerged unchallenged:

> Bearradh flaithis bhfear Lunndan
> tug dhóibh dul ó chomhurdadh:
> lá a rathuirse bás a mbróin,
> dob fhás athshoilse um iarnóin.
> (Breatnach, 'Metamorphosis', st. 12, p. 174.)

[The curtailment of the sovereignty of the men of London has enabled them to escape from the rivalry on their day of great grief their sorrow died; in the evening there was a flourish of another brightness.]

The poet's necessity to identify the new ascendant power and secure his favour is transferred here by Ó hEodhusa to James's English subjects. He is credited by Ó hEodhusa as having successfully banished the ills of Ireland too, without any qualification. As king of Ireland, James is to be hailed, just as Elizabeth was by an earlier poet. No suggestion of religion, land settlements, local independence or any other contemporary problem is specifically mentioned, or even hinted at by Ó hEodhusa in this seventeenth century poem:

> Oirchios dúin, gé a a-deirim sin,
> ceiliobhradh dár ccuing imnidh:
> súil chobhartha ar ríogh do-róigh
> tar bríogh ndomharbhtha ar ndobróin.
> (Breatnach, 'Metamorphosis', st. 16, p. 175.)

[It is fitting for us, if I say that, to bid farewell to our yoke of anxiety; the helping eye of our king reaches beyond the lasting force of our sorrow.]

Such unqualified approval of the new English monarch is echoed by a second Northern poet — Fearghal Óg Mac a' Bhaird who is entirely convinced of the legitimacy of James's monarchic claims in three countries. He introduces the poem with mention of James's charter and his rights therefrom:

Trí coróna i gcairt Shéamais
— cia dhíobh nachar dheighfhéaghais? —
críoch an sgeoil libh ga labhra,
a fhir eoil na healadhna.
(McKenna, *Aithdioghluim Dána,* No. 44, st. 1, p. 177.)

[The three crowns in James's charter — have you not seen the three of them with pleasure? — are the subject of what I shall tell thee, my friend who seekest knowledge.]

Fearghal Óg mentions the three crowns to which James is entitled [85] and goes on to suggest why it should be so:

Inneosad a adhbhar soin
na trí coróna i gcartaigh
ag rígh slóigh Gall is Gaoidheal,
ós am cóir dá chraobhsgaoileadh.
(McKenna, *Aithdioghluim Dána,* No. 44, st. 6,
p. 177.)

[I will now tell — for it is time to tell it — why those three crowns are in the charter of the king of the host of the Gaoidhil and Goill.]

According to the poet, James's greatest claim to Scotland is the antiquity of the ruling line of Stuarts from which he comes; he is the tenth ruler of Scotland of his name. His right to rule England is also based on his kinship with the Tudor dynasty:

Trí chéad bliadhan — buan a mbríogh! —
a-tá sí ag sliocht an airdríogh;

---

[85] McKenna, *Aithdioghluim Dána,* No. 44, sts. 3, 4, 5, p. 177.

fa rígh Alban ní hiongnadh
tír na n-ardbhragh n-imiolghlan.
(McKenna, *Aithdioghluim Dána,* No. 44, st. 8,
p. 178.)

[No wonder that he, Alba's prince, holds that land of bright-
bordered highlands; for three hundred years — lasting their effect! — it has been with his ancestors.]

Mac a' Bhaird then proceeds to illustrate just how selective the poets
could be in their use of information about contemporary events of
which they were undoubtedly in possession. The poet's perception of
what ought and ought not to influence his acceptance of James I is well
illustrated in his treatment of Mary, James I's mother[86] and of Elizabeth I, his cousin and predecessor on the English throne. Mary, Queen
of Scots is allotted one stanza which makes no mention of her untimely
death or alludes in any way to disharmony between Tudor and Stuart:

Badh lé Alba ó mhuir go muir
máthair an airdríogh uasail;
do chuir sí an choróin ma ceann,
onóir í ar nach fuil foirceann.
(McKenna, *Aithdioghluin Dána,* No. 44, st. 13, p. 178.)

[The noble king's mother ruled Alba from sea to sea; she put the
crown on her head, an honour never to end.]

That this 'honour' was 'ended' quite suddenly at Mary's beheading does
not prevent Mac a' Bhaird from praising James's predecessor,
Elizabeth. First, he validates James's right of charter to the Saxon
throne; this claim, like that to Scotland, has a genealogical basis,
James's claim rests on his great-grandmother Margaret, daughter of
Henry VII.[87]

Bhar seanseanmháthair — seol glan —
[inghean] airdríogh fhóid Sagsan
críoch a sgéal linn gá leanmhain

---

[86] J. Goldberg, *James I and the Politics of Literature,* pp 12-17.
[87] See William Croft Dickinson, *New History of Scotland: Scotland from earliest times
to 1603,* vol. I (Edinburgh, 1961), p. 283.

do fhéagh sinn i seinleabhraidh.
(McKenna, *Aithdioghluim Dána,* No. 44, st. 17, p. 179.)

[Following up the story which I have read in the ancient books, I find that thy great-grandmother — noble her descent! — was daughter of the king of the Saxon's land.]

Upon Elizabeth's death, James was claimed the rightful heir:

Críoch Sagsan na gcoill gcorcra
gan innte d'fhuil ríoghochta
acht éinríoghan dá gclaon coill,
craobh ler léirlíonadh Lonndoinn.
(McKenna, *Aithdioghluim Dána,* No. 44, st. 18,
p. 179.)

[That Saxon's land of purple hazels had only one queen of royal blood, the princess for whom London was thronged, the queen whom hazels salute.]

When, however, the poet considers James's claim to Ireland's charter, he appears to take his genealogical title for granted and the basis he puts forward for James's claim really lies in the fact that James already holds Ireland. It is therefore by right of conquest that James really holds Ireland — 'Éirinn armruaidh' (red-weaponed Ireland):

A lámh as díorgha dligheadh
— a-nois i gcéill cuirfidhear —
ná [bí ag] teacht ar éineing d'uaim
's do cheart ar Éirinn armruaidh.
(McKenna, *Aithdioghluim Dána,* No. 44, st. 21, p. 179.)

[O prince whose hand gives straight judgements, I will now say this to thee: talk not of 'taking in new territory' (i.e. adding Éire to your Kingdom) seeing thou hast already a right to red-sworded Éire.]

Indeed James is welcome as the spouse of Ireland, as much because he is so, as for any benefits, religious or otherwise, which the poet or his patrons and peers might hope to receive from him. The poet's interest in accommodating the *fait accompli* once again prevails:

Fada a-tá i dtairngre dhuit
críoch Sagsan — is iul orrdhruic;
duit is dú Éire amhlaidh;
is tú a céile ar chomhardhaibh.
(McKenna, *Aithdioghluim Dána,* No. 44, st. 23,
p. 179.)

[The Saxon's land has been long — 'tis well known — prophesied
for thee; so too is Éire due to thee; thou art her spouse by all signs.]

James has in fact achieved the high-kingship without 'opposition'. This
treatment of James's succession gives the poet a framework of reference
from which to view the events of the period. There is no reason to believe
that the Gaelic lords of Ireland saw James as anything other than a king
who achieved his status 'without opposition':

A mheic Hannraoi na dtreas dte
ag sin mar dleagahar dhaoibhse
gan toibhéim, a rí, ar do reacht
na trí hoiléin i n-aoinfheacht.
(McKenna, *Aithdioghluim Dána,* No. 44, st. 24, p. 179.)

[And thus, as is right, O son of hot-battling Henry, are the three
islands in thy power without any contradiction.]

Unstinting in his praise of James, Ó hEodhusa, with somewhat excessive zeal compares the purity of James's blood with that of Christ.
He also acknowledges James's foreignness, but this does not influence
adversely the praise he showers on him:

Ní fhuil fuil airdríogh eile
acht fuil meic na maighdine
ga bhfuil barr uaisleachta ar t'fhuil
guaisbhearta Gall id ghníomhuibh.
(McKenna, *Aithdioghluim Dána,* No. 44, 26, p. 180.)

[There is no blood, however noble — but only that of the Virgin's
Son that surpasses thine, the bravery of the Goill in thee.]

The acceptance of James by the poets, their enthusiasm in accommodating him in their complex historic-literary framework, and their
willingness to accommodate his administrators and officials in determining landownership and disposal of property in Ulster is discussed in

some detail by Breandán Ó Buachalla. Ó Buachalla's discussion of the poet's participation in the arrangements for the plantation of Ulster, as advisors on landownership, law and claims; and the corresponding part played by the remaining chiefs — principally junior and rival branches of the O'Neills, O'Donnells, O'Dohertys and Maguires,[88] illustrates very clearly the unanimity of attitude towards the changing conditions among those who remained of literati and the aristocracy. Poets and sept leaders alike appeared to comply alike in the new dispensation, in the piecemeal destruction of their own world.[89] In this regard, Ó Buachalla mentions Eoghan Ruadh Mac a' Bhaird (poet) and Lughaidh Ó Cléirigh (poet), who acted as commissioners of enquiry in Donegal in 1603; Eochaidh Ó hEodhusa, receiving land under the terms of the plantation in Co. Fermanagh; Pádraig Modartha Ó Donghaile acting lawyer for a principal Tyrone planter, Robert Stewart; Brian Maguire and Hugh Magennis and Sir Seán Mac Cochláin 'ag glacadh agus ag cabhrú le pleandáil a dtailte féin' [accepting and assisting in the plantation of their own territories] and Walter MacSweeny Fanad as a 'justice of the peace'.[90]

The activities of Sir Niall Garbh O'Donnell, a first cousin and brother-in-law of Red Hugh O'Donnell and Rory, are very well documented by Sir Henry Docwra, ally of Sir Niall, and commander of the Queen's forces at Lough Foyle. His career and fate are probably typical of those of many other aspiring chiefs in their dealings, both with the crown and with the senior more powerful branches of their sept. What we know of his career certainly illustrates aspects of the aspirations, frustrations and misunderstood loyalties of the majority of the Gaelic Irish aristocracy of this period.

Niall Garbh, as a representative of the lesser Gaelic lords at the beginning of the seventeenth century, displays a very complex loyalty to the demands of his own ethos. This complexity is no more so than that always demonstrated by both chiefs and poets throughout the late

---

88 Ó Buachalla, 'Cing Séamas', p. 120-4.
89 Ó Buachalla places their actions in this context:
'. . . faoi mar a bhíothas toilteanach glacadh le Séamas féin, bhíothas toilteanach glacadh leis an ordú nua freisin agus bhí an t-aos léinn, mar chuid den uasaicme, lán toilteanach dul ar aghaidh leis an dearcadh sin ach iadsan a mhaireachtaint agus a theacht slán. Is sa chomhthéacs ginearálta sin amháin is féidir iliomad sampla aonair den proiséas céanna a shuíomh agus a thuiscint . . .' in 'Cing Séamas', p. 124.
90 Ó Buachalla, 'Cing Séamas', pp 120-4.

mediaeval and early modern periods. The existence of another alternative life-style, however, as a possible viable option for the Gaelic Irish aristocracy, in general, presented the Gaelic world with an unprecedented challenge. The poets' works and the behaviour of contemporary chiefs indicate that the Gaelic Irish aristocracy perceived the challenge of the alternative system as merely a further episode in an individual experience and acted accordingly in a manner which appears curiously shortsighted and politically naïve. The loyalties are indeed both fixed and predictable — not however, to causes or to identifiable political goals, but to the perpetuation of their own existence in a manner which is explicable within the complex yet flexible framework of their own perceptions of themselves and their situation. The career of one such as Niall Garbh mirrors in a particularly graphic way the practical implications of the ethos so abstractly, yet so consistently articulated in the bardic poetry.

Niall Garbh's rivalry with his cousin Red Hugh O'Donnell for the chieftainship of the Uí Dhomhnaill in Tyrconnel, led him to join Sir Henry Docwra at Lough Foyle. Niall Garbh was a legitimate claimant for the leadership and the quest to secure this title was his fundamental motivation in his subsequent activities. Lughaidh Ó Cléirigh,[91] a member of a northern family of chroniclers, wrote a life of Red Hugh O'Donnell. As a *protégé* of the Uí Dhomhnaill, his account of the events of the final decades of the sixteenth century is heavily biased in favour of Hugh and Rory O'Donnell. Ó Cléirigh's account pays very little attention to Hugh O'Neill and his profile in the events of 1595-1603 is considerably reduced because of Ó Cléirigh's interest in promoting the Uí Dhomhnaill. Ó Cléirigh's account of the alliance between Sir Niall Garbh and Sir Henry Docwra displays his adherence to the principles we have already come to associate with the world-view of the Gaelic aristocracy. All of the individuals he deals with are soldiers, and it is within that military framework that their characters and behaviour are assessed. It is as rivals or allies of his own champion, Red Hugh, that Ó Cléirigh deals with them. His condemnation or praise is distributed not in consideration of which of the rivals has done more to preserve the Gaelic world, or attack the English or protect the catholic faith. It is the success of the participants or at least valour in their attempts to attain

---

[91] *BAR passim.*

their ends which Ó Cléirigh lauds in his life of Red Hugh. His description of Sir Henry Docwra, indicates his respect for the successful and renowned military commander. No indication is given that Ó Cléirigh saw in Docwra anything other than a leader of a number of foreign and Gaelic soldiery, threatening O'Donnell's traditional position in Ulster, — just as Niall Garbh's claims did:

> Henry Docwra was the name of their commander. He was a famous knight, prudent and skillful, with a profundity of knowledge. He was a spear-head of battle and conflict.[92]

Niall Garbh's 'defection' to this powerful warrior is dealt with in a hyperbolically condemnatory style by Ó Cléirigh. The condemnation is for Niall Garbh personally, however, and does not extend to a comment on the possible implications for Ulster as a whole, not to speak of Ireland, of this scheme of Niall:

> Woe to the mind that conceived, woe to the heart that entertained, woe to the tongue that initiated the violent, ruinous, odious, malicious scheme that was plotted then. Woe to the kinsman who forsook the race of his own flesh, and his earthly lord, his friends and blood relations, to go plotting and uniting with his enemies and foes.[93]

Ó Cléirigh mentions quite casually the fact that Niall Garbh's three brothers joined him with Docwra; again, no further comment is offered on this information:

> . . . however his three brothers joined with Niall in that revolt, i.e. Aodh Buidhe, Domhnall and Conn Occ.[94]

This casual approach is understandable when the nature of the dispute is understood; the engagements entered into by Niall Garbh against his cousins Red Hugh and Rory had all the marks of an internal O'Donnell power-struggle. In one incident Niall Garbh charged and mortally wounded Manus, brother of Red Hugh. Another brother, Rory,

---

[92] *BAR*, vol. I, pp 270-3.
[93] *BAR*, pp 265.
[94] *BAR*, pp 265.

countercharged Niall Garbh, missed his target however and succeeded merely in killing Niall's horse.[95] In spite of Ó Cléirigh's censure of Niall Garbh's alliance with Docwra, his admiration for success and bravery displayed by his own patron's rival is undiminished. His perception of the intrinsic worth of a valorous warrior is stronger than his appreciation of the issues nominally at stake. Here he commends Niall Garbh's personal bravery and resourcefulness:

> When Niall Ó Domhnaill saw his people and the English being overwhelmed in stress of combat he considered in his mind how he might relieve them. Wherefore, what he did was to escape secretly, bravely and speedily . . . where there was a large body of English and he brought them . . . to the aid of his own people and of the English . . .[96]

Ó Cléirigh likewise does not neglect his traditional duty to provide a suitable obituary notice of the fallen warriors of the Uí Dhomhnaill. Therefore, reporting the death of Niall Garbh's brother, Conn Óg, also in Docwra's camp, Ó Cléirigh records it without comment on Conn Óg's military allegiance, but emphasizes his bravery:

> There fell on the other side Conn Óg, son of Conn, brother of Niall Ó Domhnaill, and three hundred besides, including wounded and burnt. This Conn who fell was a spear-head in battle and fight and usually won victory of each first wound.[97]

It is clear that even at the time of the different military engagements comprising the Nine Years' War, that traditional perceptions of the uses of warfare and the allocation of allegiances prevailed even in areas as sensitive as Ulster. Docwra's useful bridgehead in hitherto unpenetrated Ulster was enthusiastically used by a rival branch of Uí Dhomhnaill to press their claims to sept superiority and this attitude is countenanced without adverse comment by the biographer of Red Hugh, partner to Hugh O'Neill in what has often, mistakenly, been regarded as a conscious final effort by the united Ulster chiefs to achieve local independence and eventually to create a recognizable unified Gaelic polity.

Ó Cléirigh's description of Niall Garbh's personality is essentially

---

95 *BAR*, pp 270-3.
96 *BAR*, pp 308-10.
97 *BAR*, pp 310-11.

very similar to that of Sir Henry Docwra. Both men were writing from radically different viewpoints. Ó Cléirigh castigated him primarily as a troublesome rival to the Uí Dhomhnallship. Sir Henry Docwra's description of him is that of a commander whose ally could prove more trouble than he was worth. Both writers remark on Niall Garbh's 'venomous' nature and his tendency to submit to authority only when it was manifestly stronger than he. Regarding his original submission to Red Hugh in 1592, Ó Cléirigh records:

> There came to him (Aodh Ruadh) likewise Niall Garbh, son of Conn, son of Calbhach, son of Maghnus, son of Aodh Óg, who was called Aodh Dubh. He was a violent man, hasty, unmerciful, and he was spiteful, inimical, with the venom of a serpent, with the impetuosity of a lion. He was a hero in valour and fighting. He was the head of an army and of troops in battle and war. But yet he was envious towards him (Aodh Ruadh) like the rest, though the sister of Aodh was his wife. There was another bond of friendship between them for Aodh had been fostered in boyhood by his (Niall's) parents. But yet it was not through real love for him he came, but it was wholly through fear.[98]

In Sir Henry's description of him one notices again his apparent tendency to yield to the greater power for forseeable benefits:

> . . . prone to tyranny where he may command, to proud and importunate beggary where he is as a subject, to extreme covetousness whether he be rich or poor, and unseasoned by any manner of discipline, knowledge or fear of God.[99]

The benefit rewarding Niall's alliance with Docwra was the chieftainship of Tyrconnel. Niall Garbh's grievance with O'Donnell had always centred on Red Hugh's superior position within the sept, which was due as much to the strength and insistence of Red Hugh's mother, the formidable Fionnghuala, daughter of James Mac Alasdair MacDonnell —

---

[98] *BAR*, pp 54-7.

[99] As cited in Cyril Falls, 'Neil Garve: English ally and victim', in *Irish Sword,* vol. I (1949), pp 2-7. And see the description by Moryson of Hugh O'Neill's submission to Elizabeth I cited in N.P. Canny, 'The Treaty of Mellifont and the Re-organisation of Ulster', in *Irish Sword*, vol. 9 (1969-70), p. 250 and see his (O'Neill's) letter to James I cited in N.P. Canny, 'Flight of the Earls', p. 388.

as to his traditional rights. Red Hugh's mother attended his disputed inauguration. Of her presence there Ó Cléirigh remarks:

> It was an advantage that she came to the gathering (1592), for she was the head of advice and counsel of the Cenél Conaill . . . she had the heart of a hero and the mind of a soldier, inasmuch as she exhorted in every way each one that she was acquainted with, and her husband especially to avenge his injuries and wrongs on each according to his deserts. She had many troops from Scotland, and some of the Irish at her disposal and under her control, and in her own hire and pay constantly . . .[100]

In exchange for his assistance Sir Henry Docwra promised Niall Garbh:

> . . . on behalfe of the Queene, the whole Countrey of Tirconnell to him and his heires, and my Lord Deputee and Councell at Dublin did afterwards confirme it unto him under theire hands, and his coming in was very acceptable att that time, and such as we made many uses of, and could ill have spared.[101]

Niall Garbh fought valiantly for Docwra as he had formerly done for Red Hugh. Ultimately of course Niall Garbh was fighting for himself; his perception of his rightful position; his place within the system. The system could be old or new, under Gaelic autonomy or under the crown, but he had been reared in expectation of a leading rôle for himself in conflict, or in undisputed chieftainship. The fact that the 'Tudor Conquest' and subsequently Stuart consolidation should be underway during his adulthood merely complicated his quest for power, offering him conflicting alternatives. Niall Garbh's choice was not determined by considerations of the ultimate sovereignty of Ireland. For him, alliance with Sir Henry Docwra and the Dublin administration appeared to present a more satisfactory means of achieving his aims than did a subordinate position in an O'Donnell/O'Neill confederation. When he was denied his promised rewards as a result of Mountjoy's settlement with O'Neill and O'Donnell,[102] his dissatisfaction led to him to involvement in Sir Cahir O'Doherty's rising in 1608, while in alliance with Sir Thomas

---

[100] Cf. *AFM, sub anno* 1588, and *BAR*, p. 39.
[101] Sir Henry Docwra, *Narration*, p. 264.
[102] N.P. Canny, 'Treaty of Mellifont'.

Ridgeway. Niall Garbh's everchanging alliances were not peculiar to him, but were a characteristic of all the Gaelic Irish aristocrats who in general regarded the presence of the English as welcome or unwelcome depending on their individual circumstances. When Sir Niall escaped from the custody of Sir Henry Docwra in 1603 he intended to hold out in MacSweeny na dTuath's castle '. . . reputed to be the strongest in all the North'.[103] Docwra again describes the situation:

> I had then Owen Oge in my companie, and to prevent him (Sir Niall) required he would deliver it mee, and soe hee did, onlie requesting hee might have it againe, when the Garrison I should put in it, should be withdrawn, which I gave my word unto he should . . .[104]

This Owen Oge, was Eoghan Óg mic Eoghain Óig Mac Sweeny na dTuath. His father, Eoghan Óg had been a fosterer of Red Hugh O'Donnell, he had been part of the northern alliance during their successful period. Niall Garbh's dissatisfaction with the crown's promises or those of the Dublin administration stemmed from his thwarted hope of self-aggrandisement. He was not moved to anti-government activities because of an embryonic nationalist feeling experienced by him in consideration of the events of the first decade of the seventeenth century. The same might be said of Rory O'Donnell who gladly joined with his erstwhile enemy Docwra, in pursuit of the fugitive, Sir Niall, putting his castle at Lifford at the disposal of the English being:

> glad of soe fair an opportunitie to advance his own endes by.[105]

Rory O'Donnell thus showed himself to be as traditionally motivated in his alliances as Niall Garbh or Cahir O'Doherty. He was equally quick to claim title to, and accept patents for, Niall Garbh's own land, at the hands of the Dublin administration:

> Within a while after came Roory O'Donnell to Dublin, with his Majestie's letters to be made Earle of Tyrconnell, and have all the countrey to him and his heires . . . and such lands as Neal Garvi had held . . .[106]

---

103 Docwra, *Narration,* p. 270.
104 Docwra, *Narration,* p. 270.
105 Docwra, *Narration,* p. 269.
106 Docwra, *Narration,* p. 278.

One can see that a rationale quite remote from loyalty to co-nationalists, or co-religionists, fellow chiefs, government, crown or commander operated in the Gaelic world in this period. The fluctuating fortunes of the Gaelic aristocracy had always necessitated a system of ready alliances and equally flexible loyalties. The constant factor in the everchanging political scene were the perceptions underlying the activities of the Gaelic aristocracy. One grossly misinterprets the motives underlying the activities if one places them under a rigid grid or framework of preconceived ideals of loyalties and a kind of patriotism which constituted no part either of their mental world or of their perception of their legitimate political activities. The corresponding literary articulation of the chameleon nature of Gaelic loyalties is found in the contemporary bardic literature. Eoghan Rua Mac a' Bhaird, poet to the Uí Dhomhnaill, regarded the enmity and rivalry between the brothers Hugh and Rory O'Donnell against their kinsmen, Sir Niall and his brothers, as no impediment to his professional compositions to members of both families. Likewise, Sir Niall's alliance with Sir Henry Docwra at a very sensitive period in Hugh O'Donnell's fortunes, had no effect on Mac a' Bhaird's poems for Niall and his son Neachtain on their imprisonment in the Tower.

Four different poems by Eoghan Rua Mac a' Bhaird, one for Rory O'Donnell, one for Turlough mac Airt O'Neill, and one each respectively for Niall and Neachtain O'Donnell, illustrate once again the persistence of traditional bardic, and by extension, therefore, aristocratic perceptions in the poet's treatment of the fluctuating fortunes of his patrons. Again, what is most important for the poet is the contemporary situation, balanced with expectations for the future and the traditional status of the addressee. In all four poems, deference to, and respect for, those wielding authority is in evidence. The first poem to be considered here is an address to Rory O'Donnell on his forthcoming journey to sue for terms, several months before O'Neill had 'come in'. Bergin prefaces the poem with these notes:

> Apparently he (the poet) disapproved of the surrender and the negotiations which followed it. He is careful to call his patron "O'Donnell's son" not "O'Donnell" for Rury never became chief of his clan; from Dublin he crossed over to London, and returned as Earl of Tyrconnell.[107]

---

[107] Bergin, *Irish Bardic Poetry*, p. 27.

Bergin's notes infer that the poet regards Rory's trip as a shameful surrender which must be borne on account of the defeat recently inflicted
upon him. In fact the poem is a very good example of bardic insistence
on accommodation, of themselves and their patrons, within ever-
changing conditions, while preserving very astutely their own integrity.
Therefore Rory's journey is portrayed not as an occasion of capitula-
tion but one to show his willingness to cease harrying the foreigner.
Tacit acceptance of the fact that the foreigner has power of retaliation is
inferred and the entire work is, insofar as anti-English or pro-Gaelic
political sentiment is concerned, politically neutral. The basic argument
is that Rory has decided to cease his offensive, but the damage he has
already wrought makes his journey to Dublin fraught with danger for
him; not because he is a defeated leader, but because of the justified fear
and resentment his hard battling has already occasioned among those in
Dublin. The opening stanza can be misleading in tone to a reader unfamiliar with the propensity of the poets to fill lines with proverbs:

> Dána an turas tríalltar sonn;
> fada atá ag tocht 'na thimcholl,
> geall re hoighidh an eachtra,
> doiligh earr na huaisleachta.
> (Bergin, *Irish Bardic Poetry,* No. 2,
> st. 1, p. 27.)

> [Bold is the journey attempted here; long has it been debated. The
> expedition is equal to a tragic fate; hard is the end of nobility.]

Rory's former prowess in war has hardened the hearts of those in
Dublin, he has caused much grief:

> Atáid re a ucht a n-Áth Cliath,
> óig ar ar himreadh mídhíach,
> mór ngoimhfhéchsin re a ghnúis ngloin,
> cúis roidhéisdin a rochtoin.
> (Bergin, *Irish Bardic Poetry,* No. 2, st. 5, p. 28.)

> [They are ready for him in Dublin, warriors on whom misfortune
> has been inflicted; many a painful glance at his bright
> countenance, to reach them is occasion for great loathing.]

He cannot be expected to return uharmed since he in his valour has
caused such destruction:

Iomdha cúis imnidh aca,
iomdha mairg mhná deórata,
iomdha leacht as a lossoin,
diongna a theacht ón turus-soin.
(Bergin, *Irish Bardic Poetry,* No. 2, st. 6,
p. 28.)

[Many a cause for anxiety they had, many a foreign wife's lamentation many a tombstone due to him — 'tis a marvel if he comes back from that journey.]

The onus of suing for peace is subtly placed on the 'Dublin army', who wish to cease battling against an adversary as powerful as Rory. Their craven desire for peace cancels the suggestion that Rory was in any sense summoned to Dublin in order to sue for peace on his own behalf. By this means Mac a' Bhaird neatly avoids apportioning a loser's part to Rory:

Foghla gráineamhla an ghille,
ní chuimhnigh Cath Duibhlinne,
lé fonn a síothoighthe soin
fa fhonn bhfíochfhoirbhthe bFionntoin.
(Bergin, *Irish Bardic Poetry,* No. 2, st. 13, p. 29.)

[As for the youth's dreadful forays, the army of Dublin remembers them not for their longing to be at peace throughout Fintan's land, old in wrath.]

Their formerly hostile relations are transformed to amiable relations in the interests of peace:

Tugadh leó a bfíoch sa bformad,
ar rún ceannsa ar cháonchomhrag,
fúath a-roile, a rún cogaidh,
ar rún toile tugadair.
(Bergin, *Irish Bardic Poetry,* No. 2, st. 15, p. 29.)

[They have changed their anger and envy to a resolution of gentleness and peace, their mutual hatred and warlike purpose to love.]

The ability of the 'Dublin' people to bestow or withhold pardon is inferred, and Rory's acceptance or rejection of it is indicated objectively:

A ndearna orra, as é a shuim,
maithtear do mhac Uí Dhomhnaill,
gur thaiséntor tocht 'na cceann,
aisécthar olc na hÉireann.
(Bergin, *Irish Bardic Poetry*, No. 2, st. 14,
p. 29.)

[For all that he has done to them, in short, O'Donnell's son is pardoned; until opposition is shown to them Ireland's wrong will not be repaid.]

The obscurity of some of Mac a' Bhaird's stanzas in this poem is such that they are a little incoherent to a modern reader. In the following stanza, however, the oblique nature of the statement does not obscure the recognition of 'fear ionaidh airdríogh Éireann' [the king of Ireland's deputy; Sir George Carey, the lord deputy in Dublin]:

Ón tráth fa ttáinig 'na cceann
fear ionaidh *airdríogh Éireann*,
brígh 'na ccéimiondaibh ní chuir,
sídh Éirionnaigh ní híarthuir.
(Bergin, *Irish Bardic Poetry,* No. 2, st. 18,
p. 30.)

[Since the *deputy of Ireland's king* came to them, he sets no store by their doings, peace is sought with no Irishman.][108]

Bergin interprets this stanza thus:

The meaning of this and the following quatrain seems to be that, once the O'Donnells have yielded, the surrender of the rest Ireland may be taken for granted.[109]

This is not to suggest, however, as Bergin infers, that in the contemporary context, O'Donnell represented for Mac a' Bhaird the last of the powerful Gaelic chiefs, and that his submission signalled the end of the Gaelic order. It is a further illustration by the poet of O'Donnell's power; once he has submitted, the submission of lords less powerful

---

[108] Italics are mine, and see Bergin, *Irish Bardic Poetry*, introduction, p. 30.
[109] Bergin, *Irish Bardic Poetry,* p. 221, note 5.

than he, (that is, every other chief in the country), can be taken for granted. Such is Rory's stature that his presence in Dublin guarantees peace while he stays there:

> Faigsin codhnaigh Chlann Dálaigh
> i nÁth Clíath a ccomhdhálaibh
> dáil cháomhanta do chrích Ghall,
> aonshompla síth na sáorchlann.
> (Bergin, *Irish Bardic Poetry,* No. 2, st. 20,
> p. 30.)

[The sight of the chief of Dálach's descendants at conventions in Dublin is a decree of protection to the territory, the very model of peace with the nobles.]

Eoghan Ruadh Mac a' Bhaird found himself blessing two other patrons on their respective journeys from Ulster. He commended Red Hugh O'Donnell to God's care as he set out for Spain in January 1602; 'Rob soruidh t'eachtra a Aodha Ruaidh'. He composed a poem likewise on the departure of Turlough mac Airt Óig mac Thoirdhealbhaigh O'Neill to England to claim his father's patrimony in Tyrone against the claims of Hugh O'Neill, earl of Tyrone, and those of his uncle Cormac O'Neill (*tánaiste*). The aims of both addressees appear to be diametrically mutually opposed; Red Hugh goes to Spain to secure Spanish aid in the wake of the Kinsale defeat; Turlough O'Neill travels to England to secure his claims against the earl of Tyrone. His father, Art Óg O'Neill, had allied himself with Sir Henry Docwra in expectation of being made 'O'Neill' — a situation which parallels that of Niall Garbh:

> On the first of June, Sir Arthur O'Neale, sonne to old Tirlough Lenogh that had been O'Neale, came in unto me with some 30 horse and foot, a man I had directions from the state, to labour to drawe to our side; and to promise to be made Earl of Tyrone if the other that mainteyned the Rebellion could be dispossessed of the Country . . .[110]

This Turlough travelled to London to secure his father's lands on Art Óg's death, against the claims of both the earl of Tyrone, to the entire

---

[110] Docwra, *Narration,* p. 240.

territory, and those of Cormac O'Neill, *tánaiste* and brother of the earl, Art's immediate territories. He, Turlough, was accepted by Docwra as the legitimate heir.[111] He served some time with the English in Ulster, thus proving his trustworthiness, and right to inherit. To Red Hugh, Eoghan Ruadh Mac a' Bhaird declares:

> Rob soruidh t'eachtra, a Aodha Ruaidh
> an Coimsidh do-chí ar n-anbhuain,
> gabhaidh sé t'innfheitheamh air,
> go mbé ag rinnfheitheamh romhaibh.
> (Bergin, *Irish Bardic Poetry,* No. 3, st. 1, p. 31.)

> [Auspicious be thy journey, Aodh Ruadh. The lord God who sees our distress, He takes upon him thy care, may He prepare thy path before thee.]

The poet hopes that Red Hugh will meet with no reverses of any kind on his journey:

> Go mbé an toice, a thriath Gaillmhe,
> duitse ag crúdh gach comhairle;
> ná deach faoibh fréamh ar ndoibheart,
> rob sén daoibh do dheóraidheacht.
> (Bergin, *Irish Bardic Poetry,* No. 3, st. 5, p. 31.)

> [May fortune deliberate each counsel for thee, O Prince of Galway; may the roots of our misdeeds not assail thee; may thy smile be to thee a blessing.]

Red Hugh's journey is compared with the mythical voyages of Tuathal Teachtmhar, Conghal Cláiríneach, Eoghan Mór and Mac Nia Mac Con. The journey to England undertaken by Turlough O'Neill, is approached with a slightly different emphasis by Eoghan Ruadh Mac a' Bhaird. The journey is undertaken in pursuit of the honour of Ulster and Leath Coinn:

> Rob soraidh an séadsa soir
> 'nar ghluais rí fréimhe hEoghain
> go crích Saxan na sreabh seang

---

111 Docwra, *Narration*, p. 247.

ó ghasraibh fhear na hÉireann.
(Ó Raghallaigh, *Duanta Eoghain Ruaidh Mhic an Bhaird,* No. 18, st. 1, p. 258.)

[Prosperous be thy journey eastward on which the king of Eoghan's stock went to Saxonland of the narrow streams from the soldiers of Ireland.]

Unlike the case with Red Hugh, the poet knows to whom Turlough must address himself in England. The King of England is the object of Turlough O'Neill's supplications; the poet hopes that the latter will show wisdom in his interview:

Re headh iomagallmu an ríogh
go madh ionann d'ua na n'áirdríogh
slat na bhfírfregra ngeal glan
fofhear na sír-eagna Solamh.
(Ó Raghallaigh, *Duanta Eoghain Ruaidh Mhic an Bhaird,*
No. 18, st. 5, p. 258.)

[During the time of (his) interview with the king (England) may this descendant of the high-kings — the scion of true answers(?) bright, pure — be an equal to Solomon of perpetual wisdom.]

The poet prayed, in the case of Red Hugh that his former misdeeds might not tell against him on his mission in Spain. He prayed that the understandable resentment the 'men of Dublin' felt against the powerful Rory should not prejudice his safety in Dublin. The same theme is carried into Mac a' Bhaird's poem for Turlough O'Neill. His own and his ancestors' depredations must not hinder his claims with the Saxon king. The king is regarded as an appropriate arbitrator in the question of the chieftainship of Ulster. There is no hint of, or reference to, any antagonism on the part of the poet or the claimant towards the 'Saxon king' in that capacity, just as the poet indicated no resentment at Rory's recourse to Sir George Carey in a similar connection.

Go ngabha rí Sagsan soin
briathra millsi ua Eoghain,
cisde chliar fíorghlan na bhfionn
da riar fa rioghmhagh Raoilinn.
(Ó Raghallaigh, *Duanta Eoghain Ruaidh Mhic an Bhaird*, No. 18, st. 6, p. 260.)

[May the Saxon king accept the sweet words of the descendant of Eoghan, treasury of the true poets of the Fair being served throughout the royal plain of Raoilinn [Ireland].]

The reavings of Turlough's ancestors are not to be held against him in his claims. His own security in his claim is based on the promise made to his father on his alliance with Docwra. Mac a' Bhaird makes no mention of this extra-sept connection, instead he treats of them as merely the predictable military escapades of any worthy warrior:

> Ruathair mhionca Néill Uí Néill
> dó dá dtaoibh nar thí oilbhéim,
> nó eachtra Airt uair oile
> nó an chairt fuair Ughoine.
> (Ó Raghallaigh, *Duanta Eoghain Ruaidh Mhic
> an Bhaird,* No. 18, st. 10, p. 260.)

> [May no shame reach him as a result of the frequent forays of Niall Ó Neill, or of the adventure of Art on another occasion, or of the chart Ughoine got.]

Furthermore, the poet hopes that the envy of the 'warriors of London' will not harm him:

> Nár thí choidhche re a dhreich nduinn
> d'iomthnúth na laoch o Luinnuinn;
> éag no felghníomh no folta,
> neimhdhíon na séad saoghalta.
> (Ó Raghallaigh, *Duanta Eoghain Ruaidh Mhic
> an Bhaird,* No. 18, st. 11, p. 260.)

> [May the envy of the warriors from London, death or treachery or stealthy deed never reach his noble countenance, heavenly guardian of earthly jewels.]

As a result of this journey to England, Turlough shall fulfil a prophecy made by St Patrick regarding Eoghan's race. He, Turlough, is the prophesied one assuming supremacy, succouring the race of Mil:

> Do tairngir Padraig Phuirt Breagh:
> tiocfa go mór clainn Mhíleadh
> ar feadh Banbha ó mhuir go muir

fear a gcabhra d'fhuil Eoghain.
(Ó Raghallaigh, *Duanta Eoghain Ruaidh Mhic
an Bhaird,* No. 18, st. 13, p. 262.)

[Patrick of the Fort of Bregia prophesied: 'There will come to the
great clann of Mil throughout Ireland from sea to sea a man of the
race of Eoghan to succour them.]

The prophecy is now being fulfilled, the active agent in its fulfilment are
Turlough himself and the king of England, whose authority will bestow
his patrimony upon Turlough O'Neill. This is how minor settlements
which formed part of the plantation of Ulster appeared to the immediate participants. Every episode was acted out by the Gaelic Irish
with the full panoply of traditional claim and counter-claim, expedient
alliances and of course, bardic comment. The final result of Turlough's
journey will be his assumption of the supremacy over the clan of Mil:

Toirrdhealbhach Ó Néill anos
rachaidh sé os cách a gceannas
fear a chaithmhe ba céim gar
do réir aithne na n-érlamh.
(Ó Raghallaigh, *Duanta Eoghain Ruaidh Mhic
an Bhaird,* No. 18, st. 15, p. 262.)

[Turlough O'Neill now will assume supremacy, a man who will
use it (headship) is near, according to the knowledge of the saints.]

God's help will assure his supremacy, this position is his legal right. In
declaring Toirdhealbhach to be legitimate, Mac a' Bhaird tacitly accepts
the ousting of his uncle, Cormac O'Neill's, rights as *tánaiste* to his
brother Art Óg:

Ré toil Dé da chur i gcéill
os cloinn Eoghain mac móir Néill,
do bhiaidh leannán leasa Breagh,
sgeallán feasa na bhfeinneadh.
(Ó Raghallaigh, *Duanta Eoghain Ruaidh Mhic
an Bhaird,* No. 18, st. 16, p. 262.)

[The darling of the Fort of Bregia, the kernel of knowledge of the
Fian will be over the children of Eoghan, sons of great Niall, with
God's will to bring it about.]

Mac a' Bhaird spells out the 'legality' of O'Neill's claims over those of the traditional claimant in the following stanza:

Dligid ó mhuir go muir
go mac Airt d'iúl gach ughdair,
do cheart on chuire gan locht
a dteacht uile re humhlocht.
(Ó Raghallaigh, *Duanta Eoghain Ruaidh Mhic
an Bhaird,* No. 18, st. 17, p. 262.)

[As every authority knows, it is legally due to the son of Art that the whole faultless band from sea to sea come to him in submission.]

His (Turlough's) journey is, of course comparable to those of Tuathal Teachtmhar and Niall of the Nine Hostages. He is the successor of Brian Boru, and equal of Cormac Ó Cuinn:

Brath díleas Leasa Logha,
mac ionaidh Bhriain Baromha,
aithghin do Chormac o Chuinn,
flaithghin na ndonnbhrat ndíoghuinn.
(Ó Raghallaigh, *Duanta Eoghain Ruaidh Mhic
an Bhaird,* No. 18, st. 26, p. 266.)

[Beloved expected one of the Fort of Logha, successor to Brian Boru, one exactly like Cormac Ó Cuinn, prince of ample brown mantles.]

Not only do the sons of Mil rally around him, but also do the noblemen of London:

Tiad uime cionn a gcionn
fa mac Airt ó Ráith Raoilionn,
fir ba saothroidhe glór glan
do phór laochraidhe Lundun.
(Ó Raghallaigh, *Duanta Eoghain Ruaidh Mhic
an Bhaird,* No. 18, st. 22, p. 264.)

[They come towards him one after another, towards the son of Art from Rath Raoilionn, clear-voiced lively men of the race of the London heroes.]

This Turlough is, without qualification, the single choice of the poets and of the men of Ireland, the true legitimate successor to the Uí Néill heroes:

> Oighre sleachta Néill náraigh,
> mac ionaigh an Ioldánaigh
> géag caomh abhla Chláir na bhFionn
> aon damhna áigh na hEirionn.
> (Ó Raghallaigh, *Duanta Eoghain Ruaidh Mhic an Bhaird*, No. 18, st. 25, p. 266.)

[Heir to the tribe of noble Niall, successor of their versatile one (the Ioldánach), beautiful apple-branch of the Plain of the Fair, chief cause of the valour of Ireland.]

and:

> Dósan madh réim ratha
> mac Airt ua gach ardfhlatha,
> fíor rún chléire Chláir Logha,
> lán Eire dá én rogha.
> (Ó Raghallaigh, *Duanta Eoghain Ruaidh Mhic an Bhaird*, No. 18, st. 24, p. 264.)

[For him, the son of Art, the descendant of princes, may it be a prosperous career: (he is) the true darling of the poets of the Plain of Logha — Ireland's one and only choice.]

The granting of Turlough's claims depended on the capture and dispossession of Hugh O'Neill, earl of Tyrone. The general implications of the survival of internecine sept-rivalry at this period, which was one of the major forces that eroded Hugh O'Neill's position, meant very little either to the leaders thus involved or the poets who commented on their activities. The ambition to overthrow Tyrone with a view to seizing the lordship would have been a legitimate O'Neill goal at any period, especially if the individual thus engaged was the addressee of the poem. Turlough, like his father Art, would gladly ally himself with the English to secure Tyrone's capture. Similarly, Rory O'Donnell, having made honourable terms with the English, placed Lifford castle at the disposal of Sir Thomas Ridgeway and Docwra, who had previously been his enemies, and he actively campaigned with them in order to secure the capture of his own sept enemy, Sir Niall Garbh.

Sir Niall himself, a disappointed claimant for the O'Donnell chieftainship, joined with Sir Henry Docwra to secure it with the aid of the crown. He was disappointed in the attempt and subsequently became disaffected, until finally captured by his former allies Sir Henry Docwra and Mac Sweeny na dTuath. Both Niall and his son, Neachtain, were imprisoned in the Tower until they died there about 1626. Eoghan Rua Mac a' Bhaird, supporter and eulogist of Rory O'Donnell, also eulogized Rory's greatest enemy Sir Niall, and Neachtain too. He bewailed their imprisonment in two poems, 'A bhráighe atá i dTor Lonndan. . .' for Niall and 'Mairg as bráighe ar mhacruidhe murbhaigh' for Neachtain. Mac a' Bhaird makes extensive use of the motifs and conceits usually associated with the loss of a patron to deal with Niall's imprisonment. Because Niall is in jail, the whole of Banbha is enfettered; he represents the sovereignty of Banbha. Banbha's glory, honour and hope is in bondage with Niall in the Tower:

> A bhráighe atá i dTor Lonndan,
> a ua Conuill chaomh-Ghulban,
> do gheimhil-si as lór do léan,
> ar slógh sein-Inse Saimhéar.
> (Ó Raghallaigh, *Duanta Eoghain Ruaidh Mhic
> an Bhaird,* No. 9, st. 1, p. 118.)

[O hostage in London Tower, scion of Conall of Fair Gulba, thy fetters are a great sorrow to the host of the old isle of Saimhear.]

His capture is not merely that of a single individual:

> Do ghabhail, a ghéag Eanaigh,
> lór do ghlas ar Ghaoidhealaibh;
> cách uile i láimh as a los,
> ní re duine amháin bheanos.
> (Ó Raghallaigh, *Duanta Eoghain Ruaidh Mhic
> an Bhaird,* No. 9, st. 8, 120.)

[Thy capture, o scion of Eanach, a heavy chain upon the Gaoidhil, all being captured with thee, is not the capture of only one man.]

The valour, honour and expectations of Leath Cuinn are personified in Niall, in his imprisonment Banbha is a captive:

> Dóchas laochruidh Leithe Cuinn,
> gaisgeadh curadh clann gConuill,

atáid, a Néill Ghairbh, id ghlas
a n-ainm, a gcéim, a gceannas.
(Ó Raghallaigh, *Duanta Eoghain Ruaidh Mhic
an Bhaird,* No. 9, st. 9, p. 120.)

[The hopes and valour, the name and place and power of Leath
Cuinn's warriors, Í Chonaill's heroes are bound in thy chains, O
Niall Garbh.]

Niall is compared with the Biblical Joseph, imprisoned on the false
word of a harlot. Niall too is imprisoned unjustly but there are two
powers which can be appealed to on his behalf; God can release Niall
Garbh if he wishes to; prayer to God caused the Pharoah to investigate
Joseph's imprisonment leading to his release, and not only that but to
his being made governor of Egypt:

Le toil n-Athar na n-uile
táinig dá thaom trócuire;
an rí ar gcromadh ar an gcoir,
sí ar na lomadh do láthoir.
(Ó Raghallaigh, *Duanta Eoghain Ruaidh Mhic
an Bhaird,* No. 9, st. 16, p. 124.)

[By the will of the Father, two mercies were conferred; the King
looked into the charge, and it was laid bare before him.]

When the king of Egypt examined the case, he was very impressed with
Joseph:

Ní hé amháin gur saoradh sin
rí Eigipt tráth ar n-a thuigsin
ar feadh a thíre do thogh
mar fhear ríghe do riaghladh.
(Ó Raghallaigh, *Duanta Eoghain Ruaidh Mhic
an Bhaird*, No. 9, st. 18, p. 124.)

[Not only was he set free, but the King of Egypt, leaving his case,
chose him to be a ruler throughout his kingdom.]

A direct analogy is drawn between Niall and Joseph, King James and the
Pharoah. Here, once again, Mac a' Bhaird acknowledges without comment, the supreme authority of James and his power to decide the fate of
an aspiring Gaelic lord. In this poem, Mac a' Bhaird acknowledges also

Niall Garbh's services for the crown. The poet recognizes no contradiction in hailing Niall Garbh as the hope of Ireland, and the champion of Leath Cuinn while at the same time being aware of his activities both for and against the most powerful Gaelic Ulster chiefs, and his very important services for the king's cause in Ulster. Therefore, just as the Pharoah considered Joseph's case and found him worthy, not only of his freedom but with additional honour, so too will James I examine Niall Garbh's personal history and reward him accordingly:

> Acht go gcuimhneocha an choróin
> duit arís le ro-onóir
> gach a bhfuair sibh ar a son,
> is gach buaidh libh dar leanodh.
> (Ó Raghallaigh, *Duanta Eoghain Ruaidh Mhic
> an Bhaird,* No. 9, st. 20, p. 126.)

[But that the crown may remember with all honour to thee once more, all thou hast borne for it, and every victory won by you.]

He mentions the king specifically:

> Ar an bhfáth fa a bhfuile i nglas
> acht go gcromadh Cing Séamas,
> ná meas nach saorfaidhe sibh,
> ar leas fraoch-mhuighe Fuinidh.
> (Ó Raghallaigh, *Duanta Eoghain Ruaidh Mhic
> an Bhaird,* No. 9, st. 21, p. 126.)

[If only King James examines the reason why thou art in chains, and the interests of the heather-plain of the west be sure thou shallt be set free.][112]

Niall Garbh's wife, sister of Red Hugh, daughter of the notorious Inghean Dubh — Fionnghuala, also suffers grievously because of Niall's captivity, despite the fact that her own mother had played a major rôle in his apprehension. The poet indicates Nuala's distress thus:

---

[112] Ó Buachalla remarked regarding the relations between James I and the Gaelic literati:
'Dar leis an aos léinn, pé dream a bhí le ciontú in anchás na hÉireann níorbh iad na Stíobhartaigh iad; pé duine d'áirithe a bhí le milleánú níorbh é Séamas é.' In 'Cing Séamas', p. 112.

Mó an príosún fós i n-a bhfuil
inghean ríogh fréimhe Dáluigh
a bhfuilgne ag cradh a cridhe
doilghe dál a daoirsine.
(Ó Raghallaigh, *Duanta Eoghain Ruaidh Mhic
an Bhaird,* No. 9, st. 26, p. 128.)

[Harder still the durance of the princess of Dálach's stock; more grievous is her captivity, namely, the sufferings torturing her heart.]

Bergin suggests that Nuala deserted her husband, Niall, when he deserted Red Hugh.[113] This does not mean, however, that she disapproved of conducting negotiations with the crown. And it is on record that she made several representations to the English agent in Brussels to have young Hugh O'Donnell, heir to the Tyrconnel earldom, brought from the Low Countries, where he was being tutored under the protection of the Irish Franciscans and with the patronage of the Spanish crown.[114] Her motive was to have him restored to favour with James I, and thus to his father's earldom and estates. Her departure from Niall Garbh may have coincided with his defection from Red Hugh, but it is in itself no indication of her general displeasure with the prospect of crown patronage or of any 'patriotic' impulse on her part, and must be understood as characteristic (Uí Dhomhnaill) domestic rivalry in the narrowest sense.[115]

Neachtain O'Donnell, imprisoned with his father, is the subject of a very gentle poem by Eoghan Rua Mac a' Bhaird. The thrust of the poem is that Neachtain's imprisonment is almost fortuitous for the O'Donnell sept (Clann Connell), since he is being kept from harm, because a restraint was being placed upon his natural inclinations to valorous deeds, which would have endangered his young life. The poem, however, opens on a bleak note:

Mairg as braighe ar mhacruidh Murbhaigh
mairg macaomh re na mó súil,

113 Bergin, *Irish Bardic Poetry,* introduction to No. 2, p. 27.
114 See Brendan Jennings, 'The career of Hugh, son of Rory O'Donnell Earl of Tyrconnell, in the Low Countries 1607-42', in *Studies,* vol. 30 (1941), pp 219-34, (hereafter 'The Career of Hugh, son of Rory').
115 B. Jennings, 'The Career of Hugh, son of Rory', pp 226-7.

faríor ní bhfuileam na ainbhfeas,
foireann do shíor thaibhgheas tnúidh.
(Ó Raghallaigh, *Duanta Eoghain Ruaidh Mhic
an Bhaird,* No. 5, st. 1, p. 76.)

[Alas for him who is the hostage for Murbhach's host, for youth
on whom the highest was set; we, the race ever existing in envy,
know this well.]

The poet describes Neachtain's imprisonment as though it were a traditional situation in which a hostage is retained by the victor to secure the
loyalty of the subjected sept. A compliment to Neachtain's personal importance is implicit in this stanza; he is important enough to be regarded
as a hostage who can guarantee the allegiance of the northern hosts.
Thus, what is now considered to be an event of the 'conquest' of Ireland,
is interpreted by a contemporary poet, in terms which indicate that the
attitude of the Gaelic participants in these events was not influenced by
considerations wider than their own immediate fate. The poet compares
Neachtain O'Donnell's early retirement from activities in Ulster, to Red
Hugh's clandestine abduction in his youth. Any reflection on the
dissimilar allegiances displayed by both parties regarding English activities in Ulster are unmentioned by the poet; the analogy remains true
from his perspective and it is this perspective of the poets which is one of
the keys to understanding the contemporary Gaelic aristocratic mentality:

Mar is follas da gach aoinneach
ar Aodh Ruadh do rugtha i nglas
i mbél a tharbha do thoigheacht;
tarla lén dar n-oireacht as.
(Ó Raghallaigh, *Duanta Eoghain Ruaidh Mhic
an Bhaird,* No. 5, st. 4, p. 76.)

[As we all know, Aodh Ruadh was captured before his benefits
could be realized; ruin therefore came on our assembly of nobles.]

Now, it is Neachtain's turn to be the object of the treacherous and en-
vious designs of his ill-wishers which caused his imprisonment. Indeed,
much of this 'envy' emanated from his own maternal grandmother, Inghean Dubh, mother of Red Hugh and of Neachtain's mother Nuala.

Needless to say, the poet does not identify the sources of the 'treacherous flood of envy':

Neachtain O Domhnaill fa dheireadh,
ar ndóchas lán, ar laogh búidh,
i n-aois leinbh, 'na dhamhna duine
tarla i gceilg na tuile tnúidh.
(Ó Raghallaigh, *Duanta Eoghain Ruaidh Mhic
an Bhaird*, No. 5, st. 6, p. 78.)

[And now Neachtain Ó Domhnaill, our great hope, our darling, our ungrown child, has been caught in the treacherous flood of envy.]

He, Neachtain, was the beloved of all the youth of Ireland, this popularity caused him to be suspect, leading to his captivity:

Ro-mheisde an meas, meisde an onóir,
nó an t-ainm ar tús tarrus lais,
nó an mhuirn fuair Neachtain 'na naoidhin
uainn tar sleacht-fhuil nGaoidhil nGlais.
(Ó Raghallaigh, *Duanta Eoghain Ruaidh Mhic
an Bhaird*, No. 5, st. 9, p. 78.)

[The worse for him were the respect and honour and fame won by him; and the affection which we gave him as a child beyond all the race of Gaoidheal Glas.]

This captivity, however, is fortuitous for Ireland. He is safer thus, knowing his propensity for valourous deeds and brave exploits:

Créad acht coiméad do chath Bhearnais
a bheith treimhsi mar tá sé,
ar daingion mar ghiall i ngéibhionn,
nach cailleadh fiadh Eirionn é.
(Ó Raghallaigh, *Duanta Eoghain Ruaidh Mhic
an Bhaird,* No. 5, st. 15, p. 80.)

[Is it not safety for Bearna's host that for a space he be, as he is, as hostage held in a fort, so that Éire might not lose him.]

At the same time, the poet urges prayers for the release of Neachtain;

Mary mother of God, will succour him:[116]

> Os Sí Aighne an uile gheimhligh
> guidheadh Muire, Máthair Dé,
> ag so roghain raoin gach sligheadh,
> cobhair da taoibh sireadh sé.
> (Ó Raghallaigh, *Duanta Eoghain Ruaidh Mhic*
> *an Bhaird,* No. 5, st. 21, p. 82.)

> [Let him pray Mary, Mother of God, for she has pleaded for all
> captives; let him ask help of her that is the best for all courses.]

Along with recourse to supernatural sources, however, the poet
recognizes the ultimate earthly authority over the fate of Neachtain. If
he proves his worth, by virtue of his own natural qualities and his
military efforts on behalf of the crown, 'ag cosaint chlú coróna Saxan',
he will be released again and be enabled to show his military worth:

> Acht go dtaisbeána eacht oile
> a uaisle a oirbheart re n-ég
> ag dion chlú choróna Saxan,
> 's onóra chrú gasraidh nGrég.
> (Ó Raghallaigh, *Duanta Eoghain Ruaidh Mhic*
> *an Bhaird,* No. 5, st. 17, p. 82.)

> [And that some day ere he dies he show his nobility and prowess,
> defending the glory of the Saxon's crown and the honour of Irish
> warriors.]

Again, as in the case of Niall Garbh, if the king were aware of Neachtain's true nature, he would relieve his case:

> Cosmhail da bhféachadh fir Shaxan
> a shubhailce, a cheannsa, a choir,
> nach éidir a mheas nach maothfadh
> eigean bheas go saorfadh soin.

---

[116] See a poem to another Niall Garbh O'Donnell (+ 1439) by Tadhg Óg Ó hUiginn,
written on the occasion of Niall's imprisonment in London. Particularly interesting in the
present context is the poet's appeals to the Virgin, and to Christ, note also Ó hUiginn's
declaration that but for O'Donnell's captivity, the Gael would not be disunited among
themselves (st. 11), in McKenna, *Irish Monthly,* November 1921, p. 461.

(Ó Raghallaigh, *Duanta Eoghain Ruaidh Mhic
an Bhaird,* No. 5, st. 19, p. 82.)

[It is unlikely that if the Saxons examine his virtue and gentleness
and his pledges, this will not soften their judgement of him; and
may help get him free.]

The various ways in which local chiefs in Ulster used the opportunities
provided by the English presence in Ulster are attested to by the various
activities and allegiances of Red Hugh and Rory on the one hand, and
Niall Garbh, his brothers and allies, on the other. One element in their
loyalties is clear; they made use of any opportunity to advance their own
traditional claims and their loyalty was held by the source from which
they could see the greatest amount of immediate personal advantage.
The poet Eoghan Rua Mac a' Bhaird wrote poems for both branches of
the Uí Dhomhnaill and treated all their activities as equally valid according to the world view from which they emanated; and which he in his
profession was peculiarly equipped to articulate. Evidently no 'new'
sense of Ireland as a political unit on the brink of conquest by England
and an attendant emergence of an embryonic proto-nationalistic sentiment is manifest either in the contemporary northern poetry or in the
political activities of those addressed in the poems. Likewise, Banbha
suffered no ignominy from James I's authority, indeed, his illustriousness added lustre to Banbha's glory, in fact she suffered in the
absence of this connection.

Southern poets, no less than their Northern counterparts, observed
the same rationale determining their loyalties and their interests. In the
later decades of the sixteenth century, claims to estates in southwest
Cork, originally in the Carew name, were revived by Sir Peter Carew
(+ 1575), on the basis that his ancestor Richard (+ 1199), husband of
McCarthy's daughter, Raghnailt, had received it as part of Henry II's
grant of Cork to Robert fitz Stephen.[117] Dunamark at Bantry Bay, and a
castle built there by Robert Carew, became Carew headquarters. It appears that the O'Daly poets became attached to the Carew family in the
late twelfth century along with their duties to 'O Mahoun, and . . . O
Glavin'.[118] Carew's title to the land lapsed in the mid-fourteenth century.

---

[117] See Anne O'Sullivan, 'Tadhg O'Daly and Sir George Carew', in *Éigse,* 14 (1971),
pp 27-38.
[118] O'Sullivan, 'Tadhg O'Daly and Sir George Carew', note 25, p. 34.

Sir Peter Carew amid much litigation unsuccessfully renewed the claim in the late 1560s, and his kinsman Sir George Carew, Lord President of Munster in the late sixteenth century, and envoy of James I in the seventeenth, continued the struggle to reclaim the lands.[119] The earlier agent of Carew, Sir John Hooker convened a meeting in Cork to gather information regarding his patron's claim. One of the witnesses present at the meeting was O'Daly.[120] Rivalry among senior and junior branches of the 'rhymer family' O'Daly caused dispute as to which branch ought to benefit most from the reinstatement of the Carews, who enjoyed primacy in Carbery, the area in dispute both between the poets and between Carew and the government. The significant factors for this discussion can be simplified thus; Sir George Carew (+ 1629) and his cousin Sir Peter Carew, were both active supporters of the official dispossession policy[121] that was being pursued by the crown in Ireland, and they sought to revive old invalidated titles there. Their intersts lay not only in Cork, but in Meath and Carlow also. A member of the famous O'Daly bardic family, in an effort to outdo a member of a rival branch of the family, made his loyalty to his prospective new, powerful patron quite clear. In a poem eulogizing Carew, he cites the antiquity of their mutual relations and promises to fulfil the poet's obligations in return for Carew's patronage. This poem 'Gabh mo gherán, a Sheóirse, . . .' is dated *c.* 1618,[122] a post-Kinsale period in a province which had witnessed the destruction of the Geraldine wars and the disruption of the efforts to implement the Munster plantation, not to speak of the waves of forfeiture and dispossession following these disturbances. Sir George Carew himself played a conspicuous part as Mountjoy's aid in his capacity as Lord President of Munster during this period.

In 1603 Sir Thomas Waddington submitted a report to Sir George Carew of the lands which his ancestors had allegedly held in Ireland. He described the origin of the claim and how it had lapsed and suggested

---

[119] G.A. Hayes-McCoy, *New History of Ireland,* vol. III, Chapter 3, p. 89.

[120] O'Sullivan, 'Tadhg O'Daly and Sir George Carew', p. 31.

[121] For details of Sir George Carew's effective military measures against Tyrone and his allies in Munster see G.A. Hayes-McCoy, in *New History of Ireland,* vol. III, chapter 3, pp 130-4 and *passim,* see also Aidan Clarke, in *New History of Ireland,* vol. III, chapter 7, pp 211-3, for Sir George's part in ensuring a Protestant majority for James's 1611 parliament.

[122] O'Sullivan, 'Tadhg O'Daly and Sir George Carew', note 31, p. 31.

ways to revive it.[123] He followed the Carew occupation of it down to the reign of Richard II and cited John Hooker's evidence as proof of the validity of Sir George Carew's suit.[124] Sir George Carew, therefore, as a member of the New English continued to press more ancient claims in Munster and Leinster. His exalted official position and his potential power in south-west Cork endeared him to the poet O'Daly. This O'Daly suggested that he was the true heir of a former namesake who was *ollamh* to Robert Carew, ancestor of Sir George. The material advantage of this claim was that the earlier poet had free grant of lands in Muntervary because of his position as *ollamh*. The poet wanted Sir George to champion his two claims — to ollamhship to Carew and to headship of his own sept, of O'Daly Carbery. These privileges were, it appears, being claimed by a rival O'Daly.[125]

The satisfaction of Carew's claims demanded the displacement of 'many' including Gaelic and English; McCarthy Reagh, Barry Oge, O'Mahon, O'Driscoll, O'Daly and others.[126] To these claims were added John Hooker's stipulations for '3,000 kine' and an annual 'reasonable' payment. The 'O'Daly' mentioned above belonged to the poet family of the same name. Land-ownership, privileges, hereditary rights and traditional vocations, all based on Gaelic Irish notions of the function and value of such concepts, were the principal factors of determination governing the 'response' of the Gaelic Irish bardic poets towards what has in retrospect been treated as a further instance of Tudor and Jacobite land-hunger and dismissal of native rights. Once again as has been shown to have occurred in the Ulster experience, the poets and the local native lords used the alternative options offered by the English presence in Munster to forward their own ends regardless of what are at this distance perceived as the wider consequences of these individually perceived events. Tadhg's address to Sir George Carew is full of praise for Sir George not only in his capacity as prospective overlord, but as saviour of Banbha.

The poet makes very clear the relationship in which he expects to stand

---

[123] J.S. Brewer and William Bullen, eds., *Calendar of the Carew Manuscripts, preserved at the Archiepiscopal library at Lambeth,* 6 vols., London 1867-73, (Kraus Reprint, London 1974), p. 439 (hereafter *Carew* MSS).

[124] *Carew* MSS, pp 440, 441.

[125] O'Sullivan, 'Tadhg O'Daly and Sir George Carew', pp 27-33.

[126] O'Sullivan, 'Tadhg O'Daly and Sir George Carew', note 25, p. 31.

vis-à-vis Sir George. He spells out the earlier contract between the first Carews and the O'Daly poetic family:

> Gabh mo gherán, a Sheóirse,
> cuimhnigh cion mo chineóil-se
> ag gach pór dod réimm romhuibh;
> mór dá réir do-rónabhair.
> (O'Sullivan, 'Tadhg O'Daly and Sir George
> Carew', st. 1, p. 33.)

> [Receive my complaint, o George; remember the regard that every seed of your line before you had for my kindred; you have done much to make provision for them.]

The poet makes his claims to his rights in three respects; the Carews granted a poet's portion to the Uí Dhálaigh in previous centuries. O'Daly knows this on the authority of his fellow-poets and because of the continuity in the Carew line. This land must be held free of cess by the poet since it is the poet's privilege. Tadhg O'Daly is, however, in no sense beholden to Carew. The generosity of the Carew family has been matched by the success of successive O'Daly poets in celebrating their valour and fame. He devotes much of the poem to an explanation of the landholding question:

> Rinn cheana do chinn fhine
> mar fuair cenn ar gceirdi-ne;
> déantar lat úaisle oram,
> glac an úair-se a uraghall.
> (O'Sullivan, 'Tadhg O'Daly and Sir George
> Carew', st. 8, p. 34.)

> [The head of our poetic family once got a promontory from the head of your family; deal generously, as I advise, receive now my complaint about it.]

The antiquity of the grant and the area are both emphasized; O'Daly, it must be remembered, is in dispute with a branch of his own family concerning title to the privileges of *ollamh*:

> Tug an té ó ttáinig sibh,
> a anáir ar lár ná léighidh,
> don chéidfher ór slonnadh sinn

bronnadh dárbh éigeann uirrim.
(O'Sullivan, 'Tadhg O'Daly and Sir George
Carew', st. 14, p. 34.)

[Your progenitor gave, do not disavow his gift, a grant that should
be honoured to the first ancestor from whom we are named.]

O'Daly wants the original terms to be renewed by this new/old
claimant:

Muinntear Bháire na dtrácht dte
ód shinnser fuair ar bhfine;
má tá sin daor'na dheghuidh
do bhí saor 'gár sinnseruibh.
(O'Sullivan, 'Tadhg O'Daly and Sir George
Carew', st. 15, p. 35.)

[Muntervary of the sheltered harbours [was the grant] my family
got from your ancestor; if it is taxed now, our ancestors had it
free.]

O'Daly clothes Sir George in tradition, neatly fitting him into a mould
which he, the poet, understood and thus enabled him to accept or reject
the newcomer according to traditional criteria; in a literary sense in the
poetry, and actually, in his scramble to maintain his traditional status,
O'Daly therefore equates Sir George with the first Carew, and as a corollary to this, he identifies himself with the earliest Carew's *ollamh*. This
is his 'justification' of his supplication to Sir George; and an illustration
of the scope of his own interests and principles:

An té ó dtáinig tusa.
's a' t-ollamh ór fhásus-sa,
sinn araon a ndá n-oigher;
a raon linn an leanfaider?
(O'Sullivan, 'Tadhg O'Daly and Sir George
Carew', st. 20, p. 35.)

[The progenitor from whom you are descended and the *ollamh*
from whom I grew, you and I are their heirs; shall we follow their
course?]

To press home his point, O'Daly reiterates the original strength of the
Carew-O'Daly relationship:

Ón chéadfher dod réim romhuibh
tug onóir dár n-ealadhain
féach go bhfuil ar ro-bháidh ruibh;
mh'onáir ná cuir ar chúlaibh.
(O'Sullivan, 'Tadhg O'Daly and Sir George Carew',
st. 21, p. 35.)

[From your first ancestor, the one who cherished our art, see that
we have always loved you greatly; do not abolish my privilege.]

The reciprocity which always characterized relations between chief
and poet are highlighted by O'Daly. He suggests that the loyalty of his
ancestors, and his own recognition now of Carew is of special
significance, since his particular branch of the O'Daly sept had never
sided with any foreigner but the Carews. A satire, written against the
Gaelic chiefs reputedly at the behest of Lord Mountjoy and Sir George
Carew and allegedly composed by the head of the Carbery Uí Dhálaigh
— one Aonghus Rua — would suggest that the rival branch of the Uí
Dhálaigh were also uninhibited about the acceptance of patronage by
'foreigners' or siding with them.[127] This particular branch of the sept is
that against which Tadhg O'Daly endeavours to strengthen his own
claim. He denounces the pretensions of his rivals:

An tslighe as ar íarr innmhe
fúair an cenn-so ar gcinidh-ne;
ní cóir file do rádh rinn
an tslighe ar lár do léigfinn.
(O'Sullivan, 'Tadhg O'Daly and Sir George
Carew', st. 22, p. 36.)

[The head of my family inherited the calling through which he
gained wealth; it is not right that a poet should say to me that I
should relinquish this calling.]

Intra-sept rivalry on two levels is evident here; professional jealousy
and conflicting land claims matter as much and more, to O'Daly than
the arguably invidious encroachments of an outsider. The extent to
which O'Daly is prepared to accept, and indeed champion, Sir George in

---

[127] O'Sulivan, 'Tadhg O'Daly and Sir George Carew', p. 31 and see also Brian Ó Cuív,
in *New History of Ireland,* vol. 3, chapter 20, p. 528.

his claims highlight the individually perceived nature of the advances of the Tudor conquest. O'Daly stresses his part in the O'Daly-Carew contract; he will celebrate the fame of Sir George Carew. His family perpetuated the Carew fame and valour throughout the centuries. He, as Carew's *ollamh,* will continue in this duty. The poet is convinced of the value of renown to Carew. The heroic basis of this motif forms a major part of the poet's rationale; his understanding of the contract which he can make with Carew. His expectation that Carew will both appreciate and reciprocate his submission first as a Gaelic chief might be expected to do, and then as the earlier colonists were wont to do, is illustrative of the poet's singular perceptions. O'Daly even threatens Carew with his notorious (professional) displeasure in case of default:

> Ní thuillte duid mo dhiomdha,
> fa Dhia is tú mo thighearna;
> righe ret' anáir doba áil
> dlighe gabháil ar ngeráin.
> (O'Sullivan, 'Tadhg O'Daly and Sir George
> Carew', st. 2, p. 33.)[128]

[Do not earn my displeasure, under God you are my lord; it is meet that I strive to honour you, you should accept our complaint.]

O'Daly claims his special relationship with Carew as his right; O'Dalys have always fulfilled their side of the lord/poet contract more than adequately. He is aware of disputes concerning what he perceives as his traditional rights:

> Gidh aidhbhseach é ag gach ollamh
> an fearann-so fuaramar;
> bladh as buaine iná an aidhbhsi
> do an uaine oruibh-si.
> (O'Sullivan, 'Tadhg O'Daly and Sir George Carew',
> st. 18, p. 35.)

[Though every *ollamh* thinks that this grant of land we got was enormous, we gave your family renown that stayed with [your ancestor's] name long after the chanting of [his] eulogies.]

---

128 Cf. Bergin, *Irish Bardic Poetry*, No. 20, st. 17, p. 90.

The effectiveness of the poet's efforts bear a distinct relation to the grants awarded by the lord:

> Ní buaine an toirbhert tug uaidh,
> an Carrúnach an chéadúair,
> ná a chlú gan char ar gcúluibh
> do an ar chrú an Charúnuigh.
> (O'Sullivan, 'Tadhg O'Daly and Sir George
> Carew', st. 19, p. 35.)

> [Not more enduring has been the grant that Carew gave in the first instance than the undying fame that has clung to the blood of Carew.]

The element of compliment is heavily underscored in the following stanza; the Carew grant to O'Daly is the greatest throughout Ireland, the eminence of Carew was such, however, as to afford such benevolence:

> Ar dheaghdhán dá ndernadh linn
> d'aoinfher dá uaisle a n-Éirinn,
> agad tsíol do bhí a bronnadh,
> díl mar í ní fhuaramar.
> (O'Sullivan, 'Tadhg O'Daly and Sir George
> Carew', st. 17, p. 35.)

> [For any fine poem that we have made for any man however noble in Ireland we have not got a reward like it; your family had the giving of it.]

Not only is Carew to repossess the patrimony of his worthy illustrious ancestors, but his own prowess and valour have enhanced their name and his own. Sir George Carew's part in subduing Tyrone and the disaffected elements in Munster were doubtless not unknown to O'Daly. It mattered little that Sir George's efforts were devoted to the expansion of the king's government in Ireland, and the prevention of continental catholic plots involving either the Gaelic or the Old English, all of whose loyalties he suspected because of their common catholicism.[129] Sir George causes the present poet to praise him as his ancestor was eulogized by an earlier O'Daly. Carew's battles are portrayed as being in

---

[129] *Carew* MSS, pp 305-10.

defence of Ireland and thus the cause of Tadhg O'Daly's praise:

> Mór do chuir clú do chinidh,
> ní hainm ar gcúl chuirfidhir,
> tú ad bharánta ar theacht as-tteagh
> a neart gabhála Gaedheal.
> (O'Sullivan, 'Tadhg O'Daly and Sir George
> Carew', st. 24, p. 36.)

[Greatly did our ancestor enhance the repute of your kindred, a reputation that will not be diminished; you were its guarantor when you came with a force for the defence of the Irish.]

Carew's pedigree could be accounted for, and his reputation guaranteed by munificence to the poet. The traditional validity of the poem depended on the poet's recognition of him above his rival and cousin as the senior of his sept, an oft-encountered problem in the Gaelic world of interminable intra-sept claims and counter-claims. Ó Dálaigh thereby placed Carew in a position enjoyed by many Gaelic chiefs, and all that would remain for O'Daly to do would be to apportion to him the task of rescuing Banbha from distress. This has indeed already been accomplished by Sir George. He too shall be provided with an appropriate *caithréim* (battle roll):

> Damh-sa as cóir a chur i gcéill,
> atá re cur id chaithréim,
> gan fher faghla 'ghá foghuil
> Banbha as-teagh go ttugobhair.
> (O'Sullivan, 'Tadhg O'Daly and Sir George
> Carew', st. 25, p. 36.)

[It is right that I make it known, I am going to put it in your 'battle-roll', that no raider has raided Ireland since you were brought in.]

O'Daly is under no misapprehension regarding the origin of Carew's troops. Carew banished evil from Ireland with troops from London:

> D'fhortacht Éireann, go dul duibh
> le dírmibh láech ó Londuin,
> do-chuaidh ort an ardbhladh,
> ní fhuair a holc d'ionarbadh.

(O'Sullivan, 'Tadhg O'Daly and Sir George
Carew', st. 26, p. 36.)

[Until you left London with a large body of troops, to help Ireland
she had not succeeded in banishing her evils; the fame of doing it
fell to you.]

Sir George created order and stability throughout Ireland:

Do fhágbhuis, ó chenn go cenn
an fonn aoibhinn-se Éireann
gan ghuid, gan éiginn, gan olc,
gan bhruid, darbh fhéitir fhortacht.
(O'Sullivan, 'Tadhg O'Daly and Sir George
Carew', st. 27, p. 36.)

[You left the beautiful land of Ireland free, from end to end, from
thieving, violence, evil and rapine in so far as it could be done.]

Sir George Carew, the most recent scion of an Elizabethan adventurer
family, is now hailed as the saviour of Banbha's land from civil
disorder; Sir George is the saviour of Banbha. This poem by Tadhg
O'Daly is the seventeenth century parallel of the work composed in the
early thirteenth century by Muireadhach Albanach Ó Dálaigh.[130] This
earlier Ó Dálaigh appealed to the 'foreigner' Richard de Burgo. In both
cases the poet seeks patronage, both from an acknowledged 'foreigner';
both also assign the duty and privilege of succouring Banbha to the
prospective patron, and both lords receive the poets' *imprimatur* for
power they already hold.

Clearly, the mentality underlying the poem has departed very little
from the perceptions and preoccupations articulated by the poet of four
centuries before. To avoid over-simplification it must be pointed out
that to suggest that the mentality articulated in bardic poetry changed
very little is not to suggest a state of stasis or to represent Gaelic society
as having undergone no change in four hundred years. It must be
recognized, however, that while early modern England[131] produced a

---

[130] Bergin, *Irish Bardic Poetry*, No. 17.

[131] See, Christopher Hill, *Change and Continuity in Seventeenth Century England*
(London, 1974) and J.H. Elliott, 'Revolution and Continuity in Early Modern Europe' in
Past and Present, No. 42 (February 1969), especially pp 40-4.

dynamic polity, demonstrating increased sophistication and vitality as the seventeenth century progressed, the Gaelic Irish polity experienced no such development.[132] The energies of the Gaelic Irish polity during the same period were absorbed in surviving the inroads made on it by external elements. The sophistication of Gaelic society is demonstrated only in this capacity for adaptation and survival. The strengths of one society therefore, its sophistication and expansion, cannot be compared with the strengths of the other; the compromises, accommodations and adaptations of the older society. The latter was ultimately unable to compete against the dynamic strength of the newer. One might suggest the phrase 'failure to develop' to describe the fragmented Gaelic polity of the late sixteenth century. The word failure, however suggests that an attempt had been made by the Gaelic Irish to achieve to a polity based on a rationale entirely foreign to their own perceptions and, that having consciously done so, they had failed. The elusive 'high-king', the political unity of the 'five provinces' remained elusive. The factor or factors which could forge the Gaelic and Anglo-Norman warring septs into one single recognizable polity were never produced.

James I's extension of the king's writ throughout all Ireland in 1605 was the first occasion on which Ireland was legally and politically a single administrative unit. The evidence from the Gaelic poets would indicate that this development was a welcome one. The king's administrators were hailed, his judgements applauded, himself hailed as the one for whom Banbha waited. The imposition of 'foreign' perceptions; a foreign rationale of power which accompanied the extension of the crown's administration and its officers throughout the country, more than anything else perhaps, exposed the incomprehension of the Gaelic Irish élites of this new mentality. In this context the term 'failure' is especially misleading, while individual chiefs and poets attempted to survive in a new order, and failed signally, their efforts were undertaken entirely in accordance with their own concept of survival, of values and loyalties, Gaelic aristocratic society and all its trappings failed because it wore away under the pressure exerted by a more robust society.

It is important to realize that the Gaelic aristocracy, as a facet of the Gaelic world, failed of itself. Its survival techniques were inadequate for the task of combatting the pressure of English competition. Those, of

---

[132] See Derick Thomson, *An Introduction to Gaelic Poetry* (London, 1974), p. 117.

the élites, who survived were those who consciously accepted many of the perceptions of the rival civilization. The *raison d'être* of the native aristocracy depended on the survival of the indigenous rationale of power and the methods of seeking and retaining it which regulated the active lives of the Gaelic lords and subsequently every element of their political and social self-image. The principal exponents of this rationale, the chiefs, and its articulators the poets, could accept a new set of perceptions only if they completely abrogated their own importance and position.

It is in this context one must consider the work of the Gaelic poets of the early and mid-seventeenth century. This is the period during which the autonomous and semi-autonomous and variously powerful Gaelic septs were reduced to the status of landowners at home and professional swordsmen abroad, and many of them chafed under the weight of unachievable, anachronistic claims to power, status and wealth. One does not, therefore, consider the poem of Tadhg O'Daly's for George Carew as an act of collaboration on the part of the poet with a conquering power; the treacherous self-seeking policy of a poet attempting to outwit his rival by playing the enemies game. The poet welcomes the new 'chief' as he would a powerful new O'Mahony, O'Glavin or O'Driscoll.[133]

It is appropriate for the early decades of the seventeenth century, just around the time of his composition for Sir George, that Tadhg O'Daly composed a wonderful elegy for Florence O'Driscoll:

> Sir Finghin or Florence O'Driscol, was the head of this family and was knighted. He was loyal all his life till he joined in Tyrone's rebellion; but after the defeat of the Irish at Kinsale, he was pardoned for politic reasons.[134]

This Florence O'Driscoll also, Gaelic chief of his time:

> leased the whole territory of Corca-Laoidhe Mór or Lollymore, to Thomas Crooke, Esq., an Englishman, for twenty one years,

---

[133] Cf. Tadhg O'Daly's poem for Florence O'Driscoll in O'Donovan (ed.), *Miscellany of the Celtic Society* (Dublin, 1849), Appendix pp 340-51. For problems concerning the identity of this Tadhg O'Daly see O'Sullivan, 'Tadhg O'Daly and Sir George Carew', p. 32.

[134] O'Donovan, *Miscellany of the Celtic Society,* note *e*, Appendix, p. 342.

for the sum of £2,000. [135]

This alienation of Gaelic sept lands was not exclusively a result of bloody or brutal plantations. Tadhg O'Daly sought survival on his own terms, so too did Sir Florence. The power of the chiefs died with the extension of crown administration throughout the country. The most militant chiefs left for Europe in 1607. The social degradation of the families of the ruling septs diminished their participation in and their perpetuation of, the aristocratic values and perceptions. The poets, who were in many ways the keepers of the Gaelic aristocratic code, the articulators of the perceptions and values of a dying order, maintained the edifice and subscribed to the ethos for some time after the Gaelic political order had died. Just how persistent this world view was both among the scattered remnants of the aristocracy, and among the poets, is one of the most fascinating elements of the confused decades of the first half of the seventeenth century.

---

[135] O'Donovan, *Miscellany of the Celtic Society,* note *f*, p. 342.

IV

OLD THEMES
IN A
'NEW ORDER'

'Na thráth féin ní facas linn
aon bheart do fhóirfeadh Éirinn,
mar budh cair cur an ghaiscidh
ar sgur an áigh urmhaistir.
(Williams, *Giolla Brighde Mac Con Midhe,*
No. 13, st. 17, p. 140.)

THE DISINTEGRATION OF the institutions of Gaelic society which became increasingly evident at many levels during the seventeenth century included the demise of the bardic schools of poetry. Poetry which is immediately recognizable as being different in many ways from that included in official *duanairí* and written by poets other than those of the professional bardic families, seemed to emerge into some prominence from the mid-seventeenth century onwards.[1] Many of the compositions of such 'new' poets were written not in syllabic but in accentual metres and in the increasingly popular *amhrán* metre, a metre which became popular with professional poets from the mid-sixteenth century. The increased popularity of the *amhrán* metre and the advent of newcomers to the poets' world are two elements which have contributed to the difficulty in interpreting late seventeenth century poetry. The *amhrán* metre, which made use of a simpler poetic idiom, may have made the poetry more accessible to literate individuals whose studies had not included

---

[1] Brian Ó Cuív, *New History of Ireland,* Vol. III, chap. 20, pp 528-542 and cf. Allan Macinnes, 'Scottish Gaeldom 1638-1651'. See also D.C. Fowler, *A literary History of the Popular Ballad* (Durham, 1968), pp 85-95.

the more complex language associated with the syllabic metres.[2] The fact that individuals of more diverse educational experience than that of the school-trained bardic poet, may have undertaken poetic composition, doubtless broadened the personal referential base of their compositions. It appears, however, that innovation in form should not be immediately equated with innovation in basic content or perceptions. Learned poets of the seventeenth century, writing in syllabic or accentual metres, produced few works which could be said to indicate a change in their perception of the poet's rôle which was in any way inconsistent with that of their literary predecessors. That is to say that the seventeenth century produced poets whose abiding preoccupations mirrored those of their predecessors though their social and political context was rapidly changing.

Poets depended on patronage — usually that of the native or gaelicized aristocracy. The decline of these classes in the seventeenth century meant that the poets increasingly relied on other socially or politically prominent individuals for patronage. This situation, along with the attendant elevation of the lower orders, highlighted some of the principal functions of the poets' profession in compositions where they endeavour to account for their demands under changing conditions.[3] The poets' great claim was that they alone could confer immortality even on the most renowned hero, or, conversely, on the most insignificant person. The social exclusivity which had made the poets' function important was threatened by change, social and political, or by threats specifically levelled at their profession.[4] In the seventeenth century their existence was threatened by the decline of the classes to whom they traditionally looked for patronage. Nothing could present a bleaker picture to the poet than that the elaborate structure, built on precedent and comparison and analogy, which they shaped and expanded and manipulated should be set at naught.[5] Underlying the structure was the

---

[2] See Helga Hammerstein, 'Aspects of the continental education of Irish students in the reign of Elizabeth I' in *Historical Studies,* 8 (Dublin 1971), pp 137-54, and D.S. Thomson, 'Gaelic Learned Orders and Literati in Medieval Scotland', in *Scottish Studies,* xii 1968.

[3] See N.J.A. Williams, *The Poems of Giolla Brighde Mac Con Midhe* (Dublin, 1980), poems no. 18 and 21 and see C. Mág Craith, *Dán na mBráthar Mionúr* 2 vols (Dublin 1967, 1980), poem no. 24, p. 121.

[4] N.J.A. Williams, *The Poems of Giolla Brighde Mac Con Midhe,* notes p. 340 and see also, Pádraig A. Breatnach's review of Williams in *Éigse* 19, pp 411-26.

[5] Williams, *The Poems of Giolla Brighde Mac Con Midhe,* no. 18.

heroic value of immortality among one's people. A life of heroism, bravery and acclaim, no matter how brief, is the great heroic aspiration.[6] This, however, must be balanced against the manifest willingness and ability of both chiefs and poets to attain and maintain wealth and power by unheroic means. The heroic ethos was built into the fabric of the poets' professional mentality and formed part of the rationale of the eternally warring Gaelic septs.[7] Time diluted this fundamental principle into a social exclusivity, leading to an intense snobbery on the part of the poets. To them the Gaelic world would be unthinkable without the complex structures of genealogy, the competition between septs and their professional compositions articulating its rationale. They guarded the traditional knowledge and held it for the use of the aristocracy.[8]

The search for patronage and the poet's need of appreciation for his particular function ensured that the practice of eulogizing a likely patron remained a constant feature of bardic poetry in the seventeenth century. The poet, in turn, accommodated his patron in the bardic scheme according to a rationale far more complex than the demands of the immediate political situation and therefore not specifically subject to the political vicissitudes of the moment. Success and generosity, rather than consistency[9] in politics exercised a greater attraction for the poets. Seventeenth-century learned poetry must be interpreted therefore, not only in the light of momentous contemporary political and social events, but in the reinterpretation of such events as they are articulated for us through the traditional perceptions of the poets. It is particularly interesting to examine seventeenth century poetry in the context of the earlier and contemporary professional bardic poetry because of the changes which occur in the literary form during the seventeenth century, and because of the emergence of works by poets of whose professional literary background we are unsure. The innovations in literary form lead us to expect innovation in perception, development in the rationale governing the thrust of the compositions, evidence

---

[6] *Stories from the Táin* ed. with notes and glossary by J. Strachan, and re-edited by Osborn Bergin (Dublin [1944] third edition 1976), p. 12.

[7] See Katharine Simms, 'Warfare in the medieval Gaelic lordships', *Irish Sword,* vol. 12 (1975-6), pp 98-109; and Katharine Simms, *From Kings to Warlords,* esp. pp 147-50.

[8] Williams, *The Poems of Giolla Brighde Mac Con Midhe,* poem no. 18, sts. 22 and 28, p. 210.

[9] Cf. Allan Macinnes, 'Scottish Gaeldom, 1638-51', esp. pp 84-90.

perhaps of ideological development among the literati who addressed current political developments. The most remarkable characteristic of the more well known works of the seventeenth century poetry as written by non-professional bardic poets is its adherence to the perceptions traditionally articulated in bardic poetry, to the *mores* celebrated in professional bardic poetry and to the social and political preoccupations we have come to associate with the poetry of the schools. It is appropriate, therefore, to consider some compositions of Geoffrey Keating (+ 1644?) and Pádraigín Haicéad (+ 1654); two poets of the seventeenth century whose similar backgrounds cause them to be linked together. They shared a common Old English background,[10] and both were educated for the priesthood abroad. Collections of their respective works include a typical mixture of elegy, encomium, eulogy, epithalamium and occasional poems of a more general nature. Among the poems attributed to Keating and Haicéad are a number of stylish love poems which are independent in theme of the reality of the clerical character of either poet.[11] Neither poet was a professional poet in the sense in which the traditional bardic poets are regarded as such. Both were adept users of syllabic metres however, and both frequently used the *amhrán* metre as well. Another characteristic they shared was their intimacy with, and devotion to, the Butler sept. Haicéad and Keating were probably patronized by various members of that family, especially by Edmond, third lord Dunboyne.

Keating and Haicéad belong properly neither to the category of professional bardic poet nor to the category of dilettante nobleman poet which is where their fellow poet and contemporary Piaras Feiritéir (+ 1653) belongs. Their works, which deal with the usual topics appropriate to learned Gaelic poetry of the period, have been seen by some

---

[10] See Aidan Clarke, *The Old English in Ireland 1625-1641* (London, 1966) and Aidan Clarke, *The Graces 1625-1641* (Dundalk 1968) and Aidan Clarke, 'Colonial Identity in Early Seventeenth Century Ireland', *Historical Studies* XI (Belfast 1978), pp 57-72; N.P. Canny, *From Reformation to Restoration: Ireland 1534-1660* (Dublin 1987); P.J. Corish, *The Catholic Community in the Seventeenth and Eighteenth Centuries;* Nicholas Canny, 'Identity Formation in Ireland: The Emergence of the Anglo-Irish', in Nicholas Canny and Anthony Pagden (eds), *Colonial Identity in the Atlantic world, 1500-1800* (Princeton, 1987), pp 159-212.

[11] Máire Ní Cheallacháin (ed.), *Filíocht Phádraigín Haicéad* (Dublin 1962), nos 1, 2, 3, 4, 5, 18, 28; and Eoin Mac Giolla Eáin (ed.), *Dánta is Amhráin is Caointe Sheathrúin Céitinn* (Dublin 1900), nos 4, 8, 13.

historians to carry a new message. They have been interpreted as heralding a new departure in perceptions of politics and religion indicating especially the poets' new perception of Ireland as a self-consciously single, united, catholic, political entity. [12] An examination of a selection of poems by Haicéad bemoaning the diminution of his status as poet in Ireland and in France are instructive as to his perception of his own status as poet and how the traditional sources of patronage and the traditional modes of complaint were equally suitable for his compositions and for those of the professional poet Fearghal Óg mac a' Bhaird (fl. 1600s). [13] Among the extant poems attributed to Haicéad are two poems dated 'Louvain 1630'. Their place of composition and their date do nothing more than identify these two facts, otherwise these poems might have been written by an Ulster poet in Munster or *vice versa*. Haicéad's preoccupation in the first of these two poems is the lack of appreciation shown him by foreigners surrounding him in Louvain; it was not so in Ireland, where he was esteemed among his people. The contrast in his treatment from one country to another is so stark that if those in Louvain are right, then the Irish who bestow such honours on him must be fools:

Ag ríogradh ce bhinn'se, do bharr ar chéad
fa dhíol ceana i gcríochoirear Tháil is Té,
ní saoiltear sa tír seo ach mar gharlach mé
gan aoinfhios i gcríonacht tar "as ar se".
. . . .
. . . mas saoithe na daoine bheir táir dham féin,
gur daoithe mic Mhíleadh i bhfádaibh Néill.
(Ní Cheallacháin, *Haicéad Poems*, No. 6, p. 7.)

[Though I used to be an object of esteem in Ireland (lit. land of Tál and Té) in preference to hundreds — for my compositions, in this country I am regarded as a miserable bastard, ignorant of antiquity beyond "as ar se" . . .
If those who scorn me be sages, then the sons of Míleadh

---

[12] Dunne, 'Evidence', pp 11-17 and *passim;* Canny, 'Formation', pp 104-6 and *passim.*
[13] Rev. Paul Walsh, *Irish Men of Learning,* (ed.) Colm Ó Lochlainn (Dublin 1947), pp 151-9.

in Niall's land are fools.][14]

In Louvain, therefore, we understand that Haicéad's status as a poet is unnoticed and unrewarded. Another poet, also in Louvain during the early decades of the seventeenth century made the same complaint. Fearghal Óg mac a' Bhaird (fl. 1600s), while in Louvain, appealed to the absentee archbishop of Tuam, Flaithrí Ó Maolchonaire (+ 1629). The latter belonged to a family of traditional professional historians and poets.[15] To him the poet complained that he was without due privilege in Louvain. This indignity was compounded by the fact that about him were fellow displaced countrymen of no status, now well-dressed and receiving Spanish pensions.[16] In the poem above, Haicéad suggested that in Ireland the situation is otherwise — there poets and learning are appreciated. A second poem of his however, similarly dated 'Louvain 1630' reverses this opinion. Again, failure to remunerate the poet is the primary complaint of Haicéad:

A aicme ar ar dhoirt mo thoil-se a tionngradh dil,
nár aisig dham nod do chomhall cineáltais,
don bhathlach bheag bhocht gan chothrom compánaigh,
is mairg do loisg a shop is a thiompáin libh.
(Ní Cheallacháin, *Haicéad Poems*, No. 8, st. 2, p. 6.)

[O race upon whom my goodwill poured out its loyal love, who never repaid one jot of equivalent affection to the small poor churl, without worthy companionship — I pity who would sacrifice his all for you.]

It appears that Haicéad could find a congenial audience in neither country. Yet another of his poems, from its title, probably written in France gives the lie to both:

Isan bhFrainc im dhúscadh dhamh
in Éirinn Chuinn im chodladh;

---

[14] The change of status experienced or expressed by Haicéad in this poem recalls the complaints of the painter Dürer who seems to have felt himself similarly treated in Venice: '*Hier bin ich ein Herr, doheim ein Schmarotzer,* as cited in Peter Burke, *Tradition and Innovation in Renaissance Italy,* p. 86.

[15] Walsh, *Irish Men of Learning,* pp 34-48.

[16] Flaithrí Ó Maolchonaire, *Desiderius* [Louvain, 1616], ed. T.F. O'Rahilly (Dublin 1955), Introduction, p. ix; and Mág Craith, *Dán na mBráthar Mionúr,* no. 24, p. 121.

beag ar ngradh uaidh don fhaire —
do thál suain ar síor fhaire.
(Ní Cheallacháin, *Haicéad Poems,* No. 13, p. 10.)

[When awake I am in France, in Ireland when asleep, though little
I like wakefulness, constant watching induces sleep.]

Further poems by Haicéad to Edmond, Viscount Dunboyne reveal his
preference for Ireland, simply because that is where Edmond is.[17] To
read any one of these poems by Haicéad in isolation or in ignorance of
the literary context of his compositions, would lead to a misinterpretation of the sentiments expressed in any individual poem and its relation
to contemporary events. Undoubtedly the poems have a literary validity
and artistic integrity in their own right as with all literary artefacts, but
when being interpreted as possible historical source material the literary
complexities cannot be evaluated as fact. It has been suggested that
these poems of Haicéad represent the poet's successful escape from the
localism and impersonal conventionalism of the earlier poetry and that
this development indicated a politically significant ideological advance
in the perceptions of contemporary Gaelic poets.[18] This transformation
has been seen as having been brought about by the twin pressures of the
influence of counter-reformation ideology on poets with continental
contacts and the new political awareness it fostered in them.[19] In the
literary context of *dánta deoraíochta* written principally by those clerics
who went abroad voluntarily to suffer the 'white martyrdom' of exile,
and in the context of the contradictory nature of the sentiments expressed in any two of Haicéad's 'exile' poems, it is hardly safe to assume
any new departure in political terms being expressed by him in these
compositions. It is perhaps more instructive to look at them as examples
of how the demands of the literary genre and the consciousness of the
traditional persona of the poet, shaped what each individual had to say.
What is known of Haicéad's life seems to indicate his personal commitment to the vigorous catholicism of Counter-Reformation Europe. The
extent to which this personal commitment pervaded his poetry, effec-
ting a change in the fundamental perceptions articulated is open to question. Haicéad undoubtedly used some of the more simple rhetoric of the

---

[17] Ní Cheallacháin, *Haicéad Poems,* No. 14, st. 2, p. 10.
[18] Dunne, 'Evidence', p. 17.
[19] Dunne, 'Evidence', pp 11-17.

Counter-Reformation in the course of his compositions, but in any instance where a political dimension can be ascertained, this can be shown to have been entirely at the service of the traditional demands and exigencies of the bardic convention and mentality.

The same seems to be true for the nobleman/poet Piaras Feiritéir [20] who was active on behalf of the Confederation in the mid-century. [21] His activities in the confederation military endeavour and his subsequent hanging have led some historians to suggest that his poetry reflects the exhalted standards of enthusiastically catholic Europe and the exacting standards of the revitalized Roman Catholic church. [22] Many of his compositions are love poems which owe more to the courtly love genre than they do to the Counter-Reformation. His elegy for Maurice Fitzgerald son of the Knight of Kerry, who died in the service of the king of Spain in Flanders, presents the usual features of elegy; Fitzgerald is lamented as a scion of the 'Florentine' and 'Grecian' Geraldines. [23] The territory bewailed his loss and in this particular poem the local spirits *mná sídhe* do also. This is certainly an element far removed from the standards of catholic orthodoxy. Much is made of his connections with Philip of Spain — monarch of a leading catholic power. It is neither innovative in the thematic sense nor intended to highlight the poet's personal allegiance to the catholic party. The tradition demanded that the object of elegy or eulogy be well connected socially by blood or by association of some kind. The poet's pride in these 'connections' was not necessarily guided by shared political or religious allegiances. The perceived compliment is based on the status of the individual whom the poet cited as a patron, friend or protegé of the addressee. [24]

Among the talents and accomplishments listed by Feiritéir in respect of Fitzgerald was his power of seducing women. [25] The seduction of women, polygamy and related 'vices' were among the irregularities to be reformed in Gaelic Ireland by the continentally-trained clergy. One such reforming priest was Geoffrey Keating whose prose work *Trí*

---

[20] Canny, 'Formation', pp 103-4.

[21] See P.S. Dineen (ed.), *Dánta Phiarais Feiritéir* (Dublin, 1903).

[22] Canny, 'Formation', pp 103-5.

[23] Dineen, *Feiritéir Poems,* Notes p. 131 and poem no. 1, p. 73.

[24] Cf. James Carney, *Butler Poems,* No. 16, sts. 2 and 11, pp 74 and 94; McKenna, *O'Hara Poems,* No. 3, st. 14, p. 54; and Bergin, *Irish Bardic Poetry,* No. 17, st. 12, p. 75.

[25] Dineen, *Feiritéir Poems,* No. 1, lines 57-60, p. 75; and cf. D. Greene, *Maguire Poems,* No. 20, st. 3, p. 180.

Biorghaoithe an Bháis [1631] fulminated at some length about the evil which attended irregular moral practices among the Gaelic and Old English nobles. The punishment which visited adulterers, according to Keating's work, was that the offenders would be without male heirs. He went so far as to list by name those whom he considered to have been so punished.[26] This public condemnation in the name of reform from a zealous contemporary of Feiritéir is impressive in its own context. It is an illustration of Keating as reformer. His 'warning' may have exerted moral pressure on the personal conduct of those to whom it was addressed; it may have had an impact on the morality of men such as Piaras Feiritéir. It did not, however, exert a transformation on the fundamental considerations which dictated the compositions of the poets, nor indeed did it dictate the tone of Keating's own poetic compositions. In the well known love poem 'A bhean lán de stuaim', attributed to Keating, the poet discourages the attentions of a woman to himself, emphasizing the disparity of their respective ages, not his clerical vocation. Nor does the poet take the opportunity offered by the subject of the poem to impress a facet of Counter-Reformation doctrine on the listener or reader.[27]

Feiritéir also wrote a panegyric for Meg Russell[28] a kinswoman of William Russell (Chief Justice of Ireland, 1558-1613). The poem includes a list of some of Meg Russell's socially and politically prominent relations and friends — all of whom were involved in English politics, none of whom were in any way sympathetic to, or supportive of, Counter-Reformation, or Old English or Gaelic Irish aspirations:

> Siúir Iarla Essex fuair uile,
> Is diúic dícheannta an ór fhuilt,
> lucht sugh-chorp is ngairt-phort ngaoi
> hAirfort Sufolc is Suraoi.
> (Dineen, *Feirtéir Poems,* No. 9, lines 61-64, pp 105-11.)

[She is a kinswoman of the Earl of Essex who was unfortunate [beheaded 1601], and of the beheaded golden-haired duke (?) (a

---

[26] Geoffrey Keating, *Trí Biorghaoithe an Bháis,* ed. Osborn Bergin (2nd edition) (Dublin 1931), Book III, chapter 6, p. 171.

[27] Ní Cheallacháin, *Haicéad Poems,* no. 30, p. 21.

[28] Dineen, *Feirtéir Poems,* poem no. 9 and notes p. 158.

kinswoman of) the brave strong group of the rugged fortress of Hereford, Suffolk and Surrey.]

Feiritéir makes no comment on the reasons why Essex[29] was beheaded, or how these might prove hard to reconcile with allegiances subscribed to by Hereford and Suffolk, not to speak of Feiritéir's own. Meg Russell's connections with the earl of Cork who became a great anti-Old English, anti-Catholic force, are boasted of because of his socially exalted position.

One of the poems attributed to both Haicéad and Keating[30] is a lengthy elegy on the death of Edmond Butler, third Baron Dunboyne in 1640. This Edmond had two sons who joined with Mountgarret on the Confederate side in 1642. A third son, James, who became the fourth Lord Dunboyne, was involved in the war too. He was excommunicated following the Ormond and Inchiquin peace in 1647 and left for the continent until the restoration.[31] The third baron died just before the outbreak of hostilities, Edmond Butler (nicknames *Éamonn an Chuirnín/* Éamonn of the ringlets) was a favourite of Haicéad and Keating. He was also the subject of at least two poems by Eoghan Ó Con Muighe.[32] The poems are all dated between 1630 and 1640. The poems by the three poets are particularly interesting because they demonstrate how close to the tradition the two priest/poets remained in their compositions for Dunboyne. The world-view articulated in their poems for him is no different from that indicated by the compositions of the professional bardic poet Ó Con Muighe. Haicéad and Keating, clerics of whose background and allegiances we know something, were new arrivals on the literary scene. Their continental experiences, their social background and their familiarity with foreign politics and philosophies lent their compositions a breadth of reference wider than that of the traditional repertoire. In contrast to these, Ó Con Muighe was a member of a hereditary professional family of unknown political or religious allegiances. The addressee, Dunboyne, was a member of an established Anglo-Norman sept, the senior head of which was a

---

[29] G.A. Hayes-McCoy in *A New History of Ireland,* vol. III, p. 128-9.

[30] Ní Cheallacháin, *Haicéad Poems,* No. 30, p. 21.

[31] See Mac Giolla Eáin, *Dánta Amhráin is Caointe Sheathrúin Céitinn,* p. 213; and Ní Cheallacháin, *Haicéad Poems,* Introduction, pp xiv-xv.

[32] James Carney, *Butler Poems,* nos 5, 12 and 14.

protestant. The entire family was involved in every faction of the Confederation in both the pro- and anti-nuncio parties. The obvious complexities surrounding the relations between the clerics and the baron; between Dunboyne and a Gaelic Irish hereditary poet and the complicated nature of the decade would seem to demand some manifestation in the poetry.

The poems written for Éamonn an Chuirnín by the poets mentioned above, show no significant development in the poets' mentality whatsoever; no element appears in them that might be construed as indicating any transformation of the poet's mentality as influenced by their continental experiences, their personal commitment to Counter-Reformation ideals or their conviction that a turning point had arrived in the fortunes of Gaelic Ireland. One is presented rather with a traditional elegy by Haicéad, and a number of smaller occasional poems by Haicéad, Keating and Ó Con Muighe bewailing Dunboyne's temporary indisposition.[33]

Haicéad's elegy opens with an invitation to the *lucht caointe* [keening company] to make room for the poet for his own contribution:

> Druidigh suas a chuaine an chaointe,
> tug bhar dtreas i dteas na díthe,
> Tagbhaidh feart na flatha fíre
> Fúm-sa tamall re tagra maoidhte.
> (Ní Cheallacháin, *Haicéad Poems,* No. 30, st. 1, p. 21.)

[Draw up, O mourning company, who have made your lament (lit. given your bout) in the heat of the loss. Leave the grave of the true prince to me a while for an anguished display.]

Haicéad continues the elegy in a most traditional manner; including the comparison of his loss with losses in history and mythology,[34] the planets and heavens witnessing his misfortune,[35] the baron's personal status, his fabled generosity, his illustrious social and family

---

[33] Ní Cheallacháin, *Haicéad Poems,* no. 30; Mac Giolla Eáin, *Dánta Amhráin is Caointe Sheathrúin Céitinn,* no. 18; Carney, *Butler Poems,* no. 14.

[34] Ní Cheallacháin, *Haicéad Poems,* no. 30, st. 40, p. 22.

[35] Ní Cheallacháin, *Haicéad Poems,* no. 30, lines 57-60, p. 23.

connections. Once again, the 'chiefs' nobility,[36] beauty, generosity,[37] influence over the elements and the heavens, his loss to his subjects high and low — are all recalled. His ferocity in war was equalled in intensity only by his mildness and intelligence in peace.[38] His antecedents are some among the most illustrious of Gaelic and Old English families. In a stanza acknowledging Butler's English/foreign blood, Haicéad enters into the bardic rationale of acceptance of the foreigner. His English blood is proudly declared noble by Haicéad, himself of Old English background:

> A ghallfhuil féin i réim na Raoileann,
> síorghabhla fineamhna fíre,
> isí a sgoth ba phosd dá phríomhfhuil;
> eisean a mbláth is barr na míre.
> (Ní Cheallacháin, *Haicéad Poems,* No. 30,
> lines 261-4, p. 29.)

> [His own foreign blood [is] in power in Ireland (?), eternal branch of the true vine, the best part was the foundation of his principal blood-line; and he himself its blossom and the zenith of its portion.]

For all that, he is connected too with the most illustrious southern septs, MacCarthy and O'Brien, and those of the Gall-Gael; Burkes, Barrys and Roches.[39] Haicéad thus lists both Gaelic and Anglo-Norman nobility of Munster and Thomond. Linked with this is the implied superiority of Butler over them all:

> Triatha uaisle dhó i mbuannacht do bhíodar,
> ar chíos láimhe mar ránaig ar ríograidh;
> 's do bhíodh fóir fá sdioraip ag sdríocadh

---

[36] Ní Cheallacháin, *Haicéad Poems,* no. 30, lines 93-6, p. 24; and see Knott, *Tadhg Dall Ó hUiginn,* no. 26, p. 160, esp. sts. 9, 10, p. 161.

[37] Ní Cheallacháin, *Haicéad Poems,* no. 30, line 148, p. 25; and see Canny, 'Formation', p. 104.

[38] Ní Cheallacháin, *Haicéad Poems,* no. 30, lines 149-56, pp 25-6.

[39] Ní Cheallacháin, *Haicéad Poems,* no. 30, lines 265-72, p. 29.

dob arrachta i ndánacht 's i ndíghnit.[40]
(Ní Cheallacháin, *Haicéad Poems,* No. 30,
lines 301-4, p. 30.)

[Noble lords were in military service to him, his (own?)[41] like that
which came to kingdoms, and there were assistants humbly attending at his stirrup, he was powerful in bravery and in dignity.]

Haicéad's own perception of his relationship with his patron is entirely
traditional, uninfluenced at this level by the undoubted disparity that
existed between his particular background and lifestyle and that of the
professional bardic poet whose voice, and world view, Haicéad assumed in his literary persona.

Damh is dleacht a leacht do líonadh,
damh is córa a sgeol do sgaoileadh,
damh is dual a ruaig do ríomhadh,
os damh is eolcha a ghlór 's a ghníomhra.
Tréith bheith riamh go dian le dícheall
. . . ar a bhéasaibh ag féachain go fíoghar.
(Ní Cheallacháin, *Haicéad Poems,* No. 30,
lines 115-21, p. 21.)

[I ought to compile his grave-mound, it is most fitting for me to tell
about him, it is natural for me to recount his escapades since I am
most knowledgeable of his glory and deeds.
Through continually and truly
. . . observing his habits.][42]

---

[40] See C. Litton Falkiner, *Illustrations of Irish History and Topography, mainly of the
seventeenth century* (London 1904), p. 283, in Moryson's *Itinerary:* the great lords attending Butler and the companies attending his stirrup in Haicéad's poem remind one of
Moryson's comment on the pretensions of the Irish chiefs:
'The poorest of any sept or name repute themselves gentlemen, and so will be swordmen,
despising all arts and trades, to maintain them; yet, such is the oppression of the great
lords towards the inferior sort the gentlemen and freeholders as I have seen the chief of a
sept ride with a gentleman of his own name (so learned as he spake Latin) running
barefoot at his stirrup'.
[41] Ní Cheallacháin, *Haicéad Poems,* note p. 133.
[42] See McKenna, *Magauran Poems,* no. 4, st. 21 (couch-fellow) and no. 11, sts. 10-22;
no. 19, sts. 26-32; and see Breatnach's discussion of this conceit in 'The Chief's Poet'; see
also Carney, *Studies in Irish Literature and History,* 'The Féuch Féin Controversy', pp
243-66.

Eochaidh Ó hEodhusa writing for Cú Chonnacht Maguire in the 1580s based his right to eulogize Maguire on the same grounds; his (Ó hEodhusa's) devotion to and familiarity with his lord.[43]

The two priest/poets and the professional poet Ó Con Muighe wrote poems for Dunboyne on the occasion of his temporary indisposition.[44] There is no indication in the poems that the poets were not similarly motivated in their compositions and those of Keating and Haicéad do not depart from the bardic norm as presented in the work of Ó Con Muighe. It appears that the activities of Keating and Haicéad outside of their writing did not prevent them from participating in the mental world articulated in the time-honoured formulae of bardic poetry. Their activites as priests, reformers, and political schemers on the conti- nent on behalf of the Old English, were all conducted within the world- view as they expressed it in their compositions for the various addressees of their poetry.[45] Haicéad's poem deals with Dunboyne's indisposition due to a broken leg. In the hyperbolic style in which the poets revelled, he declared that only the tragedy of Dunboyne's death could be com- pared in gravity with this present trouble.[46]

> Ní bhfuil moradh — maoite fós —
> i maoithe ar bith acht id bhás:
> faoi san gconchlann nó i gcruas
> go gcothrom nguas níor chinn cás.
> (Ní Cheallacháin, *Haicéad Poems,* No. 15,
> lines 9-12, p. 12.)

> [No greater misfortune could occur than your death short of that, no other trouble rivals that (of your broken leg)]

This poem is best read along with a frivolous stanza by the same author in which he expresses satisfaction at having broken his own leg, since it created another bond of fellowship between him and his patron.

---

43 D. Greene, *Maguire Poems,* no. 23, sts 1-9.

44 Ní Cheallacháin, *Haicéad Poems,* nos 15 and 16; Mac Giolla Eáin, *Dánta, Amhráin is Caointe Sheathrúin Céitinn,* no. 17; and Carney, *Butler Poems,* no. 14.

45 B. Ó Cuív, 'A seventeenth century criticism of Keating's *Foras Feasa ar Éirinn* in *Éigse,* vol. 11 (1964), pp 119-40.

46 See Carney, *O'Reilly Poems,* no. 15, p. 80 and no. 21, p. 100; and also Bergin, *Irish Bardic Poetry,* no. 4, p. 35.

Haicéad does not avail of the occasion to impress upon his patron or on any other audience he may have, any sentiment or doctrine other than an assurance first, of his profound grief at his patron's illness, and second, of his satisfaction at the privilege of being similarly afflicted:

> . . . dob olc 'na choimhdheacht mise, dá sbiúntaoi mé,
> 'sa chos sin brisde, muna mbrisfinn mo chrúibín féin.
> (Ní Cheallacháin, *Haicéad Poems,* No. 16, lines 3-4,
> p. 13.)

[I should be but poor company, were I to be examined, if my own leg were not broken and his to be so.][47]

The poet Eoghan Ó Con Muighe also wrote a poem concerned with Butler's illness.[48] Ó Con Muighe's poem is more elaborately structured: now that Éamonn has recovered, he should return to his wonted activities which were of course, making war for the protection and extension of his patrimony:

> Sgaoil feasda ciaich dá gcroidhe;
> tabhair d'aithle a n-eolchuire
> a-rís a n-aigeanta ar ais,
> a ghrís chaigealta an chumais.
>
> Éirigh it armaibh goile
> tóg lámh le lucht t'ionmhuine
> ísligh uaill na bhfear bhfaghla
> lean ar uaim bhur n-athardha.
> (Carney, *Butler Poems,* No. 14, sts. 13, 14, p. 66.)

[Release their hearts from sorrow, after their sadness returns their senses to them, o kindled spark of ability.
Arise with your vigorous weapons, join your beloved company, bring down the vanity of the marauders and continue the bringing together of your patrimony.]

Here Ó Con Muighe welcomes the recovered chief back into the wonted pursuits of the bardic patron; war-faring and escapades within or

---

47 See McKenna, *Magauran Poems,* no. 4, sts 22 and 23, p. 37.
48 See Carney, *Butler Poems,* p. 127.

without the boundaries of his patrimony. Such conduct was not attributable to Edmond, Lord Dunboyne, in the first half of the seventeenth century. The poet celebrated the return of the lord with whom the poetry was equipped to deal, into a life-style the depiction of which had become stylized enough to be understood immediately as an appropriate accolade. Keating's composition for Edmond Butler is more complex again. Because of the particular conceit he uses, his poem is open to misinterpretation similar to that which occurs concerning Ó Dálaigh Fionn's poem for Maurice Fitzgerald.[49] Keating's poem reads as a bitter reproach to Banbha. He castigates her for her ingratitude to her 'family'. One is presented with a picture of Banbha desolate and bereft of hope. In a seventeenth-century context, without reference to the complex literary background which provided the creative furniture for these compositions, this poem has been interpreted as being among the works which indicate a 'new awareness' among the literati of the imminence of and the malign consequences of the destruction of the Gaelic world. In its own context and in that of the mentality governing Keating's composition, this conceit of a betrayed Banbha can be shown to be an introduction to a complex compliment to Dunboyne:

> A Bhanbha bhog-omh dhona dhuaibhseach,
> is tú an bhean gan fhachuin uaille,
> Gnáth mar iarsma id' dhiaidh buaidhreach,
> is creidhm í nuidhe gach laoi dod nuachar.
> (Mac Giolla Eáin, *Dánta, Amhráin is Caointe
> Sheathrúin Céitinn,* No. 17, st. 1, p. 77.)

> [O lonely, unhappy, troubled Banbha, you are a woman without cause for pride, trouble is usually the remnant you leave in your wake, and fretfulness during the course of every day for your spouse.]

Thus Keating introduces the 'lord as spouse' motif, Dunboyne is Ireland's spouse, but she ill-treats him.[50] The continental influences

---

[49] See Bergin, *Irish Bardic Poetry,* no. 17, p. 73; and see also P. Ó Fiannachta, *Leás ar ár Litríocht,* p. 120.

[50] See Tadhg Ó Dúshláine, 'Filíocht Pholaitiúil na Gaeilge — a cineál', in *Léachtaí Cholm Cille* xiii, pp 114-29, esp. pp 120-8; Seán Ó Tuama, 'Téamaí iasachta i bhfilíocht pholaitiúil na Gaeilge (1600-1800)', in *Éigse,* vol. 2 (1965-6), pp 201-13; R.A. Breatnach, 'The Lady and the King: a theme of Irish Literature', in *Studies,* vol. 42 (1953), pp 321-36;

operating on Keating's compositions are evident in this his use of the personification of Ireland as a faithless spouse.[51] In this poem also the pervasion of English politically loaded words into the Gaelic vernacular is articulated; namely the words 'alienation' and 'plantation'. These two words and the continental flavour of the rhetoric are hardly signposts of the transformation of the Gaelic mentality however when one considers the use to which these elements are put. In this case Keating chose to employ them — not to refer to the malign advance of the Stuarts administrative power, nor indeed to the decline of the Gaelic system, but rather to highlight the culpability of Ireland in allowing the indisposition of Edmond Butler.

Do chrádh dhuit, a Éire chraobhach chnuais-gheal,
Do shliocht Gaedhil ghlais ní gabhair truaighe,
Plantation is *alienation* dá ruagadh,
Is triubhas go minic d'athchunadh do chuaine.
(Mac Giolla Eáin, *Dánta Amhráin is Caointe
Sheathrúin Céitinn,* No. 17, st. 8, p. 78.)

[O bright, fertile branched Ireland, it is to your own vexation that you do not take pity on your bright Gaelic septs, plantation and alienation causing their expulsion, and frequent attacks disfiguring your harbours.]

Keating uses the introductory stanzas to dramatize Banbha's folly. Here, carelessness towards her nobles is personified in the disability of her principal support: Edmond, Lord Dunboyne. His illness is proof that she is ungrateful to her 'family' for their loyalty. Yet, his indisposition is not to be wondered at since it is upon him that the duty of supporting ungrateful Banbha falls. It is in this stanza that Keating's eulogizing function is revealed; such is Butler's stature that his disability

---

T.C. Cave, *Devotional Poetry in France c. 1590-1613* (Cambridge 1969); C. Wells Slights, *The Casuistical Tradition* (Princeton, 1981), esp. pp 35-66; Earl Miner (ed. and introduction), *Illustrious Evidence: Approaches to English Literature of the seventeenth century* (University of California Press 1975), esp. pp xiii-xxiii and pp 41-69; John R. Mulder, *The Temple of the Mind: education and literary taste in seventeenth century England* (New York 1969), pp 89-150; Lee A. Sonnino, *a Hand-book to Sixteenth-Century Rhetoric* (New York, 1968.)

[51] Mac Giolla Eáin, *Dánta, Amhráin is Caointe Sheathrúin Céitinn,* no. 17, st. 7, p. 78.

leaves Banbha without protection. Keating, having heaped strong-worded reproaches on Banbha, now reveals the true reason for his ire:

Trian do mhí-áigh, a mhion-chláir Tuthail,
ní thig díom-sa a ríomh don chuairt seo,
Do briseadh an chos ba phort don bhuan-bhliadh,
Is níor bh'iongnadh a breodh, ba mhó a hualach.
(Mac Giolla Eáin, *Dánta Amhráin is Caointe
Sheathrúin Céitinn*, No. 17, st. 13, p. 79.)

[I cannot tell a third of your affliction o smooth plain of Tuathail; the leg which was the fortress of your lasting renown has been broken, and its crushing is no surprise, considering the weight of its burden.]

The conceit of Banbha's ingratitude, seems to have been a personal favourite of Keating's. In his arguably most famous poem, 'Óm sceol ar Ardmhagh Fáil', he makes powerful use of this conceit. Banbha in this poem is accused of suckling foreigners in preference to her 'own' children. Again, this is a motif popular in contemporary French poetry and had been so for a century previously, it finds its way into English literature too[52] and it is therefore all the more interesting to find it in Gaelic poetry; entering into a strong learned tradition of poetry and being used to convey, and strengthen if anything, the perceptions conventionally articulated in that genre. In 'Óm sceol ar Ardmhagh Fáil' Keating's intention is that of the traditional poet, seeking to present a picture of Ireland deprived of Keating's own provincial Munster lords, the Fitzgeralds of Desmond. No mention is made in this poem of the Butlers or of their territory:

Dá mba beoga ardfhlaith Áine is Droma Daoile
's na leoghain láidre ón Máigh do bhronnadh maoine,
dar ndóigh níorbh áit don táinse in oscaill Bhríde
gan gheoin is gártha os ard dá dtoghaildíbirt.
(Mac Giolla Eáin, *Dánta, Amhráin is Caointe
Sheathrúin Céitinn,* No. 3, st. 6, p. 20.)

---

[52] See Lauro Martines, *Power and Imagination: City States in Renaissance Italy* (London, 1980); Lauro Martines, *Society and history in English Renaissance Verse* (Oxford 1985); Graham Parry, *The Golden Age Restor'd: The Culture of the Stuart Court* (Manchester 1981); T.C. Cave, *Devotional Poetry in France c. 1570-1613.*

[If the great prince of Áine and Drom Daoile, and the strong gift-bestowing lions of the Máigh were alive, there would be no place in this territory of the river Bride for this horde, without their being vigorously banished with uproar and shouting.]

As in 'Óm sceol ar Ardmhagh Fáil', Keating in his poem for Edmond Butler, is at pains to point out that not only has Banbha forsaken her 'own' but that those she now 'nourishes' are low types unworthy of her. Keating is as obsessed with the status of those he considers usurprers as are the professional poets. The departure or defeat of the 'natural' leaders or their eclipse leads to social dislocation; lesser men are set to advance themselves.[53] Banbha must not countenance these while Edmond Butler is indisposed:

Do dhoirtis do dhúil a bhrúid gan tsuairceas,
Ar gach castaire ó Shacsaibh dá ngluaiseann
Saoiltear libh gur ridire ruaghmhar
Gach nduine dar bh'arm an ráca is an sluasad.
(Mac Giolla Eáin, *Dánta, Amhráin is Caointe
Sheathrúin Céitinn,* No. 17, st. 11, p. 78.)

[You poured out your favour o graceless brute, on every Saxon crook who passes. You mistake any person armed with a rake or a spade for a valiant knight.]

Keating is not worried so much about the prospect of Banbha favouring strangers, as that those she favours are socially inferior. Consciousness of the status of usurpers and foreigners is very much part of the poets' rationale of acceptance or rejection of intruders. Keating's castigation of intruding foreigners is the subject of much qualification. Keating's elegy for the two sons of Edmond Butler, John and Thomas (+ 1642), illustrates some of the criteria which governed the poets' acceptance of new peoples and new influences into the world view enshrined in the

---

[53] Any social or political disorder brought forth similar complaints from the poets — lower orders are out of control — the social structure is being attacked, see for example McKenna, *Magauran Poems,* no. 31, st. 17, p. 275; John Bossy commented on the reluctance of members of the catholic English gentry to acquiesce in the changes brought about by the reformation because of the social dislocation involved, especially the exaltation of 'basket-makers and beer-brewers', in 'The Character of Elizabethan Catholicism', in *Past and Present,* no. 21 (April 1962), p. 43.

tradition. Keating's particular interest in this poem is the accommodation of the *Sean Ghaill* [the Old English]. The criteria which govern
his powers of accommodation in the poetry are those which he already
found in the tradition; professional poets had arrived at a workable
system some centuries before. They had dealt with the emergence of the
Anglo-Norman lord and had successfully found a niche for him within
the world of bardic poetry. The political vicissitudes faced by the Old
English in the mid-seventeenth century were of an unprecedented nature
and it seems appropiate that their diminishing political status should exercise the mental and creative energies of Keating, and so it does. It is
more surprising, however, to find that his elegy for the two Butlers,
killed in an encounter of which their kinsman, Ormond, was the victor,[54] adheres to the rationale of belonging, and to the traditional
criteria of power and offers no new perceptions on what was a very new
situation. It is a measure of the validity of the perceptions articulated in
such poetry and their longevity that a poet such as Keating should have
found it congenial to produce such traditional material at such a period
of rapid change. The import of the changes occurring found no corresponding adaptation in the world view of the poetry though adaptation in language and rhetoric took place harmoniously and naturally.

For the purposes of elegiac composition, Keating recounted the woes
of Banbha which were increased by the deaths of John and Thomas
Butler. Among the calamities which had befallen Ireland was her being
overtaken by foreigners:

> Iomdha cinneamhain chorrach,
> Tarla is teidhm leath-tromach
> Do chríoch Bhreagh ghliaidh iomdha glas,
> Ar feadh Banbha conncas
> (Mac Giolla Eáin, *Dánta, Amhráin is Caointe
> Sheathrúin Céitinn*, No. 14, st. 5, p. 62.)

> [The many changing fates which have occurred to Breagh's land is
> an oppressive disease to Banbha — a conquest throughout
> Banbha.]

The foreigners who thus conquered Ireland numbered among them
ancestors of Keating and he identified himself with them:

---

[54] Mac Giolla Eáin, *Dánta, Amhráin is Caointe Sheathrúin Céitinn*, notes p. 213.

Tig na Sean-Ghoill tar sáile,
Go maicne Míle Easpáine,
Táin fhír-bheach, or bh-ionlúith inn,
Os mínleach fhionn-mhúir Féidhlim.
(Mac Giolla Eáin, *Dánta, Amhráin is Caointe
Sheathrúin Céitinn,* No. 14, st. 6, p. 63.)

[The Old English came over the sea to the plains of Míle Easbáin, a
tribe of true bees, for we were fit for service — over the meadows
and fair ramparts of Ireland.]

The fact that foreigners had overrun Ireland, however, was not in itself
either unexpected or particularly disagreeable. One is reminded of the
value placed on power successfully wielded and the alacrity with which
the victor was absorbed into the Gaelic schema. Conquest could be
qualified as good or evil. In this case Keating accepted the earlier intruders. He lists a number of reasons for their qualification as *fionn
ghaill* [fair foreigners] as opposed to *dubh ghoill* [dark foreigners]:

Báidh chleamhnais is cuisleann gaoil,
Combáidh creidimh do aon-taobh,
Air-mheas gach oirir ortha,
Cairdeas oinigh eatortha
(Mac Goilla Eáin, *Dánta, Amhráin is Caointe
Sheathrúin Céitinn,* No. 14, st. 8, p. 63.)

[Affection of marriage affinity, consanguinity and shared
religious sympathies; (they were) held in great esteem by every
region, a noble friendship between them.]

The poets at all time reserved the right to qualify their own classifi-
cations. Therefore the term *gall*/foreigner is applied with flexibility and
with contextual connotations only. Keating has both used the tradition
and complied with its demands in his accommodation of the earlier
foreign intruders who must be distinguished from their latter-day
counter-parts. The established 'foreigners' provided favourable contrast with the new intruders. These are the 'dark' counterparts of the
'fair' foreigners who had been accommodated in the bardic schema.
The *dubhghaill* display characteristics which are the converse of those of
the earlier invaders:

Tig dá n-éis ar feadh Banbha
Saoithe ain-teann allmhurdha
Gan bháidh ris an gcéad-dhroing gcóir,
Do shean-roinn chláir an chomhóil.
(Mac Giolla Eáin, *Dánta, Amhráin is Caointe
Sheathrúin Céitinn,* No. 14, st. 9, p. 63.)

[After them, throughout Banbha — to the plain of the drinking
companies — came a swarm of oppressive foreigners (who were)
without affection for the legitimate first group.]

Keating was opposed to the new intruders whose position had not yet
been determined. Battles connected with their unharmonious presence
caused the death of his patron's two sons. Keating's distinction of early
and later invaders served a number of different purposes, all of which
are elements of the great structure of accommodation and manipulation
which were at the disposal of the poet.

The foreigners, whom, in retrospect, Keating found so sympathetic
to their sometime Gaelic enemies, were not always seen thus. While they
endeavoured to settle themselves and impose their conditions on the
earlier Gaelic world, Gaelic poets writing for Gaelic lords, bitterly attacked their intrusion and counselled retribution. Their mode of dress,
language and lack of respect for the poet rendered them as obnoxious to
the fourteenth-century poet Giolla Brighde Mac Con Midhe as did that
of their later counter-parts Keating.[55] The convenient historical synop-
sis offered by Keating in the elegy for the two Butlers is a conventionalized back-drop to the main purpose of his poem, that of lamentation. The
manner in which Keating seeks to accommodate the formerly 'foreign'
elements in a situation which demands that they be treated as one with
Gaelic Irish elements is significant especially since at the time the Old
English had a particular political interest in marking the differences between the two groups.[56] Keating's disenchantment with the new

---

[55] Williams, *The Poems of Giolla Brighde Mac Con Midhe,* no. 4, stanzas 6, 27, 41, pp
40-50.
[56] N.P. Canny, *From Reformation to Restoration: Ireland 1534-1660* (Dublin 1987);
N. Canny, 'Identity formation in Ireland: the Emergence of the Anglo-Irish', in N. Canny
and Anthony Pagden (eds), *Colonial Identity in the Atlantic World, 1500-1800*
(Princeton University Press 1987); N.P. Canny, *The Formation of the Old English Elite in
Ireland* (Dublin 1975); Aidan Clarke, 'Colonial Identity in Early Seventeenth Century
Ireland', in *Historical Studies,* XI (1978), pp 57-72; A. Clarke, *The Old English in Ireland*

foreigners, predictably, does not extend to their sovereign whom he is proud to list among the relatives of James Butler, uncle of the earl of Ormond who led the party against the two men he lamented in the poem.[57] Evidently the intricacies of the bardic mentality as evidenced in the poetry was only slightly more convoluted than the intricate ties of loyalty and kinship which united and divided the protagonists and antagonists of any individual military engagement.

The poetry of the mid-seventeenth century was not characterized by xenophobia arising from increased political complications. What is perceptible in the poetry is an attitude towards political events which have been refracted through the prism of the poets' referential structure which was itself a literary articulation of the Gaelic aristocratic mentality. The fundamental principles apply in the seventeenth century as they did in the thirteenth.[58] This is not to deny change and political evolution in the Gaelic system or indeed in the political personality of the Anglo-Norman colony. Political status was not a feature of either group in the early modern period or in the seventeenth century.[59] Modifications and adjustments took place manifestly to the poet's status, his language, and his function. As the Gaelic polity changed the poets suffered great changes in status. The new emerging central administrative machine could not use the poets as their profession demanded. They found themselves eulogizing members of once-great septs whose official status was often little greater than that of a professional soldier seeking commission, much as the poet sought

---

1625-42 (London 1966); A. Clarke, *The Graces, 1625-41* (Dundalk 1968); A. Clarke, 'The Policies of the Old English in Parliament, 1640-1', in *Historical Studies,* vol. V (1965), pp 82-102; A. Clarke, 'Ireland and the General Crisis', in *Past and Present,* no. 48 (1970), pp 79-99.

[57] Mac Giolla Eáin, *Dánta, Amhráin is Caointe Sheathrúin Céitinn,* no. 6, st. 24, p. 28 and no. 17, st. 9, p. 78.

[58] See K. Simms, *From Kings to Warlords,* esp. pp 147-50.

[59] See K. Simms, *From Kings to Warlords;* Ciaran Brady and Raymond Gillespie (eds), *Natives and newcomers: essays on the making of Irish colonial society* (Dublin 1986), R. Gillespie, *Colonial Ulster: the settlement of east Ulster 1600-41* (Cork 1985); N.P. Canny, 'Hugh O'Neill, Earl of Tyrone and the Changing Face of Gaelic Ulster', in *Studia Hibernica,* no. 10 (1970), pp 7-35; Patrick J. Duffy, 'The territorial organization of Gaelic landownership and its transformation in Co. Monaghan, 1591-1640', in *Irish Geography* XIV (1981).

patronage.[60] Cadet or dispossessed branches of Gaelic septs who a half a century before fought against each other for territorial hegemony, now fought in Europe as commissioned officers or indeed as common soldiers.[61] Yet the characteristic and in most cases the only, indigenous articulation of their identity, their place in history, their biographical record, and their aspirations and status is to be found in the poetry dedicated to them or written about them. They have another life too, that which they lived in the documents of crown officials; pardons, land-grants, executions, suits at law, 'comings in', financial settlements, and provisions for education. The existence of the Gaelic leaders in crown documents is underpinned by their existence in the poetry. The end-product of decisons taken by them are what one can glean from the administrative details about their comings and goings. The rationale behind their frenetic dealings with crown officials is what one can understand from the poetry.[62]

Increasingly, in the mid-seventeenth century one comes across poems which are neither written in syllabic metres nor immediately familiar in their use of bardic motifs. Such poems do not belong to the category of bardic poetry which so far has been dealt with in this discussion. Five such poems, were edited by Cecile O' Rahilly[63] and categorized by her as 'political poems', presumably to set them apart from apolitical or non-political poems of the seventeenth century. O'Rahilly suggested that the poems thus categorized were written by non-professional poets for 'the people' and not for the 'chosen few'.[64] In the case of four of the five poems edited by O'Rahilly, the identity of the author is uncertain or no further works of the author are known. (The composition of Éamonn an Dúna is of certain authority.) None of the poets belonged to any of the well known bardic families, to judge alone by the surnames of those to whom they are attributed. For these reasons it is unlikely that any of

---

[60] Brendan Jennings, *Wild Geese in Spanish Flanders, 1582-1700;* Gráinne Henry, '*Seminarie soldiers;* connections between religious and military communities in the Spanish Netherlands', in *Retrospect* 1987 pp 41-8.

[61] See for instance Mág Craith, *Dán na mBráthar Mionúr,* no. 24, p. 121.

[62] See Sir Henry Docwra, 'A narration of the services done by the army employed to Lough Foyle . . .', in John O'Donovan (ed), *Miscellany of the Celtic Society* (Dublin 1849); T.F. O'Rahilly, 'Irish poets, historians and judges in English documents, 1538-1615', in *Proceedings of the Royal Irish Academy,* vol. 36 (1921-4), pp 86-120.

[63] Cecile O'Rahilly, *Five Seventeenth Century Political Poems* (Dublin 1952).

[64] O'Rahilly, *Five Seventeenth Century Political Poems,* p. 83.

them was a professional poet in the sense in which the bardic poet was. By the same token, neither is there any reason to believe that these five individual poems are the sole compositions of their respective authors; it is probably likely that they are not.[65] On the other hand, bardic poets quite often wrote occasional poems which were free of the restrictions of the encomiastic or elegiac forms and really amounted to either a straightforward or a fanciful account of a specific occasion.[66] Most of the poems which have survived are from formal *duanairí* and it is likely that such informal poetry was excluded in their compilation.

O'Rahilly distinguishes between what she identifies as the five 'political' poems of her collection and the usual form of contemporary and even later poetry. She sees them as having a documentary value, offering 'detailed' and 'informative' treatment of the period 1640-1659.[67] Two poems outside O'Rahilly's collection, attributed respectively to Haicéad ('Músgail do mhisneach') and Séamus Carthún (Deorchaoineadh na hÉireann)[68] display similarities in form and content to her 'five' and are similarly dated. For this discussion they will be considered along with the others. All of the poems are dated approximately within the decade 1645-1655. Of the seven poems, four are attributed to priests if we accept that the author of 'An Síogaí Romhánach' was a clergyman.[69] This is the only categorization possible in the case of the authorship of the poems. A number of other factors must be considered before one comes to any conclusion as to the nature of these poems and their significance.

The popularity achieved by these poems in the manuscript tradition decades after their composition cannot be denied. It is easy, however, to overstate or over-estimate their populist nature. It is almost impossible to argue that they are poems by the 'people' for the 'people'.[70] In Gaelic literature the 'people' are mentioned only *en masse* as either bewailing the death of a hero, welcoming his arrival or suffering grievously at the hands of usurpers. Consciousness of the 'people' and any mention of

---

[65] See K. Simms, *From Kings to Warlords*, esp. pp 1-12.

[66] See McKenna, *The Book of Magauran*, no. 15, p. 113.

[67] O'Rahilly, *Five Seventeenth Century Political Poems*, Introduction p. viii.

[68] Ní Cheallacháin, *Haicéad Poems*, no. 36, p. 38 and Mág Craith, *Dán na mBráthar Mionúr*, no. 49, p. 251.

[69] O'Rahilly, *Five Seventeenth Century Political Poems*, pp 12-17.

[70] O'Rahilly, *Five Seventeenth Century Political Poems*, p. 83.

them in Gaelic seventeenth century literature is almost entirely denigratory.[71] It is thus with these 'political' poems.[72] The suggestion that the use of the spoken idiom indicated a more popular audience does not make sense when one considers that formal bardic poetry was directed at chiefs and other prominent individuals who did not necessarily understand the convoluted bardic idiom.[73] The language of the poetry cannot be taken in isolation as a reliable indicator of audience or readership. However, the use of the plebian vernacular in the context of the narrative style of the poetry, can be regarded as a departure from the norm as it occurs in the formal *duanairí*. The straight narrative style of these poems is deceptive in its apparent simplicity. It has been suggested that these poems were greatly influenced by the stylistic structures and heavy rhetorical devices of continental baroque.[74] Indeed the great swirling structures building up to the various climaxes in the poems seem to bear this out. Such evidence points to a learned authorship versed in the poetry of sixteenth- and seventeenth-century France and England, or at least open to the intellectual movements of wider Europe. Such influences point to the cultural interchange between Gaelic Ireland and the continent; a contact which had always existed but was enhanced by the numbers of students chosing Continental colleges in the late sixteenth and early seventeenth century.

For all the innovation in the literary style of these poems, a closer examination reveals that on the level of perceptual changes and evidence of dramatic change in Gaelic political consciousness these poems prove to be as rooted in the bardic field of reference and social exclusivity as the contemporary syllabic compositions. Likewise, they contain the typical bardic blind-spots and apparently self-contradictory declarations throughout. The poems can by no means be treated as products of the poetic schools. The motifs and themes of these poems, however, and their treatment of different events, argue a dependence on the

---

[71] One of the most well known satires on the emerging lower orders is N.J.A. Williams (ed), *Pairlement Chloinne Tomáis* (Dublin 1981).

[72] O'Rahilly, *Five Seventeenth Century Political Poems,* p. 83.

[73] See however, D. Greene, *Maguire Poems,* no. 8, st. 14, p. 70 and no. 9, stanzas 6, 16 and 20, pp 80-2, in which the poet indicates Maguire's familiarity with the poet's language and learning.

[74] T. Ó Dúshláine, 'Filíocht Pholaitiúil na Gaeilge — a cineál', pp 114-29.

bardic referential framework which in turn would indicate a mentality shared with that of the bardic poet. There is indeed no evidence in these compositions of a rationale other than that to which we have become accustomed in the formal schools' poetry.

Before dealing with the thematic range of the seven poems chosen for this section, it is necessary to recognize a novelty in the situation which confronted the poets in the decade 1640-50. It was the first occasion on which the poets had to deal with a centrally organized military effort in a war context. The centralized administration of the war effort never operated effectively;[75] provincialism and individual loyalties which splintered the organization even at its inception caused it to split into a kaleidescope of factions. Yet the central administrative structure existed in the Confederation. The authors of these poems brought all their resources to bear on a novel situation. Their compositions present us with a very interesting interpretation of the decade's events using a referential structure which spanned several centuries, and reveal a fascinating patchwork of the various factions and localist loyalties militating against the ideal of central control as envisaged by the Provisional council.[76]

It is first useful to generalize on some themes common to the seven poems in question. All bewail the unprecedented destruction of Banbha and of the integrity of her leading classes. All cite Gaelic and Old English lack of virtue in different areas as factors contributing to defeat. All provide some glorified account of Gaelic pride and success before the latest disaster. Such generalizations serve only as an illustration of the

---

[75] For background correspondence illustrating the dissension which dogged the Confederation see John Lowe (ed.), *Letter-book of the Earl of Clanricarde 1643-7* (Dublin 1983); and James Hogan (ed), *Letters and Papers relating to the Irish Rebellion* (Dublin 1936); and J.I. Casway, 'Owen Roe O'Neill's return to Ireland in 1642; the diplomatic background', in *Studia Hibernica,* vol. 9 (1969), pp 48-64. Some of the fundamental differences of opinion concerning the aims and activities of the Confederation are outlined in P.J. Corish, 'Two contemporary historians of the Confederation of Kilkenny; John Lynch and Richard O Ferrale', in *Irish Historical Studies,* vol. VIII, no. 31 (March 1953), pp 217-36; P.J. Corish, 'Bishop Nicholas French and the second Ormond Peace, 1648-9', in *Irish Historical Studies,* vol. VI, no. 22 (1948), pp 83-100; D. Cregan, 'Daniel O'Neill, a Royalist agent in Ireland, 1644-50', in *Irish Historical Studies,* vol. XI, no. 8 (September 1941), pp 398-414; Tomás Ó Fiach, 'Republicanism and Separatism in the Seventeenth Century', in *Léachtaí Cholm Cille,* ii (1971), pp 74-87.

[76] Cf. Allan Macinnes, 'Scottish Gaeldom, 1638-1651'; and D. Stevenson, *Alasdair MacColla and the Highland Problem in the Seventeenth Century* (Edinburgh 1980).

propensity of the writers to follow an established structural pattern; [77] to express themselves within the literary confines of an established framework. Some of the poems are so stylistically similar as to be easily confused with each other. Their structural and idiomatic similarities can conceal some interesting divergences of opinion and allegiance evidenced within individual poems. Most interesting of all, however, is their use of the age-old motifs in a situation the political complexity of which would appear to demand a whole new approach. One is reminded once again, that far from taking a lead in dictating contemorary political or social values, the poets could only articulate the values of their social counterparts. The events of 1640-60 proved that the leaders of the Gaelic Irish remained incorrigibly individualistic in the pursuit of their political goals. The conservative attitude of the poets is consistent with the traditional perspective of their works. The general background of the seven poems considered here is that of an unresolved state of conflict; a *dénouement* has not yet occurred in the chaotic decades surrounding the 1641 rebellion and the establishment of the Cromwellian regime.

Pádraigín Haicéad, a zealous adherent of the Papal Nuncio, saw the religious issue as a matter of utmost importance in his poem — 'Músgail do mhisneach'. [78] In this poem he bewails the departure of many members of the Confederation from their original oath in spite of excommunication. [79] He likens their disobedience to that of the Israelites who chafed against their lot in the desert. The group which shared Haicéad's loyalties were praised as the rightful claimants to Ireland. The others treacherously betrayed her. [80] Several of Haicéad's near relatives were persuaded of the virtue of the Ormond truce, and must have been excommunicated as a result, and were, therefore, supposed targets of his wrath. [81] Among Haicéad's letters, however, is one addressed to the Nuncio seeking absolution from excommunication for the baron of Dunboyne. The Public Clerk of the Confederation, Philip Kearney, an

---

[77] See Aodh Mac Aingil, *Sgathán Shacruiminte na hAithridhe* [Louvain 1618], (ed.) Canice Mooney (Dublin 1952), pp 3-5; and Flaithri Ó Maolchonaire, *Desiderius* [Louvain 1616], (ed) T.F. O'Rahilly (Dublin 1955), pp 3-6.

[78] Ní Cheallacháin, *Haicéad Poems,* no. 36, p. 38.

[79] Ní Cheallacháin, *Haicéad Poems,* no. 36, p. 38.

[80] Ní Cheallacháin, *Haicéad Poems,* pp xiv-xvii.

[81] Ní Cheallacháin, *Haicéad Poems,* p. xviii.

Ormondist was Haicéad's own nephew.[82] Haicéad did not become estranged from his family or from the Butlers because of these differences. It does not mean that either he, or they took their allegiances lightly but it does provide a leaven for the excess to which he seems to have been prone in his writing.

Haicéad prefaces the poem with a prose introduction indicting those who broke their oath of association and accepted the Ormond peace. He opens the poem urging Banbha to have courage in the face of her latest distress.[83] She has been betrayed, not by foreigners but by her own disaffected family.[84]

> Móide is gráin a ngníomha
> Gaoidhil féin ar fearaibh Fáil
> d'imirt an fhill ghoimhigh ghránna,
> ann oirir is chána cháigh.
> (Ní Cheallacháin, *Haicéad Poems,* No. 36, st. 3, p. 38.)

[Their actions are all the more ugly for that the Gael themselves among the men of Fáil — leaders of the land and of everyone's tribute, were involved in ugly, venomous treachery.]

The poem introduces itself in general terms applicable to any disaster the poet choses to address.[85] The emergence of their common catholicism[86] as a significant rallying point for Gaelic Irish and Old

---

82 Ní Cheallacháin, *Haicéad Poems,* p. xv-xviii.

83 Ní Cheallacháin, *Haicéad Poems,* No. 36, st. 1, p. 38.

84 Ní Cheallacháin, *Haicéad Poems,* no. 36, lines 13-20, p. 39.

85 Ní Cheallacháin, *Haicéad Poems,* no. 36, p. 38.

86 Indeed it can be argued that their common catholicism divided rather than united the adherents of the Roman faith who belonged to different traditions of observance. The tensions and crippling disagreements which divided catholics of differing social and political allegiances are evident in the careers of some individuals, see P.J. Corish, 'An Irish Counter-Reformation Bishop: John Roche', in *Irish Theological Quarterly,* vol. XXV (1958), pp 14-32, 101-23 and vol. 26 (1959), pp 101-16, 313-30. Francis Nugent, a member of the Nugent family, barons of Delvin, was an active agent of Counter-Reformation catholicism. His efforts were entirely devoted to his own social — Old English — contemporaries in Ireland, see F.X. Martin, *Francis Nugent, Agent of the Counter-Reformation* (Rome and London 1962). Dissensions within the Catholic Church itself are discussed by H.F. Kearney in 'Ecclesiastical politics and the Counter-Reformation in Ireland, 1618-1648', in *Journal of Ecclesiastical History,* vol. II (1960), pp 203-12. John Bossy, in 'The Character of Elizabethan Catholicism', in *Past and Present,* no. 21 (April 1962), discusses comprehensively the differences in allegiance, tactics

English catholics is a tempting argument for proponents of a new catholic Gaelic political consciousness at this period.[87] There is no evidence for the development of anything like a coherent new political consciousness based on religion or race in Haicéad's poem. The perceived novel elements of nascent or emerging catholic nationalism evaporate from Haicéad's work when it is analysed within its own terms of reference rather than those imposed upon it by a retrospective synthetic appraisal of the seventeenth century literature which sees every development leading to the emergence of nationalism in the mid-nineteenth century.

Haicéad, as a poet was not professionally attached to any one sept. His personal ties were with the Butler family, the senior member of which was the foremost loyalist in the country and a committed protestant. The tendency to factionalism, individualism in power and a fundamental lack of appreciation for unanimity in action, which characterized the mentality of the Gaelic aristocracy and was faithfully articulated by the poets in their professional capacity[88] is brought into relief by the unusual circumstances which provide a background for Haicéad's 'Músgail do mhisneach'. His allegiance to the Nuncio's party in this particular quarrel, provided him with a sept-substitute. His comprehension of the complex events of the decade 1640-50 is articulated in that poem.[89] The stock-piling of motifs and references built up over centuries and the world view which such literary equipment represented, proved a strong influence on the outlook presented in the poetry because it provided both a mental touchstone and a literary vehicle. Haicéad's adoption of the nuncioist cause effectively provided him with a sept allegiance substitute, and he adapted the corresponding poem-type to his immediate needs. Once again the tradition made itself amenable to a

---

and opinions among the 'Jesuit' and 'Appellant', 'gentry' and 'clerk' factions in Elizabethan Catholic circles. Such factions had their counterparts in the Irish context and all were influenced and affected by similar distinctions in continental Europe. See also Bossy, *The English Catholic Community 1570-1850* (London 1975).

[87] N. Canny, 'Formation', *passim*, P.J. Corish, *The Catholic Comunity in the Seventeenth and Eighteenth Centuries;* see Macinnes, 'Scottish Gaeldom, 1638-1651', esp. pp 77-90.

[88] See Macinnes, 'Scottish Gaeldom, 1638-1651', *passim*.

[89] See George Steiner, *After Babel: Aspects of language and translation* (Oxford University Press 1976), esp. pp 414-70.

new situation without changing the perceptions underlying it.

The religious focus of 'Músgail do mhisneach' renders his use of the traditional format all the more interesting. The issue is that of Ireland being in danger because her leaders are not united in support of the Nuncio; Ireland is in danger because of the failure of her sept leaders to present a united front in the face of opposition, in this instance, the anti-Nuncio faction/sept — all equally close to Haicéad in background and religion. Only God's grace and repentence can ensure the future prosperity of Ireland. The way to gain the latter is to yield to the Nuncio's decision. Haicéad uses the biblical analogy of the Israelites [90] murmuring in the desert and pining for the corrupt pleasures of Egypt to illustrate the perfidy of those Gaelic and Old English who opposed the Nuncio. Haicéad's personal allegiance to the Nuncio's party dictated his attitude toward the opposing faction. His portrayal of his loyalties in 'Músgail do mhisneach' were not inspired by abstract considerations such as the good of state, nation or race, of which a corresponding sense of political expediency and compromise would play an integral part. In this Haicéad merely reflected the identical mentality predominating in the events leading to the Confederate split and the tortuous negotiations surrounding the Ormond truce and its sequel. Haicéad's allegiance to the Nuncio is translated by him into loyalty to the Roman church. His opponent's failure to acquiesce in the Nuncio's priorities above their own, is translated as allegiance to Luther — the most evocative hate object of Counter-Reformation rhetoric. His articulation of the nuances of the allegiances of both parties falls far short of the undoubted complexities of the situation. [91] It is perhaps therein more faithful to the tenor of contemporary Gaelic perceptions of loyalty and power; Haicéad saw no contradiction between his villification of fellow-Catholics, whose allegiances did not accord with his own — as

---

[90] Ní Cheallacháin, *Haicéad Poems,* no. 36, lines 29-32, p. 39 and lines 65-8, p. 40. The use of Biblical analogies in literature was especially popular in the seventeenth century throughout Europe. An early precedent for the use of the Israelite analogy is to be found in the *Cogadh Gael re Gallaibh* and see Ludwig Bieler, *The Patrician Texts in the Book of Armagh* (Dublin 1979), p. 19; Kim McCone, *Pagan Past and Present* (Maynooth, 1990); and cf. Ó Corráin, 'Nationality and Kingship in Pre-Norman Ireland', in T.W. Moody (ed.), *Nationality and the Pursuit of National Independence* (Belfast 1978); and see also Liam P. Ó Caithnia, *Apalóga na bhFilí 1200-1650,* esp. pp 136-53.

[91] See especially Haicéad's seeming rejection of the differences between *donn* and *riabhach* in Ní Cheallacháin, *Haicéad Poems,* no. 36, lines 149-52.

Lutherans, and his entreaties to Banbha to summon her courage to face the advances of her enemy — these fellow Irish Catholics. For Haicéad, the 'enemy' is any one who does not share his loyalties, and in this stark perception of immediate, short-term impact of events, Haicéad represents no development in Gaelic perceptions of power or Gaelic political destiny. He is specifically dismissive of the abstract *réasúin sdáit* as a motivating force in the decision-making processes of the leaders:

> Is mór an náire, i n-ainm fhiréin,
> d'aicme dar dhual gliocas grinn,
> réasúin sdáit ag sdiúr a n-eathar
> i n-áit iúil nach creachfadh cill.
> (Ní Cheallacháin, *Haicéad Poems*, No. 36, lines 89-92, p. 41.)[92]

[It is a great shame, in the name of the truth, that the class who were wont to be clever and cunning should direct the vessel by reason of state than by knowledge which would not destroy the church.]

The class (*aicme*) to which Haicéad referred were his fellow Old English Catholics whose rôle in Gaelic society as perceived by themselves was that of directors of the vessel (*eathar*) and who formed a percentage of the anti-Nuncio faction. Those he branded as followers of Luther, though he emphasized the fact that they shunned Calvin, according to the rhetoric of the Counter-Reformation, even more evil and corrupt than Luther.[93] In spite of the difficulties described by Haicéad he ends on an optimistic note; it was prophesied that 1646 was to be a year of deliverance for Banbha:

> Míle go leith, sé is seacht bhfichid
> annáil Íosa, iar n-uair gan ghó,
> aimsear bhuadha na bhfial bhfeardha,
> ní chuala riamh meanma is mó.
> (Ní Cheallacháin, *Haicéad Poems*, No. 36,
> lines 157-160, p. 43.)

[1646, the year of Jesus, chronologically in truth, is the year of

---

92 Cf. O'Rahilly, *Five Seventeenth Century Political Poems*, p. 91, lines 157-60.
93 Ní Cheallacháin, *Haicéad Poems*, no. 36, lines 113-6, p. 42.

victory for the generous men, I have not heard of greater encouragement (lit. high spirits).]

Haicéad proclaimed the auspicious year of victory without any qualification. There were no reasons advanced in the poem as to what political or military developments were destined to make that year, in particular, the year of victory. Any prophecy regarding Ireland's victories, however, traditionally could be applied where necessary. Haicéad does not reveal the source of such expectation. The significance of his use of such a conclusion lies in its inapplicability to political reasoning or to any recognizable development of a mode of political motivation for the leaders of Gaelic society as perceived by Haicéad. He merely clothed the new problem with old fabrics, all of which accorded with his own perception of events and with the perceptions of the Irish activists on both sides.[94] Faction, provincialism and private jealousies were thrown into high relief by the façade of unity which the Confederation originally adopted.[95] Mutual jealousy and rivalry necessitated the splitting of the military command in Ireland between Preston and O'Neill, Barry and Burke, representing respectively the four provinces. Letters exchanged between Ormond, Clanricarde and O'Neill in 1646 reveal the fears, distrusts and jealousies which prevailed in the relations between the leaders of various factions, all ostensibly involved in the same cause.[96] Clanricarde and Preston in particular were implacably opposed to O'Neill, and Clanricarde specifically objected to O'Neill's army, claiming they were more unruly and destructive than the Scots and Parliamentarian forces.[97] He requested that O'Neill be kept out of Connacht at any cost. The disparate nature of the military command, and the considerations other than those of strictly military or political import were in evidence in all the exchanges between those to whom the leadership of the united effort had been entrusted. All were independent

---

[94] See Dineen, *Feiritéir Poems*, nos. 7 and 8, p. 102 and see notes on p. 158.

[95] See for example an earlier scheme involving Flaithrí Ó Maolchonaire and the young earls of Tyrone and Tyrconnel which involved the creation of two positions of president of Ireland to accommodate the rival claims of Tyrone and Tyrconnel in Ó Fiaich, 'Republicanism and Separatism in the Seventeenth Century', in *Léachtaí Cholm Cille*, ii (1971), *passim*.

[96] Lowe, *Clanricarde's Letter-Book,* p. 239, Ormond to Clanricarde, 9 May 1646.

[97] Lowe, *Clanricarde's Letter-Book,* pp 241, Ormond to O'Neill, 9 May 1646 and p. 241-2, Clanricarde to Ormond (146), 12 May 1646.

leaders in their own spheres. A priest, Ó Melláin, travelling in the O'Neill camp kept a diary in prose of the period when he campaigned with O'Neill. He listed those whom he termed *'na huachtaráin'* (the leaders) without comment on their number or their allegiances. The descriptive qualifications attached by Ó Melláin to each character mentioned had very little to do with the abstractions of political theory and practice imputed to the principal characters in the conflicts of 1640-1650:

> An phápa, Innocentus decimus; in rígh, Sérlus; Iarla Ur(mh)umhan i nAth Cliath; Eoghan Ua Néill Gen(eral) Uladh; Preses Comhuirle (Cille) Cainnigh, A' Tigherna Buitléir; Gener(al) Leath Mogha (Tom(ás) Pristan; Primas Totus Hibern Aodh Ua Raghallaigh; Provinsial Uird S. Frions, Brian Mac Giolla Cainnigh, Connachtach.[98]

> [The leaders: the pope, Innocent X; the king, Charles; the Earl of Ormond in Dublin; Eoghan O Neill, General of Ulster; the President of the Kilkenny Council, Lord Butler; the General of Leath Mogha, Thomas Preston; the Primate of All Ireland, Aodh Ua Raghallaigh; the Provincial of the Franciscans, Brian Mac Giolla Cainnigh, a Connachtman.]

It is interesting that Ó Melláin considers noteworthy the fact that the Franciscan provincial is a Connachtman, and it is a timely reminder of the priorities of some of the participants in this extremely complex conflict. Conflicts among the clergy in the continental colleges sometimes reflecting their respective Gaelic or Old English backgrounds, sometimes reflecting conflicts traditional between their respective religious orders, contributed to the many disunities among the Confederates.[99] Ó Melláin did not find it necessary to explain or justify the

---

[98] Tadhg Ó Donnchadha (ed.), 'Cinn Lae Ó Melláin', in *Analecta Hibernica,* no. 3 (1931), p. 33.

[99] See H.F. Kearney, 'Ecclesiastical politics and the Counter-Reformation in Ireland', p. 212 — 'In essentials, the differing outlook between Ormonde's bishops and O'Neill's bishops went back to the days of Peter Lombard and Florence Conry. The religious orders also behaved in 1648 as they had done earlier. The Franciscans sided with Owen Roe O'Neill in 1648 as they had with Seán O'Neill in 1626, whereas the Capuchins maintained the outlook of Francis Nugent, backed by the Jesuits and other regulars. The new factor in 1648 was the presence of Rinuccini and it was this which accounted for Dromore, Ardagh and Cork acting, so to say, 'out of character'. But if this novelty is ignored, the features of

split command as between provinces or in any other way. It would appear, likewise, from the same source (Ó Melláin) that internal sept disputes and personal quarrels were unceremoniously settled without regard for the ostensible purpose of the military effort:

> San mBreifni ag Bél Ath hUan do mharbh Brian Ruadh Ó Neill, Aodh Mac Airt Óig, meic Toirdh, Í Néill do chuir piléir pistoil tríd.

> [In Breifne at Beal Ath hUan Brian Ruadh O'Neill killed Aodh Mac Airt Óg meic Toird, O'Neill by shooting him with a pistol.][100]

The disruption and dislocation of the period demanded that blame be apportioned for the troubles affecting Ireland. In cases where the poet found it difficult to lay the blame on the ubiquitous *Gall* — he frequently identified the lack of unity among the Gael and God's displeasure with them as the causes of Banbha's misfortunes. The thirteenth-century poet Aonghus Ó hEoghusa, bewailed the disunity among the Gael which afforded the *Gall* advantage over them. He castigated the Gaelic chiefs rather than the *Gall* in his poem for Thomas Magauran (+ 1343).[101] Thomas Magauran had been imprisoned by neighbouring Gaelic enemies. Ó hEoghusa castigated the Gaoidhael for their disunity. Their mutual jealousy was such that the *Gall* made progress against them — and deserved to do so:

> Millte Éire d'iomthnúth Ghaoidheal,
> ní gaol síodha an seol do-níad,
> a bhfíoch ga gcursun a caomhthach
> dursun nach fríoth d'aonghuth iad.
> (McKenna, *Magauran Poems,* No. 23, st. 1, p. 191.)

> [Éire is ruined by rivalry among the Gael; not mutual love in peace is their policy; their anger keeps them apart; and they cannot agree.]

All the authors of the so-called seventeenth century 'political poems'

---

the split in 1648 were essentially what they had been before the Confederation existed, and in some ways, before the seventeenth century began.

[100] 'Cinn Lae Ó Melláin', p. 44.

[101] See McKenna, *Magauran Poems,* Introduction, p. x.

would echo the sentiments of the following stanza by Ó hEoghusa in the same poem:

Méad d'iomthnúidh fa iath mBanbha
bheanas díobh Fhódhla san fheoir chuirr
an tráth badh leo léinn go Ghallaibh
gleo ar gach bhféin i gclannaibh Cuinn.

A milltear dh'Fhódhla is é mhilleas
gan mhian síodha ar sean ná ar óg;
do mhill ar n-oiléinne Éire,
soiléime linn féine an fód.
(McKenna, *Magauran Poems,* No. 23, sts. 2 and 3, p. 191.)

[The rivalry in desire of Banbha's land has deprived them of thick-grassed Fódla; instead of attacking Goill, every troop of Conn's race is in turmoil.

What ruins Fódla is that neither young nor old desire peace; 'tis Éire herself has ruined this isle of ours, we find the land too tempting an object of attack.]

This combination of disunity among the Gael and the consequent erosion of their power was a popular combination with the authors of some of the five poems selected by O'Rahilly. The fourteenth-century poet Ó hEoghusa, suggested that the capture of Magauran had hindered any hope of unity among the Gael. The capture of his patron drove him to castigate the chiefs for their internecine strife. The 'unity' aspired to by Magauran or indeed Ó hEoghusa has as little to do with political unity under a central administration as that aspired to by the poets of the seventeenth century.[102] The concept of 'unity' enshrined in the poetry had more to do with the conviction throughout Ireland that the strongest should win and that unity lasted for as long as the individual who presided over it could keep it thus. Ó hEoghusa declared that their disunity had drawn the wrath of God upon the Gael and only his mercy could enable them to overcome their adversaries. He was quite specific about the rôle of God's pardon in[103] achieving the freedom of Magauran from physical captivity by some rival lords; a theme of divine interference antedating the Reformation and Counter-Reformation.

---

102 See for example McKenna, *Magauran Poems,* no. 23, sts. 13, 14, 24, pp 191-5.
103 McKenna, *Magauran Poems,* No. 23, st. 14, p. 195.

Ní as fhiadhnaighe d'iomthnudh Ghaoidheal
gabháil mheic Bhriain an bhairr thláith;
iad ar cheann Tuama do theannadh
ní huadha as fhearr ceangal cáich.
(McKenna, *Magauran Poems,* No. 23, st. 4, p. 191.)

[The most certain example of this rivalry of the Gaoidhil is the captivity of the soft-haired son of Brian; fixing a chain on Tuaim's Prince was not the way to bind us together.]

However, while the Gael themselves captured Thomas and thereby occasioned Banbha's destruction, God could by pardoning Thomas, effect a change in Banbha's fortunes:

Mag Shamhradhan do shíodh Ghaoidheal
do ghabh Dia gá dhreich mar ghrís,
táinig an fear a hidh eile;
dhá thigh mo chean reimhe a-rís.
(McKenna, *Magauran Poems,* No. 243, st. 7, p. 193.)

[To the relief of the Gaoidheal God pardoned that hero of blushing face, and so he escaped from another chain; all hail to him now coming home.]

A sense of urgency is conveyed in the following stanza — of the inappropriateness of the internecine rivalry which leaves Banbha always at the mercy of the Gall. In a seventeenth-century context the interpretation of this stanza could serve to present false impression of the use of this particular bardic device: [104]

Ceangul síodha ar sluagaibh Banbha
beag badh iarrtha d'airgneach Gall;
cosnadh cach a orrainn d'Fhódladh;
ní tráth comainn d'fhóbhra ann.
(McKenna, *Magauran Poems,* No. 23, st. 14, p. 195.)

['Tis a small thing to ask the Harrier of the Goill that he impose peace on Banbha's hosts; let each one hold his own part of Fódla; this is no time for injuring the union (of Éire).]

---

[104] See N.P. Canny, 'Formation', esp. pp 108-110; Dunne, 'Evidence', *passim.*

It was no time to contribute to the disunity among the Gael, weakening their defences in this crucial hour which was that of a fourteenth-century local sept crisis; the capture of Magauran. The seventeenth century poet Donnchadh Mac an Caoilfhiaclaigh — to whom the poem 'Do frith, monuar an uain si ar Éirinn'[105] is attributed, also remarked upon the effects of disunity linking it with God's displeasure:

> Ní hé shaoilim acht díoltas dé uile . . .
> . . . .
> gan umhla ag dís don bhuin dá chéile
> ná d'fhearr ba thaca chum seasaimh do dhéanamh.
> (O'Rahilly, *Five Seventeenth Century Political Poems,*
> lines 150-2, p. 10.)

[Not this, I think, but God's revenge . . . and not two of the group submitting one to the other, or yet to an individual who would be a support with whom to make a stand.]

The anonymous poem 'An Síogaí Romhánach' laments likewise this 'disunity' and cites it as a reason for the chaos following the death of Eoghan Rua Ó Néill:

> Ní raibh a nglaca i nglacaibh a chéile,
> Ní raibh an tuath go fuaighte d'aontoil . . .
> (O'Rahilly, *Five Seventeenth Century Political Poems,* No. 2,
> lines 249-51, p. 28.)

[Their hands were not joined together, the country was not sown together in unity of desire . . .]

Having thus established disunity as the cause of Ireland's woes, the poet saw the necessity of enlisting a God as a *deus ex machina* to secure the restoration of Ireland to her wonted glory and to compass the defeat of her enemies;[106]

> Is treise Dia na fian an Bhéarla.
> (O'Rahilly, *Five Seventeenth Century Political Poems,*
> No. 2, line 267, p. 29.)

---

[105] O'Rahilly, *Five Seventeenth Century Political Poems,* p. 10, lines 150-1.
[106] O'Rahilly, *Five Seventeenth Century Political Poems,* No. 2, lines 305-8.

The poem titled alternatively 'Aiste Sheáin Uí Chonaill' (who is not definitively identified) or 'Tuireamh na hÉireann',[107] blames the Irish themselves for their defeat — specifically mentioning the mixed command. The poet may have preferred a military command based on racial affinities:

> . . . nach díth daoine, bíg ná éadaig
> ná neart do bhain díobh Éire
> acht iad féin do chaill ar a chéile,
> Ginerál Ghallda ar armáil Gheulaig,
> armáil Ghallda ar gineráil Geulach.
> (O'Rahilly, *Five Seventeenth Century Political Poems*, No. 4, lines 358-62, p. 75.)

[. . . not scarcity of people, food or clothes or strength which took Ireland from them, but they themselves procured their own defeat; Old English generals over Irish troops, Old English troops under Irish generals.]

Not only did they lose the battle by their own disunity, but they are helpless, the physicians of Ireland are powerless to cure her and only God can help:

> Níl ár leigheas ar liaig i n-Éirinn
> acht Dia go ghuí 's na naoimh i n-aonacht.
> (O'Rahilly, *Five Seventeenth Century Political Poems*, No. 4, lines 439-40, p. 79.)

[The physicians of Ireland do not have a cure for us but to pray God together with his saints.]

The poet identified as Éamonn an Dúna[108] identifies the moral turpitude of the Irish as a further cause for their defeat:

> Beag an t-ionadh tú thuitim, a Éire!
> Tugais crabha ar chraosaibh . . .
> (O'Rahilly, *Five Seventeenth Century Political Poems*, No. 5, lines 373-4, p. 98.)

---

107 O'Rahilly, *Five Seventeenth Century Political Poems*, no. 4, p. 50.
108 O'Rahilly, *Five Seventeenth Century Political Poems*, no. 5, p. 84.

[Your fall is a small surprise oh Ireland, you exchanged piety for greed . . .]

This poet mentions in particular the folly and treachery of the Gael who performed services for the Gall:

Is mórán fuad do chuaig mar chéird leis
ag brath ag fealla do Ghallaibh ar Ghaeulaibh
Cuid le a naimhdibh ag díol a ngaolta
is cuid ag spiaireacht i ndiag na cléire.
(O'Rahilly, *Five Seventeenth Century Political Poems*,
No. 5, lines 352-6.)

[And along with this habit (they went) in great haste spying on and conspiring against the Gael for the Gall. Some selling their relatives and others spying on the clergy.][109]

The predominence of this particular combination of themes, Gaelic disunity and God's wrath, Gaelic turpitude and God's vengeance owed something to current continental and English theological, philosophical and religious trends too. Increased familiarity with the bible and the intense sectarian politics which characterized mid-seventeenth century Europe played a part in shaping the preoccupations of the authors of these poems. These influences alone, however, do not account for the popularity of occurrence of these themes together in the non-syllabic poetry of this period. It is too easy to see the motifs of God as *deus ex machina,* and the self-deprecating tone of the poets as emanating solely or principally from the heightened sense of religious observation promoted by the Counter-Reformtion. It is similarly tempting to extend this element to a theory of revolutionary political consciousness among the poets and consequently among the social and political leaders of Gaelic society.[110] These poems are not statements of Counter-Reformation political or religious theory. They are contemporary Gaelic literary appraisals of some of the events of the mid-century.

---

[109] See Jennings, *Wild Geese in Spanish Flanders,* Introduction p. 52, in reference to spies in 1624: 'By June the rumours had grown, and a loyal-hearted Papist, as he described himself, had reported to the Lord Deputy, from a Servant of his who had served in the Low Countries under Tyrone . . .' Jennings tells us that the informant was the Superior of the Franciscan House at Timoleague, one Florence McCarthy.
[110] See Canny, 'Formation', pp 108-10.

Their tone is influenced by current events, the authors are products of their time, but the tradition from which they emerge has a powerful influence on how they treat of their subject. The priorities articulated by the poets differ not at all from those which dictated the activities of those actively participating in the conflict. In so far as the rationale predominating in the poems can be shown to be essentially that of the earlier bardic material, so the rationale of those of whose activities they celebrated can be seen as equally traditionally based.

The kernel of the Gaelic mentality as portrayed in the professional bardic poetry is presented once again in these poems in a fashion remarkably faithful both to their literary heritage and to the evidence of the survival of such a mentality stamped on every action of the Confederate Irish during the decade and a half 1640-1655. The thematic accretions displayed by these poems which owe their origin to the philosophy and politics of Counter-Reformation Europe, contribute a dimension to the traditional themes which form the basic elements of the poems. The discourse of the poetry remains entirely traditional.[111] The traditional themes of Gaelic disunity and reasons for defeat are linked together with the 'religious' themes of God's punishment, extended in some instances to analogy with the wayward Israelites who were in turn analogous with the anti-nuncio faction of Haicéad's 'Músgail do mhisneach'. The display of learning, traditional and classical, which forms a major part of each of the poems of O'Rahilly's collection causes one to doubt the spontaneity of the anguish expressed. Lack of spontaneity does not in itself invalidate the sentiments or attitudes expressed in the poetry, but it certainly points to influences other than the necessity to communicate events in their immediacy at work on the poets and casts doubt on the populist thrust of the poems.

The manner in which the author of 'An Síogaí Romhánach' dealt with the events of the 1640s indicates no development in Gaelic political perceptions from that indicated in formal bardic poetry. The same mentality dictated the perceptions articulated in both forms of poetry. The author of 'An Síogaí Romhánach' made use of a form of the 'aisling'[112]

---

[111] See *ibid.*

[112] See S. Ó Tuama, 'Téamaí Íasachta i bhfilíocht pholaitiúil na Gaeilge (1600-1800); Gerard Murphy, 'Notes on *aisling* poetry', in *Éigse*, vol. 1 (1939), p. 42; Ó Buachalla, 'An mheisiasacht agus an aisling', in de Brún (ed.), *Folia Gadelica;* Ó Cuív, 'Literary creation and the Irish historical tradition', in *Proceedings of the British Academy*, vol. xlix (1963); Tadhg Ó Dúshláine, 'Filíocht Pholaitiúil na Gaeilge — a cineál', esp. pp 124-8.

to introduce his main theme. Structurally, this poem comprises an 'aisling' introduction followed by a discussion of Banbha's ills and their source. The author uses an interrogative tone throughout with a repetition of the phrase 'Créad fá?' [113] in which the poet asks of God why the ills of Banbha should not be lessened. He traces the origins of the destruction of Banbha to the reign of Henry VIII. [114] His descendant Elizabeth I, he dismisses as a beastly individual, guilty of Mary Stuart's blood. [115] Along with Henry he placed James I and Charles I:

> I ndiaidh na mná so tháinig Séamas
> Níor thuar faoiseamh do chríocha Fhéilim.
> (O'Rahilly, *Five Seventeenth Century Political Poems,*
> No. 2, lines 89-90, p. 21.)

[After this woman [Elizabeth] came James, no auspicious event for Ireland.]

For the poet, the reign of Charles I provided no favourable contrast with that of his father, James:

> Is gearr 'na diaigh gur thionnsgain Séarlas ar nós a athar le
> cleasaibh 'se le bréagaibh.
> (O'Rahilly, *Five Seventeenth Century Political Poems,*
> No. 2, lines 95-6, p. 22.)

[Shortly afterwards Charles began like his father with trickery and deceit.]

The poet thus quickly disposes of some four generations of English monarchs. God permitted the beheading of Charles I because of the depredations of those four. He highlights Ulster as the area in which the conflicts in Ireland began:

> I gcúige Uladh do mhúsgail an chéidfhear
> Mag Uidhir fuigheall na Féine,
> is Mac Mathghamhna amhail ba bhéas dó . . .
> (O'Rahilly, *Five Seventeenth Century Political Poems,*
> No. 2, lines 116-8, p. 23.)

---

[113] O'Rahilly, *Five Seventeenth Century Political Poems,* no. 2, lines 42-62, pp 19-20; and see Tadhg Ó Dúshláine, 'Filíocht Pholaitiúil na Gaeilge — a cineál', *passim.*

[114] O'Rahilly, *Five Seventeenth Century Political Poems,* no. 2, lines 79-81, p. 21.

[115] O'Rahilly, *Five Seventeenth Century Political Poems,* no. 2, lines 83-4, p. 21.

[In Ulster the first man arose, Maguire the blossoming of the war-riors, and Mac Mahon — as was his wont.]

This mixed selection of themes and focusses in the first part of the poem, serve as an introduction for the poet's main preoccupation — the celebration of Eoghan Rua O'Neill's victory. The northern focus of the poem, stressing the Ultonian origin of the military conflicts, prepares one for the singling out of Eoghan Rua as the object of eulogy — and his victory as the subject of a typical battle-roll.[116]

O'Neill is depicted as having travelled across the sea to rescue Banbha:

> Ag so an uair do ghluais an tréinfhear
> as in Spáinn fa lán earma . . .
> (O'Rahilly, *Five Seventeenth Century Political Poems,*
> No. 2, lines 130-1, p. 23.)

[At this time the hero travelled from Spain in full armour . . .]

This is followed by seventy lines[117] of description of the victories of Eoghan Rua, and of his personal valour and prowess:[118]

> . . . leath a ghníomh a ríomh ní fhéadaim.
> Do chúige Uladh tug furtacht ar éigin,
> Do chuir sé Gaill do dhruim a chéile.
> . . . .
> Do chuir sé meatacht ar Albanaigh mhaola
> . . . Eoghan Ruadha ar ghuallaibh Gaodhal
> dá chur suas ar uachtar an Bhéarla.
> (O'Rahilly, *Five Seventeenth Century Political Poems,*
> No. 2, lines 145-7, 150-1, 182-3, pp 24-6.)

[. . . I cannot recount half of his deeds. He helped Ulster in its time of need, he threw the foreigners back upon themselves . . . he made cowards of the Scots. . . . Eoghan Rua, on the shoulders of the Gael, hampering the English nobles.]

---

[116] See Tadhg Ó Dúshláine, 'Filíocht Pholaitiúil na Gaeilge — a cineál', esp. pp 117-25.

[117] O'Rahilly, *Five Seventeenth Century Political Poems,* no. 2, lines 120-90, pp 23-6.

[118] O'Rahilly, *Five Seventeenth Century Political Poems,* no. 2, lines 184-95, p. 26; for another view of Eoghan Rua's activities during this period see Ó Fiaich, 'Republicanism and Separatism in the seventeenth century', esp. p. 85.

Eoghan Rua himself described graphically his feelings on arrival in Ulster, and gave his opinions of the 'warriors' whom he was expected to lead. His letter of 1642 to Father Hugh de Burgo [119] reveals the extent of the chaos in Ulster as it appeared to him, and the survival of the traditional war practices of booty-taking and short raiding patterns practised among the military groups there as late as the mid-seventeenth century. O'Neill's heavily qualified willingness to come to Ulster's rescue (*tug furtacht ar éigin do chúige Uladh*) is only brought into relief by his threats to quit the country if his conditions were not met:

> . . . After many hardships and sufferings usually endured by those who travel by sea. . . . I arrived in this kingdom, in a port of Tyrconnell which is called Lough Coyte [sic], expecting to find rest and quiet there after the fatigue of the sea. But the opposite was the case, for the country not only looks like a desert, but like hell, if there could be a hell upon earth; for besides the sterility, destruction, and bad condition it is in, the people are so rough and barbarous and miserable that many are little better in their ways than the most remote Indians . . .
> For on both sides I saw nothing but burning, robbery in cold blood, and cruelties such as are not usual even among the Moors and Arabs . . . no obedience among the soldiers, if one call men soldiers who behave nothing better than animals . . . for they are so disheartened and in such a state of disagreement that they are all fled together through the mountains to Connaught. [120]

O'Neill and Preston were bitter rivals and were continually in competition for prestige and supplies. Complaints about Preston entered into O'Neill's correspondence with de Burgo too and he threatened to abandon everything to Preston and return to Flanders if his complaints were not redressed.

O'Neill's own exposition of his intentions and fears fall far short of the hero presented in 'An Síogaí Romhánach'. This, however, is true of

---

[119] Jennings, *Wild Geese in Spanish Flanders,* pp 507-8; O'Neill to Hugh de Burgo, no. 25, 16-26 September 1642.

[120] Jennings, *Wild Geese in Spanish Flanders,* pp 507-8; O'Neill to Hugh de Burgo, no. 25, 16-26 September, O'Neill was not alone in comparing the Gaelic Irish in Ulster with 'Indians'. Christopher Hill cites the following in *Change and Continuity in Seventeenth-Century England* (London 1974), p. 20: 'We have Indians at home — Indians in Cornwall, Indians in Wales, Indians in Ireland' said an 'eminent person' two decades later when the conversion of the American Indians were under discussion.

all the 'heroes' eulogized by the poets; and yet the discrepancies between actual events and people and the literary exposition of those same had never been adumbrated as a reason or motive for the modification of or the cessation of either. Neither, of course, can O'Neill's less than crusading spirit [121] be seen as part of a great catholic crusade in which the poets brought the power of their pens to bear on the side of Counter-Reformation and Catholic Europe. Eoghan Rua's death was seen by the poet, not as a consequence of war or illness or of the English, but of the will of God who wished to number him among the saints in heaven:

> . . . 's nach le Gallaibh do gearradh a shaoghal,
> acht le dia lér mhian a shaoradh.
> Is gairm go neamh i measg na naomh air.
> (O'Rahilly, *Five Seventeenth Century*
> *Political Poems,* No. 2, lines 202-4, p. 26.)

[. . . his life was not shortened by the English but by God who desired to free him and called him to be among his saints.]

The poet, having disposed of Eoghan Rua in such a grand style, merely runs through a list of other Ulster 'heroes' with a brief mention of their heroic attributes. [122] Thus the bishop, Éibhear Mathghamhain, the general who replaced O'Neill in command of the Ulster forces for a short period, was commended for victories against the Parliamentarians under Coote:

> (fear) . . . do ghear gúta an Chútaigh ghaothaigh
> 's do chuir ruaig ar shluaite Shéarlais.
> (O'Rahilly, *Five Seventeenth Century Political*
> *Poems,* No. 2, lines 211-3, p. 27.)

[He cut the gout of bombastic Coote, he banished the troops of this Charles (Coote).]

The poet makes no mention of the background to some of the 'victories' he lists so proudly; Éibhear Mathghamhain and Lieutenant Farrell, having escaped slaughter at Scarifhollis were betrayed by another

---

[121] See Canny, 'Formation', pp 108-10.
[122] O'Rahilly, *Five Seventeenth Century Political Poems,* no. 2, lines 116-8, p. 23 and lines 212-20, p. 27.

Ulsterman, one Maguire, and Mathghamhain was hanged and quartered by Coote. The bishop and Farrell had ignored the advice of Henry Rua O'Neill cautioning them against a military engagement with Coote at Scarifhollis. This same Henry O'Neill, Eoghan Rua's son, is merely listed in turn without any reference to his part in the whole picture:

> Henry Ruadh dar dhual tréine,
> is Mac Mhég Uidhir an chroidhe Ghaolaigh.
> (O'Rahilly, *Five Seventeenth Century Political Poems,* No. 2, lines 216-7, p. 27.)

> [Henry Rua to whom courage is natural, and Maguire's son of the Gaelic heart.]

The author of 'An Síogaí Romhánach' celebrated the 'heroes' of the principal Ulster families without any elaboration. He looked to the ancient prophecies[123] for consolation but was in doubt as to their fulfilment considering how disunited Banbha was. Along with Haicéad, this poet was a convinced Nuncioist and any opposition to him was the basest treachery.[124] The disloyalty to the Nuncio epitomized the disunity of the Gael — and the poet's own loyalty to him made such treachery particularly pernicious. He does not lose hope entirely, however, because besides God's help there are after all, the wealth of Leinster and Munster leaders led by the legendary prophesied northern leader Aodh Buí, introduced thus:

> Gidheadh fós, mo dhóigh níor thréigeas
> 's ní bhiaidh mise gan misneach éigin.
> Is treise Dia ná fian an Bhéarla
> Mairidh fós do phór Mhiléisius
> an tAodh Buidhe sé d'fhuigheall na nGaolfhear,
> an fear do thairngir fáidh nach bréagach . . .
> (O'Rahilly, *Five Seventeenth Century Political Poems,* No. 2, lines 265-70, p. 29.)

> [Yet, however, I have not abandoned hope, and I shall not be without some courage. God is stronger than the English-speaking

---

123 O'Rahilly, *Five Seventeenth Century Political Poems,* no. 2, lines 224-8, p. 27.
124 O'Rahilly, *Five Seventeenth Century Political Poems,* no. 2, lines 23-9, p. 29.

forces; of Milesius' stock Aodh Buí yet lives — the man prophesied by the true seers.]

The poet continues with a list of Leinster and Munster heroes, presenting a series of names evocative of heroism and traditional
glory.[125]

The allegiances displayed by one individual at least indicates that the
traditional aspirations of his sept meant more to him than loyalty to the
Nuncio. Various chiefs are called upon to rescue Banbha following
Eoghan Rua's death, among them one Aodh Ó Broin:

> . . . is Aodh Ó Broin le dtuitfeadh céadta . . .
> (O'Rahilly, *Five Seventeenth Century Political Poems,*
> No. 2, line 274, p. 30.)

> [. . . and Hugh O'Byrne, by whom hundreds would fall . . .]

This Hugh, having been imprisoned in 1647 and released on exchange by
O'Neill, was appointed governor of Wicklow by Ormond in 1649.
O'Byrne's defection to Ormond and his possible 'reward' of the gover-
norship of Wicklow is understandable. Such a position was a likely attraction for any member of the Wicklow leading sept of O'Byrne. The
apparent flexibility of the loyalties of men such as O'Byrne and the concepts of power and loyalty directing their allegiances drew no censorious
comment from the poet. He castigated the anti-Nuncio faction in
general. The motivations of the individuals on either side — so long as
they belonged to the traditionally prominent septs — brought no sep-
cific disapproval from the poet. His treatment of the entire period from
that of Henry VIII to the death of Eoghan Rua is not that of a political
analyst, but rather that of an exponent of a traditional interpretation for
which the war or wars were not perceived as milestones ending finally in
political conquest but as further episodes in the on-going saga of the
fate of Banbha. Individual episodes; O'Byrne's defection to Ormond,
the betrayal by Maguire of Farrell and Mathghamhain, their disregard
for Henry Rua's advice, are all subsumed in a literary treatment which
traditionally catered for the discrete nature of such episodes in the

---

[125] See O'Rahilly, *Five Seventeenth Century Political Poems,* p. 118, note 270.

Gaelic polity.[126] The concern of the author principally with the Ulster chiefs and the reflection in his work of their adherence to the Nuncio is illustrative of the continuing links between the aspirations and values of the aristocracy and those articulated by the poets. It also illustrates the survival of the regional and provincial bases of loyalty and interest.

The poem known as 'Aiste Dháibhí Cúndún' was written in approximately the same period, and though concerned with the same historical events, deals with an entirely different cast of characters. It is the single known extant composition by the poet Cúndún and was written between 1654-7. Stylistically and metrically it is very similar to 'An Síogaí Romhánach'; but this poem is written by a poet for whom the Ulster contribution to the conflict and the Ulster warriors meant little. Its sphere of interest lies in Connacht and Leinster. The poem opens with a lament for the defeated aristocracy in general. The poet bewails their downfall and despairs of their resurrection:

> Is buartha an cás so 'd tarlaig Éire,
> 'na buaile phráisg de carna ag méirlig
> an uaisle ar lár gan fáil ar éirghe,
> 'na gcuail chnámh atáid a laochra.
> (O'Rahilly, *Five Seventeenth Century Political Poems,*
> No. 3, lines 1-4, p. 35.)

[Woe, the condition in which Ireland finds herself — a field of (wantonness) battle, being treated violently by villains, the nobles absent with no chance of return, her warriors are a pile of bone.]

The message conveyed in the introduction is that devastation has overtaken Banbha. The poet describes at length how this is manifest; women cry continually, beating their hands together in anguish, the elements

---

[126] See O'Rahilly's note in O'Rahilly, *Five Seventeenth Century Political Poems,* p. 119: 'He seems to have gone for a while over to the side of Ormond who made him Governor of Wicklow in January 1649'.

Heber MacMahon, Bishop of Clogher, was described by Rinuccini as being 'entirely swayed by political rules and motives'; see H.F. Kearney, 'Ecclesiastical Politics and the Counter-Reformation in Ireland 1618-1648', p. 209.

are at variance with one another, the moon is afire. The poet is so distracted that he cannot even beguile himself with his wonted pastimes. He continues in this vein for one hundred and seventy lines,[127] listing the great disasters of history and mythology, Irish and European, classical and biblical.[128] The poet's senses are rendered useless[129] when he contemplates Ireland's state following the victory of 'Bodaig an Bhéarla'[130] (English-speaking churls). The interest attaching to the poets listing of the woes of Banbha and his use of this epithet for the victorious English lies in the interpretation sometimes offered for it as an indication of the poet's despising anything English — a generalized hatred of anything English corresponding with his newly awakened sense of Catholic Irish nationalism and his efforts to justify the war.[131] This interpretation seems to push the evidence of the poem too far, especially when it is put into its literary perspective and not baldly presented as a factual statement. The entire tradition of the bardic poets was inseparable from that of frequent states of war. A very natural element of the bardic literary convention was the enumeration of depredations caused by defeat, or inflicted in victory. Rhetorical lists of wartime conditions, especially in defeat, and in a situation where a patron or chief had been lost, had no function of justification. Explanation of defeat, a popular element in O'Rahilly's collection, is quite different from analyses of the sources of the conflict, or justification of the activities of the participants. It is particularly inappropriate in the case of 'Aiste Dháibhí Cúndún' to suggest that he made any conscious attempt either to 'justify' the various conflicts of the decade or to use the 'English language' in any innovatively politically connotative way. Cúndún uses his poetic ingenuity in a display of his accumulated 'knowledge' of classical and Gaelic mythology, bible tales, and English and European history. The great heroes of Christendom and their most famous victories and defeats are exhaustively listed.[132] The purpose of this display was to fulfil the

---

[127] See McKenna, *Aithdioghluim Dána,* No. 4, st. 2, p. 10, a poem by Seaán Mór Ó Clumháin to Tadhg Ó Conchubhair (+ 1374); and see O'Rahilly, *Five Seventeenth Century Political Poems,* no. 3. lines 1-170, pp 35-43.

[128] O'Rahilly, *Five Seventeenth Century Political Poems,* no. 3, lines 69-173, pp 38-43.

[129] O'Rahilly, *Five Seventeenth Century Political Poems,* no. 3, lines 37-48, p. 37.

[130] O'Rahilly, *Five Seventeenth Century Political Poems,* no. 3, lines 32-5, pp 36-7; and see N.P. Canny, 'Formation', p. 107.

[131] Canny, 'Formation', pp 105-16.

[132] O'Rahilly, *Five Seventeenth Century Political Poems,* no. 3, lines 69-177, pp 38-43.

necessity of analogy and comparison. The poem's exhaustive introductory lists are justified within the tradition when Cúndún emerges from his fanciful escapades through centuries of history and mythology with the following statement:

Do-bheirim go deimhin le linn na n-Aosa. . .
nach raibh, nach fuil is nach baogal
do chur ar fhuirinn dár geineadh ó Éabha
samhail na bruide fár cuireadh críoch Fhéilim.
(O'Rahilly, *Five Seventeenth Century Political Poems,*
No. 3, lines 174, 181-3, p. 43.)

[I deem it certain that throughout the ages, there never has been, never will be and that there is no danger that an oppression comparable to that under which Ireland has been placed, shall ever again be imposed on any group descended from Eve.]

Cúndún's articulation of his desolation because of Banbha's stricken condition is emphatically traditional. The poet's individual loss, or his articulation of loss in a more general context, is always the most unsurmountable loss ever inflicted on him personally, or on Banbha as a whole.

A poem by Tadhg Mór Ó hUiginn on the death of Brian Magauran (+ 1298), provides an early illustration of this particular conceit; Magauran was killed in a battle after a stormy career during which he had spent some time in captivity. The poet blamed Magauran's mercenaries for lack of vigilance in protecting him.[133] His loss is greater than that of almost all the kings ever in Ireland. Ó hUiginn lists in nine stanzas other great losses he knew of in the Gaelic tradition:

Níor marbhadh Ghaoidheal ngeal
go bás Briain is nír báidheadh,
nír loisg teine riamh roimhe
Brian eile badh easbhoige.
(McKenna, *Maguaran Poems*, No. 4, st. 27, p. 37.)

[Never was slain by a Gaoidheal's bright sword, never was drowned, no fire ever consumed, a Brian whose death was a sorer loss than (this) Brian's death.]

---

[133] McKenna, *Magauran Poems,* no. 4, st. 18, p. 35.

Ó hUiginn stated that though some individual deaths could have been more grave, no loss was inflicted which quite equalled that of Brian's:[134] the untimely and tragic deaths of eight other heroes are listed[135] by Ó hUiginn as a preface to the stanzas announcing his most recent loss. Like Cúndún, Ó hUiginn sees their loss as nought when compared with his present distress. He suggested that unless God came to his assistance he should never assume his wonted state again:

> Is beag orainn n-a fharradh
> na huile eile fhuaramar;
> gach easbhaidh dar bhean riamh rinn
> go Brian nochan eadh airmhin.
>
> Acht muna fhuil go Dia dhamh
> éirighe n-a dhiaidh do dhéanamh
> ní éir me do eadar as,
> leagadh mar é ní fhuaras.
> (McKenna, *Magauran Poems,* No. 4, stanzas 38 and
> 39, p. 41.)

[Compared with that grief, small are all the other disasters that have befallen us; I think it not worth mention the losses that befell us up to Brian's death.

Except God help me to rise hereafter, I shall never rise again, I feel; no fall like this have I ever experienced.]

Like Ó hUiginn, Cúndún's sense of loss and defeat was unprecedented, like him also, the source of his sense of loss could be pinpointed to the immediate impact of the setback experienced by his patrons or his local leaders. Cúndún's sense of loss was confined to his distress because of the reduction of some prominent southern septs. He made no mention whatever of the Ultonian contribution to the wars of any individual hero involved in the Ulster sphere. Indeed, Cúndún's aspirations for Banbha do not extend much further than that the two southern septs of O'Brien and McCarthy be reinstated.[136] The evocation of McCarthys and O'Briens to the prejudice of any other leaders or province is articulate of

---

[134] McKenna, *Magauran Poems,* no. 4, st. 28, p. 37.
[135] McKenna, *Magauran Poems,* no. 4, stanzas 29-36, pp 37-9.
[136] O'Rahilly, *Five Seventeenth Century Political Poems,* no. 3, lines 296-9, p. 48.

the poet's aspirations for Ireland as a whole. No latent sense of a burgeoning catholic nationalism is evident in this articulation of the poets supposed political hopes.

It is inappropriate to suggest that the poet's condemnation of the English language had anything to do with a feeling of political nationalism either. Cúndún refers to the English language three times in his poem. The three occasions are mutually contradictory if one wishes to attach an interpretation of nationalistic xenophobia to them.[137] No contradiction is perceived when the poem is interpreted according to the poet's own frame of reference. He describes the devastation of Ireland during the recent wars. The nobility have disappeared, the towns are under the control of the English, and the charters have been lost by the Irish:

> Do measadh a stát is tá ar láimh na méirleach,
> is táid a mbailte faoi bhastartaibh Béarla,
> is táid a gcartacha daingean le tréimhse
> ar láimh na nGall nach ceannsa céadfa, . . .
> (O'Rahilly, *Five Seventeenth Century Political Poems,*
> No. 3, lines 208-11, pp 44-5.)

> [Their estates have been measured and are in the hands of villains, and their towns are under English-speaking bastards, and their charters are for some time firmly in the hands of the insensitive English.]

Cúndún used 'bastardaibh an Bhéarla' and 'bodaig an Bhéarla' as alternative identifications of Englishman/foreigner. The language is used to denote the race of the people referred to, and is unconnected with simple political allegiances. Cúndún used language on two occasions in a socially connotative way. In one instance Cúndún lists the English language among his pleasurable accomplishments, along with chess, harp-playing, speaking Spanish, hunting, riding, spear-throwing, and dogs:[138]

> Ní labhraim ceachtar díobh, Laidean ná Béarla,
> is orm is dall Franncais is Gréigis,

---

137 See Canny, 'Formation', p. 107.
138 O'Rahilly, *Five Seventeenth Century Political Poems,* no. 3, lines 49-61, pp 37-8.

ní chanaim Spáinnis ná ráite Éibhir
is teanga no mháthar, mo chrá má's léir dham.
(O'Rahilly, *Five Seventeenth Century Political Poems,*
No. 3, lines 55-8, pp 37-8.)

[Oh woe is me, I speak neither Latin or English, I am blind to
French and Greek, I speak neither Spanish nor Gaelic (lit. the
speech of Éibhir), my mother tongue.]

Mastery in the English language in this context is a status-symbol, rank-
ing along with other gentlemanly pursuits. A poet who composed an
elegy on the death of Piaras Feiritéir, who died at the hands of the
English-speaking parliamentarians, commended him on his fluency in
the English language as part of a list of his accomplishments. Cúndún's
expressions 'bodaig an Bhéarla' and 'bastardaibh an Bhéarla' are ex-
pressive, not of Cúndún's dislike of 'Béarla' but of his abhorrence of the
low status of the intruders; his hatred of the social upset caused by the
wars in which status-less individuals could thrive. It is a fear which
echoed that of the poet Maol Seachluinn Ó hEoghusa in his elegy for
Thomas Magauran (+ 1343). Along with the disorder manifest in nature
and in the poet's life, the social order [139] was disturbed by Magauran's
death and menial folk took the opportunity to defy their superiors.

Ní frioth orraim d'fhior uainne
i nGlinn Ghaibhle gheaguaine
ré ndul do ghríbh Chúnga a chach,
do rígh nírbh urra a óglach.
(McKenna, *Magauran Poems,* No. 31, st. 17, p. 275.)

[No (other) man ever got homage from us in green-valleyed
Gleann Gaibhle till Cunga's Griffin died, (and) no common
soldier ever dared to act as lord to a lord.]

Cúndún's villification of intruders as 'English-speaking' refers pe-
joratively not to the language but to the status of those involved.

Cúndún concluded his poem on a pessimistic note; the poet expresses
a desire to die until God sees fit to rescue Banbha. [140] Such was the
destruction wrought by the conflicts of the decade 1642-52 that the poet

---

[139] McKenna, *Magauran Poems,* no. 31, stanzas 15-26, pp 273-7.
[140] See Dunne, 'Evidence', p. 21.

could see no other relief to his distress. The conclusion of his poem, is so structured as to provide a literary *dúnadh*.

An uair nach faighim-se leigheas na gcréacht so,
leagfad mo shúile dúnta i n-aonacht,
ní chuirfead mo dhúil re smúine ar aonrud
is ní chuirfead cor dom chois go n-éagad,
bíodh Críoch Fáil mar atá le tréimhse,
go dtigid grása ó árdMhac Dé ghil,
'na buaile phráisg dá cárna ag méirlig.
(O'Rahilly, *Five Seventeenth Century Political Poems,* No. 3, lines 309-15, p. 49.)

[Since I cannot find a cure for this wound, I will close my eyes together, and I shall not move my feet until I die; let Ireland be as she has been for some time now — a battle-field, being violently dealt with by villians, until the grace of God's bright sons shall come.]

Cúndún's resolution for the woes of Banbha is the restoration of the McCarthys and the O'Briens, the replacement of his provincial leaders. His desolation and distress focussed entirely on his own relationship with the polity of his native province. His articulation of the situation is within the conventionalized ethos which was celebrated in bardic poetry in which each loss is subjectively evaluated. His pessimism is born of the absence of the rightful rulers of Munster and the customary articulation thereof is the stuff of his composition. The mentality articulated in Cúndún's concluding lament could be understood and shared four centuries earlier by the poet Lucas Mac Naimhín who lamented the death of Fearghal, son of Brian Magauran. He especially mentioned the dispersal of poets and nobles following Fearghal's death. His followers and poets had no future in the devastated territory:

Ag sgaoileadh dúinn n-a dhiaidh sain
gan arbhur d'aithle an fheolmhéigh;
ar ndul uainn do chraoibh Choraidh
laoigh ar mbuair far mbeathoghadh.
(McKenna, *Magauran Poems,* No. 5, st. 4, p. 43.)

[We (have to) scatter after his death; now that he is a corpse we have no corn; now that the hero of Cora is gone, the calves of our flock are our food.]

Both the territory and the people suffer his loss. Mac Naimhín specifically mentioned those who will have to disperse in the absence of the leader:

D'éis a mharcaigh Mhuighe na bhFeart
budh oilithrigh ar n-oireacht;
biaidh aithne na sligheadh sair
ga chineadh d'aithle Fhearghail.
(McKenna, *Magauran Poems,* No. 5, st. 8, p. 45.)

[After the passing of the Hero of Magh na bhFeart our nobles will be pilgrims; Fearghal's race, now he is gone, will come to know the roads of the East.]

A final complimentary stanza for another patron — Mathghamhain Mag Raghnaill (+1315) which concludes this elegy for Fergal Magauran, is illustrative of the literary nature of the grief thus conventionally expressed. Mac Naimhín, having declared his devastation of Fearghal's demise, then described his equally inconsolable grief at the death of another:

Mathghamhain Mag Raghnaill réidh,
ar gcara fíre an feirséin;
do-bhéara mhe odhar ann
no go mbé tolamh taram.
(McKenna, *Magauran Poems,* No. 5, st. 42, p. 53.)

[Generous Mathghamhain Mag Raghnaill was a true friend of mine; he (by his death) will keep me pale till the earth covers me too.]

The poet had no interest in the disrupted life and unnatural order which followed first, the death of Fearghal, and second, that of Mathghamhain. Cúndún's expressions of grief at the reduction of the Munster nobility is traditionally excessive and focuses entirely, as did that of the earlier poet, on the individual loss and its consequences.

It is tempting to suggest that Cúndún's final resigned lines indicate that he has indeed accepted the disappearance or imminent destruction of the Gaelic world. Political realities of the 1640s-'50s must have presented some problems of interpretation for the traditional framework which was so much part of the poets' equipment for the articulation of the priorities of the Gaelic aristocracy. It is not necessary to deny the existence of these complex areas where the perceptions of a relatively new and robust polity met the stylized, conventionalized and arguably decadent perceptions of a much older polity. The Gaelic and Old English efforts during the so-called Eleven Years war are ample proof of how unsuccessfully they attempted to incorporate the concepts of united effort and military coördination, and many of the values necessary and generally taken for granted in a polity which had achieved a centrally organized effective administration some centuries earlier, as in England. It is more than tempting to interpret Cúndún's final note of despairing lethargy as a poet's politically prescient comment on the political situation as a whole and its effect on the Gaelic world, according to a posterier analysis of the momentous events of the period, or more important, that which followed it.[141] It hardly makes sense, however, to divide the poet's composition into areas in which we identify and interpret separately, traditional display and rhetoric, contemporary realistic commentary, and finally a genuine *crie de coeur*. This is, in effect, the kind of interpretation which has been offered in respect of Cúndún's poem and by extension, other compositions edited by O'Rahilly.[142] The entire composition must be accepted as a statement with its own integrity within a tradition, or it must not be used as a historical document. In the case of this poem, it can be used as such because it has been firmly placed in the perspective of its tradition in literature. The conservatism of the poets, and the conservative goals of those whose views they articulated must indicate the survival of traditional views and perceptions among the literati and aristocracy. The extent of the poets' participation in the decline of their élite civilization socially and culturally, is evident in their adherence to traditional expression of problems which by the seventeenth century were only superficially comparable to those addressed when the literary tradition assumed the form in use by the poets.[143]

---

[141] See O'Rahilly, *Five Seventeenth Century Political Poems*, Introduction, *passim;* Dunne, 'Evidence', *passim;* Canny, 'Formation', *passim.*

[142] Dunne, 'Evidence', pp 16-22, 'Formation', pp 105-10.

[143] See Canny, 'Formation', p. 96.

Cúndún's participation in the tradition which allowed him to draw on the most popular bardic motifs of loss and defeat automatically places his composition in the traditional context. The fact that his composition contains long drawn out lists of his fancied incarnations:

> Do bhíos san each do cheapadar Gréagaigh . . .
> (O'Rahilly, *Five Seventeenth Century Political Poems*, No. 3, lines 69-136, pp 38-41.)
>
> [I was in the horse which the Greeks made . . .]

and so on for one hundred-odd lines which allowed him to witness some legendary scenes of destruction, demonstrate his participation in the bardic rationale which demanded structures for comparison and analogy.[144] This fundamental element in the composition cannot be considered apart, and representative of a mere traditional aberration in his composition. The mentality which governed his approach and which assured him of the relevance of such traditional material, dictated his account of those events; developments which one recognizes as 'historical fact' and his 'vague account' of transplantation in the same poem. Cúndún's composition, therefore, and his lethargic conclusion must not be interpreted as either pessimistic or prescient. It must be read as his choice of responses from the bardic storehouse which continued to subscribe to the fundamental world-view of which they were eloquent. The mentality which dictated the poets' attitudes as expressed in their compositions is the literary articulation of values and perceptions stylized and conventionalized into manageable literary forms.[145]

The poet identified as Éamonn an Dúna[146] begins his composition on the same note of resignation on which Dáibhí Cúndún concluded his:

> Mo lá leóin go deo go n-éagad
> 's go dul am luí fán líg am aonar
> 's go héirí suas dam Luan an tSléibhe,
> ruaig an ráis si ráinig ort, a Éire,
> d'fhág mo cheann gan mheabhair gan éifeacht, . . .)
> (O'Rahilly, *Five Seventeenth Century Political Poems*,
> No. 5, lines 1-5, p. 86.)

---

[144] O'Rahilly, *Five Seventeenth Century Political Poems*, no. 3, lines 69-174, pp 39-43.
[145] Allan Macinnes, 'Scottish Gaeldom, 1638-1651', esp. pp 77-94.
[146] O'Rahilly, *Five Seventeenth Century Political Poems*, p. 84.

[Woe until the day I die and lie buried (lit. under the stone) alone, until I rise again on the last day, this rout of the race which has come upon you Ireland has left me senseless, . . .]

Munster is the area upon which the poet focused his attention and the plight of the nobility of that province, especially of the Old English, is the subject of his lamentations. In this poem the Ulster hero Eoghan Rua is merely mentioned once.[147] An extensive list of Old English nobles, mainly of Munster and the Pale is provided. The list is very similar to that in 'Tuireamh na hÉireann'. Éamonn an Dúna commends the members of 'An Gallfhuil Ghaeulaig'[148] because of their displaying traditional virtues of generosity to poets, vigour in battle and hospitality.[149]

Ó Conaill, in 'Tuireamh na hÉireann' is also very favourable to the Old English nobles and praised their traditional virtues too. Otherwise he lists them exhaustively without comment on their undoubtedly mixed political and religious affinities.[150] Like Keating, Ó Conaill emphasizes the compatibility of the Old English with the Gaelic Irish and how the two had become one:

Do bhíodar caoin sibhialta tréitheach,
ba mhaith a ndlithe, a gcreideamh 's a mbéasa,
Gach duine d'úmhlaig, do bhí a chuid féin leis.
Do bhíodar ceannsa mar cheann cléire.
Do shíolraigh a bhfuil trí na chéile,
do bhí an Gaeul Gallda is an Gall Gaeulach.
(O'Rahilly, *Five Seventeenth Century Political Poems,*
No. 4, lines 275-280, pp 71-2)[151]

[They were gentle, civilized and talented, their laws, religion and manners were good. Anyone who submitted, held onto his own property. As ecclesiastical leaders they were gentle. They inter-married and the Irishman was English and the Englishman Irish.]

---

147 O'Rahilly, *Five Seventeenth Century Political Poems,* no. 5, line 404, p. 99.
148 O'Rahilly, *Five Seventeenth Century Political Poems,* no. 5, line 25, p. 87.
149 O'Rahilly, *Five Seventeenth Century Political Poems,* No. 5, lines 25-8, p. 87.
150 O'Rahilly, *Five Seventeenth Century Political Poems,* no. 4, lines 381-96, pp 76-7.
151 See O'Rahilly, *Five Seventeenth Century Political Poems,* no. 2, line 155, p. 24; no. 4, lines 361-362, p. 75.

The poet once again drew the fine distinction between the 'intruders' whom he chose to accept or reject. At the time of writing the unacceptable intruders were Cromwellians of low status; and Éamonn an Dúna in his poem specifically excluded English nobility from any culpability in the contemporary intrusion:

> Ní Gaill uaisle luaim san méid si,[152]
> atáid gan chúis acht cúrsa an éigin;
> gérbh' éigean dóibh don fhórsa géille,
> bíon a bpáirt do ghnáth le Séarlas,
> Acht sluaite Chromuil chuthuig chraosuig . . .
> (O'Rahilly, *Five Seventeenth Century Political Poems,*
> No. 5, lines 305-9, p. 96.)

[I do not mention the English nobles among these (despoilers), they are without cause of accusation except that of necessity. Though they had to yield to force, they usually side with Charles. But Cromwell's raging, gluttonous mob . . .]

This support for Charles and the Royalists[153] is not echoed by the author of 'An Síogaí Romhánach' or by Donnchadh mac an Caoilfhiaclaigh (Do fríth monuar . . .) both of whom reckoned Charles no improvement on James I. Mac an Caoilfhiaclaigh mentions no English monarch before James I, unlike the author of 'An Síogaí Romhánach' in this respect, who dates Ireland's troubles from the reign of Henry VIII. In 'An Síogaí Romhánach', the poet describes landownership changes under James I[154] and concludes that Charles continued the same land policy:

> I ndiaigh na mná so tháinig Séamas,
> Níor thuar faoiseamh do chríocha Fhéilim,
> an fear do thógaibh a bpór as a bhfréamhaibh,
> is d'órdaigh a dtalamh do thamhas le téadaibh, . . .
> . . . .
> Is gearr 'na diaigh gur thionnsgain Séarlas
> ar nós a athar le cleasaibh 's le bréagaibh.

---

[152] See O'Rahilly, *Five Seventeenth Century Political Poems,* no. 5, lines 289-96, p. 95.
[153] See Gerard Murphy, 'Royalist Ireland', in *Studies,* vol. xxiv (1935), pp 589-604.
[154] See Breandán Ó Buachalla, 'Cing Séamus', *passim.*

(O'Rahilly, *Five Seventeenth Century Political Poems,* No. 2, lines 89-92, 95-6, pp 21-2.)

[Following this woman cames James, and it was no portent of relief for Ireland, the man who pulled the seed up from its roots and ordered the assessment of land with measures, ... shortly afterwards Charles began with the same habits of trickery and deceit as his father.]

Mac an Caoilfhiaclaigh who begins with James I merely throws the two Stuarts together and reckons Ireland's oppression from the accession of James I — having described the valour and bravery and success of the various Gaelic heroes until then:

> . . . go teacht iona rí do rí Séamus
> is dá mhac 'na dhiaig do riar Rí Séarlas,
> Atáid ó shoin 'na dtocht fá dhaorsmacht . . .
> (O'Rahilly, *Five Seventeenth Century Political Poems,*
> No. 1, lines 109-11, p. 8.)

[. . . until the accession of James I and his son King Charles after him, they are since firmly in bondage . . .]

Séan Ó Conaill, author of 'Tuireamh na hÉireann' like the author of 'An Síogaí Romhánach', lists Henry VIII and Elizabeth and James among the oppressors of Ireland, but indicates his loyalty to Charles I by listing his death among the contemporary woes of Ireland:

> Sin mar d'imig an donas ar Éirinn
> bíodh nár imig an tubaist le chéile
> nó gur thionnsguin an coga so Fhéilim
> is gur chaill a cheann 's a theann Séarlas.
> (O'Rahilly, *Five Seventeenth Century Political Poems,*
> No. 4, lines 349-53, p. 75.)

[That is how misfortune befell Ireland, though it did not all happen together until this war of Felim's began and Charles lost his head and his strength.]

Éamonn an Dúna (Mo lá leóin go deo go n-éagad) is positively inclined towards Charles and like Ó Conaill bemoans Charles' beheading. Listing Ireland's losses Éamonn an Dúna creates a decreasing scale of loss; Ireland has lost her head, her family and her spouse. Her head is Charles, her family are the nobles, and her spouse is Eoghan Rua:

> Do chaillis do cheann, do chlann is do chéile,
> mar atá Séarlas séanmhar séadach,
> t'iarlaí, do thiarnaí, do thréinfhir,
> is Eoghan na gcath, mac Airt uí Néill,
> t'fhior.
> (O'Rahilly, *Five Seventeenth Century Political Poems,*
> No. 5, lines 401-4, p. 99.)

> [You lost your head, your family, your husband; namely jewelled, prosperous Charles, your earls, your lords, your warriors, and your husband — Eoghan mac Art O'Neill of the battles.]

Quite obviously the poets' differences in evaluation of the several English monarchs reflects the nuances of allegiance and loyalty among their politically active peers. This diversity dogged the efforts of the Confederation to arrive at a consensus of loyalties for the four provinces, or even within an individual province.

The traditional nature of the poets' treatment of their subject makes such differences unremarkable in the context of the poets' adherence to the store of references built up for a referential structure which subscribed to a world-view which accepted such diversity of opinion; and yet shared fundamental perceptions of power and authority. One must reiterate once again a fundamental precept of the poets' mentality: where authority was established and effectively wielded — and was acquiesced in to some extent by the poets' patron or patrons, the poets supported it too. Ó Conaill, in 'Tuireamh na hÉireann' made explicit this precept in his rationalization of the position of the Old English as deserving intruders on the Gaelic polity:

> Do bhíodar caoin sibhialta tréitheach,
> ba mhaith a ndlithe, a gcreideamh 's a mbéasa.
> Gach duine d'úmhlaig, do bhí a chuid féin leis.
> (O'Rahilly, *Five Seventeenth Century Political Poems,*
> No. 4, lines 275-7, pp 71-2.)

> [They were gentle, civilized and talented, their laws, religion and manners were good. Anyone who submitted, held onto his own property.]

Ó Conaill did not object to conquest out of hand, he objected, like all the Gaelic poets, without exception, to the preponderance of individuals of low status in prominent positions in the parliamentarian forces. It was a matter of individual choice on the part of the poet, usually influenced by the allegiances of his perceived patron(s), whether or not to champion the king, the native lord or indeed any claimant of sufficient authority and perceived status. Such support was always contingent on a suitable professional position being found for the poet in whatever regime was established. Unfortunately for them, the poets no less than the chiefs, lacking political prescience, did not always appreciate or foresee the accumulative effect of the accommodations which their flexible traditional rationale allowed. Instability of land-titles and inconsistencies in the application of the law, unscrupulous practices and general insecurity was not a unique phenomenon of the mid-seventeenth century. Lists of wrongs and grievances can appear as new and urgent to those who come upon the O'Rahilly collection without experience of earlier material. With such a self-consciously conventionalized, and historically allusive literary genre, the entire body of work, must be taken into account at all times if the poetry is to be used effectively to add a dimension to our view of the Gaelic world's response to the various phases of what eventually amounted to total conquest.

In the fifteenth century, the poet Tadhg Óg Ó hUiginn supported the MacWilliams of Connacht, in the person of Éamonn na Féasóige (+1458). Ó hUiginn felt that where the MacWilliams were concerned, it behoved him to support the king's law and therefore the earls, as its champions and protectors. Ó hUiginn supported the Anglo-Norman MacWilliams against the Gaelic O'Neills and recommended that the king's law be enforced more consistently throughout Banbha. He mentioned especially the insecurity of land-titles in the unsettled conditions perpetuated by flouters of the king's law. He suggested that since the English law is now being shamefully disregarded, the only saviour of Ireland will be the new lord, Éamonn na Féasóige. The object of this poem is one of anticipatory eulogy for Éamonn the MacWilliam. Until he is established the customary chaos is depicted, the chaos which in the poets' idiom always characterized a lordship in dispute. The first stanza of Ó hUiginn's poem sets the scene of disarray:

> Do briseadh riaghail ríogh Sacsann,
> seadh cairte rí chomhaill Gall;

gan neach ann do réir a ríaghla
gach Gall féin is iarla ann.
(McKenna, *Aithdioghluim Dána,* No. 38, st. 1, p. 152.)

[The law of the Saxons' king has often been broken; the Goill set
no store by legal document; none of them obeying the king's law;
each of them is an earl for himself.][155]

He mentions in particular the greed which causes each lord to become a
law unto himself. He bewails the insecurity of inheritance brought
about by the breaking of the king's law, because it is for an Anglo-
Norman lord, whose liege is properly the king of England, in Ó
hUiginn's poem the old good law, which he enjoins on the leaders of
Ireland, is that of the king:

Lorg na n-iarlaidh ní headh leantar
gan luadh cirt ag an chath Ghall;
a gras nochan uighe oidhreacht
duine go fás oirbheart ann.
(McKenna, *Aithdioghluim Dána,* No. 38, st. 3, p. 152.)

[The way of the old earls is not followed, the Gall making no account of justice; a man's inheritance will get no recognition except
when he has the strength to fight.]

Ó hUiginn thus complained about what appears to have been the most
enduring principle of the Gaelic polity; might is right. In this instance he
really uses the same principle with the legal jargon of the law to en-
courage Mac William to seize Eamhain Macha[156] from the O'Neills. In
summary, Ó hUiginn suggested that lack of respect for the law had
created a situation where each man scrambled to retain or expand his
own power, — leading to vicious and unscrupulous practices, making
land-titles unsound.

Éamonn an Dúna (Mo lá leóin go deo go n-éagad) cited similar conditions as the sources of the unsettled state of Ireland. Lack of respect for
the law has condemned Ireland, the king's law he had in mind:

. . .
Toisg aindlíthe h'andaoine dhaor thu

---

[155] See also McKenna, *Aithdioghluim Dána,* No. 38, stanzas 2 and 3, p. 152.
[156] McKenna, *Aithdioghluim Dána,* no. 38, st. 8, p. 153.

gan ciorrú, bac ná smacht 'na n-éirleach.
(O'Rahilly, *Five Seventeenth Century Political Poems,*
No. 5, lines 321-2, p. 96)

[. . .
Because of the lawlessness of your great men which condemned
you; without curtailment, resistance nor control of their destruction.]

The poet deplored the lack of due respect shown to the legal process, and
the king's law in the circumstances:

Bíd céad smacht gan acht i n-Éirinn
do ghlac go sanntach cuid Gall is Gaodhal
is gan a gclocha ná a gcrocha 'na n-éiric.
(O'Rahilly, *Five Seventeenth Century Political Poems,*
No. 5, lines 338-40, p. 97.)

[A hundred laws are illegally enacted in Ireland, which greedily
claims the property of English and Irish, without their (the
perpetrators) being hanged or stoned in retribution.]

The poet claimed that sharp practices continued unchecked and led to
an accumulation of unscrupulous cheating which destroyed Ireland.[157]
Ireland would remain thus until her rightful rulers were restored, in this
poet's case, Charles II and the Duke of York.

Aitchim Íosa díbhse céasadh,
d'fhulaing an pháis do ghrá úr saortha,
mar tháinig ar dtúis cúis úr ndaortha,
go dtí chum críche díbhse an méid si;
teacht díbh fé neart tar ais gan bhaoghal,
is úr Rí corónta reóaibh 'na léadar,
is *Duke of York* mar phosta cléire,
ag teacht fé mheadhair 'núr n-oighreacht
féin cheart.
(O'Rahilly, *Five Seventeenth Century Political Poems,*
No. 5, lines 409-16, pp 99-100.)

[I implore of Jesus who was crucified for you and who suffered the

---

157 O'Rahilly, *Five Seventeenth Century Political Poems,* No. 5, lines 341-51, p. 97.

passion to save you from the original cause of your condemnation, to accomplish this much; your return in strength and without danger, with your crowned king before you as leader; with the Duke of York as a support for the clergy, returning joyfully to your rightful heritage.]

Until Charles II and the Duke of York are restored, Ireland will not resume her true form, and her nobles will remain dispossessed. As it is she exhibits all the characteristics of a lordship bereft of its chief:

Bilí gan bhláth acht bárr baothghlas,
gan iasg ar inbhear ná innilt ar éanlaith,
gan tairbhthe ar thráigh ná trácht ar thréithibh.
(O'Rahilly, *Five Seventeenth Century Political Poems,*
No. 5, lines 405-7, pp 99.

[Trees (are) without blossom, but a vain green top, harbours are without fish and the birds are without protection; there is no wealth on the strands and accomplishments go unmentioned . . .]

When, however, the leader is re-established, the territory and its inhabitants regain their equilibrium. The leader sought could be a local Gaelic or Anglo-Norman/English lord, or the monarch of England. The important factor was that the leader be successfully established.

In the poem 'Tuireamh na hÉireann', the poet Seán Ó Conaill, displays the same interest in those who are, or were powerful; 'heroes' in the poets' terms, regardless of their record in conflicts which in retrospect appear as milestones in the Tudor 'reconquest' and the Stuart consolidation of power. Biographical details of many of the individuals listed for instance in 'Tuireamh na hÉireann' show them to have been less than totally committed to any one course of action or any one cause. This has already been pointed out in the instance of 'An Síogaí Romhánach' where the defection of Hugh O'Byrne goes unmarked by the poet.[158] The apparent flexibilty of the loyalties of men such as O'Byrne and the concepts of power and loyalty directing their allegiances drew no censorious comment from the poet. Likewise, the indiscriminate nature of Éamonn an Dúna's distribution of accolades

---

[158] O'Rahilly, *Five Seventeenth Century Political Poems,* no. 2, line 274, p. 30.

for the élites of his province[159] is entirely in accordance with the rationale of the poets as it has been illustrated so far. One Mac Giolla Choda, head of a branch of the O'Sullivans,[160] had not taken arms during the wars until 1648, showing himself unmoved by any element of the conflicts in their more chaotic period. He is, however, listed among the Munster chiefs who suffered for their efforts on behalf of Banbha.[161] No adverse reflection is cast upon Bishop Boetius Mac Egan for levying troops in Kerry on a commission from Ormond — the latter a stumbling-block in the achievement of freedom of catholic worship.[162] O'Rahilly expressed surprise that Edmund FitzGibbon, the White Knight of Clangibbon, should be listed among the heroes:

> . . . Ridire an Ghleanna 's an Ridire gléigeal
> . . .
> (O'Rahilly, *Five Seventeenth Century Political Poems,*
> No. 4, line 344, p. 75.)
>
> [. . . the Knight of Glin and the White Knight . . .]

O'Rahilly considered Clangibbon's participation in the betrayal of the Súgán Earl, a disqualification for inclusion in Seán Ó Conaill's list:

> He the (White Knight) entered into an alliance with James Fitz-Maurice against Desmond. He also betrayed the Súgán Earl in 1601. It is curious to find his name given in such a list of Seán Ó Conaill.[163]

Seán Ó Conaill writes within an ethos which appreciated the discrete nature of every military and political event even while viewing the whole much as a seamless garment. The bardic ethos reflected the values of the polity in which it survived — the value of short-lived success was enshrined in the world-view perpetuated through the poetry and it was of

---

[159] Note however distinct echoes of the Leath Mogha v. Leath Cuinn controversy in 'Tuireamh na hÉireann' in the poet's incidental mention of the seniority of the southern dynasties descended from Éibhear: '. . . a sinnsear uile gan imreas Éibhear' in O'Rahilly, *Five Seventeenth Century Political Poems,* no. 4, line 121, p. 64.

[160] O'Rahilly, *Five Seventeenth Century Political Poems,* note 419, p. 155.

[161] O'Rahilly, *Five Seventeenth Century Political Poems,* no. 4, line 419, p. 78.

[162] O'Rahilly, *Five Seventeenth Century Political Poems,* note 427, p. 157.

[163] O'Rahilly, *Five Seventeenth Century Political Poems,* note 344, p. 145.

such individual events as the White Knight and the Desmond betrayal that the various 'heroic' activities of the poets 'heroes' were made. Edmund FitzGibbon belonged to a firmly established prestigious southern sept. His political activities could not affect his status as one entitled to be listed among the Munster heroes. Nor did Seán Ó Conaill make any anachronistic distinction between 'Mág Uidhir Gallda' and 'Mág Uidhir Gaeulach' [164] who are given equal attention in his list of northern chiefs. From O'Rahilly's perspective it is therefore equally curious to find Sir Niall Garbh O'Donnell listed along with O'Rourke of Breifne, since Sir Niall was responsible for introducing Sir Henry Docwra and his troops into Ulster, giving him a bridgehead and assisting him against Sir Niall's own cousin Red Hugh O'Donnell:

> . . . is Ó Ruairc uasal tiarna Bréifne . . .
> . . Niall garbh sa Túr 's a mhac Maonas . . .
> (O'Rahilly, *Five Seventeenth Century Political Poems,*
> No. 4, lines 328 and 333, p. 74.)

> [O'Rourke, noble lord of Breifne, . . . Niall Garbh in the tower and his son Maonas . . .]

Ó Conaill was unstinting in his exoneration of Muskerry, Ormond, Inchiquin and Clanricarde from some unspecified accusations of negligence in their conduct of the war. The poet insists that there is no truth in the rumour that any one of them proved negligent in his prosecution of the war: [165]

> Do bhí cáil amhrais — níl acht bréag ann —
> go raibh Donnchadh, Murchadh is Séamus
> is Uiliog a Búrc mar chúl daortha

---

[164] O'Rahilly, *Five Seventeenth Century Political Poems,* no. 4, line 329, p. 74.

[165] See O'Rahilly, *Five Seventeenth Century Political Poems,* p. 149, note 369 for a discussion of the card metaphors in seventeenth century literature relating to the Eleven Years' war. See also O'Rahilly, *Five Seventeenth Century Political Poems,* p. 149 for the conspiracy theory popularized concerning the parts played by the four nobles, Ormond, Muskerry, Inchiquin and Clanrickard in contemporary reports. O'Rahilly has pointed out that in some manuscripts of 'Tuireamh na hÉireann' an interpolation apparently in defence of Muskerry occurs; Donnchadh MacCarthy's losses in the war are emphasized, thereby possibly hoping to infer that of all people, Muskerry stood to lose most by perfidy in the confederate or loyalist cause.

ar mhá an stainncáird ag imirt na hÉireann.
(O'Rahilly, *Five Seventeenth Century Political Poems,*
No. 4, lines 365-8, p. 76.)

[There was some suspicion, it is merely a lie — that Donnchadh
[McCarthy], Murcadh [O'Brien] and James [Butler], with Ulick
Burke as a support in the guilt; played but a poor trump in the
game of Ireland.]

The poet is unwilling to apportion a loser's or a betrayer's part to any
one of those illustrious names. The extent to which the poets dealt with
the conflicts making up the 'Eleven Years'' war as a further discrete
historical episode is illustrated by the traditional manner in which they
rationalized victory or defeat. The struggle for supremacy in Banbha is a
basic theme of bardic poetry — the most worthy character won. If he
lost, he, as an individual could not be blamed; a whole series of rational-
izations could be adduced to ensure that the 'heroes' reputation remained untarnished. Therefore the portrayal of the struggle as a 'game'
was a useful conceit when culpability had to be removed from the principal 'players'. The effort to reduce the responsibility for defeat on the
leaders was closely linked with the poets' propensity to acquiesce in the
the new order following defeat; in that way the good fortune or ill-luck
attending a 'game' had to be accepted. The poet neither castigated the
former leader now defeated, nor shunned the new lord, the victor; and
so survived another period of upheaval.

The great gaming metaphors in Seán Ó Conaill's 'Tuireamh na
hÉireann' and in Éamonn an Dúna's 'Mo lá leóin go deo go n-éagad'
and later in the eighteenth century repeated in Aoghán Ó Rathaille's
'Cabhair ní ghairfead', have become especially associated with this
period and with the political context of this time. The duke of Ormond
was a gambler of some repute and the metaphors used by Éamonn an
Dúna and Seán Ó Conaill relate to card games. The theme of the rights
of the winner was used prosaically by William Petty in his justification
of the carving of Irish territory in the Cromwellian period:

But upon the playing of this Game or Match upon so great odds,
the English won and have (among) and besides other Pretences a
Gamester's right at least to their Estates. But as for the Bloodshed

in the contest, God knows best who did occasion it.[166]

Ó Conaill suggested that Clanricarde, Ormond, Muskerry and Inchiquin had let the game slip from their grasp:

Do sginn eatorra cíoná spéireat
do rug an bun 's a' ghoin i n-aonacht,
Olibher Cromuil, cura na féine,
's a mhac Hénrí go cróga taobh leis.
(O'Rahilly, *Five Seventeenth Century Political Poems,*
No. 4, lines 369-72, p. 76.)

[They let the five of trumps slip between them — and Oliver Cromwell the hero of the troop and his son bravely beside him, took the tricks and the jinx hand together.]

It is to be noticed that Ó Conaill applied the adjectives suitable to the victor to both Oliver Cromwell 'cura na féine', and his son, 'go cróga taobh leis'. Éamonn an Dúna considered Banbha — through her lawlessness, to have indulged false players in a crooked game:

Do bhí agat co ceanúil cearúig chlaona
do bhí ró-chliste san imirt do-bhéaradh
ar chur cártaoi 'na bhfághthaoi céadta,
san imirt chaim do bhí suim a gcéille.
(O'Rahilly, *Five Seventeenth Century Political Poems,*
No. 5, lines 341-4, p. 97.)

[You indulged crooked sharp players who were too clever in the game, placing cards for great gains in crooked play they placed all their interest.]

While the loser must accept defeat, God can be enjoined to help reverse the decision in any game. In 'Tuireamh na hÉireann', and in Éamonn an Dúna's 'Mo lá leóin go deo go n-éagad' God was implored to reverse the verdict on Ireland. In an elegy for Brian O'Neill in 1260, the poet, Giolla Brighde Mac Con Midhe, likened the death and defeat of Brian to a game; chess rather than cards was the metaphor used by Mac Con

---

[166] Compare, William Petty, *Anatomy of Ireland* [London, 1691] (reprint Shannon, 1970), p. 24.

Midhe. The attitude to defeat was the same however; the game was lost, only God could help:

Cogadh Gaoidheal re Gallaibh
imirt ar nguin ghallbhrannuibh;
fian Ghall do ghuin ar mbranáin
ní fhuill ann ar n-ionghabháil.
(Williams, *Giolla Brighde Mac Con Midhe,* No. 13,
st. 14, p. 138.)

[The war of the Irish against the Foreigner is a game of chess after the king has been check-mated; a foreign set of pieces checked our king; there is no way to protect yourselves.][167]

According to Mac Con Midhe, the Gaelic chessmen were put in check because of their being guilty of negligence in their organization of the war effort against the English:

Fáth ar mbeart bheith i gcoire
'mun gcath ar ceann Maonmhaighe;
dá mbeartha ar chách gan an cath
ní ba tráth deabhtha an Domhnach.
(Williams, *Giolla Brighde Mac Con Midhe,* No.
13, st. 21, p. 141.)

[The reason for our failure was our being in guilt concerning the battle about the leader of Maonmhagh; if everyone had been induced not to fight, that Sunday would not have been the time of battle.][168]

---

[167] Compare Seán Ó Tuama, *Filí faoi Scéimhle,* p. 119;
'Do bhodar an tSionainn, an Life 's an Laoi cheolmhar,
abhainn an Bhiorra Dhuibh, Bruice 'gus Brid, Bóinne,
com Loch Deirg 'na ruide 'gus Toinn Tóime
ó lom an cuireata cluiche ar an rí coróinneach.'
[168] See McKenna, *Magauran Poems,* No. 14, st. 10, p. 107 in which the poet likens the chief to a chess-king [branán]; and see Greene, *Maguire Poems,* no. 24, st. 11, p. 228 in which the poet declares that it is time for Maguire to 'win the game' [. . do uair do bhreith an bháire]; and see also McKenna, *O'Hara Poems,* No. 8, st. 4, p. 112, in which the poet likens the continual contention to 'a game' [beart cluiche ní dheachaidh dhe . . .]

Quite recognizable in that stanza is the implication of disunity among the warriors as to a suitable time or day for the engagement. Until the death of this thirteenth-century chief, all the conflicts for Ireland had been but a game. Now however, the loss of the leader and defeat changed the foreign threat from a game into reality. In a seventeenth-century context the following stanza would be hailed as an admission of defeat by the poets, a sign of their awareness of the 'true' impact of the foreign intruders — of an awakening of a new sense of Catholic nationalist consciousness perhaps:

> Cluiche go bás Briain Bhanna
> creacha is marbhtha is madhmanna;
> eachta Gall go guin Í Néill
> nochan fhuil ann acht oilbhéim
> (Williams, *Giolla Brighde Mac Con Midhe*, No. 13,
> st. 51, p. 151.)

> [A game till the death of Brian of Banna were the plunders, killings and routs; the deeds of the Foreigners until O'Neill was slain were mere impediment.]

For Mac Con Midhe, the death of O'Neill was tantamount to the beheading of Ireland, for Éamonn an Dúna the death of Charles I was a double decapitation:[169]

> Buille dicheannta bhfear bhFáil
> bás Í Néill Oiligh fhodbháin;
> cuibhreach Gaoidheal an geal-seang
> agus sgaoileadh fhear nÉireann.
> (Williams, *Giolla Brighde Mac Con Midhe,* No. 13,
> st. 53, p. 151.)

> [The death of O'Neill of Aileach of the white turf was the blow that beheaded the men of Ireland; the pale, slender one was the bond of the Irish and the scattering of the men of Ireland.]

The dead nobles are listed by Mac Con Midhe in some thirty stanzas, like those in Éamonn an Dúna's poem, without qualification except as to their having died at that engagement. Mac Con Midhe, however, at a

---

[169] O'Rahilly, *Five Seventeenth Century Political Poems,* no. 5, line 401, p. 99.

loss to rationalize the defeat inflicted on the Ulster warriors and the intolerable loss of Brian, introduced a note which seventeenth-century
poets could equally employ:

Go lá an Dúin nír cuireadh cath
ar mhuintir Mhíleadh Teamhrach;
mar bhíos i ndán do dhroing dol
nocha phoinn agh ná eangnomh.

Na thráth féin ní fhacas linn
aon bheart do fhóirfeadh Éirinn,
mar budh cáir cur an ghaisgidh
ar sgur an áigh urmháistir.
(Williams, *Giolla Brighde Mac Con Midhe,* No. 13,
stanzas 16 and 17, pp 140-1.)

[Until the day of Dúin, no battle was won against the people of Míl
of Teamhair; when it is fated for a people to die, valour and prowess are of no avail.
We have not seen in its own time a plan that would rescue Ireland,
for it would be right to lay down arms when valour that is smitten
has been given up.]

The latter couplet would indeed appear to sum up the most enduring
philosophy of the Gaelic Irish in the face of defeat, and underlie their
perceptions of the value of power and the striving to attain it. God en-
compassed the defeat and O'Neill's death for his own reasons; therefore
the best efforts of the Ulster warriors were doomed. It will be
remembered at this point that according to the author of 'An Síogaí
Romhánach', the seventeenth-century O'Neill was removed by God
too, not by the English. Such reasoning exonerated the champions from
any charges of inability or cowardice and allowed the poet to indulge in
despairing lamentations following the departure of his champion win or
lose — since in spite of their valour, God had seen fit to move against
them. The chiefs' guilt in their choice of an unsuitable battle-day,
played some part in the thirteenth-century defeat. However, in no other
circumstance did O'Neill conjure God's wrath and Mac Con Midhe insists that O'Neill did not exploit the poor, disrespect the clergy or violate
the church; the leaders of the 1640s, according to the poets, were guilty
of all three, drawing God's wrath upon themselves. Mac Con Midhe's
explicit references to O'Neill's faultlessness in the matters of the poor

and the church and the later poets' highlighting of such violations [170] illustrate the longevity of such reasoning in the conventionalized literary
world. It hardly needs to be pointed out that such a conceit ante-dated
the Counter-Reformation influence and formed part of the mental furniture of the learned poets independent of that influence, though, of
course it may well have been reinforced or enhanced by such influence.
Evidently the many strands which woven together made up the fabric of
the world depicted by the poet in the thirteenth-century composition
proved durable for use in the seventeenth century.

Three poets out of O'Rahilly's collection of five, indicate that the
author was a supporter of the Nuncio. Haicéad's work is manifestly
supportive. Their interest in the destruction of the church and its supporters can be confused with their declared allegiance to the Nuncio faction and seen as an element of that allegiance and even as a
distinguishing characteristic if considered apart from its literary milieu.
It is important therefore to emphasize that the poets' articulation of
concern for the church and their dismay at its physical or metaphorical
destruction is independent of the immediate circumstances of the mid-
seventeenth century, and is not characteristic of the pro-Nuncio faction
only. It has been contended that the Counter-Reformation focused the
poets' imaginations on denominationally religious matters and caused
them to be more assertive for the claims of the church and clergy. It is interesting to note first, how closely this 'new' interest paralleled that of
the poets four hundred years earlier, second, how the anti-Nuncio priest
Séamas Carthún expressed similar interest in the welfare of the church
and third, how a poem written by the clergyman Patrick Dunkin seems
to echo the loyalties of the author of 'An Síogaí Romhánach'.

Extravagance of sentiment had become part of the customary expression of the poets. In times of turmoil, poets, nobles and the land itself
suffered if defeat or loss of the lord were the outcome of the conflict. Indeed, anything which nominally or actually came under the lord's
authority and influence was adversely affected by his departure. The
protection of the church and churchmen could also be the responsibility
of a chief or lord and would be included in the lists of those which suffered in the social and political (and often cosmic) disruption which accompanied the lord's departure. The poet, Giolla na Naomh Ó hUiginn,

---

[170] O'Rahilly, *Five Seventeenth Century Political Poems*, no. 2, lines 238-55, pp 28-9;
no. 4, lines 55-6; no. 5, lines 369-80, p. 98.

lamented the death of Thomas Magauran in 1343. His departure caused the poets and the churches to be without protection; life henceforward would no longer be ordered and secure:

Budh oilithrigh ar éis Thomais
a theaghlach ag triall don Róimh;
dá dhíoth rugadh crodh gach croise
tugadh cor coise don choir.
(McKenna, *Magauran Poems,* No. 10, st. 34, p. 79.)

[Now that Thomas is gone, his household will go as pilgrims to Rome; for lack of his protection every church is robbed of its goods, and justice is trampled on.]

In this particular instance, the poet is concerned for the hazards to unprotected churches. It is easy to see how complaints and fears about the violation of churches in a pre-Reformation context could easily be extended to accommodate church violations in a post-Reformation and Counter-Reformation context.

The priest/poet Séamus Carthún OFM, a late conversion to the Nuncioist cause,[171] described the state of the churches in the aftermath of the decade of conflict:

Do díbreadh tar fairrge a tréinfhir;
Atáid a teampla — mar barr péine —
gan altóir, gan aifrionn, gan sléachtuin,
'na stábluighe each — is truailliadh an sgéal so —
Nó gan cloch dá gclochuibh re chéile.
(Mág Craith, *Dán na mBráthar Mionúr,* No. 49,
lines 14-18, p. 252.)

[The warriors were banished abroad; in addition to the torment,

---

[171] An account of Fr James Caron, OFM is given by McKenna in Mág Craith, *Dán na mBráthar Mionúr* vol. 2, pp 236-8. In an account taken from the *Aphorismical Discovery,* Mág Craith points out that not only did Caron defy his superiors until 1650, but that he endeavoured to bring other friars over to the anti-Nuncio side:
. . . and such as are irreligious, to God, Kinge, and nation refractorie, must continue, whose names are these, Fr Patrick Plunkett . . . Fr James Caron . . . Fr Thomas mac Kiernan . . . endured much trouble, by his apostate friers, Fr Patriik Plunkett and Fr James Caron, every day resortinge to him . . . to vex and trouble him, to reduce or rather seduce him . . . unto the obedience of theire then corrupt government.

their temples are without altars, without mass, without worship, nor a stone of their stones together, they are horse's stables, this is a miserable story.]

The desecration of church and clergy has occurred because of the banishment of the lords. This motif of dislocation suits Carthún's attempt to articulate some of the distress felt after the upheaval of the previous decade. In this particular instance he chose to adapt a well-used bardic expression of disorder. It is of major importance to note the tone adopted by the 'apostate'[172] Carthún in his composition, concerning the reasons for the current distress of Banbha. Just as the author of 'An Síogaí Romhánach' and other pro-Nuncio poems edited by O'Rahilly use the bardic theme of Banbha divided to explain her fate, so too does Carthún. Carthún, though, is doubtless to be numbered among the faithless 'faction' castigated by Haicéad and must be considered among those subject likewise to the fulminations of the other Nuncioists. Carthún's own composition, however, reproduces the identical rationalization of Banbha's defeat; never has Banbha been reduced to such a state. Unless God helps she is utterly helpless; her misfortune stems from her own perfidy and the disunity[173] among her leaders. Like his erstwhile opponent, Haicéad, Carthún uses the analogy of the Israelites:

Ó bhí clann Israél san Éigipt,
Faoi bhruid 's faoi dhaoirse i n-éiniocht,
nar sgríobhadh i leabhar 's ní fhacuigh éinneach
Annró mar annró na hÉirionn.
(Mág Craith, *Dán na mBráthar Mionúr,* No. 49,
lines 19-22, p. 252.)

[Since the children of Israel were in slavery and oppression in Egypt, nobody has seen, nor has an account been written of, distress as grave as that of Ireland.]

Carthún then cites disunity and negligence as the sources of defeat.

Ní neart sluaigh, ní heasbuidh bheatha,
ní marcshluagh Gall dar ghluais ó Bhreatuin,

---

172 Mág Craith, *Dán na mBráthar Mionúr* vol. 2, p. 238.
173 Mág Craith, *Dán na mBráthar Mionúr,* vol. 1, no. 49, lines 20-3, p. 252, lines 90-121, pp 254-5.

ní clíth cumuis, ní díth spracuibh
Do chuir sluaite na hÉironn chum ratha. . .
. . . .
Ní rabhamar ariamh i lúib a chéile
Acht bó faoi cheangal is bó faoi réiteach; . . .
(Mág Craith, *Dán na mBráthar Mionúr*, No. 49, lines 90-93,
p. 254 and lines 115-116, p. 255.)
[It was not for lack of hosts, nor want of spirit, nor because of the
foreign cavalry who travelled from Wales, nor from failed ability,
nor want of energy that put the hosts of Ireland to flight, . . .
They were never yet hand-in-hand, but each one settled for
himself (lit. 'but a cow for guarantee and one for settlement') . . .]

Carthún is quite obviously expressing no individual assessment of the
previous decade in a way which gives any indication of his own committment. We are aware of his particular allegiance, his late conversion to
the Nuncio, because of independent accounts of his career. For the
authors of the five O'Rahilly poems we have no evidence of their
allegiances other than their individual compositions. It is quite within
the bounds of possibility that, far from being committed Nuncioists as
one is led to believe from the aura their poems have assumed, some of
these authors, were, like Carthún, late conversions. So much again, for
the 'documentary' value of such poems as 'detailed' and 'informative'
sources of the political facts of the period.[174] Carthún expressed himself
in terms one has become accustomed to associate with a party to whom
Carthún was supposedly anathema, because of the predomination of
pro-Nuncio sentiment in the O'Rahilly selection, when the author's
committment is expressed at all.[175] Carthún's poem presents no feature
which marks him out as one who has changed allegiance as late as 1650.
The poets' use of and selection of motifs and themes is independent of
the transient allegiances and divisions occurring within the fundamentally culturally homogeneous community.

    Indeed, participation in the literary tradition automatically exercised
an influence on the mentality projected by the poet. The traditional bardic articulation of dislocation and defeat proved stronger than, or at

---

[174] O'Rahilly, *Five Seventeenth Century Political Poems,* Introduction, p. viii.
[175] O'Rahilly, *Five Seventeenth Century Political Poems,* no. 2, lines 256-8, p. 29; no.
3, line 245, p. 46; no. 4, line 355, p. 75.

least, unconcerned with, sectarian nuances. In this connection, it is of interest to consider a poem attributed to a protestant minister, one Pádraig Ó Duincín.[176] The following note occurs with the poem in one manuscript copy:

> Being the composition of a Protestant Ministers, viz. Mr Patrick Dungin, bred in the College of Dublin, who in the tyrannical time of government was banished out of his native soil, the County Downe to the Isle of Man by three Presbyterian ministers, viz., Hamilton, Loe and Brown and being somewhat settled in Man among his other amusements he sung the above consoling *dán* or poetical verse.[177]

Ó Duincín returned to Ireland around 1666.[178]

In his poem, Ó Duincín laments his departure from Ireland, he castigates the 'perverted' theology of the 'puritans', and he lists those to whom he would naturally look for protection and support. Like the bardic poets, Ó Duincín is inclined to have recourse to his native lords, in this case, the O'Neills, including the great 'Catholic champion', Eoghan Rua O'Neill. Ó Duincín's composition, is in the bardic tradition, though he did not share in the religious allegiances of nearly all seventeenth-century Gaelic poets; Ó Duincín's personal circumstances are articulated in a manner indistinguishable from that of poets whose circumstances differed substantially. His composition might be attributed to any banished layman or cleric of Ulster:

> Truagh mo thuras ó mo thír
> go crích Mhanannáin mhín mhic Lir,
> idir triúr Piúratán — meabhal géar —
> gearr mo shaol más buan na fir.
> (*Nua-Dhuanaire,* No. 29, st. 1, p. 38.)

> [Woe is the journey from my own country to the Isle of Man amid three puritans — a bitter disgrace — if they be long lived, then my life will be short.]

---

[176] Pádraig de Brún, Breandán Ó Buachalla, Tomás Ó Concheanainn (eds), *Nua-Dhuanaire* cuid 1 (Dublin 1975), pp 112 and 182.

[177] P. de Brún, B. Ó Buachalla, T. Ó Concheanainn, *Nua-Dhuanaire* 1, p. 112.

[178] P. de Brún, B. Ó Buachalla, T. Ó Concheanainn, *Nua-Dhuanaire* 1, p. 182.

Ó Duincín uses the 'exile' poem introduction. He then lists his three persecutors; Hamilton, Loe and Brown, three presbyterians. Like Haicéad,[179] Ó Duincín deplores their 'crooked theology':

> Claon a gcogús, saobh a gciall,
> easpag ná cliar ní mian leo;
> ní abraid paidir ná cré —
> freitim féin bheith dá sórt.[180]
> (*Nua-Dhuanaire*, No. 29, st. 4, p. 38.)

[Their conscience is perverted, their minds crooked, they desire neither cleric nor bishop; they say neither creed nor prayer — I myself refuse to be among their number.]

Among the perverted values of these three puritans were ignorance of the saints' festivals and of the Virgin. They disrespect the cross and the church and reject the religion of Patrick. Thus, Ó Duincín adopts the religious rhetoric of the tradition, which clearly requires no sectarian analyses:

> Troscadh ná féilte na naomh —
> olc an taom — ní chongbhaid siad;
> ní mó leó Muire ná brobh,
> pór gan mhodh nár bheannaigh Dia.
>
> Fuath leo baisteadh, cros is ceall,
> bunadh na bhfeall; truagh, a Dhia,
> creideamh Phádraig do dhul ar gcúl
> 's creideamh gan stiúir a bheith dá thriall.
> (*Nua-Dhuanaire*, No. 29, stanzas 5 and 6, p. 38.)

[Grave the blow — they observe neither saints' festivals nor vigils, they honour Mary no more than a wisp (lit. blade of grass), — a disrespectful group, unblessed by God.
They hate baptism, cross and church. The basis of the treachery — pity oh God, is that Patrick's religion is being ignored, and a religion without direction is being advanced.]

---

[179] Ní Cheallacháin, *Haicéad Poems*, no. 36, p. 38.
[180] See O'Rahilly, *Five Seventeenth Century Political Poems*, no. 5, lines 298, p. 96.

These two stanzas could have been written by any Counter-Reformation priest or poet, or indeed any of the poets who chose to address the religious element as part of the social disorder. Another element of abiding interest to the poets is raised by Ó Duincín in the following stanza; that of the low social status of those responsible for his banishment. All the poets of the mid-seventeenth century were very quick to indicate that the true culprits involved in the uglier aspects of the conflicts were invariably of lowly status:

> Deir gach bodach ceannchruinn cruaidh
> "dibirt bhuan ar Chlanna Néill
> 's ar shíol ríogh, ughdar gach uilc" —
> is leó do thuit mo mhuintir féin.
> (*Nua-Dhuanaire,* No. 29, st. 7, p. 38.)

[Every hard roundhead churl says: "eternal banishment to the O'Neills and to the king's line — author of every evil", it is at their hands that my own people fell.]

Having outlined his complaints, Ó Duincín lists those from whom he might have expected succour; Fearghus mac Róigh and Cú Chulainn head the list, heroes from Gaelic mythology, and Murchadh the son of Brian Bóraimhe.[181] He follows on with a more detailed list of recently departed O'Neill leaders, including Shane O'Neill, Fear Dorcha, Baron of Dungannon, Eoghan Rua O'Neill and the Clandeboye O'Neills.[182] If all of these were alive, Ó Duincín would not have to suffer as he does. No allusion is made to any possible impediment his protestant ministry might have on his expectations to their protection. Like the author of 'An Síogaí Romhánach', Ó Duincín is particularly attached to the O'Neills; like that of 'Tuireamh na hÉireann',[183] he also appeals to more recent arrivals — Savages and Russell, settlers of the Norman period:

> — nó Sabhoise ó Loch Cuan,
> nó sliocht Fheidhlim na ruag ngarg,

---

[181] P. de Brún, B. Ó Buachalla, T. Ó Concheanainn, *Nua-Dhuanaire* 1, no. 29, lines 33-6, p. 39.

[182] P. de Brún, B. Ó Buachalla, T. Ó Concheanainn, *Nua-Dhuanaire* 1, no. 29. lines 37-40; lines 45-8, p. 39.

[183] O'Rahilly, *Five Seventeenth Century Political Poems,* no. 4, lines 385-400, p. 77.

nó Ruiséalaigh, m'olc is mo bhruid,
d'éireódh a bhfuil is a bhfearg.
(*Nua-Dhuanaire,* No. 29, st. 13, p. 39.)

[— or the Savages of Loch Cuan, or the line of Felim of the
vigorous routs, or Russels — my sorrow and woe — their anger
and blood would be roused.]

Of the five poems edited by O'Rahilly and of the two others I have
linked with them, in this section, no one poem can be said to represent
any great political development or transformation of the poets' perceptions in the matters of power and authority. They are the subjective
though traditional compositions of learned poets expressing a predictable horror at the temporary dislocation of their world. The poets'
scope of interest lies very close to, or within, the province of those whom
they regard as their leaders, so that Éamonn an Dúna's poem is
recognizably of Munster origin and that the author of 'An Síogaí
Romhánach' is more likely to have been of Ulster origin. No two poems
looked forward to a single *dénouement.* Éamonn an Dúna looked to the
restoration of Charles II, while Dáibhí Cúndún hoped for a restoration
of the O'Briens and the McCarthys. The author of 'An Síogaí
Romhánach' looked to an assured general revival of the Gaelic and Old
English lords, principally under Aodh Buí O'Neill, Felim O'Neill and
Richard Farrall. The poems reflect the continuing interest of the poets in
the regional successes of local heroes and in the careers of illustrious
names.

While the literary expressions, structures and reference-bank of the
poets remained intact, the world of which they were an integral part
disintegrated. The seven poems dealt with above are in part evidence of
the collapse of the integrity of the literary structure, since they belong to
a learned tradition in terms of reference but a more popular tradition in
execution. For this discussion it was necessary to emphasize their traditional qualities in order to give them a realistic framework and in order
to dispel some misinterpretations as to their value as factually explicit
documents of seventeenth century history. Their value for the historian
lies in understanding just how close to the bardic tradition these poems
prove themselves to be in perceptions, though not in language or metre.
Poets whose experiences and learning evidently involved intellectual
and physical exposure to continental Europe found the rationale

established by the conventionalized, professional writings of a profoundly conservative literary élite adequate in essence to the expression of their understanding of the events of the mid-seventeenth century. The reality they addressed became even more distorted when the bardic rationale was applied to it, as can be seen in the political illogic in each of the poems. None of them could be said to have represented any particular political coterie in Ireland at the time, and yet the very confusion of the loyalties they depict, the unexpected influence of the Nuncio, the fierce adherence to him, the frantic opposition to him, are all credible viewed in the light of the convoluted sense of political priorities depicted in these poems. The activities of Gaelic and Old English leaders of the period show just how closely the poets reflected the kind of reality with which they were equipped to deal — that is — with the fundamental rationale governing the activities of the Gaelic political élites. The whole mass of the poetry will not be useful to the historian who takes as it were a mental still photograph of the poetry of a single decade and analyses it at face value. Poets of the seventeenth century who drew from the same selection of references were participating in, and subscribing to, the world-view contained in the bardic poetry; they were ambiguous about 'historical fact', and their own or their patron's loyalties, and expressed themselves in a genre in which they felt comfortable. This is true of the poems written in the accentual metre considered above. It is even more true and more obvious in poems written in the same period in the syllabic metres by poets bearing surnames traditionally associated with the profession.

Tadhg Dall Ó hUiginn considered himself specially attached to the O'Hara family;[184] late into the seventeenth century, different members of the Ó hUiginn family were still eulogizing members of the O'Hara family. One Oilill O'Hara (+ 1685), son of Cormac Óg O'Hara, grandson of the chief Cormac O'Hara (+ 1612), was the recipient of several poems by members of the Ó hUiginn family. This Oilill[185] had taken part in the 1641 rebellion and because of it, had been deprived of his lands. The poet Maol Muire Ó hUiginn's poem for him, welcomes Oilill back to his ancestral lands. His father, Cormac Óg, died in 1642, so the poem is probably dated sometime after that date. The poet in this welcoming composition makes extensive use of the motif of the territory

---

[184] E. Knott, *Tadhg Dall Ó hUiginn Poems,* nos 25, 31 and 38.
[185] McKenna, *O'Hara Poems,* Introduction, p. xvii.

welcoming her true ruler. Luighne (ancestral O'Hara land) has cast aside her recent gloom (the death of Cormac Óg?) and revived herself to greet Oilill.[186] The poem may have been written during the tumultuous period 1642-1652. Even if it is of a later date, the poet continued with the metaphor:

> Do theilg dhí a deilbh mbrónaidh,
> do dhúilt dá dúil n-ochónaidh,
> do reac uaidh a dreich ndubhaidh,
> do theith gruaim ón ghealtuigh.
> (McKenna, *O'Hara Poems,* No. 25, st. 2, p. 258.)

[She has cast off her sad mien, and has checked her mood of lamentation; a grave mound has changed its look of gloom, and the sad cloud has fled from the sunny hill.]

If Ó hUiginn wrote this poem during the Eleven Years' war, conditions in Luighne can hardly have been reflected in this idyll. If it is dated after this period of conflict, the O'Hara territory to which O'Hara returned was reduced. Nothing daunted either way, the poet described the marvellous changes which the chief's return occasioned in the territory; the trees bowed low with the weight of fruit, grass took on an added bloom, and the territory prepared itself for her lords return.[187] Ó hUiginn introduced the classical legend of Demophon and Phyllis as analogies of Luighne and Oilill O'Hara. It is hardly likely that the poet visualized as 'reality' the situation he described so graphically in this stanza:

> Leag do chíos, cuir do chánaigh
> bóruimhe n-uill n-éadalaigh
> mun thír mbratghlain ngéilshlim ngloin;
> glantar géibhinn red ghiallaibh.
> (McKenna, *O'Hara Poems,* No. 25, st. 45, p. 270.)

[Lay thy rent upon her, put thy cess, a great valuable cattle-cess, upon this bright-cloaked shining smooth land; let chains be polished ready for thy hostages.]

---

[186] McKenna, *O'Hara Poems,* no. 25, stanzas 1 and 2, p. 258.
[187] McKenna, *O'Hara Poems,* no. 25, stanzas 3 and 10, pp 258-60.

Ó hUiginn addressed O'Hara as a king of an important territory — with the power attaching thereto. This poem illustrates the survival of the most ancient bardic motifs, and the poets' seeming compulsion to express themselves in this convention. Oilill O'Hara's circumstances must have been at some appreciable remove from that so attractively and flamboyantly depicted in the poem. It is indeed difficult to determine whether or not the scenes habitually described by the poets ever existed at all in fact. The explanation of the poets' continued use of such language, motifs, references and sentiments must be that this body of literary expression represented a conventionalization of fundamental social, political and cultural beliefs, aspirations and ideals. Ó hUiginn could not express the appreciation peculiar to the poet for his chieftain in any other comparable way. The same could be said for the bardic poet, Pádraig Óg Mac a' Bhaird's poem for Rory O'Hara, great grandson of the chief Cormac O'Hara (+ 1612). His mother was Máire, daughter of the last O'Flaherty chief.[188] O'Hara died in 1702 in the service of the King of Spain in Italy. The poet flourishing around the 1690s [189] must have written the poem in the latter decades of the seventeenth century. The poem written by Mac a' Bhaird, celebrates O'Hara as the scion of the O'Hara sept. No mention is made anywhere in the poem of the changed world of the seventeenth century, O'Hara's interesting continental military career, or indeed of any of the 'facts' which the poets needed to mention at their own discretion. There was no new standard by which the poets could measure the successes or failures or the kinds of life-style enjoyed by such as Rory O'Hara as a successful foreign mercenary. The poet eulogized him as a traditional hero, guarding the borders of his territories.[190] He could hardly exhort him to follow a sedentary career. In its final stages, the literary structure was all that remained of the aristocratic world of the chiefs and the poets which had endured in different ways for so long. The structure through which this ethos was articulated outlived the order from which it received its social, political and cultural support.

The evolution of the Gaelic elites into a ruling class subject to a centralized Gaelic administration never took place. The indigenous evolution of the Gaelic polity was interrupted in a manner which destroyed

---

[188] See McKenna, *O'Hara Poems,* Introduction, pp xx-xxviii.

[189] McKenna, *O'Hara Poems,* Introduction, p. xxviii.

[190] McKenna, *O'Hara Poems,* no. 26, stanzas 1, 2, 9, 23, 31, pp 276-84.

native Gaelic capacity for further development, or ability to evolve a system compatible with the demands of other elements traditionally supportive of the polity. Ruling members of Gaelic septs, often impoverished and dispossessed, could not participate as leading members of the polity which developed in the seventeenth century, and simultaneously maintain their cultural integrity. The poets, like the chiefs had become casualties of the obsolescence of their traditional society. Their survival and development depended on the success of their patrons. Their literary conventions admitted of change, their survival through over four hundred years proved their ability to absorb change and move on.[191] This could only happen where the chiefs were successful in war, in peace and in the subtle social and political adjustments which are usually within the capabilities of a viable polity. In the seventeenth century, the greater number of Gaelic lords were unable to adjust any further to the contemporary upheaval, without major cultural alterations in areas of language, religion and lifestyle. The lords who survived as peers of the realm adjusted accordingly. The remainder lost status and wealth in varying degrees.

Gaelic society produced no powerful indigenous replacement for the old ruling elites. The mental world of that order was not outgrown or discarded by an emerging ruling class from within the Gaelic world, rather its proponents and perpetuators were entirely replaced during the course of the seventeenth century. No Gaelic polity existed which consisted of successful or victorious Gaelic leaders and their retainers, which had consciously or purposefully rejected or replaced the traditonal rationale which dictated the choices made, objectives striven after, and methods employed by the leaders of Gaelic society — facets of which were articulated faithfully in the bardic poetry. Since Gaelic leaders produced no sustained, innovative political initiatives in the mid-seventeenth century, the poets could reflect no new rationale by which to eulogize, castigate or lament the leaders who remained.

It may be useful therefore, not simply to divide up the poet's composition into areas which we identify and interpret separately as traditional display and rhetoric, contemporary realistic commentary and finally a genuine despairing cry from the heart. This is in effect, the kind of interpretation which has been offered for instance in respect of the O'Rahilly

---

[191] K. Simms, *From Kings to Warlords.*

collection and other seventeenth century accentual poetry. It may be more useful in the light of the ultimate collapse of the Gaelic world in this period to see them as belonging, in ethos, if not in literary form to the world celebrated for centuries in bardic poetry and not lightly discarded for an ethos in which the leaders of the Gaelic world found no natural place.

This approch may eventually provide a flexible framework and a realistic field of reference in which to study such singularly elusive subjects as Dáibhí Ó Bruadair and Aoghán Ó Rathaille. Until the works of these two poets in particular are given a realistic place within Irish social and literary history, the link between the Gaelic Ireland of the sixteenth century and colonial Ireland of the eighteenth century will never be understood.

CONCLUSION

Literature, in any language, can provide insights into the society in which it is produced. The nature of the insights thus attained depends on the quantity and quality of the literature and the context in which it is approached. Historians who look to literary works to assist them in their discovery and interpretation of the past, attempt to use a very rich and worthwhile source of information. It is also fraught with complications. The separate disciplines of literature and history have their own specialists. The interpretations proper to one are not always so to the other. This is true for all literature and all history. In the particular context of bardic poetry, this tension seems to be especially appropriate. Rarely have scholars of literature and history combined their expertise to provide more than a cursory context or an apt illustration one for another.

The work of Katharine Simms, Breandán Ó Buachalla, Tom Dunne, Nicholas Canny, Ciaran Brady and Brendan Bradshaw has attempted to draw together the disciplines appropriate to the study of literature on the one hand, and of history on the other to produce insightful and stimulating interpretations of Irish history and literature. I have attempted to contribute to this growing body of material by exploring some interpretations of bardic poetry and its use as historical source material. A certain reluctance to attempt to work on material which has long been the preserve of linguists and literateurs is apparent among historians. Familiarity with literature in general and with Gaelic literature in particular, is naturally a prerequisite for such interdisciplinary work. It is unlikely that either discipline will ever be entirely satisfied with the resulting work. One is reminded, however, of Austin Clarke's claim that 'grumbling grammarians and thin textualists' tried to discourage him from literary criticism in his case, with 'ogreish frowns and fee-faw-fummery' (*Irish Times,* 6 January 1945). Some historians are discouraged in this way, many scholars of literature are simiarly scared away. Those who brave the 'ogres' of either discipline are providing material which challenges the experts in both fields.

Challenging accepted interpretations of history is the stuff of which historical literature is made. Revisionism and reinterpretation can never be an end in itself however, and unless it provide new insights, it is counter-productive. No one could argue that the history of Gaelic Ireland in any period, especially in the late mediaeval and early modern period is an overworked field. In many ways its study has only begun. No source material can be overlooked in the study of this crucial period of Irish history, and no theory can go unchallenged.

BIBLIOGRAPHY

I have omitted most standard general works in this bibliography, except in the case of very recent publications. A full bibliography of standard works can be found in J.G. Simms, 'Bibliography' in *New hist. Ire.,* iii. Full references for works referred to within the text are in the following bibliography which is simply divided in three parts:
1. published collections of poetry
2. printed sources
3. secondary works

1. PUBLISHED COLLECTIONS OF POETRY:

O. Bergin (ed). *Irish Bardic Poetry,* 1970.

P.A. Breatnach. 'Marbhnadh Aodha Ruaidh Uí Dhomhnaill'. In *Éigse,* vol. 15 (1973).

_____. 'Metamorphosis 1603'. In *Éigse,* 17 (1977-8).

P. de Brún, B. Ó Buachalla and T. Ó Concheanainn (eds). *Nua-Dhuanaire 1.* Dublin, 1975.

J. Carney (ed.). *Poems on the Butlers of Ormond, Cahir and Dunboyne (A.D. 1400-1650).* Dublin, 1945.

_____. *Poems on the O'Reillys.* Dublin 1950.

M. Ní Cheallacháin (ed.). *Filíocht Phádraigín Haicéad.* Dublin, 1962.

P.S. Dineen (ed.). *Dánta Phiarais Feiritéir.* Dublin, 1903.

W. Gillies. 'A Poem on the Downfall of the Gaoidhil'. In *Éigse,* 13 (1970).

D. Greene (ed.). *Duanaire Mhéig Uidhir.* Dublin, 1972.

J. Hardiman. *Irish Minstrelsy* 2 vols. [London, 1831] Irish University Press [reprint] 1971.

E. Knott (ed.). *The Bardic Poems of Tadhg Dall Ó hUiginn.* London, 1922.

S. MacAirt (ed.). *Leabhar Branach.* Dublin, 1944.

E. Mac Giolla Eáin (ed.). *Dánta, Amhráin is Caointe Sheathrúin Céitinn.* Dublin, 1900.

J.C. McErlean (ed.). *Duanaire Dháibhidh Uí Bhruadair: The Poems of David O Bruadair.* 3 parts (London, 1910-17).

L. McKenna (ed.). *The Book of Magauran.* Dublin, 1947.

_____. *Aithdioghluim Dána.* Dublin, 1939.

_____. *Philip Bocht Ó Huiginn.* Dublin, 1931.

——. *The Book of O'Hara*. Dublin, 1951.
——. *Iomarbháigh na bhFileadh*. 2 vols, London, 1918.
——. 'Some Irish Poems'. In *Studies*, vol. 38 (1949).
O. McKernon. 'Treoin an Cheannais, Gofraidh Óg Mac a' Bhaird'. In *Éigse*, vol. 5 (1945).
C. Mág Craith. *Dán na mBráthar Mionúr*. 2 vols (Dublin, 1967, 1980).
B. Ó Cuív. 'A sixteenth-century political poem'. In *Éigse*, vol. 15 (1973).
——. 'Mo thruaighe mar atá Éire'. In *Éigse*, vol. 8 (1957).
T. Ó Donnchadha (ed.). *Leabhar Clainne Aodha Buidhe*. Dublin, 1931.
D. Ó Muirithe. *An tAmhrán Macarónach*. Dublin, 1980.
T. Ó Raghallaigh (ed.). *Duanta Eoghain Ruaidh Mhic an Bhaird*. Galway, 1930.
C. O'Rahilly. *Five Seventeenth Century Political Poems*. Dublin, 1952.
T.F. O'Rahilly (ed.). *Dánta Gradha*. Cork, 1926.
A. O'Sullivan. 'Tadhg O'Daly and Sir George Carew'. In *Éigse*, 14 (1971).
A. O'Sullivan and P. Ó Riain (eds). *Poems on the Marcher Lords: from a sixteenth-century Tipperary Manuscript*. Dublin, 1987.
N.J.A. Williams (ed.). *Riocard Bairéad; Amhráin*. Dublin, 1978.
——. *Dánta Mhuiris Mhic Dháibhí Mhic Gearailt*. Dublin, 1980.
——. *The Poems of Giolla Brighde Mac Con Midhe*. Dublin, 1980.

2. PRINTED SOURCES:

E. Bourke. 'Irish levies for the army in Sweden 1609-10'. In *Studies*, vol. xlvi (1918).
R.B. Breatnach. 'Donal O'Sullivan Beare to King Philip III, 20th February 1602'. In *Éigse*, vol. 6 (1962).
J.S. Brewer and W. Bullen (eds). *Calendar of the Carew Manuscripts*, preserved at the Archiepiscopal library at Lambeth, 6 vols., London 1867-73 (Kraus Reprint, London 1974).
R. Butler (ed.). *Tracts relating to Ireland II*. London, 1904.
M.J. Byrne (ed.). *Ireland under Elizabeth . . . being a portion of the history of Catholic Ireland by Don Philip O'Sullivan Beare*. Dublin, 1903.
T. Carte. *A History of the life of James, the first Duke of Ormonde*. 6 vols. Oxford, 1951.
D. Cregan. 'Irish Catholic admissions to the English Inns of Court 1558-1625'. In *Irish Jurist* n.s. vol. 5 (1970).
Sir John Davies. *A Discovery of the True Causes why Ireland was never entirely subdued . . . until . . . His Majesty's Happy Reign*. [London, 1612] (facsimile reprint, Shannon, 1969).
C.L. Falkiner. *Illustrations of Irish History and Topography, mainly of the seventeenth century*. London, 1904.

J.T. Gilbert (ed.). *A Jacobite narrative of the war in Ireland, 1688-1691.* [Dublin, 1892] (reprint, with introduction by J.G. Simms, Shannon, 1971).

J. Hardiman (ed.). R. *O'Flaherty, A Choreographical Description of west or h-iar Connaught written A.D. 1684.* Dublin, 1846.

L.W. Henry. 'Contemporary sources for Essex's lieutenancy in Ireland, 1599'. In *Irish Historical Studies,* vol. xi, No. 41 (1958).

J. Hogan (ed.). *Letters and Papers relating to the Irish Rebellion.* Dublin, 1936.

B. Jennings (ed.). *Wadding Papers 1614-38.* Dublin, 1953.

G. Keating. *Foras Feasa ar Éirinn: the History of Ireland.* (ed.) David Comyn and P.A. Dineen, 4 vols (London, 1902-14).

———. *Trí Biorghaoithe an Bháis.* (ed.) Osborn Bergin, (2nd edition) Dublin, 1931.

J. Lowe (ed.). *Letter-Book of the Earl of Clanricarde 1645-1647.* Dublin, 1983.

A. Mac Aingil. *Sgathán Shacruiminte na hAithridhe.* [Louvain, 1618], (ed.) Canice Mooney, Dublin, 1952.

F. Mac Raghnaill (ed.). B. Ó hEodhasa, *An Teagasc Críosdaidhe.* [Antwerp, 1611], Dublin, 1976.

J.C. O'Callaghan (ed.). Charles O'Kelly, *Macariae Excidium, or the destruction of Cyprus.* Dublin, 1850.

B. Ó Cuiv (ed.). *Parliament na mBan.* Dublin, 1952.

———. 'Flaithrí Ó Maolchonaire's catechism of Christian doctrine'. In *Celtica,* vol. 1 (1950).

———. 'James Cotter, a seventeenth-century agent of the Crown'. In *Journal of the Royal Society of the Antiquities of Ireland,* vol. lxxxix (1959).

T. Ó Donnchadha (ed.). 'Cinn Lae O Melláin'. In *Analecta Hibernica,* no. 3 (1931).

J. O'Donovan (ed.). *Annála Ríoghachta Éireann; Annals of the Kingdom of Ireland by the Four Masters from the earliest period to the year 1616.* Dublin, 1851 [reprint, New York, 1966].

A. Ó Fachtna (ed.). *An Bheatha Dhiadha.* Dublin, 1967.

F. Ó Maolchonaire. *Desiderius.* [Louvain, 1616], (ed.) T.F. O'Rahilly (Dublin, 1955).

T.F. O'Rahilly (ed.). 'Irish Poets, Historians and Judges in English Documents, 1538-1615'. In *Proceedings of the Royal Irish Academy,* vol. XXXVI, sect. C (1921-4).

W. Petty. *The Political Anatomy of Ireland.* ed. by John O'Donovan [reprint Shannon, 1970].

M.V. Ronan. *The Reformation in Dublin, 1536-1688: from original sources.* London, 1925.

J.E. Spingarn. *Critical Essays of the Seventeenth Century.* 3 vols, Oxford, 1908.

P. Walsh (ed.).   Lughaidh Ó Cléirigh, *A Life of Aodh Ruadh O Domhnaill, transcribed from the Book of Lughaidh Ó Cléirigh.* 2 vols (Dublin, 1948, 1957).

———.   'A memorial presented to the King of Spain on behalf of the Irish Catholics A.D. 1619'. In *Archivium Hibernicum,* vol. 6 (1917).

———.   *Gleanings from Irish Manuscripts.* Dublin, 1900.

———.   *The Will and Family of Hugh O'Neill, Earl of Tyrone.* Dublin, 1930.

———.   *Tadhg Ó Cíanáin, The Flight of the Earls.* Dublin, 1916.

J. Waterworth (ed.).   *The canons of the Sacred and Ecumenical Council of Trent.* London, 1848.

3. SECONDARY WORKS

K.R. Andrews, N.P. Canny, P.E. Hair (eds).   *The Westward Enterprise.* Liverpool, 1978.

E. Benveniste.   *Indo-European Language and Society.* Coral Gables, Florida, 1973.

O. Bergin (ed.).   *Irish Bardic Poetry.* Dublin, 1970.

L. Bieler.   *The patrician Texts in the Book of Armagh.* Dublin, 1979.

A. de Blacam.   *Gaelic Literature Suveyed.* Dublin, 1929.

J. Bossy.   *The English Catholic Community 1570-1850.* London, 1975.

———.   'The Character of Elizabethan Catholicism'. In *Past and Present,* No. 21 (April 1962).

———.   'The Counter-Reformation and the people of Catholic Ireland, 1596-1641'. In *Historical Studies,* 8 (1971).

M. Bowra.   *Heroic Poetry.* London, 1952.

B. Bradshaw.   *The Irish Constitutional Revolution of the Sixteenth Century.* Cambridge, 1979.

B. Bradshaw.   'Native Reaction to the Westward Enterprise: a case-study in Gaelic ideology'. In K.R. Andrews, N.P. Canny, and P.E. Hair (eds), *The Westward Enterprise* (Liverpool, 1978).

———.   'George Brown, first reformation Archbishop of Dublin, 1536-1554'. In *Journal of Ecclesiastical History,* vol. 21 (1970).

———.   'Sword, word and strategy in the Reformation in Ireland'. In *Historical Studies,* vol. 21 (1978).

———.   *The Dissolution of the religious orders in Ireland under Henry VIII.* Cambridge, 1974.

C. Brady and R. Gillespie (eds).   *Natives and Newcomers: essays on the making of Irish Colonial Society 1534-1641.* Dublin, 1986.

J. Brady.   'Catholics and Catholicism in the Eighteenth Century Press'. In *Archivium Hibernicum* vol. xvi-xx.

P.A. Breatnach.   'Marbhnadh Aodha Ruaidh Uí Dhomhnaill'. In *Éigse,* vol. 15 (1973).

____. 'Metamorphosis 1603'. In *Éigse,* vol. 17 (1977-8).

____. 'The Chief's Poet'. In *Proceedings of the Royal Irish Academy,* Sect. C, vol. 83, No. 3 (1983).

R.A. Breatnach. 'The Lady and the King: a theme of Irish Literature'. In *Studies,* vol. 42 (1953).

A. Bruford. *Gaelic Folktales and Medieval Romances.* Dublin, 1967.

P. de Brún. (ed.) *Folia Gadelica.* Cork, 1983.

P. de Brún, B. Ó Buachalla, T. Ó Concheanainn (eds). *Nua-Dhuanaire 1.* Dublin 1975.

P. Burke. *Popular Culture in Early Modern Europe.* London, 1978.

____. *Tradition and Innovation in Renaissance Italy; a sociological approach.* London, 1974.

____. *The Renaissance Sense of the Past.* London, 1964.

____. *Venice and Amsterdam: a study of seventeenth-century Élites.* London, 1974.

J.E. Caerwyn Williams. *The Court Poet in Mediaeval Ireland.* London, 1978.

N.P. Canny. *The Elizabethan Conquest of Ireland: a pattern established 1565-76.* Hassocks, 1976.

____. *From Reformation to Restoration: Ireland 1534-1660.* Dublin 1987.

____. *The Formation of the Old English Elite in Ireland.* Dublin 1975.

____. 'Hugh O'Neill, Earl of Tyrone and the Changing Face of Gaelic Ulster'. In *Studia Hibernica,* no. 10 (1970).

____. 'The Flight of the Earls 1607'. In *Irish Historical Studies* XVII, No. 67 (March 1971).

____. 'The Treaty of Mellifont and the Re-organisation of Ulster'. In *Irish Sword,* vol. 9 (1969-70).

____. 'The Formation of the Irish Mind: Religion, Politics and Gaelic Irish Literature 1580-1750'. In *Past and Present,* no. 95 (1982).

N.P. Canny and A. Pagden (eds). *Colonial Identity in the Atlantic World, 1500-1800.* Princeton University Press, 1987.

J. Carney. *The Irish Bardic Poet.* ⌐1967⌐, reprint 1985.

J. Carney. 'The Féuch Féin Controversy'. In J. Carney (ed.), *Studies in Irish Literature and History.* Dublin, 1955.

____. *Studies in Irish Literature and History.* Dublin, 1955.

G. Castor. *Pléiade Poetics: a study in Sixteenth-Century Thought and Terminology.* Cambridge University Press, 1964.

J.I. Casway. *Owen Roe O'Neill and the Struggle for Catholic Ireland.* Philadelphia, 1984.

____. 'Owen Roe O'Neill's return to Ireland in 1642; the diplomatic background'. In *Studia Hibernica,* vol. 9 (1969).

T.C. Cave. *Devotional Poetry in France c. 1570-1613.* Cambridge, 1969.

M. Ní Cheallacháin (ed.). *Filíocht Phádraigín Haicéad.* Dublin, 1962.

A. Clarke. *The Old English in Ireland, 1625-42.* London, 1966.

_____. *The Graces, 1625-41.* Dundalk, 1968.

_____. 'Colonial Identity in Early Seventeenth Century Ireland'. In *Historical Studies,* XI (1978).

_____. 'Ireland and the General Crisis'. In *Past and Present,* no. 48 (1970).

_____. 'The Policies of the Old English in Parliament, 1640-41'. In *Historical Studies,* vol. V (1965).

_____. 'Ireland and the general crisis'. In *Past and Present,* No. 48 (1970).

R. Clifton. 'Popular fear of Catholics during the English Revolution'. In *Past and Present,* no. 52 (1971).

T. Corcoran. *State Policy in Irish Education 1536-1816.* London, 1916.

P.J. Corish. *The Catholic Community in the Seventeenth and Eighteenth Centuries.* Dublin, 1981.

_____. 'An Irish Counter-Reformation Bishop: John Roche'. In *Irish Theological Quarterly,* vol. XXV (1958) and vol. XXVI (1959).

_____. 'Bishop Nicholas French and the second Ormond Peace, 1648-9'. In *Irish Historical Studies,* vol. VI, No. 22 (1948).

_____. 'Two contemporary historians of the Confederation of Kilkenny; John Lynch and Richard O Ferrale'. In *Irish Historical Studies,* vol. VIII, No. 31 (March 1953).

_____. 'The Reorganization of the Irish Church 1603-1641'. In *Proc. of Irish Catholic Historical Committee,* 3 (1957).

_____. 'John O'Callaghan and the Controversies among the Irish in Paris, 1648-54'. In *Irish Theological Quarterly,* Vol. 21 (1954).

D. Cregan. 'Daniel O'Neill in Exile and Restoration 1651-64'. In *Studia Hibernica,* no. 5 (1965).

_____. 'Daniel O'Neill, a Royalist agent in Ireland, 1644-50'. In *Irish Historical Studies,* vol. XI, No. 8 (September 1941).

W. Croft Dickinson. *New History of Scotland: Scotland from earliest times to 1603 vol. 1.* Edinburgh, 1961.

L. Cullen. *Life in Ireland. London, 1979.*

B. Cunningham. 'Native Culture and Political Change in Ireland, 1580-1640'. In C. Brady and R. Gillespie (eds), *Natives and Newcomers: essays on the making of Irish Colonial Society 1534-1641* (Dublin, 1986).

B. Cunningham and R. Gillespie. 'The East Ulster Bardic Family of Ó Gnímh'. In *Éigse,* 20 (1984).

E. Curtis. 'The O Maolchonaire Family'. In *Galway Archaeological and Historical Society,* vol. 19 (1941).

J. Delumeau. *Catholicism between Luther and Voltaire: a new view of the Counter-Reformation.* Introduction by John Bossy (transl. by Jeremy Mosier) London, 1977.

P.S. Dineen (ed.). *Dánta Phiarais Feiritéir.* Dublin, 1903.

T. Dowling. *The Hedge Schools of Ireland.* Dublin, 1968 ⊤2nd ed.⊥.

P.J. Duffy. 'The territorial organization of Gaelic landownership and its transformation in Co. Monaghan, 1595-1640'. In *Irish Geography*, vol. 14 (1981).

_____. 'Patterns of landownership in Gaelic Monaghan in the late sixteenth century'. In *Clogher Record,* x (1981).

T.J. Dunne. 'The Gaelic response to conquest and colonisation: the evidence of the poetry'. In *Studia Hibernica,* no. 20 (1980).

J. Dwyer, R.A. Mason, A. Murdoch (eds). *New Perspectives on the Politics and Culture of Early Modern Scotland.* Edinburgh, nd.

U. Eco. *Semiotics and the philosophy of Language.* London, 1984.

_____. *The Role of the Reader: Explorations in the semiotics of texts.* London, 1979.

J.H. Elliott. 'Revolution and Continuity in Early Modern Europe'. In *Past and Present,* No. 42 (February 1969).

S. Ellis. *Tudor Ireland: Crown, Community, and the Conflict of Cultures.* (Longmans, 1985).

C. Falls. 'Neil Garve: English ally and victim'. In *Irish Sword,* vol. I (1949).

B. Farrell (ed.). *The Irish Parliamentary Tradition.* Dublin, 1973.

C. Geertz. 'Centers, Kings and Charisma: Reflections on the Symbolics of Power'. In C. Geertz (ed.), *Culture and its Creators, Essays in honor on Edward Shils.* (University of Chicago Press, 1977).

C. Geertz (ed.). *Culture and its Creators: Essays in honor on Edward Shils* (University of Chicago Press 1977).

R. Gillespie. *Colonial Ulster: the Settlement of east Ulster 1600-41,* Cork 1985.

W. Gillies. 'A Poem on the Downfall of the Gaoidhil'. In *Éigse, 13 (1970).*

J. Goldberg. *James I and the Politics of Literature.* Baltimore and London, 1983.

J.K. Graham. 'The birth-date of Hugh O'Neill, Second Earl of Tyrone'. In *Irish Historical Studies,* vol. 1, no. 1 (1938).

D. Greene (ed.). *Duanaire Mhéig Uidhir.* Dublin, 1972.

J.R. Hale. 'Sixteenth-century explanations of war and violence'. In *Past and Present,* no. 51 (1971).

H. Hammerstein. 'Aspects of the continental education of Irish students in the reign of Elizabeth I'. In *Historical Studies,* Vol. 8 (1971).

G. Henry. 'Seminarie soldiers: connections between religious and military communities in the Spanish Netherlands'. In *Retrospect* no. 7, 1987.

C. Hill. *Change and Continuity in Seventeenth-Century England.* London, 1974.

_____. *The World Turned Upside Down: radical ideas during the English Revolution.* London, 1972.

J. Hardiman. *Irish Minstrelsy.* 2 vols. ⊤London, 1831⊥ Irish University Press ⊤reprint⊥ 1971.

J. Leersen. *Mere Irish and Fíor Ghael.* Amsterdam, 1986.

J.R. Goody (ed.). *Literacy in Traditional Societies.* Cambridge, 1968.

B. Jennings. 'The career of Hugh, son of Rory O'Donnell Earl of Tyrconnell, in the Low Countries 1607-42'. In *Studies,* vol. 30 (1941).

——. Mícheál O Cléirigh, chief of the Four Masters, and his associates. Dublin, 1936.

H.F. Kearney. 'Ecclesiastical politics and the Counter-Reformation in Ireland 1618-1648' in *'Journal of Ecclesiastical History,* vol. XI, No. 2 (October 1960).

M. Kerney Walsh. *'Destruction by Peace': Hugh O'Neill after Kinsale.* Armagh, 1986.

E. Knott. *Irish Classical Poetry.* Cork, 1960.

C. Lévi-Strauss. *The Savage Mind.* ⊤La Pensée Sauvage⊥, (3rd ed. London, 1974).

K.J. Lindley. 'The impact of the 1641 Rebellion on England and Wales, 1641-5'. In *Irish Historical Studies,* vol. xviii, no. 70 (1972).

S. MacAirt (ed.). *Leabhar Branch.* Dublin, 1944.

P. MacCana. 'Notes on the concept of unity'. In *Crane Bag* 2 (1978).

B. MacCurtain. 'An Irish agent of the Counter-Reformation: Dominic O'Daly'. In *Irish Historical Studies,* vol. xv, no. 60 (1967).

A.I. Macinnes. 'Scottish Gaeldom, 1638-1651: The Vernacular Response to the Covenanting Dynamic'. In John Dwyer, Roger A. Mason, Alexander Murdoch (eds), *New Perspectives on the Politics and Culture of Early Modern Scotland,* Edinburgh (nd).

C. Marstrander (ed.). 'A new version of the Battle of Mag Rath'. In *Eriú* V, 1911.

F.X. Martin. *Francis Nugent, Agent of the Counter-Reformation.* (Rome and London, 1962).

L. Martines. *Power and Imagination: City States in Renaissance Italy.* London, 1980.

——. *Society and History in English Renaissance Verse.* Oxford, 1985.

C.P. Meehan. *The Fate and Fortunes of Hugh O'Neill, Earl of Tyrone and Rory O'Donel, Earl of Tyrconnel.* Dublin 1868.

J. Miller. 'Thomas Sheridan (1646-1712) and his 'Narrative'. In *Irish Historical Studies,* vol. xxx, no. 78 (1976).

J. Miller. 'The Earl of Tyrconnell and James II's Irish policy 1685-1688'. In *Historical Journal,* vol. xx, no. 4 (1977).

E. Miner (ed.). *Illustrious Evidence: Approaches to English Literature of the seventeenth century.* California, 1975.

T.W. Moody (ed.). *Nationality and the Pursuit of Naitonal Independence.* Belfast 1978.

J.R. Mulder. *The Temple of the Mind; education and literary taste in seventeenth century England.* New York, 1969.

G. Murphy. 'Notes on *aisling* poetry'. In *Éigse*, vol. 1 (1939).

_____. *Saga and Myth in ancient Ireland.* Dublin, 1961.

F. O'Brien. 'Florence Conry, Archbishop of Tuam 1608'. In *Irish Rosary* (1928).

B. Ó Buachalla. 'Na Stíobhartaigh agus an t-aos léinn; Cing Séamas'. In *Proceedings of the Royal Irish Academy,* Sect. C, vol. 3, No. 4 (1983).

_____. 'An mheisiasacht agus an aisling', in P. de Brún (ed.), *Folia Gadelica,* Cork 1983.

L.P. Ó Caithnia. *Apalóga na bhFilí 1200-1650.* Dublin, 1984.

T. Ó Concheanainn. 'A feature of the poetry of Fearghal Óg Mac a' Bhaird'. In *Éigse,* vol. 15, 1974.

B. Ó Conchúir. *Scríobhaithe Chorcaí 1700-1850.* Dublin, 1982.

D. Ó Corráin. 'Nationality and Kingship in Pre-Norman Ireland'. In T.W. Moody (ed.), *Nationality and the Pursuit of National Independence,* (Belfast, 1978).

B. Ó Cuív. *Seven Centuries of Irish Learning 1000-1700.* Dublin, 1961.

_____. *A View of the Irish Language.* Dublin, 1969.

_____. 'A seventeenth century criticism of Keating's Foras Feasa ar Éirinn'. In *Éigse,* vol. 11 (1964).

_____. 'Literary creation and the Irish historical tradition'. In *Proceedings of the British Academy,* vol. xlix (1963).

P. O'Dea. 'Father Peter Wadding SJ: Chancellor of the University of Prague, 1629-41'. In *Studies,* vol. xxx (1941).

S. Ó Domhnaill. 'Sir Niall Garbh O'Donnell and the Rebellion of Sir Cahir O'Doherty'. In *Irish Historical Studies,* vol. iii, no. 9 (1942).

J. O'Donovan (ed.). *Miscellany of the Celtic Society.* Dublin, 1849.

M. O'Dowd. 'Gaelic Economy and Society'. In C. Brady and R. Gillespie (eds), *Natives and Newcomers: essays on the making of Irish Colonial Society 1534-1641,* (Dublin, 1986).

T. Ó Dúshláine. *An Eoraip agus Litríocht na Gaeilge 1600-1650: Gnéithe den Bharócachas Eorpach i Litríocht na Gaeilge.* Dublin, 1987.

_____. 'Filíocht Pholaitiúil na Gaeilge — a cinéal'. In *Léachtaí Cholm Cille* XII, Maynooth, 1982.

T. Ó Fiaich. 'Republicanism and Separatism in the Seventeenth Century'. In *Léachtaí Cholm Cille* II, Maynooth, 1971.

P. Ó Fiannachta (ed.). *Léann na Cléire.* Maynooth, 1986.

_____. *Léas ar ár Litríocht.* Maynooth, 1974.

S. Ó Tuama. *Filí faoi Sceimhle: Seán Ó Ríordáin agus Aogáin Ó Rathaille.* Dublin, 1978.

_____. 'Téamaí iasachta i bhfilíocht pholaitiúil na Gaeilge (1600-1800)'. In *Éigse,* vol. 2 (1965).

M. Olden. 'Counter-Reformation problems in Munster'. In *Irish Ecclesiastical Record,* 104 (1965).

_____. 'From Kinsale to Benburb — a valuable breathing space in Irish history'. In *Léachtaí Cholm Cille* ii (1971).

G. Parry. *The Golden Age Restor'd: The Culture of the Stuart Court.* Manchester, 1981.

D.L. Patey. *Probability and literary form; philosophic theory and literary practice in the Augustan age.* Cambridge, 1984.

L. Price. 'Notes on Feagh McHugh O'Byrne'. In *Journal of the Royal Society of the Antiquities of Ireland,* vol. lxvi (1936).

_____. 'The Byrne's country in the County Wicklow in the sixteenth century'. In *Journal of the Royal Society of the Antiquities of Ireland,* vol. lxiii (1933).

A. and B. Rees. *The Celtic Heritage.* London τ1961ι, 1976.

C. Ryan. 'Religion and State in seventeenth-century Ireland'. In *Archivium Hibernicum,* vol. 33, (1975).

M. Scowcroft. 'Miotas an Gabhála i Leabhar Gabhála'. In *Léachtaí Cholm Cille* XIII, (1982).

M.A. Shaaber. *Some Forerunners of the Newspaper in England 1476-1622.* τPhiladelphia, Univ. Pennsylvania Press, 1929ι reprint London, 1966.

J.J. Silke. 'Hugh O'Neill, the Catholic Question and the Papacy'. In *Irish Ecclesiastical Record,* 104 (1965).

_____. 'Primate Lombard and James I'. In *Irish Theological Quarterly,* 22(1955).

_____. 'Irish scholarship in the Renaissance 1580-1673'. In *Studies in the Renaissance, vol. 20, (1973).*

K. Simms. *From Kings to Warlords; the changing political structure of Gaelic Ireland in the Later Middle Ages.* The Boydell Press, 1987.

_____. 'Warfare in the medieval Gaelic lordships'. In *Irish Sword,* vol. 12 (1975-6).

J.G. Simms. 'John Toland (1670-1722), a Donegal heretic'. In *Irish Historical Studies,* no. 15, (1966).

L.A. Sonnino. *Hand-book to Sixteenth-Century Rhetoric.* New York, 1968.

G. Steiner. *After Babel; Aspects of language and translation.* London, 1975.

_____. *In Bluebeard's Castle; some notes towards the redefinition of culture.* London, 1971.

_____. *Language and Silence; essays 1958-66.* London, 1967.

D. Stevenson. *Alasdair MacColla and the Highland Problem in the Seventeenth Century.* Edinburgh, 1980.

J. Strachan (ed.). *Stories from the Táin.* τDublin, 1944ι, reprint 1976.

G.H. Tavard. *The Seventeenth-Century Tradition: a study in Recusant Thought.* Leiden, 1978.

K. Thomas. *Religion and the decline of magic.* London, 1971.

D.S. Thomson. 'Gaelic Learned Orders and Literati in Medieval Scotland'. In *Scottish Studies,* xii 1968.

D. Thomson. *An Introduction to Gaelic Poetry.* London, 1974.

N. Wachtel. *The Vision of the Vanquished: The Spanish Conquest of Peru through Indian Eyes 1530-1570.* (translated by Bert and Sîon Reynolds), London, 1977.

P. Walsh. *Irish Men of Learning.* (ed.) Colm O Lochlainn, Dublin 1947.

C.Z. Weiner. 'The Beleagured Isle: a study in Elizabethan and Jacobin Anti-Catholicism'. In *Past and Present,* No. 52 (May 1971).

C. Wells Slights. *The Casuistical Tradition in Shakespeare Donne, Herbert and Milton.* Princeton, 1981.

A. Williams (ed.). *Prophecy and Millenarianism: Essays in honour of Marjorie Reeves,* Longman, 1980.

N.J.A. Williams (ed.). *Pairlement Chloinne Tomáis.* Dublin, 1981.

_____. *The Poems of Giolla Brighde Mac Con Midhe.* Dublin, 1980.

_____. *I bPrionta i Leabhar.* Dublin, 1986.

. 'A note on *Scathán Shacruiminte na haithridhe'. In Éigse,* vol. 17 (1978).

INDEX OF PLACENAMES

INDEX OF PERSONAL NAMES

317

GENERAL INDEX

Accentual metre, 215-6, 295
administration, 13-14, 67, 91, 158-9, 183, 212, 237, 240
aisling, 255-6
'Aiste Sheáin Uí Chonaill', 253
amhrán metre, 215-6, 218
'An Síogaí Rómhánach', 252, 255-62, 273-4, 279, 287, 289, 293-4
anachronisms, in interpretation, 20, 50-51, 102, 124, 180, 185, 187, 222, 230, 281; in poetry, 240
analogies, instances of, 6, 20, 30-2, 37, 50-1, 57-9, 78, 114, 121, 134-5, 154, 176, 189, 193, 196-7, 216, 225-6, 242, 245, 255, 262-3, 289
ancestry, 30, 32-7, 56-7, 104-7, 168-9, 173-4, 206, 226; *see also* 'genealogy'
Anglo-Irish Catholics, 13
Anglo-Normans, 43-4, 56, 67-8, 103, 131-2, 160, 224, 277; *see also* 'De Burgo', 'foreigners'
annals, 70; *see also* 'Four Masters'
apologues, ix, 5, 36 & passim, 51
aristocracy, literati and, 2, 9, 64, 157; world view of, 2, 29, 36, 53-4, 117, 120, 122, 152, 177-8, 183-4, 199, 244, 262, 270, 275, 295; decline of, 6, 13, 119 & passim, 124-8, 152, 212-3, 262; *see also* 'chieftainship', 'foreigners'
audience, and symbolism, 6; nature of, 239-40

Banbha, sovereignty of, 4, 21, 41, 59, 91, 105, 146, 182; unity of, 21,

62-118 passim, 120, 164, 250; deliverance of, 23, 29, 39, 41, 58-60, 71, 98, 109-10, 158, 204, 210-11, 212, 246-7, 251, 257, 261, 267-8; espousal of, 36, 39, 51, 56, 60, 66, 79, 98, 112, 175, 230, 296; fertility of, 39, 137-9, 170; desolation of, 52-55, 101, 121, 124-9, 131, 134, 139, 195, 230, 241, 243, 256, 262-4, 274, 289; unification of, 62-3, 66, 69, 91, 97, 101; treachery of, 5, 46, 129, 219, 232-3, 280
banishment, 40-3, 91, 99, 109-10, 147-8, 166-7
bardic poetry, as historical source, ix & passim; as literary genre, 2, 6, 16, 20, 92, 125, 140, 211-3; continuity in, 8, 97, 108, 119-20, 122, 134, 152, 177-8, 216, 222, 240-1, 268, 271; as propaganda, 45, 123; and Christianity, 2, 69-70; as embodiment of political principles and philosophy, 101, 117, 163, 165, 168, 184, 280-1, 294, 298; *see also* 'interpretation', 'poem-types', 'poet', 'themes'
bardic schools, decline of, 215
baroque, 240
battle rolls, 72-9, 81-90, 118, 141-2, 145-50, 210, 257-62
belligerence, as social factor, 10, 72; poets' incitement to, 105; *see also* 'warfare'

caithréim, *see under* 'battle-rolls'